Fourth Edition

Introducing Religion
Religious Studies for the Twenty-First Century

Robert S. Ellwood

University of Southern California

Routledge
Taylor & Francis Group

LONDON AND NEW YORK

First published 2014 by Pearson Education, Inc.

Published 2016 by Routledge
2 Park Square, Milton Park, Abingdon, Oxon OX14 4RN
711 Third Avenue, New York, NY 10017, USA

Routledge is an imprint of the Taylor & Francis Group, an informa business

Cover Designer: Bruce Kenselaar

Cover Image: Top left: © Creativa / Fotolia, top
  right: © Zoonar GmbH/Alamy Stock Photo
  Corbis, bottom right: © L. Shat / Fotolia, bottom
  left: Dan Herrick/Getty

Credits and acknowledgments borrowed from other sources and reproduced, with permission, in this
textbook appear on the appropriate pages within text for photos, and text credits appear in the Credits
section on page **292**.

Library of Congress Cataloging-in-Publication Data
Ellwood, Robert S., 1933-
    Introducing religion : religious studies for the 21st century / Robert S. Ellwood, University of Southern
California.—FOURTH EDITION.
        pages cm
    Rev. ed. of: Introducing religion : from inside and outside. c1993.
    Includes bibliographical references and index.
    ISBN 978-0-205-98759-7 (alk. paper)
    1. Religion.   I. Title.
    BL48.E43 2014
    200—dc23
                                        2013046886

ISBN 13: 978-0-205-98759-7 (pbk)

My feet were set upon a narrow pathway
Crossing worlds of worlds to find Love's Center;
I shall not return as I.
—G.F.E.

For Fay Elanor Ellwood
May she find that path.

BRIEF CONTENTS

Chapter 1   How to Study Religion   1

Chapter 2   History of Religion on Planet Earth   14

Chapter 3   Myth: Our Lives, and the World's, Are Stories   31

Chapter 4   Magic Doorways: Symbol, Rite, and Religion   47

Chapter 5   Oases of the Mind: The Psychology of Religion   60

Chapter 6   Inner Adventure: The Way of Realization, the Way of Faith   76

Chapter 7   Why Evil?   92

Chapter 8   Faith Through Form: Religion and Art   107

Chapter 9   Ghost Marriages and Country Music: Popular Religion   130

Chapter 10   Infinite Information, Worlds Without End: The Internet, Religion, and Virtual Realities   147

Chapter 11   Traveling Together: The Sociology of Religion   166

Chapter 12   Truth Messages: The Conceptual Expression of Religion   186

Chapter 13   Worlds to Come: Religious Eschatology and the Afterlife   202

Chapter 14   How Shall We Live? Religion and Ethics   218

Chapter 15   Horror and Glory: Religion Confronting War   242

CONTENTS

Foreword   xiii

Chapter 1   **How to Study Religion   1**

Pictures of Religion   2

Another Reality   5

Definitions of Religion   6

Three Forms of Religious Expression and a Working
Definition   8

The Structure of this Book   11

Summary   12   • Key Terms   13

Chapter 2   **History of Religion on Planet Earth   14**

Human Religious Beginnings   15

The Religion of Early Gatherers and Hunters   17

Archaic Agriculture   20

Ancient Empires   21

The Axial Age   22

The Great Religions   25

Five Stages in the Development of Great Religions   27

Apostolic   27

Empire and Wisdom   28

Devotionalism   28

Reformation   28

Modern   29

Summary   29   • Key Terms   30

Chapter 3   **Myth: Our Lives, and the World's, Are Stories   31**

Your Story as Myth   32

Stories Before Writing   33

Coyote   35

Kinds of Myth and the Creation Myth   37

The Myth of the Hero   40

The Warrior Hero   41

The Savior Hero   44

Myth and Meaning   45

Summary   46   • Key Terms   46

Chapter 4   **Magic Doorways: Symbol, Rite, and Religion   47**

Signs and Symbols   48

Audio Symbols   50

Nonverbal   51

Nonconceptual Verbal   52

Conceptual Verbal   52

The Orchestration of Symbols in Rite   53

Public Worship   54

Pilgrimage   56

Initiation   57

Summary   59   • Key Terms   59

Chapter 5   **Oases of the Mind: The Psychology of Religion   60**

Mental Shifts   61

Subuniverses   62

Development and Change   64

Religious Experience   70

Psychological Interpretations of Religion   72

Summary   75   • Key Terms   75

Chapter 6   **Inner Adventure: The Way of Realization,
the Way of Faith   76**

Ways to Go   77

The Way of Realization   80

Awakening   81

Preparation   83

Illumination   83

Dark Night of Soul   83

Unitive State   83

Insight   84

Faith, and Monks Who Hated God   86

The Meeting of the Twain   90

Summary   90   • Key Terms   91

Chapter 7   **Why Evil?   92**

What Exactly is Evil?   93

Myths of the Origin of Evil   94

Evil Ritual, Evil Initiation: Can Religion Create Evil?   98

Why Do Bad Things Happen? Religious Thought
and Evil   100

Summary   106

Chapter 8   **Faith Through Form: Religion and Art   107**

Stained-Glass Windows   108

Painting   110

Sculpture   113

Architecture   116

Music   118

Poetry   120

Drama   122

Novels and Stories   124

Summary   128   • Key Terms   129

Chapter 9   **Ghost Marriages and Country Music: Popular Religion   130**

Two Kinds of Religion   131

Popular Expressions of Mainstream Religion   131

The Devil's Share   135

Global Christianity   136

Theories of Popular Religion   137

Camouflages of the Sacred   140

Are They Religion?   144

Summary   146   • Key Terms   147

Chapter 10   **Infinite Information, Worlds Without End: The Internet,
Religion, and Virtual Realities   147**

The Way We Live Now   148

Levels and Life   149

Information Please   151

Alone Together: Religious Talk Online   154

Gamesmanship   157

Gateways to Wonder   162

Cyber Apocalyptic   163

Summary   165

Chapter 11   **Traveling Together: The Sociology of Religion   166**

All Religion is Social   167

Religious Groups   168

Established Religion   169
Three Kinds of Religion   172
Emergent Religion   172
Religious Personalities and Roles   177
The Transformation of Society By Religion   180
Image of the Normative Nature of Society   180
Worship and Sociology of Religion   181
Historical Impact of Religion   181
Prophetic Teaching and Religious
Demands for Justice   181
Religion and The Interpretation of History   182
Religion Today   182
Summary   184 • Key Terms   185

Chapter 12   **Truth Messages: The Conceptual Expression
of Religion   186**
Ways of Thinking about God   187
God   188
Determining Truth in Religion   189
Reason   190
Experience   192
Empiricism   193
Authority   193
Sociological Factors in Religious Preference   194
Existential Choice   194
Are Religious Beliefs Irrefutable?   196
Essentialism and Deconstructionism   197
The New Atheists   199
Summary   200 • Key Terms   201

Chapter 13   **Worlds to Come: Religious Eschatology
and the Afterlife   202**
On the one Hand, on the Other . . .   203
How Important Is It?   203
Now or Later   206
Islamic End-Time   207
Christian Judgment   208

One Death or Many: Heaven and Hell Versus
      Reincarnation   209

Eternal Recurrence   212

What Kind of Heaven?   213

Near-Death Experiences   215

Summary   217   • Key Terms   217

Chapter 14   **How Shall We Live? Religion and Ethics   218**

Taking it to the Streets   219

Ethics and Morality   220

Down from on High   221

Kinds of Ethical Thought   222

Similarities and Differences in Religious Ethical
      Traditions   226

Contemporary Issues in Religious Ethics   227

   The Abortion Controversy   228

   The Right to Die   231

The Role of Women in Religion   234

Religion and Ecology   236

Summary   241   • Key Terms   241

Chapter 15   **Horror and Glory: Religion Confronting War   242**

Introducing War   243

What is War?   244

The Feel of War   244

Just War Theory   245

To the Right and Left of Just War   247

A Remarkable Discovery   250

Protection and More Than Protecton   251

Living the Dream   251

The Joy of Battle   254

Terrorism   255

Mythic Time and Ourselves Again   255

The Horror of War   257

The Nonviolent High   258

War and Moral Meaning   259

Summary   261

Journey's End 262

Appendix 263

Glossary 272

Notes 279

Credits 292

Bibliography 293

Index 300

FOREWORD

Gratified by the response which this introduction to the academic study of religion has received, I have prepared a fourth edition of *Introducing Religion: Religious Studies for the 21st Century* in the hope of making it still more useful to college and university students—and to all who are interested in exploring different ways of looking at religion in the new world of the twenty-first century.

The overall scope and organization of the book has remained unchanged, although some of it has been rewritten. Study aids, in the form of statements of chapter objectives, summaries, and a glossary were added to the second edition. Entirely new chapters on religion, art, and ethics were put into the third edition, together with a new appendix giving students suggestions for ways of writing and studying in religious studies classes.

The present fourth edition has been expanded with new chapters exploring certain topics of contemporary interest: myth, spiritual paths, religion and popular culture, religion in the computer age, religion and war. It is hoped these are areas that will help students relate the subject matter to life in the world around them, and offer lively topics for discussion and research.

A couple of caveats about this book. First, it is intended only as an introduction to academic religious studies. Much that is important in the religious world, and even in the academy as it looks at religion from the perspective of its various disciplines, may here be mentioned only in passing. One hopes that fields of inquiry only introduced in these pages will whet the appetite for more, encourage good classroom presentations, and stimulate students to find in them material they want to explore further in research projects.

Second, this project is not a world religions textbook, but an introduction to religious studies as a discipline. The emphasis is therefore on learning how one thinks in academic religious studies and its main areas: sociology of religion, psychology of religion, history of religion, religion and art, ethics, and so forth. Examples are selected worldwide to some extent to display the worldwide, multicultural nature of human religion. On the other hand, when illustrations and terminology seem to reflect largely a North American or other English-speaking context, perhaps Christian and monotheist as well, that is due to no particular favoritism but only because that is likely to be the cultural background of a majority of students using this book. Modes of analysis like those of the sociology or psychology of religion, as well as every day cybernetics, pop culture, or ethical issues, are likely to be best understood in the beginning through observations and experiences to which one can personally relate. There is the teaching principle of starting where the students are. Ideally, this book might be employed in conjunction with a fine textbook on world religions.

May you find this study an adventure in expanding your knowledge of one of the major areas of human life and culture, and beyond that of the visions and experiences behind that knowledge.

R. E.

P.S. As you read this book, look for important words and be sure you understand them before going on. The key words defined in the glossary at the end of the book are in boldface type at their first use in the text.

NEW TO THIS EDITION

- Brief summaries of major contributors to understanding religion, from Friedrich Schleiermacher to William James, Sigmund Freud, Mircea Eliade, and Jonathon Z. Smith.
- Enhanced discussion of the Axial Age and the religious founders, analyzing their nature and subsequent significance.
- A new chapter on myth, emphasizing its relation to understanding our own lives as story, and such major kinds of myth as creation, origin of evil, hero—as warrior or as savior—and eschatological.
- New material on initiation and its relation to religious symbol and rite.
- In the chapter on psychology of religion, an updated presentation on the psychology of religion, including the work of James Hillman and recent debate about a "God gene" and neurological sources of religious awareness.
- A new chapter on spiritual paths, presenting both the classic graduated path (for example, Evelyn Underhill's interpretation), and its rejection by such figures as Luther and founders of Pure Land Buddhism.
- A new chapter on evil: mythic and philosophical accounts of the origin of evil; initiation and evil (including an example from a recent fraternity scandal); Eastern and Western views of evil or suffering compared.
- A new chapter on popular religion, discussing examples from Sallman's famous Head of Christ to religious themes in country music, Chinese "ghost marriages," Navajo witches, the "Satanic panic" of the 1980s, world pentecostalism. Are "superheroes," the quasi-religious cult of Elvis, or Disneyland "camouflages of the sacred," as had been proposed? The chapter includes recent theories of popular culture and religion.
- A new chapter on religion and the Internet, examining its role as a locus of religious information, dialogue, and ritual enacted in cyberspace; computer games and their mythology and influence; the "cyber apocalyptic" some have predicted as computers and humanity merge to create a whole new kind of life: cyborgs. What does all this mean for religion?
- In the chapter on sociology of religion, an enhanced discussion of religious personalities and roles, such as the shaman, priest, prophet, etc., and a presentation of recent (2012) figures on religious demographics in the United States, including the rise of the "nones," especially in the younger generation.
- In the chapter on religious thought, a fresh discussion of recent revivals of the ontological argument, as by Charles Hartshorne and Alvin Platinga, of religion and Deconstructionism, and a description and critique of the "new atheists" and their positions.
- A new chapter on religious eschatology and the afterlife, involving discussion of their relative importance in different cultures, individual versus "Last Day"

judgment, heaven or hell versus reincarnation, theocentric versus anthropocentric heavens, ancient and Nietzshean eternal recurrence, and near-death experiences.

- In the chapter on religious ethics, a new section on ecological ethics, with statements representative of major religions, and of a new "dark green" eco-centric religion.
- As an example of ethics, a new chapter on religion and war: its human origins; literary descriptions; presentations of "just war" theory; the power of religious mythology based on the warrior ethic, and related speculation on the significance of the recently discovered "Staffordshire horde" of Anglo-Saxon weapons glorified with invaluable gold, silver, and jewel ornamentation as though sacred; why it is possible to love war; religious dimensions of terrorism, moral equivalents of war, including the Civil Rights struggle of the 1960s and the exploration of space.
- A largely new Appendix on Studying Religion, with suggested student projects to go with nearly every chapter: how to do, and report on, a meditation experiment; how to write a sociological-type report on a visit to a religious group or activity; how to organize a debate on a topic such as the existence of God or the ethics of war; how to write a paper analyzing a myth, novel, or religious Internet site; or a historical paper on a past religious figure, group, or event.

CHAPTER

1

How to Study Religion

The door to an ancient temple at Angkor, Cambodia,
suggesting the mysterious adventure of a spiritual quest
(Chris Lees/Alamy)

LEARNING OBJECTIVES

After reading this chapter, you should be able to:

- Explain why you think it is, or is not, important to study religion today. Then offer examples of your own of what religion is in the twenty-first century and has been in the past.
- Say what is meant by referring to religion as postulating "another reality."
- Explain the definitions of religion of representative thinkers past and present.
- Formulate and defend the *descriptive* definition of religion that seems best to you. (This means a definition *not* based on what you believe is the right or true religion but one which simply describes what religion is in human life.) Compare the definition you formulate now with what you would have said before reading the chapter.
- Explain Joachim Wach's three forms of religious expression.
- Reflect on what might be the view of religion appropriate to different disciplines, such as history, sociology, and psychology.
- Understand the arrangement of chapters in this book.

PICTURES OF RELIGION

What does it mean to study religion in the twenty-first century? In our generation, one finds many different attitudes toward religion. However, most agree that it is important to understand religious faith for several reasons.

Religion is essential for understanding history, including the history of art, architecture, and literature. Flip through any history book, and see how many conflicts, and significant causes from the spread of Islam to the abolition of slavery, are linked to religious movements. Go to an art museum, and note how much traditional painting and sculpture is religiously inspired. Check out the great buildings in any traditional society, and see how many cathedrals, temples, or mosques are among them. It would be hopeless to try to get inside this history and art without some comprehension of the motivation inspiring religious works and their creators.

Nor is it just a matter of times past. Any reading of or listening to the news, including the speeches of politicians, reminds us that religion has considerable social, political, and even economic influence today. Its institutions, and people's beliefs toward marriage, medical procedures, the role of women, the role of the state in education and welfare, all are major parts of the debates of our times. On a larger scale, religion is still invoked on behalf of war and the foreign policy of several nations, even if it may not be the only factor involved.

It is also the case that religious attitudes and experiences continue to have an effect on personal psychology, and so can help us understand why some people act and feel the way they do.

Finally religious claims raise important philosophical questions that thoughtful people should want to think through. Is there a God? What is the real nature and purpose of human life? How should I act when ethical decisions are difficult? And much else.

Clearly, this is something we should know more about.

What is **religion**? Everyone has some idea, perhaps some mental picture, to go with the word. If one tries to turn that idea or picture into a clear, comprehensive definition, however, the task may be surprisingly difficult.

First, then, let us look at two quite different examples of the phenomena often called religious.

Picture the great shrine at Ise (pronounced Ee-say) in Japan on the eve of the Harvest Festival. Ise is the preeminent place of worship of Shinto, the religion of the ancient gods of the island nation. Here at Ise are worshiped Amaterasu, the solar goddess said to be ancestress of the imperial family, and Toyouke, goddess of food and bestower of plenty. Each of these high goddesses has her own shrine, the two nearly identical temples being about 5 miles apart. Each shrine is a simple, rustic house of unpainted but gold-tipped wood set in a rectangular field spread with white gravel. The field, which holds three or four auxiliary buildings, is surrounded by four wooden palisades. Every 20 years, the entire shrine complex is rebuilt with new wood in exact imitation of the old on an adjacent alternative site, also spread with white gravel.

On the night of the Harvest Festival, torches flare in the crisp October air when a procession of white-robed **priests** bearing boxes of food offerings, their black wooden shoes crackling like snare drums on the white gravel, approaches the shrine. The priests enter behind the fences and are lost to the observer's view as they carefully spread the plates of rice, water, salt, rice wine, vegetables, and seafood before the encased mirror that represents the presence of Amaterasu. One can, however, hear the shrill, mysterious music of the reed flutes, so suggestive of uncanny divine activity. A prayer is read, and then the offerings are slowly and solemnly removed from the boxes and presented on an offering table. The priests next proceed to a smaller shrine on higher ground above the principal temple. This is a shrine to the *aramitama*, the "rough spirit" or aggressive side of the divine Amaterasu. Here offerings are also presented. Later, in early morning while it is still dark, the whole **ritual** is repeated. The following night it is repeated—again, twice—at the shrine of Toyouke. Why it is done twice and why it is done at night are matters lost in centuries of tradition at the Ise shrines (if there ever existed an explicit reason). The very sense of mystery evoked by the feeling of something lingering from a half-forgotten past, and the atmosphere of mystic wonder in which actions seem weighted with meanings the human mind does not quite grasp, give Shinto rites their particular kind of religious aura.

Now turn to another scene. It suggests not only one kind of religious experience, conversion, but also one major type of religious personality, the founder of a great religious movement lasting many centuries, in this case Jesus. Although based on real experiences, the following retelling is a stylized and idealized account of religious experience in a Christian context. It is not presented as being representative of all Christian experience. It offers, however, a **subjective** counterpart to the preceding religious expression in **rite**.

An American girl was in her room reading the New Testament and praying. As she read, a vivid image came before her mind's eye. She saw Jesus on a hill, and he seemed to be surrounded by beseeching figures in ragged garments, some clearly sick

The Grand Shrines of Ise, consisting of the Kotai-jingu, or Naiku (Inner Shrine, pictured here), and the Toyouke-daijingu or Geku (Outer Shrine)   (Gideon Mendel/Corbis)

or deformed. He stood out because he was taller, was dressed in something a bit fuller and whiter, and was on higher ground. Above all, he had an air of power and calm amidst the suffering, and his hands were raised in healing. His face possessed a simple majesty, and his eyes made you want to keep looking at them. Then he seemed to step out of the gospel scene to look directly at the American girl. He beckoned.

She prayed on. Deep and warm feelings about the image sang through her, rising and falling like cresting surfs of molten light. She saw other scenes from the story—the manger, the cross with the bleeding flesh on it, and the garden where the ecstatic women saw the same person in calm white outside the empty tomb. These tableaux grew brighter and brighter. In contrast, her life, as it came into view beside the mind-painted images, was gray, lacking all sparkle or color. Indeed, much in it seemed worse than gray as she thought of things she wished could be washed out or made to belong to another life. She recalled people she liked and even envied who talked of accepting Christ and of being forgiven or being saved. She saw the beckoning hand wanting to make her a part of this story.

She felt herself entering the vision and prayed still more deeply. She then sensed clear and distinct words being spoken in her, almost as though by a new person coming into being within her mind and body, words of accepting Jesus Christ as the center of her personal faith. She arose, tingling, feeling full of light, and almost floating, with a queer but beautiful sort of quiet deep-seated joy. She sat down, with little sense of time or place, just bathing in the new marvelous experience.

ANOTHER REALITY

You have just read two very different vignettes that have one thing in common. Both would be accepted by most people as expressions of human religion or culture, first of all because they are thoughts, feelings, or actions that do not meet ordinary, practical needs in ordinary, practical ways. They do not directly spin cloth or pick grain. Even if they were directed toward a practical end, such as a better harvest, they do not go about it through a practical course of planting and cultivating. They add to what is practical by implying another point of reference and another level of activity. If that point of reference or level is more than human, probably it would be called religious.

Even if a religious act is a dance or prayer for rain, it does not set about meeting this practical need by using ordinary deduction about cause and effect. Contrary to what some have believed, primitive peoples are nearly as aware as moderns of the distinction between the practical and the nonpractical. Certainly modern Shinto priests at a Harvest Festival are as aware of the facts of meteorology and agricultural science as are Americans expressing gratitude to God on Thanksgiving Day.

Religion, however, adds other dimensions full of color, stylized acts, and symbols that outsiders sometimes see as bizarre and totally nonsensical. In this they are akin to such human practices as wearing clothes even in hot weather, writing poetry, or flying to the moon. These are also impractical things that like religion must be profoundly human, for they are only dimly foreshadowed in the behavior of our animal kin. Something in these gestures must be making a statement about a side of being human that is not just concerned with practicality. They must be trying to tell us—emphatically—that there is another side to being human. Apart from speech and fire, in fact, what most obviously separates even very primal human societies from animals are such artifacts as haunting masks, paintings on stones of spirit ancestors, and the magic rocks or tufts of grass of sorcerers. They tell us across great gulfs of cultural development that here were creatures who did not just deal in practicalities but who feared pictures in the mind; thought about who they were and where they came from; told stories; sensed the working of indirect invisible currents of force in the cosmos as well as the obvious; and doubtlessly knew wonder, humor, joy, and dread.

We could go back to the very beginnings of human culture as we know it, the stunning cave paintings of such sites as the Lascaux and Chauvet caverns in southern France. The latter, discovered only in 1994, contains the oldest known cave paintings of all, the earliest made perhaps some 35,000 years ago, and was the subject of a remarkable documentary by Werner Herzog, *Cave of Forgotten Dreams*. These incredibly dynamic and graceful pictures, nearly all of powerful animals, drawn far underground in pitch darkness except for the light of torches, may—according to various theories—have represented hunting magic, the site of initiations, myths told in a sort of code, or the visions of shamans. We may never know. But clearly they had some significance far beyond the immediate and practical in the everyday sense; they were a way of enhancing the meaning of human life through symbol and creativity.[1]

DEFINITIONS OF RELIGION

Now let us summarize the definitional and interpretive ideas about religion of a few representative philosophers and scholars to give an impression of their range and perspective.

An important reminder: Bear in mind the difference between a personal definition of religion—what religion means to *me*—and a general, descriptive one that would enable one to answer the question—what is the religion of this or that society? For religious studies, one needs to have a working view of what religion is generically, whether or not one agrees with or likes it.

This is looking at religion from the *outside*. It is, of course, all right to have one's own religious beliefs and practices—religion looked at, as it were, from the *inside*. For purposes of religious studies, it is important to try to keep them separate. However, sometimes it is hard to keep the two apart, and even the best scholars have not always been successful at this. Here are some scholarly examples of definitions of religion.

For Friedrich Schleiermacher (1768–1834), generally recognized as the founder of modern liberal Protestant theology, who under the influence of the romantic movement recognized the importance of emotion as well as logic in religious understanding, religion is an individual expression of a "feeling of absolute dependence."[2]

Émile Durkheim (1858–1917), one of the founders of modern **sociology**, viewed society as the real **sacred**, and therefore society and religion as virtually inseparable and indispensable to each other. Moreover, "religion is a unified system of beliefs and practices relative to sacred things, that is to say, things set apart and forbidden."[3] However, this does not set those things apart from society, but only from the ordinary, everyday, "profane" aspects of society; religious rites and objects are special precisely because they are that which unifies and legitimates society on a higher level than the everyday. That all-important role comes out in ceremonies such as sacred dances. Religious occasions happen when the social "effervescence" generated by the group makes real a sense of the people's sacredness as a society.[4]

William James (1842–1910), the American pragmatic philosopher and psychologist, swung back toward a more individualistic view of religion as grounded in personal experience in his great work, *The Varieties of Religious Experience*. Religion is "the feelings, acts, and experiences of individual men in their solitude, so far as they apprehend themselves to stand in relation to whatever they may consider the divine."[5] As to what lies behind that sense of the divine, James tells us it "consists of the belief that there is an unseen order, and that our supreme good lies in harmoniously adjusting ourselves thereto."[6] This could, of course, be a society's collective adjustment, but clearly for James the real locus of religiosity is in the individual, not the Durkheimian society as a whole. Perhaps that is because James' book dealt with personal religious experiences, many of them in more individualistic recent times, whereas Durkheim treated of primal societies like those of Australian aboriginals. However, it is also a matter of perspective; we will later reflect on ways in which religion is inevitably a social experience in its language and concepts even when it most seems individual, even when it is secret.

For Karl Marx (1818–1883), whose ideas greatly influenced modern socialism and communism, religion was basically the result of an unhealthy society, in which one class—capitalist owners of the means of production—exploited another—the workers—for their labor. For the exploiting class, religion could justify their privileged place by saying it was God's will, and they could use it to control the masses. For the exploited, religion offered the consolations of piety and the hope of a better world after death. In this context Marx made the famous statement that religion is "the opium of the people."

However, Marx deserves that his whole statement be heard:

> Religious distress is at the same time the expression of real distress and the protest against real distress. Religion is the sigh of the oppressed creature, the heart of a heartless world, just as it is the spirit of a spiritless situation. It is the opium of the people.
>
> The abolition of religion as the illusory happiness of the people is required for their real happiness.[7]

For another major figure in the modern critique of religion, Sigmund Freud (1856–1939), the father of psychoanalysis, faith was a symptom or expression of incomplete or pathological development within a personality. It might take the form of an adult still yearning for an all-perfect, problem-solving, rule-enforcing parent figure remembered from childhood, now "projected" into a divine Father or Mother on high. Or it may be the "oceanic" consciousness of the infant before her limits are well understood, now become **mysticism**. The point is that, amidst the confusion, disappointments, and frequent feelings of helplessness in life, we desperately want these concepts to be true. Religious ideas, Freud said, are "illusions, [but] fulfilments of the oldest, strongest and most urgent wishes of mankind. The secret of their strength lies in the strength of these wishes."[8]

For Freud's one-time disciple, Carl Gustav Jung (1875–1961), who broke with the older man largely because of Freud's emphasis on the sexual and pathological explanation of religion, religion is instead a treasure house of resources for understanding our innermost nature. The world's myths and rituals are like a diorama of great figures that occur over and over in story, and also in dreams: the Wise Old Man, the Great Mother, the Hero, the Maiden, the Shadow. These are real aspects of the self, and can be rightly aligned as one individuates, or becomes who one truly is, through inner processes somewhat parallel to religious initiation and ritual. Jung has had considerable influence in religious studies, above all in the study of myth.

Moving back to immediate psychological experience, the German theologian and historian of religion Rudolf Otto (1869–1937) perceived religion as experience of the Holy, or the **numinous**. The Holy, when truly met in revelation or when inwardly felt, is *mysterium tremendum et fascinans*, always mysterious, strange, tremendous, and fascinating. It draws us by its uncanny power, yet also fills us with dread. Religion evokes a kind of feeling, but Otto heavily stressed the difference between a God evoking the numinous kind of feeling from the God of reason, or even the deity of ethics or devotion. Writing of Yahweh in the Hebrew Scriptures, Otto contended that this deity's "holiness," like his "fury," his "jealousy," his "wrath," his nature as a "consuming fire," is the result not only of divine "righteousness" or humanlike emotion, but is all "enclosed and permeated with the 'awfulness' and the 'majesty,' the 'mystery' and the 'augustness,' of His non-rational divine nature."[9]

Several of these strands of social and experiential religion come together in the work of the historian of religion Mircea Eliade (1907–1986). The title of one of his basic books, *The Sacred and the Profane*, is a key to his thought. Drawing from Durkheim's work, he perceived humankind yearning for **transcendence** of the ordinary, "profane" world of everyday space and time. We want, at least some of us, also to share in the mythic and absolute world of origins, the "other time" when the gods made the world and heroes walked the earth. Times of religious festival and rite are sacred times that try to recapture the strong primal time; temples, holy mountains, and sacred trees represent sacred space, places set apart as ways of access to that other world. Religion, then, is that which shows ways in which *homo religiosus*, "religious man," "attempts to remain as long as possible in a sacred universe."[10] Looking for such patterns or structures as sacred space and time, symbolic ways of transcendence, and the importance of a New Year's festival, consistent through many religions though the names and externals may change, characterized the work of Durkheim and Eliade, and is called **structuralism**.

Finally, we will mention certain recent scholars of religion who have taken a quite different, untraditional approach. Recognizing the immense complexity and diversity of what has been called religion, whether by religious practitioners themselves or by students like those above endeavoring to find some common theme that would enable to say what is or is not religion anywhere, at any time, they have concluded that this is the wrong way of going about it. It is asking the wrong question. Acknowledging that a tremendous amount of data exists out there about myth, ritual, and all the rest, no one such thing as "religion" as a collective term or concept appears, they say. It's all facets of culture, psychology, or history, which could be looked at in several ways, but not necessarily as "religion" in the sense of something special or unique. As Jonathan Z. Smith, a progenitor of this school, put it in arguing that religion as we study it in the classroom is an artificial construct, "It is the study of religion that invented 'religion.'"[11] We call something religion in order to define and study it, just as a biologist might define a fish as belonging to a particular species, but that does not mean our human labels have any meaning outside the laboratory, or the library.

Russell McCutcheon has gone on to insist that this labeling happens out in the culture as well. Religion as social formation is so branded by the culture, and different cultures may have different ways of using this nomenclature. Therefore, following John F. Wilson, McCutcheon contends that "the study of religion has no special methodology," but rather is, or should be, "a nonessentialist, multidisciplinary field."[12] (As we will see later, "essentialism," a notion much criticized by some philosophers today, means attributing a special character to a whole class of entities, like religion in all its variety, as in saying that religion as such is *sui generis*, of its own type and like nothing else.) Another scholar, Talal Asad, has narrowed the definition down to the point of calling religion social and ritual activities that possess special authority within their particular culture.[13]

THREE FORMS OF RELIGIOUS EXPRESSION AND A WORKING DEFINITION

Clearly a definition of religion adequately covering everything usually considered "religion" in a balanced way is very difficult. Indeed, as W. Cantwell Smith has pointed out, religion in the sense the word is used today, to speak of different "religions" such as Judaism or Hinduism, is a modern idea.[14] So, to an increasing extent, is the idea that one's religion is entirely personal and as it were detachable from the rest of culture, so that one can consider oneself a good citizen without adhering to the religion of that society. There are no words in classic languages such as Greek or Sanskrit meaning exactly what religion now means, and most ancients would not have thought of the cultus of Athena or the Vedic sacred fire as "their religion" in the modern sense of something separate from the rest of their culture, which you could either participate in or not according to your personal "beliefs." It was just part of who they were, like the kind of food they ate or who they might marry.

So it is that today, to a significant extent, religion is a matter of what individual students, including yourself, want to call religion. In this book, we will find examples of everything from "hardcore" Islam or Christianity to Disneyland or the "cult" of Elvis spoken of as in some way religious. You decide.

For the purposes of this book, though, here is what we will regard a working definition of religion. We will start with William James' reference to belief in a transcendent or "unseen order." Then we will say that, to be religion in the full historical sense of the term, that "unseen order" must be visibly expressed through the three **"forms of religious expression,"** proposed by the sociologist of religion Joachim Wach.[15]

According to Wach, the three basic forms of religious expression are the **theoretical**, which covers what is thought and said, the stories, rhetoric, doctrines, and ideologies of religion; the **practical**, which includes what is done, the rites, worship, spiritual techniques, and customary practices; and the **sociological**, referring to the types of groups, leadership, and interpersonal relations that appear. All these are best understood if they are seen as ways in which one component of experience—the transcendent experience—evokes response in ideas and stories, in actions, and in forming

A girl praying, suggesting the inner life of religion   (robyelo357/Fotolia)

groups. (Later in this book, we look in more detail at these three forms. Chapter 4 deals in large part with the practical form of rite and related practices. Chapter 11 treats the sociological side of religion, showing how a religious group or institution is in itself a symbol of transcendent reality. Chapter 12 discusses the theoretical form of religious expression and endeavors to demonstrate how religious words, sentences, stories, and concepts are symbols at the same time.)

A word might be said about this "working definition" in response to the critiques cited above of the academic study of religion as too much is based on an "essentialist" (that is, having its own unique nature) view of the subject. These critics, discussed further toward the end of Chapter 12, very rightly point out that different people respond differently to religion, some being nonreligious virtually by nature. From the subjective human perspective, certainly there is no one unique thing that is religion, but practically as many religions, or nonreligions, as there are people.

However, it could be responded that to look at the matter just from the subjective angle is one-sided. That may be a scholarly bias here akin to that of those styles of religion that put all their emphasis on inner faith or feeling. We could also ask what is "said" by such outer structures usually regarded as religious as art, architecture, and ritual, regardless of the feeling they evoke, or do not evoke, in various persons. The Shinto *torii* or distinctive gate of itself may suggest a passageway from the secular world to a sacred space, whether or not everyone who passes through it has such a feeling. In the same way, Christian Holy Communion, or Muslim prayers toward Mecca, or Buddhist monks in their saffron robes seem to make a statement to the world whether all the world hears

Prehistoric cave painting or cow and horses at Lascaux, France, recalling the distant beginnings of symbolism and perhaps sacred rites   (Glasshouse Images/Alamy)

it or not. As the structuralist would point out, these are often consistent: Many religions have sacred times, like festivals; demarcate sacred places, like temples or shrines or churches or even an inward sacred place in the heart; and designate people who have special religious roles sometimes marked by special dress.

Whether one calls a view like this "essentialism" or not may be a matter of choice, but in any case it would not necessarily imply any supernaturalist view of religion, only that for whatever reason our human ways of expressing an "unseen order" tend to fall into common patterns or forms of expression.

Religion, in short, has many sides. As we will see in various ways throughout this book, its origin and meaning has been understood as an evolutionary adaptation in early humans, with roots in animal behavior; anthropologically and sociologically as a system of social identity and control; and psychologically, for its role in dealing with problems, or even neurologically, "hardwired" into the biology of the brain. It is no less understood experientially, if one takes into account experiences of "the Holy" or "the Sacred," whether in revelation or in **mystical** experience. Last, but not least, there is the role of religion as response to intellectual and philosophical questions about the origin, nature, and destiny of the world and humanity; about evil; about ethical obligations; about justice and the social order. In the chapters following, we will suggest, at least, the place of all these perspectives in religious studies.

THE STRUCTURE OF THIS BOOK

After this introductory chapter, and after one giving necessary background on the history of religion, we will get down to business with a series of chapters on different ways of looking at religion, followed by example chapters.

The sequence of chapter topics seeks, broadly speaking, to follow the way a person like you or me might actually become acquainted with a religion, whether it is a familial religion learned in childhood or an adult encounter. By extension, we can take that same process to escort us through familiarization with the broader social and scholarly meanings of religion.

By and large, it is not really the abstract doctrinal concepts or advanced philosophical arguments that one first meets, but rather a faith's stories, symbols, rites, and sociological matrix. Here we strive to follow the order in which religion is learned: beginning with childhood or novice listening to myth or story, then going on to seeing symbol and rite, then to the psychology of religion to keep pace with the new feelings and thoughts one has had in hearing the stories and seeing the rites. On from there we engage with the religious groups our growing child or seeker will inevitably encounter on his or her quest, and then will face religion in its artistic and popular forms, including today's religion on the Internet. The quester will next want to deal with the philosophical and belief issues the journey presents, and finally with its expression in action: How does one then live?

Described topically, then, the chapters will be as follows:

Chapter 1. We first present this Introduction to religious studies.

Chapter 2. In order to get a larger perspective, we then survey the history of what we call religion on planet earth.

Chapter 3. In this book, after each substantive chapter, will come one presenting a concrete example of the topic. Following history, the example will be mythology, a form of religious discourse undoubtedly known to humanity from our earliest origins as speaking and imagining beings.

Chapter 4. Along with myth, the first humans must have made or done things, like the cave paintings mentioned above, to create what we would call symbol and rite. These will be the topic of this chapter; anyone encountering a religion is likely first to hear its stories and see its symbols and practices.

Chapter 5. It will now be time to reflect on the psychology of religion, to understand what is going in the mind as it deals with myth and symbol as the individual matures in the faith.

Chapter 6. To provide examples to go with the psychology of religion, we will look at various spiritual paths and means of salvation presented in religion.

Chapter 7. Perhaps the deepest problem dealt with by religion in its myths and practices as well as its psychology and philosophy is the problem of evil. It is time now to look at it.

Chapter 8. Next comes the sociology of religion, the groups, institutions, and forms of leadership incumbent in religion as we know it.

Chapter 9. All of the forgoing is expressed in religious art, from the colorful images embedded in its mythology to the architecture of the buildings within which its people gather, and the music performed therein, together with its poetry and stories.

Chapter 10. A special case of the expression of religion is its popular forms; popular religion offers examples of religious art and groups.

Chapter 11. By way of further example of religious art and sociology, we will consider the remarkable role of religion in the computer age, which is changing so much about how we live.

Chapter 12. It is now time to deal with religious ideas, doctrines, and philosophy; they did not come first, since religion is most often encountered first in its more everyday phenomena, but a faith's great ideas are very important.

Chapter 13. As examples of religious doctrine, we will study beliefs about the afterlife and the end of the world.

Chapter 14. Finally, how does religion affect the way we made decisions about right behavior? We come now to religion and ethics.

Chapter 15. As a case study in ethics, we will take the all-important issue of religion and war.

SUMMARY

In this chapter, we have first asked the question: What does it mean to study religion in the twenty-first century? Some reasons are: It is important for understanding history, including the history of art and literature; it still has important social and political influence; and it influences the behavior of people in many ways, whether medical choices or in personal psychology; the philosophical questions raised by religion remain important.

Examples of religion are given from Shinto ceremony to American conversion; we may see how they all reflect awareness of another reality from the ordinary.

We next examine definitions of religion presented by a number of important thinkers, noting the wide variety of approaches to this topic represented by them.

Our own working definition is James' "unseen order" expressed through Joachim Wach's three forms of religious expression: the theoretical, practical, and sociological.

The chapters in this book are arranged roughly so as to present the way in which a child would gradually learn about the religion of his or her family and culture, or in which a person encountering a religion would perceive and begin to understand it, go through the historical, mythological, practice, sociological, philosophical, and ethical dimensions of religion.

KEY TERMS

mystical, p. 11

mysticism, p. 7

numinous, p. 7

priest, p. 3

rite, p. 3

ritual, p. 3

sacred, p. 6

sociology, p. 6

structuralism, p. 8

subjective, p. 3

three forms of religious expression, p. 9

transcendence, p. 8

CHAPTER 2

History of Religion on Planet Earth

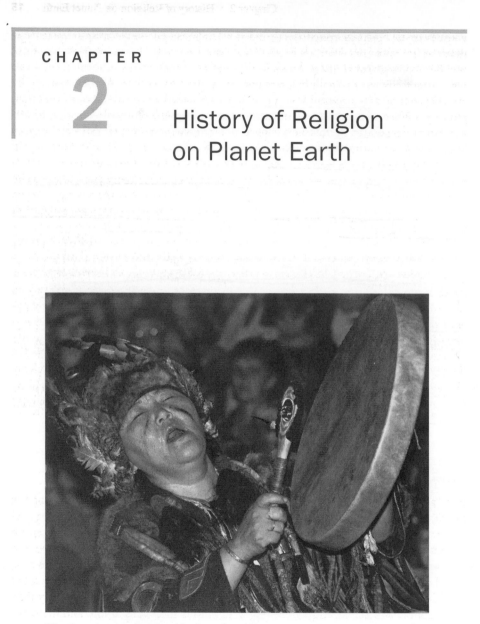

Siberian shaman beating his drum in ecstasy   (Ilya Naymushin/Reuters)

LEARNING OBJECTIVES

After reading this chapter, you should be able to:

- Characterize the earliest stages of human religion.
- Describe some basic features of the religion of prehistoric hunters and gatherers, such as initiations, shamanism, and the sacred meaning of land and plants, and of the animal and the hunt. Define the term animism.
- Discuss new developments that came to religion with the emergence of agriculture: the importance of mother goddesses, seasonal festivals, and sacrifice, including human. What is the relation of all these to archaic agriculture?
- Interpret the religion of the ancient empires, with their sacred kingship and elaborate polytheism. Discuss the significance of the emergence of the great religions in the "Axial Age" and the time of the ancient empires, when writing was becoming widespread, society was becoming more and more complex, and trade and political units were expanding.
- Present very briefly the names and basic characteristics of the world's great religions: Hinduism, Buddhism, the faiths of China and Japan, Judaism, Christianity, and Islam.
- Present and discuss the stages of development of the great religions as suggested by this book: apostolic, consolidation, devotional, reform, modern. Discuss some different ways religion has responded to modernity around the world.
- Talk about what you think the future of religion will be.

HUMAN RELIGIOUS BEGINNINGS

How did religion begin? This question has not been definitively answered and is probably unanswerable because it is put the wrong way. The words *religion* and *begin* are misleading here. The discussion in Chapter 1 on the way religion, as we understand it, is a modern concept may have suggested this to you. If you were to visit a tribe of very early humans, and you tried to ask them what their religion was, the chances are they wouldn't know what you were talking about, because what we think of as the special religious dimension of life was just part of the way they lived. As we will see in Chapter 3, they told stories that were at one and the same time entertaining, imparted practical information, and dealt with questions about the origins of life and death. Before they went out on a hunt, they danced, perhaps acting out the way a primal ancestor hunted, but that was as much getting instructions as religion. If they returned successful, they might dance, feast, and make an offering to the spirit of that primal hunter, but that was just gratitude, not religion in some modern sense. These gestures were at one and the same time prayer, celebration, and passing tribal ways on to the next generation. It was just a part of the process of becoming human. They were ways of learning to think as humans in the universe.

Myth, **magic**, ritual, sacred art, and beliefs in gods and spirits were more than just chapters in the process of becoming human. In a real sense they *were* the process, because fundamentally the components of religion, as we now think of it, were not abstract "beliefs" but tools with which to think, talk, and know about self and world.

You learn something by telling a story about it, or dancing it, or doing ritual for it, and why shouldn't these stories and dances include the invisible world one sensed all around as well as the visible?

The stories and dances were all a kind of language. Learning the secrets of hunting meant talking about it and acting it out; it meant telling stories about it and doing ritual-like hunting plays or energizing dances in which the souls of animals and the controlling forces in the forest come alive as spirits and gods. These dramas may have included cave paintings such as those we considered in Chapter 1 and other forms of art.

So people were learning to think. The formation of human thought was likely *inseparable* from the use of mythic "pictures in the head" and ritual gestures as pegs on which to hang thoughts and memories. Ideas about birth, feelings, and death arose also; these too needed symbolic pegs in thinking and doing, but they would not have thought of them as "religion" in the modern sense.

The notion of a beginning to human religion is equally misleading. There certainly was no single dramatic moment when it all started. Humankind brought over from the animal world raw material with which to make religion, including instinctive capacities for ritual, hierarchy, and social morality; for territoriality; for play as a means of setting apart separate time and space for learning by acting out, in ways sometimes not far from creative ritual; and for sensing depth and meaning in certain events.

In 1970 Jane Goodall, the famous student of chimpanzee behavior in Africa, observed chimps doing a kind of ecstatic dance at a waterfall, sometimes singly and sometimes in groups, apparently excited by the awesome beauty and energy of this dramatic natural display. She believed the activity was like an expression of the awe and joy that led to religion in early humans.[1] That may well be so, but unless the animals were able to articulate what they experienced there at the "sacred" waterfall in language—and there is much we do not know about animal communication—it would not yet be religion in the human sense. So it's the words, and hence the group, that make it religion. And there's more to religious groups than that.

It remained, as the human mind undertook that strange and unprecedented expansion endowing it with capacity for concepts and choices, to get all these things together in a way that would help humans to think about and handle their world and above all themselves—and to find words for them, for they were now also alive with human-scale memories, moods, and awareness of birth and death.

The most important, distinctively human inputs into religion were the discovery of death and the articulation of memory into stories, both dependent on language. When some protohuman first saw the body of a dead comrade, and generalized in his or her mind from that grim observation to the realization that all, including oneself, will die, that must have been an awesome moment and one important for religion. Both death and memory were reinforced by association with the sacred and the numinous. Most likely both were first thought out through stories, as were all other complex ideas; we first think in stories because we learn sequences of action from the memory that makes one's past a story.

Stories themselves are a way of talking and of exploring new ideas. When the development of language along with a mind powerful enough to use it opened up past and future as well as present, people began to query where they had come from and what their destiny was. At first, the answers were in terms of stories, just as our own memories come out as stories that help to tell us who we are today. We put word symbols around birth, life, and death; talk and chatter about them; tell stories about them; feel their glory or horror in new and different ways; and sometimes forget about them in the fascination of a tale.

These stories were (at least the most significant of them) what is called in religious studies myth. "Myth" does not here mean a story that is not true. Rather, a myth is a story that presents in the form of narrative the basic worldview of the society. Whether it tells of the world being made by the gods from the body of a monster or emerging from a cosmic egg or of the first man and woman rising out of the ground, it tells a great deal about how the society views itself and about the relation of people to earth and universe.

Memory is a rough instrument in humans. We do not remember everything that ever happened to us with equal clarity but only certain things, generally those that have a major symbolic or actual bearing on who we think we are today. They are what has gone into making you or me who we are. In the same way, myth and religion do not remember everything just as it was in the sacred past but concentrate on moments from the past that cast a bright light on the present. Nearly all societies have narratives about gods, animals, divine ancestors, or heroes that help explain who the people of today are. Most have some concrete idea expressed in myth and funeral practices about what happens to a person after death—for all humans confront death.

A key feature of early religion, and of tribal, indigenous, and folk religion down to the present, is what sometimes is called **animism**. This term, from the Latin *anima* for **soul**, has nothing particularly to do with animals but refers to belief in innumerable finite spirits or souls around, whether ancestral, inhabiting particular trees or stones or places in nature, protecting the house, or visiting one in dreams. Often small shrines to animistic spirits, like those to the *nats* of Thailand, coexist with faith in a major religion, in this case Buddhism. Indeed, much contemporary belief in angels and other spirits intermediate between humanity and a high God is like a continuation of animism.

THE RELIGION OF EARLY GATHERERS AND HUNTERS

The earliest humans were gatherers and hunters. The hunt, mainly a masculine business, was very important to men and was often a partly ritual affair. It was typically undertaken after fasting, dancing, and magic. After an animal was taken its spirit might be propitiated, for the archaic hunter saw himself as part of a web of life through which all souls, animals and human, circulated.

The gathering of roots, nuts, seeds, fruits, and other plant products was largely women's work; its spiritual significance prior to the discovery of agriculture was no less vital, though sometimes less public. Indeed, in many religions women have had their own rituals that were considered extremely important, even more important than the men's, for the maintenance of the society, but were kept secret. Usually they were addressed to goddesses. This was the case in ancient Greece, where the penalty for a man intruding on a woman's secret ritual to a goddess such as Artemis or Demeter was death. The culminating ritual at the famous shrine of Eleusis in ancient Greece, though a mystery of life and death in which both men and women were initiated, was kept secret for some 2,000 years, and is still unknown today, and one reason is that it centered on a goddess, Demeter.

Another characteristic feature of primitive religion is **initiation**. Typically all young men, and often young women, experienced an initiation into adulthood, or into a special mystery like that of Eleusis. A serious initiation usually involved isolation and pain, in effect becoming a symbolic death and rebirth. Going through initiation was a way of acquiring the society's memory and its knowledge of death. Indeed, initiation was really a way of learning the symbolic language of the society, for initiates would be taught the myths in the context of experiences to reinforce them.

The most striking representative of early religion is the **shaman**. This is the title, derived from Siberia, given to a figure common in primitive religion (though not universal) who foreshadowed much of what religion was to become. The shaman is about the same as the person more popularly called "witch doctor" or "medicine man." The shaman, through a process usually involving an altered state of consciousness, is able to contact spirits, find lost or strayed souls, heal, and ascertain the will of the gods, all the while providing a dramatic performance that in itself is a religious experience for his public.

According to commentators such as Mircea Eliade, the most important fact about shamans is the means by which they come to their office.[2] Theirs was not always an easy accession through heredity or professional schooling. Rather, in Eliade's model, the shaman has felt called out by the gods or spirits and has then acquired mastery over them through an intense initiatory ordeal. He or she has, in the process, felt torn apart, nearly killed, by invisible entities. One then goes through an arduous training to control them—perhaps given by a senior shaman, perhaps imparted in dreams or visions, perhaps alone deep in the woods or mountains.

As a result, shamans are reborn as new persons able to use the spirits as **supernatural** allies. They are subsequently able to divine and heal; often, they enact dramatic scenarios in which, entranced by the beat of drums or the throb of chanting, they fly invisibly to the lands of the gods and the dead to intercede or seek out lost and stolen souls. The Altaic shaman in Siberia, for example, sacrifices a horse and transfers its spirit into a wooden mount. For his public performance, he seats himself astride it and beats his drum as he enters a light trance. When fully in the spirit, he moves to an upright tree trunk, representing the axis of the world, to which platforms have been attached—each of these stands for one of the nine heavens. He climbs them, calling down to the assembled tribes people his dialogue with the gods at each level. This shaman also has a scenario in which he rides his wooden steed to the underworld, bearing messages to and from the departed souls of his people.

Shamans are key figures in human religion and culture because they early made the transition from the parareligious behavior of animals to that of beings for whom religion is a quest for human knowledge and power. In many archaic societies the shaman is the principal custodian and creator, out of visions, of what art and poetry there is. Their vocabulary is often much larger than that of ordinary people, and they are said to speak the language of birds.

The shaman's vocation is perhaps the first example of division of labor in which an individual is set apart and supported by the rest, on the grounds of a subjective experience he or she has had and for the sake of his or her contribution to the spiritual, psychological, and cultural good of the whole. However bizarre the shaman's behavior may seem (though the psychotherapeutic value of much of what shamans do is increasingly appreciated), the paleolithic shaman advanced human society far along the road toward the kind of community it now is. Shaman's healed mind and body, saw visions, told the future, spoke to the gods, made costumes and artwork rich with symbols from out of his supernatural encounters, and chanted the lore of the gods and the tribe. In his craft lay the seeds of those cultural growths that would lead to the physician, the psychiatrist, the scientist, the priest, the **mystic**, the magus, the poet, the artist, the actor, and the spirit medium. These callings are now quite diverse and not always temperamentally sympathetic to each other, but they have in common a creative use of human inner life and spirit, and can be traced back to shamanism.

Perhaps more than anyone else in earliest times, shamans articulated the most distinctive and striking idea in religion: the existence of gods, supernatural beings, or a supreme God. Shamans, in their vision flights, were not bound by ordinary perception but met and even married spirits and gods who transformed them, or they encountered a high God who had made the world. These perceptions moreover were expressed, not only in story but perhaps also in art such as the earliest cave paintings.

For a hundred millenniums or more, human societies subsisted by hunting and gathering. As is always the case, the forms of religious expression were deeply interwoven with crucial material sources of life. The animal, as the most imposing source of food and clothing, might be a symbol of life's ultimate sources, hunted, worshiped, storied, sacrificed. As sacrifices they were messengers from one world to another; as totem of a tribe they represented its life.

When looking into the animal's shining eyes, early humans saw an ambivalent spiritual power with which they had to establish a harmonious working relationship, learning the skills and magic that would enable sufficient animals to be taken and the propitiations that would satisfy the spirits of the killed animals and their divine protectors, thus allowing them to return and be taken again. The famous cave paintings of animals perhaps represent this spiritual power seen in animals, as well as shamans' visions of them. Over the years, as good a spiritual balance as one could hope for in this uncertain world was achieved by the hunting society. Human population was sparse and could not grow beyond what could be supported by a fairly mobile life of following game. Although certain species, such as the giant ground sloth of North America, may have been driven to extinction by paleolithic hunting, archaic hunters learned their ecological niche in the world and generally took no more than was needed. Also, men and women, leaders and followers, were often more equal in the small bands and tribes of archaic hunters than they have been in the later more complex, male-dominated societies of kings and slaves.

ARCHAIC AGRICULTURE

The next development shattered forever this equilibrium. It set humankind off on a course of meteoric growth and change that was very sudden from the perspective of geological or biological timetables. Population grew phenomenally, as it still sometimes grows, when fertile areas were suddenly able to support many times the people they could from hunting. Towns and finally cities appeared where once there had been only wandering bands, and empires where before had dwelt only tribes. Humanity was off on its careening ride in history as we know it, with its incredible misery and splendor and above all the rapid rate of change in the world—a world in its horrors and glories alike so different from those of animals or even primeval hunters.

The catalyst of all this change was, of course, agriculture. Planting and harvesting crops and keeping domestic animals meant a change in the way most people spent most of their time and in the relationship between them and the earth on which they lived. It meant also a partial shift from the animal to the plant as an ultimate source-of-life symbol, indicated in goddesses representing mother-earth and vegetation gods who die and rise with harvest and seedtime.

Agriculture emphasized the idea (although the thought was not new) that the earth was like a mother; in the religion of archaic agricultural societies appeared a new emphasis on the mother goddess. The turning of the seasons and the sacredness of place understandably became newly important, for agricultural people were nonmigratory and bound to the cycle of planting and ingathering, expressed in anxious planting and protective rites and joyful harvest festivals such as that of Ise, or the American Thanksgiving.

At the same time a darker side of spiritual experience also appeared. This was the relationship of death to life, the experience that blood and death were necessary for life to flourish, analogous to the seed that seemed to die and be buried in the soil or the animal whose slaughtered body gave life to many. Archaic agriculture was the milieu

Dancers in a harvest rite widely celebrated in northern India, suggesting joy and thanksgiving at the end of the agricultural year   (Channi Anand/AP Images)

in which animal and human sacrifice, cannibalism, and headhunting most prospered. Myths of the origin of agriculture often involve the killing of an earth-maiden out of whose body food crops are taken.

As indicated, however, archaic agriculture also made possible a great increase in population—even if, as many studies have shown, ancient peasant farmers were likely to be less healthy and shorter-lived than nonfarming hunters and gatherers, owing to overcrowding and disease, less-varied diet or famine. The mythological association of agriculture with death as well as life was not misplaced. Nonetheless, a given amount of land, if fertile, could support far more farmers than hunters. Furthermore, farmers were bound to one place and often dependent on organized systems of trade, irrigation, and defense against raiders. For this reason agriculture led to the creation of larger political units, particularly along the banks of great rivers where commerce and massive hydraulic works were feasible—the Nile, the two rivers of Mesopotamia, the Indus, the Yellow River in China.

ANCIENT EMPIRES

Let us imagine one of those ancient riverside empires, so important as transitions between prehistoric and semimodern culture. In their bosoms appeared writing, philosophy, and the great religions that still flourish.

Here, along the banks of a wide watercourse, such as the Nile or the Yellow in China, a procession of singing priests is moving with the slowness of ancient ritual. Behind them, surrounded by courtiers, comes the king, resplendent in gold cloth and green jade. He is making progress toward the vast burnished temple of the young god who returns to these riverbanks every spring and then grows old with the year. The sacred king opens the planting time by ritually plowing three furrows in the temple courtyard, while incense burns and trumpets blare.

The ancient empires above all idealized order, both human and cosmic, and the two were thoroughly integrated. In them, if all went well, humans dwelt harmoniously with the seasons and the gods. Order was far from consistently achieved, but it was the ideal toward which religion, politics, and philosophy strove. That was understandable, for order was the supreme good down on the farm; what the farmer even today desires above all else of the universe are security and reliable seasons. The ancient empires, profoundly attuned to agriculture, wished a universe as regular as planting and harvest in a good year. Generally they held a concept of a universal law or regulating principle: Maat in Egypt, Rita or Dharma in India, Tian or Heaven in China. It embodied the order, and gods above, like kings below, were themselves servants of order and its exemplars and upholders.

The sacred king symbolized and maintained this order. The sovereign would ritually fight and defeat the forces of chaos to create anew the world every year, as in ancient Babylon, or begin the new planting season by wearing colors appropriate to the force of growth and creativity and by plowing the first furrows, as in China. The ruler, such as the pharaoh or the Chinese emperor, was no mere political figure. He was a part of the divine order. He represented heaven—the sacred law and primal power—to his people, even as he represented them to heaven. His ritual actions, which occupied a large part of his time, were deemed crucial to society because they mystically harmonized human life with the power of the turning of the seasons and the life-producing work of the gods. It was usually felt that if the king performed his ritual and moral obligations wrongly, nature itself would respond with flood or drought, and society with war or revolution.

The ancient empires also represented the beginning of widespread religious networks, for priests or scholars allied with the court were the king's representatives in far-flung provinces and incorporated the common people (and their gods) into the religious system centering on the king. The religion of the ancient empires exhibited a rich polytheism. Primitives had, to be sure, accepted a plurality of gods and spirits, even as they also often venerated a high God who represented the steady, creative, and regulative force. The ancient empires brought together many tribes, each contributing its own deities to a common pool. Furthermore, the increasing complexity and variety of the new imperial and urban ways of life suggested divine functions unthought of before. The pantheon tended to become a heavenly court that was a celestial model of the earthly, as in China, or a set of options for spiritual experience to match the many temperaments and ways of life of humankind, as in Egypt or India.

Polytheism thus came to full flower in the ancient empires. It meant not only that there were a great number of gods but also that spiritual life had a special quality. For the polytheist, the universe is a rich spiritual complexity with every time, place, and occasion having its own sacred meaning, being in a deep but finite sense its own spiritual center. It was in every grove, mountain, and hearth and in every hour whether of war or love, dread or rapture. Polytheism is different from monotheism, belief in one God, not just in terms of quantity, the number of deities, but also of quality, the kind of religious life it represents.

THE AXIAL AGE

Something else was going on as well, for the age of the ancient empires culminated in the time of the religious founders—the likes of Confucius, the Buddha, Jesus, Muhammad—who started the great religions we know today. These half-dozen or so men have had an incomparable influence on world history, and the lives of countless individuals. Their time began in the period known as the Axial Age, commencing about the fifth century BCE by the western calendar. It was called Axial by the philosopher Karl Jaspers, because it was a time of decisive turning in human history, above all religious history.[3]

What happened? One place to begin would be with the invention of writing. That innovation significantly preceded the religious founders and their written scriptures by a few centuries. Writing meant chronicles, and history as we now know it. It meant we now had records, and not just myths, about what had happened in ages past. It meant we had to realize the world didn't start over about the same with each new year, or each new generation, but that things changed and did not change back as empires rose and fell, and peoples moved about over the face of the earth.

For most ordinary people this was not necessarily good. Farmers want stability, but what they often saw was one army after another marching across their fields, followed by exorbitant tax collectors, and in between the likelihood of drought, flood, famine, or plague.

Meditating Buddha image in a garden   (d100/Fotolia)

Another important factor was that the time of the ancient empires was also a time of the mixing up of peoples as settlers, soldiers, and slaves moved about, inhabiting the new cities and spreading new religious ideas; they also, taken out of old tribes and towns, were often lonely and lost, thrown on individual spiritual resources, and so more interested in individual salvation than communal gods. For their needs the old religion of many gods and sacred kings had no real answers.

Innumerable new religious movements emerged in this time of change, like those of the old salvation-oriented mystery religions, such as Eleusis, of the Mediterranean world, and the mysticism of ancient India. However, two developments are especially important to our story.

One was the idea of **eschatology**, that history is leading up a final point when all will be made right. Things may be pretty bad now, but lift up your eyes to look into the future, when God will judge the world and create a new heaven and earth, or a new Buddha will arise in a paradisaical age. Then all will be explained and made worthwhile, and all tears will be wiped away.

Even more important was the Axial Age belief that a new divine revelation had appeared in the midst of historical time, here and now: Moses and the Commandments on Mt. Sinai, the Buddha's enlightenment, Jesus with his cross and empty tomb, the Prophet Muhammad receiving the Qur'an—all events in our world, in our time. Now the most sacred events are not those of the creation and the beginning, but happened in history well afterward. Significantly, the major holidays of these religions commemorate events they see as historical, such as the Passover or Easter, Christmas or the Buddhist Wesak marking in the spring the Buddha's birth and enlightenment. They carried over innumerable features of pre-Axial Age religion—the very name Easter comes from an Anglo-Saxon goddess of spring—yet while keeping enough to quiet the anxieties of people turning to a new faith, gave the old a new meaning.

It is just as important that the Axial Age religions rejected the polytheism of the ancient empires in favor of a single **monotheistic** God in the Western faiths, Judaism, Christianity, and Islam, or a single **monistic** (unified) reality in the east. It must be noted, however, that the appearance of polytheism, as of animism, was often carried over in them, in the cults of saints, buddhas, bodhisattvas, immortals, and Hindu deities occupying, as it were, the space between the human and the ultimate one divine. For all their inner radicality, the Axial Age religions made many adjustments to the prevailing spiritual culture.

Most important of all, Axial Age religions are generally centered on a **founder** and a revelation that appeared in the midst of historical time, basically between Moses (c. thirteenth century BCE) or Zarathustra (628–551 BCE?) and Muhammad (570–632 CE). The founder represents something new: the conveyor of an absolute revelation of the divine in the midst of real history, as Jesus was born in the days of Caesar Augustus, a quite historical Roman emperor of two thousand years ago, but of Jesus's birth, in the words of the Christmas hymn addressed to Bethlehem, the traditional town of his nativity, "The hopes and fears of all the years/Are met in thee tonight."

This is quite different from a religion based on mythical events that happened in a misty, undated "other time" at the Beginning. Significantly, these founder, Axial Age religions tend to be named after that founder, as are Buddhism, Christianity, or Confucianism. (However, Islam should not be called Muhammadanism, as it once was by non-Muslims, because Muslims insist it is not based on the Prophet as a divine person, but on *islam* or submission to God as taught in the Qur'an received by Muhammad.)

The founder of a new religion (the vocation commonly ascribed to persons such as the Buddha, Jesus, Confucius, and Muhammad) has, needless to say, a very rare calling, but one which has affected human life immensely. He or she must have an especially comprehensive religious personality, together with a special charisma and the right historical setting. The founder must become a symbol in his or her personality of both complexity and clarification. The great founders have had a reputation for being able to cover enough of the diverse roles of religion to provide models in themselves for all the strands a great religion needs to have: a spiritual way, an attitude toward society, a common touch, deep wisdom.

The founder must also appear at a point of historical transition when religious symbols are still persuasive but new ones or new arrangements of old ones are needed. The founder must be able to facilitate the transition because he or she has links with past, present, and future. People were reassured by Jesus, for example, because he did not reject the tradition, only its abuses; yet he also gave new symbols, himself and his cross, for a new age and suggested meaning for the future as well, in the kingdom of God. What the founder does is like opening up a heretofore shuttered window, so that new light revealing new patterns and meanings falls on a preexisting mosaic, or adding a few final pieces to a jigsaw puzzle already in process.

An important aspect of the founder is the fact that he or she has a small band of disciples—the **disciple** being still another religious type. The disciple is a special type of religious personality in his or her own right and is essential to the founder by providing an intimate audience for the message in a group that will prepare the lasting institutionalization of the newly founded religion.

The Axial Age religions with their founders have a view of historical time stretching from creation to a glorious end, or in the case of Buddhism and Hinduism (the latter in some ways like an Axial Age religion in its modern form, but without a historical founder) moving in great cycles of creation and destruction, but always swinging back to begin each cycle with a Golden Age. All these faiths have a written scripture, obviously dependent on the invention of writing. They put emphasis on individual responsibility for one's faults or sins, and one's salvation through right faith and right action.

Fundamentally, of course, what was happening was that a new image of what it meant to be human was emerging as experience taught new meanings for life and time. A person was not just a part of nature or of a sacred order ruled over by a sacred king, but an individual who had to find salvation amid change and even chaos in a hard world. Now let us turn to look for just a moment at those religions.

THE GREAT RELIGIONS

We cannot here discuss in any detail the history and teachings of the major world religions. Other books are devoted wholly to this task.[4] What we shall do is name and identify the most important faiths, discuss briefly the significance of their appearance in history around the time of the ancient empires, and survey the principal stages of their development.

Hinduism is perhaps the most difficult to encompass in a few words, for it includes the vast complex of ideas and practices associated with the culture of India, from yoga to village shrines. Although it has no single founder, its chief philosophical and devotional traditions first emerged in roughly the same Axial Age period as the founding of the other major faiths. Especially on an intellectual level, its main emphasis is on seeing the divine in all things and in oneself, then realizing this divinity through meditation or devotion to the gods.

Buddhism started in India with the teaching of Gautama, called the Buddha or Enlightened One (563–483 BCE), but is now established mostly outside of India in Southeast and East Asia. Centering around the *sangha*, the order of monks who are successors of the Buddha's disciples, Buddhism teaches that one attains liberation through meditation and related methods that counteract our usual attachment to partial realities.

Chinese religion should be considered as a whole, even though it comprises several strands. Confucianism is based on the teaching of Confucius (551–479 BCE), which emphasize the good society based on virtue, family loyalty, and a respect for tradition and ancestors affirmed by solemn rites. Daoism, according to tradition ascribed to an older contemporary of Confucius called Laozi, inculcates a more romantic and mystical path aimed at oneness with the Dao. The Dao (sometimes Tao) means the Way. It refers to nature, the cosmos, and human life as like a vast stream down which we are moving, and the idea is to live in harmony with its flow. Buddhism and folk religion were also very important in China. Most prerevolutionary Chinese had some relation to all these faiths.

Japanese religion is a comparable matter. Here both Buddhism and Shinto, the latter being the veneration in lovely shrines of the polytheistic gods of ancient Japan, have a place in the lives of most people. Confucianism has been very influential too as a moral system, and more recently a number of new religions have flourished.

In the West, three great monotheistic religions have dominated the spiritual scene for centuries. All three worship a single personal God, and all are rooted in the spiritual experience of Jews in Ancient Israel. For this reason they are often called the Abrahamic faiths, because they trace their lineage back to Abraham, the first patriarch of the Hebrew people.

The faith that most directly continues this heritage is Judaism, found in the state of Israel and as a minority around the world. Believing that God has a special calling for them in world history, serious Jews have kept their identity intact by being faithful to the moral and ceremonial norms of the Law and the passion for righteousness of the **prophets**.

Christianity traces its origin to the ministry of Jesus, called the Christ or Anointed One (about 4 BCE–30 CE). Traditional Christianity is based not only on following the moral teachings of Jesus but also on the belief that in Jesus, God worked in a special way for the salvation of humankind. Christianity has taken many forms throughout history, but all have been seen as ways of identifying oneself with God's work in Jesus.

Islam (the name means "submission," submission to the will of God) derives from the work of the Prophet Muhammad (570–632 CE) in Arabia. This faith believes that the Qur'an, the Islamic scripture, is the final revelation of God given through Muhammad. Islam is concerned with applying the teachings of God in all areas of life, from the Muslim's devout life of prayer to the organization of society. Islam is a simple, deep faith with both legal and mystical aspects.

These great faiths and the five or six human beings who have been founders of major religions have influenced human history far more than countless kings and presidents. On the other hand, kings and states have been deeply intertwined with their histories. Faith has provided integration for large and complex cultures, such as those of India, Japan, and medieval Europe. Religions sweeping across many diverse lands (such as Buddhism, Christianity, and Islam) have carried innumerable cultural gifts with them and have helped missionized lands awaken into the mainstream of history.

Sometimes, as in Christian Europe, the great religion arose to power only toward the end of the ancient empire stage. Sometimes the great religion aligned itself with an empire (Christianity with the late Roman Empire under the Emperor Constantine, Buddhism with the empire of Ashoka) or even helped create one (Islam and the

York Minster Cathedral in England, bespeaking the Great Religions in full development
(David Bank/John Warburton-Lee Photography/Alamy)

Damascus-Baghdad caliphate). In retrospect, though, we can see these Axial Age religions as being born in the world of the ancient empires, but finally helping people go beyond sacred king and agrarian/cosmic cycles. These new "great" religions instead help people gain a sense of internationalism, history, and universal truth. This was particularly true of the three most intercultural faiths, Buddhism, Christianity, and Islam, together with Judaism.

FIVE STAGES IN THE DEVELOPMENT OF GREAT RELIGIONS

Let us now trace, roughly and in outline, the stages of development through which the great religions have passed.[5] Each stage can best be understood as presenting one religion's interpretation of a common process.

Apostolic

The first period may be called the apostolic. It is the first few generations after the founder in founder religions. It is a time of expansion within a culture ostensibly devoted to other values. It is also a difficult time, because the transition from a religious founder to the next generation of leadership, usually by his one-time disciples, is always problematic, and because the new religion will be at odds with many of the values of the environing society. There is tension and perhaps persecution. It is a time of rapid change in the new religion and of deep-seated personality conflicts and doctrinal debates. Indeed, the forms the religion takes in all the forms of expression are in flux at first. For a religion that is to survive, enthusiasm is even greater than these difficulties and prevails. During this period the basic doctrines, organizational structure, and canon of scripture (the list of books considered authoritative scripture) are made firm.

Empire and Wisdom

The next period is one of doctrinal and institutional consolidation after a measure of success has been achieved and the religion has attained some political recognition. If the new religion is to become world class, inevitably it becomes aligned with a major empire at the onset of this second period. This period is Buddhism in the empire of Ashoka, Confucianism in Han China, Christianity in the Roman and Byzantine empires after Constantine, and Islam under the Caliphate. Councils of religious leaders now present dogmatic definitions, forms of worship are devised that meet the needs of both peasants and converted intellectuals, and institutional structures are erected appropriate to the dominant imperial faith that parallels the state.

Doctrines are probably made to tie in with existing traditions of wisdom but are deepened by new symbols from the erstwhile underground faith. One thinks of Han Confucianism, Christian and Islamic philosophy appropriating forms from Neoplatonism at this stage, and of Buddhism relating to Vedanta thought. The theological emphasis is likely to be a reaction against the radical discovery of history implied by the life and work of the original founder. The movement is now toward putting his message in terms of eternal truths behind all changes in history, behind all existing forms of worship, and behind the rise of the new religious institutions.

Devotionalism

The next style to emerge is characteristic of high medieval religion in the Christian, Jewish, Muslim, Hindu, and Buddhist spiritual worlds alike. In Hindu **bhakti** (devotion to the great gods) in India, Pure Land in Chinese and Japanese Buddhism, or the Franciscan style of devotion in medieval Europe, the emphasis is on the ability of even the simplest to achieve the highest sanctity through devotional fervor, faith, and love for God, saints, or buddhas and bodhisattvas. In fact, according to some popular teachers, this goal might take the wise far longer to achieve because of their insistence on proper technique or theological wisdom. In a subtle way, medieval devotion undercuts the hierarchical structure of the medieval type of society by saying it does not matter what class or caste or gender a person is, or how wise, so long as the person loves the Lord in her or his heart.

Reformation

In the next stage, reform, there is an intensification of the devotional mood within a major segment of the religion to the point of a radical break with the tradition, ostensibly in favor of return to its original or pure essence, and also a kind of radical purification in favor of simple faith. This generally occurs after about 1,500 years of development. One thinks of Pure Land Buddhism (belief one is saved by the grace of Amida Buddha) in China and Japan; the kind of radical Hindu bhakti represented by Chaitanya, spiritual father of the modern Krishna Consciousness movement; and the

Reformation of Luther and Calvin in Europe. All of these taught something comparable to Luther's insistence that one is saved by God's grace received through pure faith, not by any "works," however devout or moral or wise, one might do on one's own. Perhaps Islam, only some 1,500 years old now, is now moving into this stage, expressed in its current resurgence.

Modern

The last stage we shall here consider may be called the modern. Unlike the previous stages, it does not occur only because of the internal dynamics of the history of the particular religion but is also induced by developments in the world as a whole. For the last 150 years or so, all the world religions have had to adjust to the whole panoply of developments we call modernization: the Industrial Revolution; Western expansion (and then retreat); a rapid pace of change; new scientific ideas; population growth; educational growth; the worldwide spread of consumerism, nationalism, and Marxism. They have reacted to all this in many ways. Different parties in each religion have, in fact, taken diverse tacks: rigid conservatism, reformism, nationalism, thorough-going adjustment to the new. None, however, are what they were before. In some cases we see religion remaining as a kind of folk or popular religion, though its one-time intellectual and political influence is much diminished.

SUMMARY

The roots of the planet earth go deep into geological time, and so do the roots of religion, for there are parallels or apparent parallels between certain forms of animal behavior—such as territoriality, ranking, ritual, and play—which remind one of religious behavior or behavior sanctified by religion in human society. However, religion does not emerge until the human awareness of time and death, the use of language and story, and above all a sense of real self appear.

The earliest stage of religion is that of prehistoric hunters, in which there is typically a sense of the animal or its guardians as sacred and needing to be placated; there is also initiation and shamanism.

After the discovery of agriculture, new emphasis is placed on mother goddesses, seasonal festivals, and sacrifice, all understandable among sedentary farmers dependent on the fertility of the earth, seasonable weather, and the power of new life unleashed by death.

When societies coalesced into the large units we may call the ancient empires, such as those of Egypt, Mesopotamia, or China, the underlying desire of these agricultural communities was for stability, expressed in sacred kingship, seasonal rites, and a bureaucratic polytheism. Underneath, however, a thirst for new revelation, **monotheism** or **monism**, and personal liberation or salvation was on the increase.

That tendency was expressed in the great religions that emerged in the world of the ancient empires. They are characterized by emphasis on sacred scripture, a historical founder who is in some way a unique expression of divine reality, revelation in historical time, a monotheistic or monistic thrust, and means of personal salvation or liberation. (Not all the great religions have all these characteristics to the same degree or at all, but all have most of them.)

The great religions have subsequently gone through several stages of internal develop-ment, which may be summarized as apostolic, consolidation, devotional, reform, and modern, the last representing the crisis that all religions have undergone in the last century or two in responding to the modern world.

KEY TERMS

animism, p. 17

bhakti, p. 28

disciple, p. 25

eschatology, p. 23

founder, p. 24

initiation, p. 18

magic, p. 16

monism, p. 29

monotheism, p. 29

mystic, p. 19

myth, p. 16

polytheism, p. 22

prophet, p. 26

shaman, p. 18

soul, p. 17

supernatural, p. 18

CHAPTER 3

Myth: Our Lives, and the World's, Are Stories

Perseus, a hero from Greek mythology, holding the snake-covered head of Medusa (Pierrette Guertin/Fotolia)

LEARNING OBJECTIVES

After reading this chapter, you should be able to respond to these queries:

- How would you tell the story of your own life? What does this exercise tell you about myth?
- What role do myths or stories play in groups, such as schools or workplaces?
- What is the difference between preliterate and literate cultures in the way they see the world?
- What is a trickster and what are trickster myths?
- What are some different kinds of creation myths?
- What is the significance of the myth of the hero? What is its characteristic outline?
- What are the two kinds of hero myths?
- Do you consider myths significant? Why or why not?

YOUR STORY AS MYTH

If someone asked you to tell the story of your life, and you agreed, how would you tell that story?

Obviously you can't tell everything. In fact, you probably can't remember everything. If you're like most people, the chances are you cannot remember more than a few days or events from the earlier years of your life. Perhaps those days are the ones remembered because they were really the most important—the day a brother or sister was born, a key birthday, an honor at school—or perhaps just because they were representative, highly typical of what it was like to be a third grader.

In short, when you tell that life-story, you relate only a small selection of everything there is to say. Undoubtedly what you do narrate—what you remember—will be the story of your life as it tells who you are today, and why.

That account of past years may well be disproportionate in terms of the way things seemed back then. (I recall once discovering some letters I had written years before while in college that my mother had saved. I was amazed to read of events I had totally forgotten, but which apparently were important at the time. But they didn't make the unconscious cut of what ought to be in a story explaining who I am *now*. So they were left out of my current autobiography as I tell it to myself.)

You may even unconsciously reconstruct some happenings to fit the story as it now seems it ought to be told. (Psychologists are well aware of what are called false memories. Fantasies, separate events conflated together, even a gripping tale read or seen in a movie grafted onto your real memories, can quite innocently be reconfigured as a remembrance of something one now sincerely believes happened to oneself, and of course there are also pathological liars.)

All this can help us understand **myth**. We are here using the word in the positive sense, as a story that presents in narrative form the basic beliefs and values of people, just as your own singular life-story as remembered and told by yourself, your own personal myth, does for you individually. When a myth, then, tells about the creation of the world, the first humans, the foundation of a nation, and the lives of the gods and heroes whom it honors, what it does is tell stories that explain who we—our country, our culture, our religion, ourselves—are *now*. They may not be accurate in every detail—indeed, much may be read back into the story—but they speak of what is really important to us *now*. That is why such stories should not be thought of as science in the modern sense, but as self-understanding.

Moreover, myths are not just stories for the self alone. Anyone who has been part of a body such as a school, military unit, business, or corporation knows there are certain stories that are part of the lore of that group, that help explain what and who it really is. Knowing these stories helps make one an insider instead of just a newcomer. Stories of what it was like when so-and-so was here, why another person didn't fit in, this-or-that eccentric individual, the big fire or break-in. . . These accounts are often not told officially; in fact, they may be particular to a subgroup, even subversive. There are stories students tell when the teachers aren't listening, or that employees tell out of earshot of the bosses. Nonetheless, the stories are part of the lore and distinctive culture of that institution, and so are part of belonging.

Why story? Why not some more abstract scientific kind of exposition? First, we need to be able to relate *personally* to the narrative. We can slip our own lives more easily into a larger, more general story that gives it meaning, than into an abstraction. *Our lives, after all, are not abstractions but stories.* We are not just good or bad, or just oxygen, carbon, and other elements, but a *life-story*. So this personal story might aspire to share in the greater story of a heroic or divine exemplar. I might model my life on Hercules, or see my meditations as like those of the Buddha even if less deep, or my suffering as my way of sharing in the world-saving agony of Christ.

Such tales impart certain fundamental values through the story and the way it is told. It probably would not occur to primal peoples to ask whether the narratives are literally true in a modern scientific sense, even though they may deal with such ultimate questions as where the world came from, and why is there life—and death. They are just tales, and sometimes there are several alternative stories about those matters told by the same people.

The style of the story, and the way it is told by a master storyteller, solemnly or with a wink and a chuckle, can say quite a bit about our world, how we respond to its buffeting, and how we live our own lives. The bard's voice and expression suggest an attitude one could take toward this beautiful and baffling planet. Much out there is lovely as a sunrise, yet also much makes us weep, up to the brutal cutting-short of a life just as it was getting well underway. Do we laugh at the incongruities of our world, or cry, or shout angry defiance, or just blank out the bad and try to see only the good?

There are myths for all these responses.

STORIES BEFORE WRITING

Second, we must remember that these stories may well go back, in their ultimate sources, to tales told even before the invention of writing. Back then, stories were the best means by which a tribe's crucial information was passed on from one generation to another, because they were the form in which it was most easily remembered. Oral cultures—those without writing—think as well as tell stories differently from those with writing.

Aleksandr R. Luria, a Soviet psychologist, interviewed illiterate and newly literate peasants in Uzbekistan and Kyrgyzstan in the 1930s. He found that differences did indeed exist between writers and tellers.[1] Illiterates talked in pictures and stories, while literates were far more ready than they to speak of abstract categories and hypothetical situations. In one experiment, illiterates were shown a picture containing a hammer, a saw, an ax, and a log, and were asked to name the three that were similar.

The nonreaders said they were all useful. If pressed, they would exclude the hammer on the grounds it could not be used to cut the log like the saw or ax. Clearly, they were not thinking in terms of generic categories like "tools," but rather they immediately wanted to begin a story—a tale of doing something with the objects, like cutting wood.

When told that some viewers had grouped the three tools together, excluding the log, they laughed, saying "That person must have enough firewood already." When shown a picture of three adults and a child and asked which one of those didn't fit, they refused to exclude the child, saying he needed them and the adults needed the child to run errands—again, the picture immediately becomes not a puzzle but a story. *To think something through you tell a story about it.* In the same way, to pass on important information, such as where a water hole is and how to hunt a certain animal, you tell a story, perhaps of a primal god who put the water hole there, or of a primal hero-hunter whose tactics we always emulate.

For nonliterate oral culture, then, understanding immediately becomes story making rather than abstract logic. Orals store their thoughts in stories. There is more. As another student of orality and reading, Walter J. Ong, has pointed out, to be memorable, and so remembered, a story needs protagonists and opponents, us and them. It calls for conflict, and violent and passionate events, to summon up the "juices" that energize good memorization—the tale must become myth, not mere chronicle.[2] To make it more interesting, the primal hero might have been opposed by evil entities who wanted to keep all the water or game to themselves. It also helps if the narrative is put in verse and meter, as were stories as old as the *Iliad* and the *Odyssey*, for rime is much easier to recite in long memorized stretches than prose.

The distinguished anthropologist Claude Lévi-Straus has examined myths from a structuralist point of view. For him, they expressed binary, or sets of opposites, patterns. The world is thereby organized and made intelligible. Although controversial, this approach is worth studying. This scholar made three basic points about myth in his essay "The Structural Study of Myth."[3] Here they are:

1. Myth is a kind of language—that is, it has a message and is trying to make a statement.
2. A myth is composed of all its variants—to know what the message is, one looks not only, as a historical scholar might, for the earliest form but also at every way the myth is expressed. To know the full message of the Buddha in human experience, for example, one would not only look at the life of the historical Buddha but also at all the ways he has been represented and talked about down through two and a half millenniums of Buddhist history.

3. A myth is based on pairs of opposites. The movement of myth is from awareness of opposites to not bring the two sides together. Polarities such as male and female, man and nature, youth and age, or locality and world are reconciled.

Let's look at an example. One figure who brings two sides together—gods and humans, humans and nature, good and bad—is the "trickster," such as Coyote in Native North American mythology, who manages by his wits to touch all the bases.

COYOTE

Let's then take as an illustration of myth that well-known trickster, Coyote, and his role in the creation of the world and the setting-up of human life the way it is.

A trickster is a mythic figure—other examples are the Greek Hermes and Nordic Loki—neither wholly good nor bad, but full of jokes and the unexpected. Generally male, he tends to have extreme appetites for food, drink, and sex, and is often a thief and deceiver. Yet he can also be helpful to us humans when he feels like it. But, as we will see, sometimes even his well-intended attempts at innovation get out of hand and lead to trouble.

The Native American Coyote is wily, cunning, ruthless, and unwilling to defer to anyone else, man, beast, or god. Coyote is out only for himself, even his sense of humor has an edge to it, and his "jokes" can be cruel. Yet like many other tricksters, he can also serve as a "culture hero," a divine or semidivine figure who gives humans valuable tools such as fire or irrigation, or even helps in the creation of the world.

No less than humans of the same stamp, Coyote can be appealing in his cleverness, his disguises, and his ruses, by which he sometimes outsmarts even himself. For all his unscrupulousness and bad conduct, like some children he's cute even when he's bad. His limitless energy and seemingly inexhaustible bag of tricks fascinate, and those who have made Coyote's acquaintance rarely tire of his exploits. Native Americans have enjoyed listening to his tales around the campfire for centuries.

(One can think of Coyote, and most other tricksters, as like Jack Sparrow, performed for laughs and thrills by Johnny Depp in the *Pirates of the Caribbean* movies. Jack is clearly just playing his own game, and sees others mostly as toys or as means to get what he wants for himself. Yet he cannot help but catch every eye and steal every heart when he's on screen, with his liquid eyes, his gymnastics, and clever ploys; you can't help cheering him on even as you're appalled.)

What do Coyote and his stories say about our world? His set of tales suggest a wondrous and beautiful world, but. . . something went wrong. The gods, humans, and animals running around the earth, trying to scratch a living from it or trying to improve it, are not always good or reliable, though always entertaining. They can send currents in contrary directions and go beyond what was intended. Even so, what can we do but laugh and enjoy the story?

Here is a Coyote story from the Maidu people of California.

At the beginning, when nothing lay below but endless waters, two beings looked down and began talking about what they could do next to make it into a better place. They were Earthmaker and Coyote. Earthmaker, a respectable god, wanted to create a good, decent world in which pain and death were not, and spouses remained faithful to one another. But Coyote said in effect, "Why not make it a little more interesting?"

He's not exactly evil, and at first he and Earthmaker get along; the two are like good buddies talking enthusiastically about their new project, Earth. But clearly they are of different temperaments. One is straight, well meaning, but a little dull and unimaginative; the other more interested in angles and bursting with imagination: more than is called for, and enough to get him into trouble. Clearly the Maidu considered the world offered plenty of evidence for both these personalities at work in its dramas.

In time, Earthmaker and Coyote had a falling out. Earthmaker wanted the people he was making, when they died, to be placed in water overnight and then be able to rise up again the next morning; and he wanted even married couples to be celibate, as there was no need for procreation in a world without death. Coyote said of this:

> But you, Earthmaker,
> are not speaking for human contentment and joy!
> But I speak for a world where men can laugh
> and feel good and come to take delight in themselves
> and in the women they care for.
> So then, an old man,
> flirting and playing around with a young woman,
> should feel like a lad again.
> And women should feel that way too.

Coyote obviously felt that a world without flirting, love, and sex was hardly worth living in, even if the price was death, for immortal life in such a world would be bound to get very boring.

To this, Earthmaker had no answer, so

> . . . he thought to himself:
> "You, Coyote, have overcome me in everything;
> so then, without my saying so,
> let there be Death in the World."

But, as happened more often than not, Coyote's victory came back on himself. Not long afterward he sent his own fine son to fetch some water. On that simple expedition the boy was bitten by a rattlesnake, and died.

> Then Coyote cried out [to Earthmaker]
> "May I never say such things again!
> You must make my son come back to life!"

But Earthmaker paid no attention, and Coyote, full of anger and remorse as he learned what death meant in personal as well as theoretical terms, could only say of Earthmaker, "I will chase him no longer. . . I will never catch up with him."[4]

What do we learn from this myth? First, that life is made up out of two forces, sometimes in harmony but more often pulling against each other: a serious, constructive side, and a fun, but rebellious and potentially destructive side. Most of us have both sides in ourselves. Yet they are not deadly antagonists like, say, the Christian

God and Satan; rather the whole interplay is more like a game, or even a joke on the protagonists' propensity for going beyond their limits. We may as well take the world that way.

KINDS OF MYTH AND THE CREATION MYTH

This Maidu Coyote myth includes two themes, creation and the origin of death, both common motifs in myth. Basic mythic types include **cosmogonic** or creation myths, myths of the origin of evil and death, myths of the hero (both warrior and savior types), and the myth of the end of days (**eschatology**). We will look at examples of each, though eschatology will be considered in later chapters.

As for creation, generally (because it is hard for humans to imagine absolute nothingness) at first there extends a simple but virtually endless something, the empty stage before the play begins: yawning chaos, clouds or vapor, vast barren plains, or shoreless seas like the waters over which the Spirit of God brooded at the commencement of creation in Genesis.

How one says that the world came into being tells a great deal about how one thinks of the world, and one's place in it, today. In India one of many accounts of the beginning of this world tells of a primal man who is also God dividing himself up in a sacrifice to make the many things. The Judaeo-Christian account in the Book of Genesis relates that God literally created the universe as something outside of himself and subject to him.

These two narratives suggest two different views of the total meaning of the world in relation to God. In the first, God is hidden in the world. All parts of the cosmos, stars, mountains, trees, and people, are really God in disguise, God self-sacrificed so the many can flourish.

In the second, God is not the same as the world but views it as a craftsperson views the exquisite work of his or her hands, or as a sovereign views his or her subjects, expecting love and obedience from them.

In both cases, the myth implies that if we know the real origin of something, we can understand it much better than otherwise right now. Myth is then a tool and a source of power.

Here are some cosmogonic myths.

Dark and endless desert was the primal world of one of the Australian aboriginal peoples, the Arrente. All was night and without life, and beneath that earth slept the first ancestors. Finally the firstlings awoke, or at least moved into a dreaming sleep, for their minds rose into what is called the Dreamtime. Wandering and chanting, they sang sun and moon into life, then various plants and animals. Finally, they carved into completion half-made forms of men and women they found. The creators then went back to sleep, but they left the trail of their Dreamtime peregrinations in the form of signs, often enhanced by rock paintings, across the immense land. Even now, one can follow these markings in traveling from one part of the country to another, or to return spiritually to that time of origins. For the Dreamtime is ever with us, set over our ordinary world. Today as in the past, the first people of Australia return to it in dreams and festive dance, as they dance the steps and sing the songs of the Beginning.[5]

The Australian creation was by walking and singing; the ancient Greek, according to the version in Hesiod's *Theogony*, "Birth of the Gods," was genital, like normal human procreation.

At first only chaos ruled everywhere, but at the right time out of it appeared Gaia, the earth-goddess. Mating with Ouranos, the overarching sky-father, she gave birth to the Titans, who in turn engendered countless features of the Mediterranean world, and whose difficult intergenerational conflicts eventually produced the well-known gods of Olympus, such as Zeus, Hera, and Poseidon.[6]

A fundamental message of this account is that despite appearances, nature is alive and on some profound level it shares our experience as living beings. These procreating deities represent, and in some way *are*, natural features, such as sky (Zeus), fertile fields (Demeter), and sea (Poseidon). For one basic point of creation stories is always to make the universe humanly significant; to show that we humans have some connection to the purpose and inner character of the big picture.

The Babylonian account in a text called the Enuma Elish, which undoubtedly influenced the Hebrew creation narrative in Genesis, begins not with endless desert or endless chaos, but with endless water, some fresh and some salt.[7] The fresh fluid belonged to the god Apsu, salt water to the stormy goddess Tiamat. That tumultuous pair begot more gods in several generations. But when the irascible Tiamat decided to destroy some of the younger gods, only the heroic deity Marduk was able to confront her. In a great battle of wind and storm, of magic and force, he managed to split her body in half, making the lower part earth, and the upper sky. He then developed the earth, creating humans as slaves of the gods to work it, especially in digging irrigation ditches, and he gave them the great city of Babylon. There offerings would be returned to the gods in a great temple, and the king, as chief of the slaves, would confess sins on behalf of the people, and play the role of Marduk in a New Years reenactment of the defeat of Tiamat.

One other example, out of many: the cosmic egg. Variants of this myth occur, alongside other accounts, in many societies: China, Finland, Borneo, Greece, and North America, among others. Imagine that you, as the first conscious being, first opened your eyes not to vast vistas of endless land, sea, or chaotic air, but to utter darkness, cribbed and confined inside an egg. Perhaps you were trapped in that tiny, curved, lightless prison for a day, perhaps a million years. Who knows?

In the Polynesian South Pacific, it is said the primal being Tangaroa so first came to awareness of himself squeezed into an egg-shell. Eventually, pushing and squirming in his cramped quarters, that first god managed to crack it open, and was amazed as his eyes swept across a much wider universe of endless space than he had imagined possible inside his oval prison. But he was disappointed not to see a world in which he could live, or the companions or attendants to which he felt entitled. He wanted more. You too might want all you could get, if you had just broken out of such tight confinement. So Tangaroa made the sky of half the shell, and the earth out of his own body. Then, being lonely, he created other gods, including a female consort for himself, and other humans he made to be his servants.[8]

What do such myths of beginnings tell us? Much, no doubt. But two points stand out in Babylon and Polynesia: First, the creation of the earth as we know it was the result of ferocious divine struggle, however differently conceived; and second, humans were made to be slaves of the gods, so must obey and fear punishment.

Carving of Tangaroa from the Cook Islands   (NZGMW/Shutterstock)

(By contrast, the Greek accounts, while presenting much brawling among the gods, say little about the creation of humankind, as though we just came along with the mountains and islands. The gods don't need humans and don't care too much about them so long as they receive offerings, though these offerings are necessary for them to maintain their own divine strength. On occasion they can hate some one individual, as Hera did Hercules, or love another, as Aphrodite favored Odysseus. But generally their unconcern beyond the routine offerings left us humans with some degree of freedom, and the Greeks developed that gift of freedom well.)

Finally, one last category of creation: repetition. In the great Asian religions of Hinduism and Buddhism, as well as in some strands of Greek philosophy, the world goes through long cycles of creation and destruction, then reforms and starts the sequence all over again. Generally it begins with a golden age, delightful with its exceedingly long lifespans and paradisaical conditions. But gradually conditions of life deteriorate until we reach what in Hinduism is called the Kali-yuga, when life is short and brutish. It is said that even then an avatar (appearance of Vishnu) called Kalki will come on a white horse to save those who can still be saved under the worst conditions. Then the world will disintegrate, and the god Vishnu will sleep on the cosmic ocean atop a serpent made up of the world-fragments, until time to wake up and start the process again. This has happened an infinite number of times, and will another infinite number; each full cycle, called a "Day of Brahma," lasts over 4 billion human years.

Clearly, repetition represents a different way of experiencing the universe than seeing it as in linear time, with a definite beginning and end. Because these religions also countenance individual reincarnation, one can picture oneself, and all other

The Hindu God Vishnu, whose repeated awakenings begin a new creation of the world   (Dmitri Mikitenko/Shutterstock)

beings, on pilgrimage through these endless worlds, systems, and universes, enjoying countless adventures and learning much. But ultimately, by means of the enlightenment they also teach, one may leave the cycle and unite with the whole, like a very long river finally flowing into the sea.

THE MYTH OF THE HERO

We have creation; evil, as we will see in Chapter 7, soon enough tarnished the beautiful original work of the gods, and probably sent them away, out of touch with us here below. How do we reverse the rot and get back to the way things were before the shadow fell? That is the work of the hero, from Hercules to today's superheroes, from the founders of the great religions to contemporary saints. The hero defeats an expression of evil or chaos, usually personified as a demon or monster or master criminal, and so at least at one time and one place allows the joy of the beginning once again to reign. Because we are still in this imperfect world, the victory is not for all times, but it is a sign, and opens a way the rest of us can follow if we will.

The hero appears in two different modes: the fighter and the saint or savior. The fighter is the warrior hero, such as Rama, St. George, or one of the knights of King Arthur's Table Round, or an independent superman, such as Hercules or Captain Marvel.

The saint or savior, the religious or spiritual variant or hero, follows the same overall stages—he sets out on a mission, defeats a foe, returns with benefits for all humanity—but the mission is of the spirit and the foe as much within human beings as demonic entities without. This hero would be the Buddha, Jesus, or many of the saints or holy ones of all religions.

Let us take a look at the stages through which a mythic hero's career usually passes. A source often used is a work by Joseph Campbell, *The Hero With a Thousand Faces*.[9] Here this scholar laid out a series of events he saw occurring over and over in the myth of the hero. Though sometimes controversial, this model has had considerable influence and has suggested to many moderns the value of ancient myth in understanding the stories of our lives today.

It has also had a literary and artistic impact. The hero's adventure in the *Star Wars* movies—that of Luke Skywalker—was modeled on Campbell's stages. L. Frank Baum's 1900 novel, *The Wizard of Oz*, and its famous 1939 movie version, anticipated the stages remarkably. Read or watch one of these epics and see if you can pick out Campbell's stages in it.

The list in *The Hero With a Thousand Faces* has three parts: Departure, Initiation, and Return. Under the first is the Call to Adventure, Refusal of the Call, Supernatural Aid, the Crossing of the First Threshold, and the Belly of the Whale. Initiation entails the Road of Trials, the Meeting With the Goddess, Woman as Temptress, Atonement With the Father, Apotheosis, and the Ultimate Boon. Before Return, there is Refusal of the Return, then the Magic Flight, Rescue from Without, the Crossing of the Return Threshold, Mastery of Two Worlds, and Freedom to Live.

THE WARRIOR HERO

As an example of the fighter hero, let us take the story of Hercules, or Herakles as he was in the original Greek. This hero was the son of Zeus, king of the gods, and Alcmene, beautiful wife of Amphitryon, son of a local king now exiled to Thebes. Zeus, in one of his many infidelities to his consort Hera, tricked Alcmene into believing he was her husband as he approached the marriage bed. But even though the name Herakles may mean "Glory of Hera," and while Zeus allowed the child to nurse at Hera's breast, thus accounting for his superhuman strength, the goddess was enraged. Taking out her anger on the faithless husband's infant son, she sent serpents into his crib to kill him and his twin brother, but the mighty baby strangled them.

Hercules grew up happily, married a Theban princess, Megara, and successfully took part in several heroic endeavors: killing a fierce lion and making his trademark lion skin wrap out of its pelt, taking part in a raid on Troy, joining Jason and the Argonauts in the famous quest for the Golden Fleece, later founding the Olympic Games. But Hera's wrath was not quelled. She sent madness to the great man, causing him to kill his children, and leaving Megara to die of a broken heart.

The Greek Hero Herakles (Hercules) and the three-headed dog Cerberus   (Davor Pukljak/Shutterstock)

Filled with remorse, Hercules almost killed himself. But he betook himself to Delphi to gain wisdom at the oracle of Apollo. The entranced priestess there told him to go to his cousin Eurystheus, king of Mycene, and enter his service. That monarch, fearing his mighty suppliant as a rival, hoped to get rid of him by sending him on a series of dangerous missions. These are the famous Twelve Labors of Hercules.

He was successively to kill the Nemean lion; destroy the hydra (a nine-headed water snake); capture alive the Ceryneian hind (a deer of extraordinary beauty with golden antlers); trap and bring back alive an enormous boar; clean the Augean stables in a single day (a well-known task that he accomplished by diverting a river); destroy a flock of noisome birds with metallic wings, beaks, and claws; capture a troublesome white bull on Crete; go to Thrace and round up four mares that fed on human flesh; bring back the girdle or belt of the queen of the Amazons on the faraway shores of the Black Sea; steal the cattle of a three-headed ogre on an island out in the unknown Atlantic; fetch apples from the paradisal garden of the Hesperides, also far out in the mysterious direction of the setting sun; and finally as the twelfth labor, to descend into the Underworld and bring up the fearsome three-headed dog Cerberus who was its guardian for a brief visit to Eurystheus.

Hercules fulfilled all these tasks, each of which is a wonderful story in itself, not only through brute strength but also through clever—and sometimes none too scrupulous—tactics that show him as agile of mind as of body, both qualities much admired by the Greeks. It is worth noting that his labors sent him farther and farther afield from his native parts of Greece, till finally he was venturing to the legendary Hesperides and then to the Underworld itself.

His violent temper was not abated, however, and after these triumphs the hero committed further follies leading to more punishment. His trials included 3 years as a slave to the beautiful queen of Lydia, who not only had him rid her realm of robbers and wild beasts, but also sometimes amused herself by forcing on her burly hero the indignity of dressing like a woman and spinning with her handmaidens.

Eventually, however, he was able to leave and marry again, now to the lovely princess Deianira. This union was to lead to Hercules' death. One day, out to visit a friend, the couple had to cross a river. A centaur, Nessus, offered to carry Deianira across. Centaurs, half horse and half human, are known for their lusty character, and once he had the princess on his back, Nessus could not resist dashing away with her, obviously with ravishment in mind. But he was no match for Hercules, who quickly dispatched him with an arrow. Then, as he lay dying, Nessus took final revenge on his enemy. He told Deianira to dip a cloth in his blood, saying it was a love potion that would win her husband back should his affections ever stray; sprinkle some on Hercules' clothes and he would remain true to her. In fact, the blood was a deadly poison.

Years later, the day came when Deianira believed she saw a rival in Iole, a stunning princess her spouse had previously wanted to marry, but had been refused, and now had captured in a war and brought into their own house. The wife secretly rubbed some of Nessus' blood into Hercules' shirt. Putting it on, far from growing amorous the hero began writhing in agony. When Nessus' cruel trick became apparent, and it was clear Hercules was dying, Deianira took her own life in atonement.

As he lay on his funeral pyre, calmly resting on his lion skin, the heavens briefly opened in a flash of lightning as Zeus took back his son. In a consummation very rare even for a half-god like him, Hercules was taken to Mt. Olympus and allowed to join the company of the fully divine as an immortal.

What shall we make of this story in relation to Campbell's stages of the hero's quest? Hercules' Call to Adventure was built into his half-human, half-divine nature. Someone born the son of the King of the Gods is not likely to have just an ordinary life, even if his mother is human, and the strangeness began in infancy, provoked by Hera's antipathy. But after the challenge of the two serpents, perhaps in a sense he refuses a further call, growing up as a normal though exceptionally strong and able boy.

Supernatural Aid and the Crossing of the First Threshold may be suggested by his joining the quest for the Golden Fleece, since that journey was under the protection of the divine Athena, and sailed out to what then was virtually the ends of the earth, the far side of the Black Sea. Certainly the Belly of the Whale, a low point for the hero which is also a decisive transition for him, would be the mad crisis of the death of Megara and the children, and his encounter with the priestess of Apollo.

The centerpiece of the Hercules myth, the Twelve Labors, is surely the Road of Trials, up to and including the slavery in Lydia. Meeting with the Goddess (who does not need to be literally divine) may be his happy and generally improving nuptials with the worthy Deianira. Then Woman as Temptress leads the hero to stray from his quest in the form of the princess Iole (though through no fault of hers). Certainly his death brought about Reconciliation with the Father, as Zeus brought his mighty offspring up to Olympus, Apotheosis as he himself became fully a god, and the Ultimate Boon in the powers this final completion of his heroic career gave him.

However the stages of the third and last part of the paradigm, the Return, do not seem as well represented in Hercules as they are in the chronicles of Jason and of some, though not all, other heroes of antiquity. Return to a (somewhat) normal life is also an important climax of several modern hero epics, from *The Wizard of Ox* to *The Lord of the Rings* and Harry Potter's final installment, *Harry Potter and the Deathly Hallows*, which ends by showing the principals 19 years later, married and taking their own children to the train for Hogwarts. But Hercules' Olympian reward was even greater, and the Mountain of the Gods became for him a truer home than any on earth.

THE SAVIOR HERO

Let us now compare the life of Jesus as presented in the Gospels to Campbell's stages, and see how their narratives compare with the stages. Theologically, Jesus is for traditional Christians far more than a human hero, or even a half-divine hero such as Hercules, since he is defined as both fully human and fully divine. His death on the cross is not just part of his own story, but of that of all humankind. Nonetheless, as ancient as well as modern Christian commentators have pointed out, the Galilean's life-story often suggests the same pattern as lives of classic heroes. This, they agree, is significant.

The Christ's heroic destiny was preset at conception, when he was conceived in the Blessed Virgin Mary by action of the Holy Spirit, the human/divine nativity common to the myth of the birth of the hero—Hercules' sonship to Zeus. His first real Call to Adventure was when he heard the preaching of John the Baptist, and was baptized by him. On that occasion he received Supernatural Aid, for "when he came up out of the water, immediately he saw the heavens opened and the Spirit descending upon him like a dove; and a voice came from heaven, 'Thou art my beloved Son; with thee I am well pleased.'" (Mark 1:10) A sort of first Refusal of the Call may be combined with The Crossing of the First Threshold in the way that next "The Spirit immediately drove him out into the wilderness," (Mark1:12), and certainly there he experienced the Belly of the Whale, the separation from the hero's previous world, a low point yet also a transformational experience, for "he was in the wilderness forty days, tempted by Satan; and he was with the wild beasts; and the angels ministered to him." Luke 4: 1–13 expands on those temptations, saying that Satan challenged him to turn stones into bread, to miraculously lower himself down from the pinnacle of the temple, and finally to accept all the kingdoms of the world if he would worship him, but Jesus refused.

He was then ready to set out on the Road of Trials, which can be taken to be his public ministry with all its successes and difficulties, leading up to the greatest testing of all, the events of the last week, the arrest, the trial before Pilate, the crucifixion.

As for meeting with woman, John's Gospel tells us that Jesus' mother Mary was standing by the cross with him, and all the Gospels that it was women who first came to his tomb the morning his remains were not found, for he had risen. These women included Mary Magdalene, whose complex role in Jesus life and work has been explored by scholars, speculators, and novelists both ancient and modern, but is more than we can enter into now.

In any case, Jesus' death on the cross and subsequent resurrection, according to traditional readings of the Gospels and all traditional Christian thought, meant Atonement With the Father, Apotheosis (being deified, or shown to be divine), and the Ultimate Boon—achieving the goal of the quest, or in this case the ministry of Jesus.

The Return stages can be assimilated to the events of Jesus' postresurrection life, the so-called Great Forty Days between Easter and the Ascension. If there was at any point a Refusal of the Return, we would not know about it; however, the Magic Flight might be suggested by his going into Galilee, his earthly homeland, right after the resurrection, an unexpected venture mentioned in the Gospels of Mark and Matthew.

Rescue from Without is hinted at by his insistence, in the postresurrection appearances, that the work is now in the hands of the disciples, prepared or not. The Christ's visible mission on earth is accomplished, and his power is now passed into their hands. "And he said to them, 'Go into all the world and preach the gospel to the whole creation. . . And these signs will accompany those who believe: in my name they will cast out demons; they will speak in new tongues; they will pick up deadly serpents, and if they drink any deadly thing, it will not hurt them; they will lay their hands on the sick, and they will recover.'" (Mark 16: 15, 16)

Finally, the Crossing of the Return Threshold, Master of the Two Worlds, and Freedom to Live are all surely contained in the Ascension, Jesus' return to his eternal home, from where he exercises ability to work in both worlds freely: "So the Lord Jesus, after he had spoken to them, was taken up into heaven, and sat down at the right hand of God. And they went forth and preached everywhere, while the Lord worked with them and confirmed the message by the signs that attended it." (Mark 16: 19-20)

MYTH AND MEANING

We have looked at two basic themes of myth: creation and the adventure of the hero both warrior and spiritual. As stated, the origin of evil and another important type of myth, stories of the afterlife and the end of days, will be considered in later chapters. A further aspect of myth studies, their interpretation from the perspective of the psychology, sociology, and philosophy of religion, must be referred to our chapters on those topics.

For now let us close our brief foray into the world's mythologies by noting again that myths may be considered stories about both our own life and that of the world. For their whole purpose is to show how those two sides fit together: myth makes the world alive and so fully meaningful to the individual, and it makes his or her life more than just that of one person in one time, for we humans are parts of larger dramas.

The distinguished American philosopher Susanne Langer wrote insightfully about the meaning of drama. Langer said that drama creates a kind of "virtual future," in which we are made to see how each moment of action grew out of what went before, and leads to its inevitable fulfillment. "As literature creates a virtual past, drama creates a virtual future."[10] Insofar as this is true, myth is on the side of drama. While myth may be set in the remote past, indeed at the time of the Beginning, we sense that myths display gestures which set in motion chains of event extending down to the present.

In fact, from the myth point of view, our present experience is enmeshed and explained in the myth of creation, and in the myths of heroes who came soon after but whose words and ways still resonate today. In myth we sense actions that are larger than themselves in significance, from the first coalescence of primal chaos to something like the story of Jesus; even the freedom of action claimed by individual characters in myth, real as it is, somehow is part of that larger meaning, somehow both free and meant to be. We are part of the story too, and so myth does not die.

Furthermore, regarding myth and drama, myth is arguably still best appreciated as dramatic recitation, whether sung by the bards of old, as stage drama or, today, as cinema. In the voice of a great storyteller, on the stage, or on the screen, myth lives in a way harder for it to achieve in the more unnatural format as something just read in a book. If you can, don't just read myths, as engrossing as they often can be even on the page, but hear them told and see them skillfully enacted before your eyes.

SUMMARY

Myths are stories that tell in narrative form the basic values of a society, and how it got to where it is now. The point of a myth is not whether it is accurate in every detail, but what it says *about* the subject and, beyond that, about the kind of world we live in and what our lives should be like. We need such stories because our *lives* are stories, not abstractions.

Myths, the telling of important truths in story form, go back to oral culture before the invention of writing, and they reflect a different way of thinking from what emerged with literacy. They say the way to pass on important information is by telling a story about it. One example is trickster myths like that of Coyote.

Kinds of myth include cosmogonic or creation accounts, myths of the origin or evil and death, hero myths, and eschatological myths or stories of the coming end of days. Creation myths tell in story form a great deal about how we are to think of the world by telling how it was made, or how it repeats itself in endless cycles. The hero myth can be divided into myths of the warrior hero, such as Hercules, and the **savior hero**, such as Jesus.

In reflecting on the meaning of myth, we can think about how they tell us how chains of event were set in motion, or exemplified, that affect our lives today.

KEY TERMS

cosmogonic myth, p. 37
eschatology, p. 37

hero/savior myth, p. 46
myth, p. 32

CHAPTER

4

Magic Doorways: Symbol, Rite, and Religion

Gold cross with crystals, symbol of a faith
(Margo Harrison/Shutterstock)

LEARNING OBJECTIVES

After reading this chapter, you should be able to:

- Understand the difference between sign and symbol, and present a good definition of the religious meaning of symbol.
- Discuss how religious symbols help the mind relate particular issues to general religious patterns of meanings, like those of Christianity or Buddhism, and thereby help people make decisions. Think of some concrete examples of how this relationship might work.
- Discuss how sounds and words, including stories and doctrines, can also serve as audio symbols. Define the main categories of audio symbols in religion: nonverbal, nonconceptual verbal, and conceptual verbal.
- Explain how doctrine, as a statement of a religion's beliefs in abstract, propositional form, differs from its narrative expression. Explain the nature and use of "religious rhetoric" in preaching and inspirational writing.
- Discuss rite as "orchestration of symbols," by which a special time and place is set apart wherein the religion's world comes alive and its reality is enacted. Explain the use of "condensed symbols" and of religious rite as a ritual perpetuation of the past. Summarize the stages a worship rite typically goes through.
- Explain pilgrimage as also an orchestration of symbols and a religious rite. Emphasize particularly the pilgrimage experience of going from ordinary to "liminal" reality, and back.
- Do the same for religious rites of initiation.

SIGNS AND SYMBOLS

Perhaps you have read a story in which a very ordinary entryway, a closet door, or a garden gate, turns out to lead into a fabulous other world. Sometimes even a click on a remote, when it opens a drama such as *Star Trek*, reveals another world. This chapter is about symbols in religion, and symbols for religious believers are like such doors, gates, and television controls. Even the plainest symbols can open the door to a virtual universe of transcendent feeling and meaning for those who feel and understand. Those particular portals are magic gates into another world where the truth of a religion is visible, felt, and may overshadow the inconsistent ordinary world. A symbol may be a work of art, the architecture of a temple, a church service, or a sacred book. The Ise shrine and the figure of Jesus, as described in Chapter 1, are good examples of religious symbols that have this kind of door-opening power.

   To comprehend how symbolism works, a couple of distinctions have to be made: first, the distinction between **sign** and **symbol**; second, the distinction between the religious and the nonreligious meanings of both terms.

   Consider this. All sorts of indicators bombard us from all sides, and the structure of our thought processes continually construes them to tell us things not literally contained in the words as noises or the objects as things. We constantly make out certain squiggles of ink, like those before you now, to be more than just black-on-white patterns, but full of meaning: words, ideas, emotions, on and on. We read significance into colors, gestures, and even the arrangement of the stars. We understand significance through associations we have been taught, or that the mind makes on its own from past experience, or from its own ways or working. Language itself is sign and symbol; the noise of most words has no relation to the meaning, yet words immediately call to mind, to one who knows the language, what is being communicated. *Cat* does not sound or look like the animal, yet when we hear or see the word, we call up a visual and even audio idea of the furry creature that meows.

Many such verbal units as well as countless nonverbal indicators, from traffic lights to the dial tone on the telephone, come to us as little more than *signs*. They are just indicators that have no essential relation, except convention, to the thing signified. The sign can be thought of as like a stop sign, or a freeway exit marker. But what about the cross or a Christian church, the Star of David on a synagogue, the star and crescent on a Muslim mosque? If you were a believer in one of these faiths, just seeing that token might well evoke more inner response than just saying, "Well, now I know what that building is." It might even evoke a whole rush of thoughts. These indicators are *symbols*, not just signs.

The theologian Paul Tillich said that a symbol *participates* in that which it symbolized. It not only points in the right direction but calls up feelings, memories, ideas, and even aspirations associated with that object. It probably comes out of the tradition and represents some important aspect of its story.

Now imagine you have gone into the building that evoked a religious response from you, and have begun participating in its religious life: praying, observing a ritual, taking part in a service. Now you are involved in many more symbols, even immersed in them, because practically every part of religious life has symbolic meaning, representing some part of the faith, and also, in a real sense, serving as a symbol of the whole. For Christians, Holy Communion evokes symbolically the whole life of Christ and its meaning. For Muslims, praying in the direction of Mecca recalls the holy city and the life there of the Prophet Muhammad, together with the full teaching of the Holy Qur'an revealed through him.

We might say, then, that every part of a religion is a symbol of the entire religion. Advertisers constantly tell us that how one brushes one's teeth or what kind of soft drink one imbibes can identify the person's whole lifestyle and generation. The principle behind such claims, however excessive they may be, contains some truth. For a cultural style, like a personality, is made up of a thousand details that are interrelated, reveal something of the totality, and are capable of serving as a symbol of the whole lifestyle of one who participates in it. Toothpaste tubes and carbonated soft drinks, like stop signs, are significant symbols of modern American civilization. They participate in it not only metaphorically but also as million-dollar industries with high advertising visibility. They reveal important attitudes in the culture toward health and happiness. They are telling details in a way of life quite different from that of the Middle Ages, or of primal humanity.

In passing, we might also distinguish between **private** and **public symbols**. Most people have symbols that are personal to them, or maybe to a very few others: the place you fell in love, a "charm" that seems to bring you luck, a picture that reminds you of a secret dream. Some of these may be highly personal religious symbols, but they are different from common, public symbols, such as a flag or cross or star, that would be equally recognized and accepted as symbols by a community. The private symbol's full meaning for you is known only to you. Public symbols, conversely, serve to link us to others who share them.

If the part serves as symbol of the whole in ordinary society, it does so to the highest degree in religion. Religion is the greatest of all redoubts of symbolism, especially if the vast realms of art and music associated with religion are included. Everything in religion is a symbol, since the object of religion is the transcendent that cannot be pictured but can only be pointed toward. A religion's art can recall its ideas, its ideas can evoke one's experiences of worship and meditation, all these can remind one of family and friends associated with the religion, and so it goes, all the way through all the faith's forms of expression.

Religious symbols, however, are not merely passive clues to identity or meaning. They are also aids to thought, and so to decision, just as are language symbols. Thus, in the example of the girl converted to Christ presented in Chapter 1, accepting Jesus really meant accepting the whole of Christian life, doctrine, worship, and fellowship as she understood it, along with transforming grace through Christ; however, focusing just on the figure of Jesus clearly facilitated her decision. Encapsulating a total world of experience in a single symbol can sometimes be misleading, but it also helps one clarify distinctions and make choices.

We want maps to put the separate choices we encounter into a simple, comprehensive pattern, as scrambled iron filings leap into line when a magnet is brought near. We want a *pattern* that fits over them and lines them all up—right versus wrong, good versus bad. We want this pattern to have ultimate meaning, like the good and evil forces in myth as presented in Chapter 3. Then, as we pick the right side, we feel part of the pattern too—a somebody who really fits in.

AUDIO SYMBOLS

We may think of symbols first of all as visual, but it is important to realize that sounds, not to mention stories and ideas, can function just as powerfully as do visual symbols. When a worshiper enters a church, he or she is lifted into the religious world as much by the organ music, the choir, the words of prayer, or the sermon as by what is seen. Shinto worship begins with drums, Islamic with the chanted call to prayer.

Therefore, now we turn our attention to the religious symbolic role of what is heard. The symbolic role of the written word is included in this discussion because in religion it is never wholly detached from its parentage in the spoken word and shares its meaning.

It should not be thought that visual and audio symbols always work together in religion in mutual reinforcement and grand harmony. In fact, an aspect of the history of religion that might seem puzzling to the proverbial man from Mars has been a seesaw war between the respective symbolisms of the two distance senses—a war sometimes only latent but sometimes rising to furious battle in which people have killed and died for the sake of the word against the picture or vice versa. Sometimes religion has been most conspicuous as the patron of sacred painting and sculpture, has made the fruits of this patronage the foci of worship, and has communicated to most people a preeminently visual suggestion of the sacred. Medieval Catholicism and Mahayana

Audio symbolism: Tibetan monks performing a religious ceremony with music and chanting   (Victor Paul Borg/Alamy)

Buddhism veered in this direction. At other times, religion has generated iconoclasm (the destruction of images) in favor of upholding the spoken and written word as the most reliable conveyor of truth. Protestantism and Islam are examples.

The written word in religion is an extension of the spoken word and shares its spiritual attributes. Reading may be visual but is not usually mistrusted by those who suspect visual symbols of a nonverbal nature. The origin of writing in the spoken word is more decisively recognized in religion than anywhere else; silent reading is rarely allowed to stand alone in one's relation to the verbal symbols of faith. In Protestantism one is certainly encouraged to read the Bible and religious books, but doing so does not take the place of formally hearing the Bible read in church and a sermon preached—so with Islam and the Qur'an.

Audio symbols fall into three categories: nonverbal—music and sound; nonconceptual verbal—words such as chants and spells used chiefly for effectiveness in the word itself as opposed to the concept the word conveys as verbal communication; and conceptual verbal—story, myth, rhetoric, and doctrine.

Nonverbal

Music is virtually universal as an important accompaniment of religion, except in Islam in which chanting and rhythmic recitation take its place. Music's importance in facilitating the basic task of religious symbolism, helping the participant to make the transition from ordinary to sacred reality, is unsurpassed. Whether the solemn and mystical Gregorian chant, the fast-paced hums of Buddhist sutra reading, or the gladsome notes of gospel singing, music in religious worship sets the altered emotional tone of worship and does much to bring the participant into the service's universe of meaning. In worship, religious music is often secondary to word—scripture and sermon—and to visual art, such as statues or pictures used as actual sacred objects, despite music's great importance to many people for setting a religious tone. The music of a religion is mostly specific to its cultural context and drawn from it, although a great religion may spread across many cultures and carry various musical traditions with it, along with other cultural baggage. We look more at religious music in Chapter 8.

Nonconceptual Verbal

Although it may be less familiar to some Westerners, sacred words as **nonconceptual verbal audio expression** are extremely important in the history of religion. In some cases, such as the distinctive chants of Japanese Pure Land and Nichiren Buddhism, they rise to the role of being the religion's preeminent symbol, that by which it is best known.

Very often the nonconceptual feature is not absolute. Religious scholars within the tradition may appreciate the meaning, and it may in fact be known to ordinary practitioners. Nevertheless, as in the case of the Nichiren chant *Namu Myoho Renge Kyo* ("Hail the Marvelous Truth of the Lotus Sutra"), the literal meaning is not as important to ordinary devotion as the mantic or evocative power of the formula, which just through the vibrations of the sounds themselves is believed to align one to rich spiritual forces.[2] Other examples are the mantras of Hinduism and Buddhism, recited in formal prayer and private meditation to create an atmosphere of the presence of divinity and peace; the *dhikr* chanted ascriptions of praise to Allah in Islam; and such comparable Christian devotions as the Jesus prayer in Eastern Orthodoxy, the rosary in Roman Catholicism, and the repeated utterance of familiar prayer phrases and hymns in Protestantism.

The use of special or sacred language, from Latin and Sanskrit to the archaic English of the King James Bible, is a closely related matter. The idea is widespread that solemn religious words, such as those of scripture or prayer, ought to be in an ancient language, or at least in a very formal and archaic version of the current tongue. Think of the tendency of many Christians to use language reminiscent of the King James Bible, with "thee's" and "thou's," in prayer.

Conceptual Verbal

Conceptual verbal expression in religion takes several different forms. As one grows older, the words about religion that one hears change. One may at first be told about religious heroes, later may learn the faith's creeds and catechisms and be taught something about the abstract meaning of the doctrine, and finally may see it expounded in mature philosophical form. Without implying that one or the other forms is better, most religions have words that fit all these categories.

Myth is one example of conceptual verbal expression. We have pointed out in Chapters 2 and 3 that myth in religious studies means a story that expresses in narrative form the basic world view of the culture.

Doctrine is also a symbol of the religious world one is in. It differs from myth and narrative in that it usually comes later and sums up in more abstract language what they said in story format. Doctrine asks and answers the question, "If such and such is what the divine did on this and that occasion, what can we say about it that is true all the time?" Responses are such general statements as that God, or the sacred reality, is always near at hand, knows all things, can transform people, and so forth. Specific religious doctrines are discussed in Chapter 12.

In connection with myth and doctrine as symbols, a word might be said about sacred texts—that is, the scriptures of the religion—as themselves symbols. These may be the sources for the basic stories and doctrines of the faith, but it is worth noting how much they are often venerated even when not being read. In Christianity, many Protestant churches have the Bible as the central symbol on the altar; in Judaism, as we noted, the Torah in preserved centrally in the Ark at the front of the synagogue; in Nichiren Buddhism, invoking the Lotus Sutra is the main act of worship. Moreover, texts such as these are frequently carried around in a quasi-devotional way by believers, or chanted and recited inwardly in the midst of everyday life. In Sikhism, the Guru Granth Sahib, the basic scripture, is chanted continuously at the Golden Temple in Amritsar, the central temple of the religion. The Qur'an is memorized by many devout Muslims. Scripture, then, *itself* becomes symbol as well as conveyor of symbols.

Religious rhetoric, language that is conceptual but intended to persuade or to construct religious reality through its interweaving of concepts, is found in preaching and inspirational writing. It blends the second and third forms of audio symbolism, verbal nonconceptual and verbal conceptual, and perhaps even has a hint of the first, music, when the rhythm and intonation of a voice are used to create a special state of consciousness. Chiefly, though, preaching and other rhetoric is the use of words and concepts not so much as doctrinal statement or sustained logical argument but as triggers to enable the hearers (and perhaps the speaker) to make the leap of transition into the religion's alternative worlds where its values are plain and true. Key words, phrases, and ideas potently recall the root images and metaphors and experiences of the faith, bringing them back if one has known them before, suggesting their transformative power if one has not. Religious rhetoric constructs religious reality rather than describing it and enables experiences of it rather than mere knowledge about it.

THE ORCHESTRATION OF SYMBOLS IN RITE

It remains to say a few words about symbols in relation to the practical form of religious expression, that is, expression in acts such as worship, pilgrimage, art, architecture, or private prayer and meditation. Rite or public worship, the fullest of all these practical forms, is an orchestration of symbols to evoke the religious alternative world through several media simultaneously—the "distance" senses of vision and hearing, perhaps also the "proximity" senses: smell, touch, and taste (e.g., incense, kissing of sacred objects, eating of offered or consecrated food). The most effective worship is a network of many small things, all of which converge to bring the participant into the alternative reality of the religion. It becomes a total perception. When such a total environment is constructed, there is no objective reference point from which to judge it, and even one's inner thoughts may be brought into alignment with it.

Religious rites perpetuate in the present sacred times and persons from out of the past, help simplify and clarify feelings, and, above all, create through the impact of many symbols at once a special time and place in which the religion's view of reality is enacted, making it, for those able to respond fully to the symbols, entirely real.

These concepts have been applied to theater by the dramatist and critic Richard Schechner.[3] His approach to theater, centering on the ideas of environment and performance, depends heavily on studies in traditional religion, especially shamanism, and in turn does much to illuminate the meaning of rite as orchestration of symbols. Schechner emphasizes the theatrical experience as a total experience—a "total immersion" in the drama, which therefore becomes transformative for cast and audience alike. For there to be a total environment, of course, the audience cannot be just spectators *outside* the drama but must be participants, a part of the environment that makes the drama. The fact that there are people present is a major factor in what goes on.

In the same way, a religious rite (whether a shaman's trance, a High Mass, or a Protestant service with sermon) may be an effective performance by the religious specialist, but the total experience for those present is affected also by the presence of the whole group of participant-observers. The rite is probably the act of a community of some sort, and its meaning is completed by the fact that there are others besides the performers present and by the transformative impact it has on those others.

Transformation means mental movement from one world or reality to another. Very often, that "reality" is a symbolic or condensed re-creation of a sacred past. Thus the Christian holy communion is an enactment of Jesus' last supper, which in turn is believed to sum up symbolically his life and, above all, his sacrifice. The Jewish Passover expresses in a similar symbolic, condensed way the beginning of the Exodus out of Egypt of the ancient Israelites. The Hindu Diwali, or "Festival of Lights," with its lighting of lamps as though to greet a returning hero, expresses the joy people felt of old in several victories, including that of Krishna over forces of evil and the triumphant return of the hero Rama from exile. On a more personal level, simple forms of worship, and familiar old spiritual songs, may recall childhood innocence, and the presence of loved ones now gone. Religion is then often like a ritual perpetuation of the past, above all in its orchestration of symbols.

We consider three settings for the orchestration of symbols: public worship, pilgrimage, and initiation.

Public Worship

All rite and worship involve a combination of symbols. Even worship as simple as a Quaker meeting speaks through several symbols and senses—silence, the spoken voice and words, austerity of surroundings, the presence of other people. There is a message about any religion in the structure and symbolism of its worship, just as much as in what is outwardly said. In all religion worship is a form of expression. It is simply a matter of ascertaining *what* its message is wordlessly saying about how one best comes into rapport with the transcendent through this form of expression.

If it is an elaborate and traditional rite, like a Shinto rite such as that described in Chapter 1 or a Greek Orthodox liturgy, it says one best transcends finitude through participation in something with strong aesthetic appeal and a sense of getting beyond the limitations of the mere present through forms that come out of, and call back, the past.

Bartholomew, Ecumenical Patriarch of the Eastern Orthodox Church, during an Easter
service in Istanbul   (Mustafa Ozer/AFP/Getty Images/Newscom)

If it is very plain or free-form, it says one achieves the same end best through a
minimization of impediments to knowing the divine inwardly or to expressing oneself
freely. This would be plain meditation, even if done in a group, or the kind of worship
in which participants speak and pray their concerns in ordinary language.

We now look at some of the stages by which worship as orchestration of symbols
typically enables the transformative process. The order of the internal stages may vary.

Opening   The rite begins with a gesture that marks and enables a transition from
the ordinary to religious reality. It may be a rite of purification, such as the Shinto
priest waving a wand over the assembly of worshipers. It may be a hymn, a dramatic
procession, the beat of drums, or the sound of a conch, but it marks a transition and
may even induce a sort of shock to assist the subjective shift. In Hindu temple worship, the beginning may be marked by the waving and presentation of lamps and singing *bhajans* or hymns.

Prayer or Establishment of Rapport with Transcendence   The next
stage is likely to be a verbal process of becoming synchronous with the sacred—
chanting, praying, or reading of sacred texts. It is quieter but more prolonged than the
opening drama, indicating a more deeply meditative adjustment to the other reality. In
the Hindu temple, the deity image may be bathed with milk and water.

Presentation of Offerings   This stage is many things, such as placing of food
on Shinto or Hindu altars, offering the sacramental bread and wine in Roman Catholic

and Eastern Orthodox liturgies, and offering money in Protestant churches. Some rather ceremonial collections and presentations of offerings relate important material symbols, like food and money, to the divine. This is often an active and dramatic moment.

The Message   In most, but not all, worship there is a sermon or at least the reading of a sacred text by a religious specialist as instruction or inspiration and the use of religious rhetoric in the very supportive setting of temple and rite. This is a reversal of the previous action—the people then communicated to the divine; now the divine communicates to them.

Participation   In this culminating stage, the people and the divine come most together and are thoroughly mixed. Divine life comes into the people, perhaps altering behavior, and people feel closest to God. There is likely to be some motor activity and the use of some of the proximity senses: taste, touch, and smell. This is the point of Holy Communion, of Pentecostal speaking in tongues, of the Shinto festival climaxing in sacred dance, carnival, and the rapid procession of the deity through the streets. In the Hindu temple, individual worshipers may process by the image to offer their personal prayers and simple offerings, such as garlands of flowers.

Closing   At the end there is another moment of transition in the termination of the sacred experience and return to ordinary life, though it may be eased by blessing, music, final prayers, and socializing among participants.

Practical expression is not limited to settings of worship. It can also be done individually. A person alone can move himself or herself through these stages and enter the alternative world or actualize the real self in prayer and meditation. The process can be achieved with the aid of sound or visual accouterments, such as a sacred picture or image upon which one concentrates, or it can be accomplished with only the evocation of what is within one's mind.

Pilgrimage

The process of transformation through orchestration of symbols can be accomplished geographically. Pilgrimage—travel for religious renewal to a special place that is itself a sacred symbol, such as Rome, Jerusalem, or Mecca—is a prolonged and spatially expressed rite. Traditional customs of pilgrimage have the same sense of opening, transition, offering, learning, and participation, but they may go on over days or weeks, and each stage is done at a different place along the route. The entire journey is like a rite and amounts to a temporary movement into the religious alternative world or into liminality, to a place where the map of the alternative world coincides with geography as we know it. The pilgrimage site is a place where one can be a real self.

For example, the well-known Muslim pilgrimage to Mecca begins with separation from ordinary life as the visitor dons simple pilgrim's garb at the port of Jidda several miles from the holy city. From then on he or she will take no life, cut neither

Mecca, with Islamic pilgrim crowds around the Kaaba or sacred stone   (Ayazad/Shutterstock)

hair nor nails, and abstain from sex. At Mecca, he or she will circumambulate the shrine of the Kaaba seven times, stand on the side of Mount Arafat (to hear a sermon) all afternoon, and then, leaving the sacred state, ritually sacrifice a goat or sheep and have a haircut—all over a period of two or three days.

Traditional pilgrimage sites, such as Mecca and many others, are themselves complex symbols. Their buildings and temples reproduce the organization of the heavenly realm of their gods or God. In Mecca, for example, the throne of Allah above is said to be directly over the Kaaba, and angels continually circle around it even as do the faithful below. Kyoto, the ancient capital of Japan, is patterned on a mandala or Buddhist sacred diagram of the relationships of cosmic Buddhas and has monasteries or temples guarding its approaches.

Religious symbols, then, are magic doorways into worlds where religious meaning becomes the overt and apparent meaning of things, rather than the hidden meaning as in our ordinary world.

Initiation

A special word must be said about the initiatory rites of religions. Most religions have some means by which persons are brought into the household of the faith: Christian baptism, Jewish bar mitzvah, Hindu samskaras, the elaborate initiations of many primal societies, even fraternity and sorority initiations. These are, first of all, freighted with the binary symbolism of moving from outside to inside, from darkness to light, from one group and one world to another. The anthropologists Arnold van Gennep and Victor Turner have proposed a threefold structure to initiation: separation, marginality or liminality (from *limen*, "threshold"), and return with reincorporation into a new role.[4] The first is when the initiate leaves the ordinary world. The second, the heart of the rite, is a time apart when, presumably, he or she being detached from the ordinary is especially open to divine influx: the knight at vigil all night before his dubbing; the young Native American away from camp on the vision quest or in the sweat lodge; the prospective shaman out in the wilderness. For as an Eskimo adept told the Danish explorer Rasmussen: "All true wisdom is only to be found far from men, out in the great solitude, and it can only be acquired by suffering. Privations and sufferings are the only things that can open a man's mind to that which is hidden from others."[5]

Initiations also have a symbolism specific to the religion: washing, in Christian baptism, as a cleansing from sin; reading a bit of the Torah in bar-mitzvah, as incorporation into its sacred world; in some primal initiations, liminality means separation from society for a time, even symbolic burial. For major initiations are, above all, grounded in the symbolism of death and rebirth. The word initiation means a beginning, and the new start it implies is not meant to be merely perfunctory, but to indicate a real change of consciousness, or awareness, or how one perceives the world. This is accomplished through the combination of ever-present symbols with physical and emotional shocks that imprint their message on the initiate. One who has been so ritually scarred does not easily forget the pain or the emotional trauma. In this way the initiation is meant to leave the individual forever different from others outside the initiatory circle, and bind him or her with whom this irreversible experience has been shared.

Consider the initiation of boys in traditional New Guinea. As for separation, the young men would be taken from the village to the sound of whirring bullroarers, symbol of the voice of gods. The women, believing or pretending to believe they would never see them again, would weep. Supposedly they would be eaten by a monster; and it is true they would not come back again as boys, for when they returned they would be men of the tribe. But they were told the youths could be redeemed by the offering of pigs, in many south Pacific societies the general symbol of wealth and of communication between the gods and humans.

The initiates were actually taken to a secret lodge in the forest said to be the belly of a ghostly monster. There they would be painfully circumcised, a complex symbol in itself, taught the lore of tribe, and eat the flesh of the sacrificed pigs. Then, finally, after several months they would come back home to the village—the return. The initiates are ready to celebrate their victory elaborately decorated with paint and mud, prepared to feast and celebrate, but first they are given only soft food, like a baby, to symbolize their death and rebirth.[6]

Initiations can be just for groups such as this, or more individual as for shamans and priests. They can even be private, as in the initiations some have believed they received in experiences of conversion or mystical realization. They can be public ceremonies, or restricted to the initiators and initiates, even secret. However, in all cases they will involve an elaborate display of symbols keyed to significant and, ideally, unforgettable action. An initiate should never again be what she or he was before. Initiation is discussed more extensively in Chapter 5.

SUMMARY

The fundamental distinction between sign and symbol needs to be understood. A sign, such as a road sign, merely points to what it indicates, but a symbol participates deeply in what it symbolizes, being derived from a figure or object close to its heart—the cross in Christianity or the figure of the meditating Buddha in Buddhism. It is not only a signpost but it also itself helps a person enter into the experience of the religion. Further, each symbol is a part of the whole religion and opens into the whole pattern of meaning it sets up. By thinking of what is compatible with the major symbols—the cross or the Buddha—and what is not, we are aided in making choices. That is, by letting the symbol lead us into the religion's "world," with its values and experiences, our eyes are opened to its pattern of meaning and so much further helped in decision making. Audio symbols or symbols in music, chant, or word as of scripture or sermon are as important as visual symbols.

Religious rite may be spoken of as an "orchestration of symbols." Public worship, pilgrimage, and initiation are important venues of symbolic orchestration. Visual and verbal symbols, perhaps also symbols reaching the senses of smell, taste, and touch, are brought together. Religious rites perpetuate the sacred times and persons of the past, help simplify and clarify feelings, and, above all, create through the impact of many symbols at once a special time and place in which the religion's view of reality is enacted, making it, for those able to respond fully to the symbols, entirely real.

KEY TERMS

audio symbols, p. 51
doctrine, p. 52
nonconceptual verbal expression, p. 52
private symbol, p. 49

public symbol, p. 49
religious rhetoric, p. 53
sign, p. 48
symbol, p. 48

CHAPTER

5

Oases of the Mind:
The Psychology of
Religion

A woman Buddhist monk in England meditating
(Imagestate Media Partners Limited - Impact Photos/Alamy)

LEARNING OBJECTIVES

After reading this chapter, you should be able to:

- Describe the shifts in "state of consciousness" that we go through as we move from one mood or mode of mental and emotional activity to another, and then discuss how religion accepts the reality of these shifting states of consciousness and evaluates some as better, higher, and closer to the real self in relation to Ultimate Reality than others. These "states" can be understood as "subuniverses of meaning."

- Show how our human capacity for development and change through life interacts with religion and religious experience, including the possibility of experiences of conversion and initiation.

- Describe what Maslow means by the "peak experience" and what Turner means by "liminality"; discuss the meaning of both in and for religion.

- Summarize the position of such major psychological interpreters of religion as Freud, Jung, and the humanistic psychology school.

- Construct your own model, based on the section on religious development and personal observation and experience, for the role of religion in the various stages of human growth, from infancy to old age.

- Present your views on why childhood seems to be so important to religion, both as an ideal and as something to be gone beyond.

MENTAL SHIFTS

Our discussion of the psychology of religion will begin with the concept of different **states of consciousness**, that is, different ways in which one is aware of oneself and feels oneself, together with the resultant shifts in the way one perceives the world.

Think about it this way. In ordinary life we pass through many transitions of consciousness every day. To pass from sleep to wakefulness, or from sleep without dreams to sleep with dreams, is to go from one state of consciousness to another, so is passing, as one nods over studies, from focused attention to diffuse reverie. The state of consciousness during a game is quite different from that of war, or from the deadly serious scavenging of a famished man. Intense emotional states, such as fear or rage, bring about their own state of consciousness.

Psychological researcher Stanley Krippner has listed 20 basic states of consciousness that range from dreaming, lethargy, hysteria, and rapture to trance, reverie, and those induced by drugs.[1]

Think of spending a summer day at the beach. The day may seem wholly uneventful and pointless except for relaxation and fun. Even on such a day, though, one moves through a number of states of mind, most of which in fact have religious parallels. Strenuous physical activity such as swimming or playing ball makes the mind alert and under a certain tension to perform, and bathes the mind in mild joy as performance is achieved. In times of quiet reading, the mind is passively receptive and the body is in repose. A special concentration and excitement ripples through one's senses when talking animatedly with friends, conversation full of warmth and humor. Parents and children together at the beach feel the special warmth of enjoying one another in a situation of considerable freedom and lack of pressure. Finally, there are those contemplative moods that the beach seems especially able to induce. One looks at the enjoyment of others and the sun sinking over the sparkling water in an almost god-like way, and begins to intuit some sort of unity behind it all. One's ongoing stream of consciousness comprises an unceasing series of shifts like these.

One can think of the mind as a piano or organ and of these transitions as continuing but ever-changing music. Musical possibilities are virtually infinite, owing to the great number of possible combinations of a much smaller number of notes and tempos. In the same way, the almost infinite shadings of consciousness we experience are the product of combinations of a smaller number of basics, such as Stanley Krippner's 20 basic states of consciousness, together with varying circumstantial factors.

The idea that different states of consciousness each have their own way of knowing self and world, so that moving from one to another can both provide valid knowledge of Ultimate Reality and facilitate self-transformation, is fundamental to religion. One person might say that only the mind in a calm rational mood can truly see the world aright. But many religious persons, similarly to the poet, might counter that love—as of God and of God's children—has also its eyes and ears, as might also fear—the "fear of the Lord"—or even anger, like the righteous anger of the prophet against injustice. (At the same time, we ought to bear in mind as we noted earlier that, in the words of the sociologist Max Weber, some people are "religiously unmusical.")

Equally fundamental is religion's assumption that some states of consciousness are better—more valuable to these ends—than others and its provision of extrinsic guidelines for evaluating them. These presuppositions underlie religion's emphasis on such states as meditation, conversion, worship, and philosophic or moral reflection and its characteristic denigration of strongly sensual or negatively emotive states.

Entering into a religious situation always, at least on a symbolic level, implies entering a different state of consciousness or "reality" with its own way of seeing things. A rock in a temple may be a divinity; a rock outside may be just a rock. Standing or kneeling in church may be praising or praying to God; outside it may be just standing to look out the window or kneeling to work in the garden.

If religion means moving into (and later out of) a different reality, the process of moving in and out is of great interest. We need to reflect on this process and these realities.

SUBUNIVERSES

Any concept of different realities intermixed with different states of consciousness is reminiscent of the great nineteenth-century psychologist William James' concept of **subuniverses**. Shift in states of consciousness is like moving from one "subuniverse of meaning" to another. For James, outside reality, in any sense meaningful to humans, is something "out there" that interacts with our emotional and active lives. When something stimulates one's interest, and so comes into relationship with that person, the combination creates a special reality, a subuniverse of meaning.[2]

James's subuniverses have more recently been explored by Alfred Schutz.[3] He sees our experience as made up of countless "finite provinces of meaning." The paramount one is the world of everyday life, our "working world." It is the mode of experiencing oneself and the universe that is the point of reference for all others. It is probably the reality created by the culture whose worldview one accepts, and so is in practice the norm for evaluating other perceptions. Schutz tells us there are other worlds too—"the world of dreams, of imageries and phantasms, the world of scientific contemplation, the play world of the child, and the world of the insane."[4] These each have a "cognitive style," a way of knowing, unique to that world, and so each creates a realm of experience with inner consistency, even if different from the cognitive style of the "working world," or everyday life.

The world of religious meaning can be one of those subuniverses for a person. For some, those whom we consider very religious, it can be the keystone by which all others are assessed and understood. For others, such as those who participate in religion—attending church, visiting a temple or mosque, taking part in a festival—as one of several more or less equal "realities," along with family, work, sports, and entertainment, it may have its place but not be central.

A particularly important point in Schutz's discussion is transition from working reality to one of the others. The transition, he says, is accompanied by a sort of shock, such as falling asleep to enter the world of dreams or awakening to leave it. The transition may be marked by signs that indicate one is suspending one reality in favor of another while reading or hearing a story, playing a game, or starting a ritual. Anyone who has known the subtle but meaningful inward jolt or transition that marks entry into a meditation state, or the outward thrill of response to the drums or organ music or processional panoply opening a splendid religious service, knows the meaning of Schutz's words for understanding religious states of consciousness and their entry. More intense examples would be the jerking phenomena often observed as shamans or mediums go into trance or the strong psychoemotional effects, sometimes experienced as rhythmic waves of feeling, that can accompany intense prayer or meditative rapture.

Religion fully and enthusiastically accepts the reality of different states of consciousness or subuniverses. If it did not, it would not be easy for it to postulate, as it must, transcendent patterns and the possibility that the real meaning of things can be better perceived if looked at in other than the ordinary way. The sociologist Peter Berger once remarked that religion is man's audacious attempt to see the whole universe as humanly significant. This statement implies that ordinary perception does not render the universe humanly significant but that religion's task requires looking at things in a nonordinary way. Entering the reality of other subuniverses and their corresponding states of consciousness (because it can be postulated that different realities and different states of consciousness come and go together), it sees, for example, the same deity behind sea and stars as behind human love.

What religion does is establish a scale of values among states of consciousness, whether or not everyone accepts its scale. It says that certain states are highly valuable for perception of transcendent reality and for acting out the dramas in which one is a real self and others are counterproductive to this end. Therefore, religion provides techniques and situations to induce the desired states, and sanctions to discourage the undesirable ones. Religion is a matter of the mind, and with its continuing music of ongoing states of consciousness, the mind is an instrument on which one can learn to play different scores. States of consciousness are the raw material with which religion works, as an artist works with oils or clay. With states of consciousness, religion makes a picture of a real self in tune with infinite reality.

This artistry can work because the psychology of religion has certain principles. It is extremely important to understand that states of consciousness do not remain the same. Not only do they change, but we humans appear to have a need for them to change. It seems to be almost a natural law that a particular state of consciousness sooner or later wants to be supplanted by a contrasting state—a calm contemplative state with an active one, a highly emotional state with a clear tranquil one. When these changes do not occur, it is a sign of severe mental illness.

Religion, therefore, can speak of getting to more desirable states of consciousness, such as one embracing devotion and love of God or the joy of enlightenment, because all of us have gone through at least a limited range of different states and through the different ways of seeing the world that accompany them. Moreover, the principle of alteration in states of consciousness indicates that we have a need for states and realities that contrast with what we take to be ordinary consciousness and reality, for every state wants to be followed by a contrasting state. The more monotonous a person's life is, doubtlessly the more intense is the need for something else, like intense religious experience.

Innumerable people around the world live practical, commonsense lives close to the soil and to family and friends, for the most part. They are concerned chiefly with crops and prices, buying homes and planning parties—except in certain religious situations, when events long ago and far away but kept alive in stories and temples arise in vivid color in their minds and conversation. They may perceive miracles or real-life dramas that confirm the power of those times for today.

This other world is a part, a necessary contrasting part, of the lives of crops, houses, and families. Just as the people need the commonplaces of life, they also need the states of consciousness that open doors to an alternative reality of prophets, gods, and wonders. Tradition, temple, church, music, rites, preaching, and feeling open invisible doors to that other world, utterly remote though it may be in time and place, can brighten the skies of this world more than a thousand sunrises. Indeed, that other world goes into this one like mother's milk and love, giving point to the institutions that cement families and communities.

DEVELOPMENT AND CHANGE

Now let us see how religion relates to our capacity for development and permanent change. Alterations of consciousness do not need to go around and around a limited cycle. People can experience changes in the whole structure of the cycle, and very often religion is the major symbolic factor in this change. Something in nearly everybody wants to find a way of life in which he or she knows a more desirable, perhaps because more intense, state of consciousness a larger part of the time. For this some turn to adventure, romance, or drugs. Others, recognizing that religion deals in states of consciousness and with the highest and widest ranges of being, turn to it.

Sometimes the permanently changing effect of religion is sudden. Consider a young man following a very ordinary life—getting up, getting dressed, going to work or school, worshiping perfunctorily in the way of his people, eating, and sleeping. One fine day he has an experience. A tremendous power enters his life, in a vision or jarring psychological experience along the road or at the back of the barnyard, and he knows that from then on his life will be entirely different. Afterward, he leaves home, wandering and possessing nothing, yet (in his mind) possessing all things. In ancient times, he might have become a disciple of the Buddha or Jesus, in the Middle Ages a Franciscan friar or itinerant yogi or dervish, nowadays a missionary or Zen monk. The religion-connected change was fast and deep; the new states of consciousness that now ring his mind make him feel more like who he was really meant to be.

The change may also be gradual and, rather than wholly spontaneous, deliberately sought through religion. Indeed, it is a mistake to think the sudden, unexpected conversion is typical. Without going into the issue of what sort of unconscious psychological preparation there may be even for a change as dramatic as Paul's on the road to Damascus, it is safe to say that most people are first drawn to religion by hope for change, sudden or gradual, and that many subsequently find it.

Chumash Native American teen dancing   (Eyal Nahmias/Alamy)

On the other hand, personality change is not necessary to the practice of religion as such; there is also the way of those ordinary believers for whom religion is a contrast within normal life rather than a radically new life. Even when extensive change occurs, it may be more a spiritual parallel to the radical enough changes nature itself gives than something of a wholly different order.

Quite apart from any effects of religion, everyone's life is a series of immense changes. We move from infant to child, from child to adult, and from student to sage, from maiden to mother. All these require giving up one pattern of thought and life and taking on another. The reprogramming of mind and feelings is never easy. It requires effort, some tension, and probably some symbolic reinforcement through such means as graduation and wedding ceremonies. New titles and status may go with the new role to uphold the individual's sense of new identity and meaning during a difficult adjustment.

Everyone who survives infancy goes through changes like these. In the course of such transitions almost everyone experiences significant problems, moments of poignant regret for what he or she is leaving behind, and the excitement of attaining the new. The adult may wish to be a secure and happy child once more, the harried mother a glamorous maiden again.

Here, in conjunction with the ordinary transitions of life, religion provides assistance. It does so in three ways that may appear contradictory but that nevertheless seem to work well enough together.

One way is to offer times and places for symbolic returns to earlier stages, such as childhood, under controlled conditions. It can hardly be denied that much of religion does suggest, in contrast to the ambiguous adult world, a return to the subuniverse of the child's perception of things. Morality may be delineated by simple rules, such as those of the nursery. Practices such as kneeling, chanting, and singing simple songs symbolically hint at returning to the child's height and modes of expression. Pentecostals often talk of their tongues as "babbling like babes," which shows the speakers are reborn "babes in Christ." For many people, temporary returns to the world of childlike values, actions, and perceptions are doubtlessly of great benefit in maintaining psychological equilibrium.

Yet religion also works to support adult life and to reinforce the idea that one can and must transit from earlier to later stages. It marks these transitions with rites such as confirmation and marriage. It gives prestige to heads of families and the elderly, and it supports their authority. It portrays adult vocations as divine callings that must be exercised morally and cannot rightly be refused; they are parts of the pattern that makes each person within society a real self. These two sides of religion—the return to childhood and the sanctification of adult life—are ideally kept in equilibrium.

Finally, religion contends that it can offer religious parallels to the transitions of life. If one has found life after physical birth to be empty and off-center, one can be reborn spiritually, start again, and make right what went wrong the first time out. If one has inadequately moved from childhood to adulthood, one can become an adult spiritually, doing right through a new process of spiritual growth what was done wrong when the process was only physical and social. Mystics talk of spiritual marriage to Christ or deities. Just as one can grow, learn, and marry in secular life, so one can in spiritual life.

The greatest natural and spiritual transition of all is birth itself, apart from the equally great transition of death. Birth is the transition from nonexistence, at least in terms of this world, to existence. Beside the momentousness of this event, other transitions, such as those of maturation or marriage, pale.

It is no wonder, then, that religion has seized on birth and often made it the most important symbol of all on its dynamic side. The idea of **rebirth** is a concept around which the most powerful forces of religious psychology revolve. In this idea everything potent is pulled together. Through rebirth one is able to negate one's previous life and to start again, doing right what then went wrong. This experience immediately suggests the reality of two contrasting modes of being and so of ordinary versus transcendent planes of reference. Rebirth suggests the return to childhood, indeed to the womb and the very roots of childhood, yet it also indicates sanctifying a new life here and now as an adult. It also infers passing through a mysterious alternative reality, thereby indicating that one who is truly reborn has knowledge, if not mastery, of other realities. He or she is one who has spiritually gone through death and come back, having dealt with all significant corners of the sacred, met the numinous and taken it into himself or herself, and built a symbolic bridge from here to there.

Not all religions, of course, put equal emphasis on the symbols and language of rebirth. However, if it is interpreted broadly to include any extensive change in one's state of consciousness, whether sudden or gradual, rebirth seems an apt symbol for the dynamics of religion within personality. Rebirth can also be called initiation, and as we have seen the rites of initiation are often full of rebirth symbolism. We do not speak of just those traditions in which spiritual rebirth is expected to be sudden and dramatic. In an arduous but gradual process such as yoga, undertaken as serious spiritual training, much in the traditional literature suggests a psychic return to the womb, gestation, and reemergence as a new person with a new and powerful mode of being in the world. In all sorts of religion and amid all kinds of technique, the prevalence of initiatory and rebirth motifs reminds us that at heart religion is, in Frederick Streng's term, "means toward ultimate transformation."[5]

Indeed, virtually every religious tradition has some process of initiation, introduced in Chapter 4, for all members, for religious specialists, or for both. These are commonly rife with symbolism of dying and then coming to life again, or returning to the womb and being reborn.[6] One good example is Christian baptism. Going into the waters as into a grave and then emerging clearly represents, as the apostle Paul stated, dying with Christ and rising again with him. It also suggests returning to the watery depths of the womb and being reborn as a new person with new values and a new life.

Among Native American tribes, such as the Algonquin of the Northeast, a young man undergoing initiation spends several days in a round sweat lodge. In its center is a fire, representing the center of the world, surrounded by rocks on which water is thrown to produce steam. While in this hut full of fire and steam, the initiate neither eats nor drinks nor sleeps. He does, however, occasionally smoke the sacred pipe and endeavor to travel to the realm of the gods, see a vision of his guardian spirit, and perhaps receive from him a new name. After this experience in the warm, dark, and mystical world of the lodge, he emerges, clad only in a blanket like a baby, and ritually receives his first food and drink.[7]

Yoga in India and elsewhere is a comparable process but enacted more within the self—although sacred environments and regimens reminiscent of the Algonquin are not unknown to yoga. Indeed, yoga, as we know it, has partial roots in ancient sacrificial rites centering on fire. Its main emphasis is on inward control of the mind and senses, and inwardly the yogi strives to pass through a mystical death and rebirth. After mastering techniques of posture and breathing that give yogis tranquility together with mastery over their moods and desires, they are able to withdraw their senses from the outer world and become unaware of external events. They then find developing within themselves a whole new equivalent of the nervous system and the mind, as though a new person were forming. The power of the new yogic men and women compared to that of the old is as a superman to a baby; they have access to marvelous psychic senses (the tradition tells us) that enable them to know and control things near and far, and their consciousness is bathed with a calm light beyond the keenest joy of ordinary folk.[8]

These examples suggest deliberate techniques for inducing subjective rebirth, or moving from one state of consciousness to another, more desirable one. It is important to realize that much of religion consists of just such techniques and the concepts that go with them.

It is equally important to balance that realization with the understanding that although experiences of transformation can be prepared for by prayer, study, meditation, psychosomatic procedures, and association with spiritually significant people, when religious experiences occur they feel unexpected and spontaneous. They are a breakthrough that liberates something previously dammed up within the self. Far from feeling induced, they may feel like the most free and genuine being the self ever had. One thinks of the great **conversions**, from those of Paul and Augustine in the West and Chaitanya or Shinran in the East to modern converts.

Group practicing yoga   (Anna Furman/Shutterstock)

The experience may have been sudden or gradual; in many cases it can be convincingly argued that there was unconscious preparation; it may also have been strongly suggested by factors in the cultural environment or by specific events in the individual's prior life. The fact remains, however, that conversion differs from something planned. It feels like a new and unexpected gift, a grace. Instead of merely using a technique based on an already accepted worldview (though this may come later, as the convert endeavors to hold or recapitulate his or her experience), it moves the recipient into an altered worldview and behavior pattern along with the new state of consciousness.

Many conversions have involved significant symbols that seemed to trigger the transformation. St. Augustine heard a child chanting in a singsong voice from some neighboring garden, "Take and read, take and read," and opened a New Testament to a passage that deeply changed his life.

Hui-neng, a Ch'an, or Zen, patriarch of the seventh century CE in China, sold firewood to support his mother after his father's death. One day he carried wood to a customer's shop. As he left he saw a man reciting a sutra. It was the Diamond Sutra, with such lines as the following: "As the raft is of no further use after the river is crossed, it should be discarded. So these arbitrary conceptions of things and about things should be wholly given up as one attains enlightenment. So much more should one give up conceptions of non-existent things, and everything is non-existent."

Hui-neng was immediately awakened. He talked with the man and found he was a monk from a certain monastery. After provision was made for his mother, the young Hui-neng left to join the monastery and eventually became one of the most influential figures in the history of Chinese Buddhism and Zen.[9]

A modern spiritual figure of India, Mcher Baba, first awakened to his spiritual vocation from a rather ordinary student life when, at the age of 19, he passed a famous and very aged Muslim female saint called Hazrat Babajan. She was sitting under a tree but silently arose and embraced the young man unexpectedly. Not a word was spoken, but from then on the youth's life was deeply changed. He visited her every day for a time thereafter and soon was spending many hours in deep meditation.[10]

So far our reflections on the psychology of religion have led to the following observations: (1) Human beings are capable of different states of consciousness; (2) religion accepts this fact enthusiastically and is concerned with distinguishing the states and giving them differing values; (3) religion offers techniques and symbols for inducing or giving meaning to changes in consciousness of religious significance. These operations of religion work against the background of the changes of consciousness that inevitably occur with human growth and alterations in life. Life is a series of initiations—of developmental changes, natural or induced, that produce lasting changes in one's *patterns* of states of consciousness, or at least in the meaning and symbolization one gives them—from birth through education, marriage, and parenthood. Religion relates itself to this process of life-stage initiations both by providing occasions of release from their inevitable tensions and parallel ritual or psychologically transformative initiations with religious symbolic completion. We next look at some important states of consciousness to see what meaning religion gives to them.

RELIGIOUS EXPERIENCE

What do we mean by religious experience? Psychologist Abraham Maslow has written of what he called the **peak experience**.[11] Though Maslow's peak experience is not explicitly or necessarily a religious state, he has taken pains to show its general similarity to the experiences reported by religious mystics in the past. It is primarily the feeling of joy and creativity that comes to anyone at high moments, whether in something done well, in love, or in spiritual ecstasy. It is a state suffused with absolute being, sufficiency, wholeness, and effortlessness. In a peak experience, Maslow says, a person feels integrated, able to fuse with the world, at the height of his or her powers, spontaneous, natural. Creativity flows out of the person, and he or she needs nothing outside of himself or herself. Because the person has no sense of dependence or goal orientation toward anything outside, she or he is complete within and so has little sense of time or space. It is akin to joyfully playing a piece of music one has mastered, so that the performance seems effortless. The person in a peak experience often has a sense of luck, fortune, or grace. All this is analogous to what many have described as religious experience.

The ways in which this state can offer a contrast to ordinary self-awareness should be obvious. Here is a condition in which, for the moment, meaningful awareness of bounding by birth and death, and the stress engendered by unfulfilled needs, falls away. When you are swimming, skiing, loving, writing, painting, reading, or just contemplating and there wells up a sense of deep fullness in the here and now so great that it needs no outside justification, that is the peak experience. Give it a religious content, call it an experience of God, and it is explicitly a religious experience. Intense conversion and mystical experiences have qualities of peak experience (although they may include others too, such as intense awareness of guilt, especially related to the religious content). Both involve a melting down, so to speak, of the ordinary structures of thought shaped by self-cognition or self-awareness, thus enabling these structures to be reformed. One emerges from the experience with new systems or states of consciousness and new internalized symbols to stimulate them.

This is what really happens psychologically during an initiation, rebirth, or conversion such as those previously described. As we saw in Chapter 4, the anthropologist Victor Turner, following the classic work of Arnold van Gennep, distinguished three stages of initiation: separation, liminality, and rejoining.[12] The previously presented Algonquin Indian initiate, for example, first passed through a process of separation from ordinary life—he underwent a preliminary fast and purification, then entered the hut. Next followed the most interesting state, the liminal, or marginal, state of the novice during the heart of the transition, when he is in neither his former nor his new status, but is cut off from both, as well as from the mode of existence on which ordinary self-awareness or self-cognition is based. He is in a place with virtually no contact with the outer world but open to the depths of his consciousness and to the gods. The **liminal state** is tomorrow's knight during his nocturnal vigil, a future king during his coronation, the novice in the initiatory lodge.

In a broader sense, Turner points out, certain categories of people are in a permanent state of liminality against the structures of society: outcasts, monks, hobos, unassimilated minorities, alienated youth, or whoever finds his or her role to be on the borders or margins of structure. Attention to these persons is very important to under-standing religion, because the religious world is full of them, both official and unoffi-cial. Often this role, as in the case of the monk or Hindu *sadhu* or "holy man," may be a symbolic gesture toward antistructure which is actually accepted and semiritualized by society, and so (like initiation) a part of its structure in a larger sense. Nonetheless, the liminal person is in principle not bound by all of society's rules or a participant in all its privileges, and he or she has thoughts of a different sort, being oriented toward different values. The liminal person serves as a standard symbol of the possibility of alternative ways of life and climates of consciousness, as do all sorts of people in American life, from Trappist monks to rappers. Also, at certain times or occasions, groups of people, or society as a whole, enter a state of liminality in comparison with ordinary life—in festival or carnival, in pilgrimage, in revolution.

The ordinary initiate or convert, however, only briefly passes out of structure into antistructure, with the aim of returning to the same structural world as a person changed within. The initiate is, as we have seen, spiritually reborn; he or she has returned to the forge of making and has built new structures out of the breakdown of previous ones. The new structures include new vision, perhaps a new name. The initia-tory experience, in other words, functions to induce a transition state comparable to that of a peak experience. Both provide an alternative to ordinary life.

Another state of consciousness related to the peak experience is that of **meditation**—basically a pleasant and restful quietness or stillness of mind. It may involve imagery (of a religious nature, if the meditation is religious), or it may be focused on a chant, a point of visual concentration, or a formless mental quietude. This singleness makes one feel he or she is living close to the ground of consciousness. Meditation, whether in prayer or dance, is a common religious way of perpetuating or recovering or, one could say, enjoying the effects of a transformative experience.

Still another religious state of consciousness, related to the foregoing in a nega-tive way, is **guilt**. A sense of guilt—that is, of severe disconnect between what one feels oneself to be and one's ideal self-image—is a state of consciousness markedly different from both ordinary self-cognition and the peak experience. It implies intense feeling-laden introspection. In it, as in conversion, values are polarized into broad blocs of feeling, essentially good versus bad, with the present self identified with bad. One can continue in a state of moderate guilt for some time and be motivated by it to a high level of religious activity that simultaneously activates and alleviates it. The guilt state can also lead to conversion, especially as it becomes intense. It is perhaps less likely, psychologically, that a person with a strong sense of guilt would be successful in meditation or other peak experience, since they fundamentally require a positive valuation of the accessible self. It can be observed that religious traditions in which the guilt state is prominent tend to stress active or emotionally intense forms of reli-gious expression more than meditation.

Often, religion is also connected with a state of consciousness centered on a sense of immense power. One may emerge from initiation or conversion feeling that one has transcended all ordinary limits and is full of great power, immune to what can hurt and able to do almost anything. The power state of consciousness may result from the very close identification of the self with the paramount symbol that the rebirth experi-ence can afford, so that symbolically one *is* Christ or Buddha and is as immune and transcendentally powerful as he, or it may simply be that because one has enjoyed the sort of peak experience that alternates with ordinary self-cognition, one is infused with the alternative consciousness's indifference to the normal awareness of bounding and finitude.

Another characteristic religious state that can be psychologically defined is attachment or dependency. The religious personality frequently attaches itself in an emotionally powerful way as a disciple to a particular person, a savior, teacher, or guru. The attachment can also be to a particular symbol, idea, or slogan that is emotively powerful, perhaps one that emerges in a transformative process. One can see religious dependency psychologically (again, much else may be operative on levels beyond the psychological) as a process internalizing something initially outside the self as a pivot around which the consciousness revolves. Because the symbol is still outside as well, continual contact with it is needed to maintain the pivot in a central place, at least until it is well fixed. Thus, disciples may spend several years in almost continual attendance upon their master, then leave and not see him again physically for many years. Yet they continue to keep him in mind and heart, worship him from far off, and perhaps believe he is still teaching and guiding them in their thoughts.

PSYCHOLOGICAL INTERPRETATIONS OF RELIGION

We now look at some important modern psychological interpretations of religion. Some of these figures were also discussed in chapter 1.

First mention might go to the American psychologist and philosopher of pragmatism William James (1842–1910). James' classic work, *The Varieties of Religious Experience*, presents a remarkable cornucopia of spiritual phenomena, from visions to trances, from what he called the "healthy-mindedness" of the "once-born" to the "twice-born" state of the convert.[13] He recognized that some religion is bizarre and pathological. In this and other writings, however, James did not allow himself to be drawn into one single view of religion, as good or bad, but respected anyone's right to believe, allowed that feeling was as valid as reason as grounds for belief, and was willing to judge religion by its fruits.

For the father of psychoanalysis, Sigmund Freud (1856–1939), religion was a symptom of incomplete development within a personality. It perpetuates childish or repressive attitudes toward the world in place of the "reality principle," that is, the way things really are. Religious notions are retentions of childhood concepts of internalized father, mother, mystical feelings, and magical power as ways of dealing with the world and one's place in it.[14]

For example, a person facing a difficult problem in adult life might turn to a divine father figure, recalling the time in childhood when the father seemed able to solve all problems. Or he or she might turn to prayer, a magical rite, or a mystical state of consciousness, harking back to the infancy in which cause and effect were not well understood, and it seemed that repeating something over and over, or ritualized gestures, might make it happen.

A more positive assessment of religion was made by a student of Freud who later broke with him, Carl G. Jung (1875–1961). Jung taught that life is a quest for *individuation*, that is, for unifying the various constituents of one's mind into a harmonious pattern. These constituents are basically aspects of masculinity and femininity, together with the dark negative principle, called the Shadow, and the emerging ideal self. Each of these parts has a root image called an archetype. Traditional religious myth and ritual, together with dreams and fantasies, are seen by Jungians as treasure troves of images that represent these archetypes. The feminine side, for example, presents itself to us as the elderly and wise Great Mother (goddesses such as Cybele or Isis) or as the eternally young anima (youthful maidens such as Persephone or the Virgin Mary). The masculine may be the Wise Old Man, such as Merlin, or the youthful Hero. The emerging individuated self may be represented by the archetype of the Marvelous Child or by a Hero triumphant through a struggle, such as Christ.

The archetypes and the psychic force behind them are normal constituents of the mind. Everyone has something of all of them, and if any are repressed, it may cause trouble. Equally unhealthy is inflation by an archetype, so that one acts *only* the Great Mother or the Hero. They must instead be arranged into a pattern, a Mandala, so that they balance each other off and the ideal self emerges in the center. Religious rites, myths, and art (as well as those of traditions such as alchemy) are seen by Jungians as

Psychiatrist Carl G. Jung   (Bettmann/Corbis)

able to help one greatly in the process of rightly placing the archetypes and attaining the individuation process. They give one symbols for understanding aspects of oneself that correspond to the dynamics of the Great Mother or the Hero. Traditional rites can help insofar as they are basically aimed at aligning the archetypes and enabling a true self to emerge out of them.[15]

Mention should also be made of James Hillman (1926–2011), a post-Jungian who developed what he called archetypal psychology. Hillman emphasized the distinctiveness of each archetype, or "personality," within the individual, arguing that none should be suppressed by a single dominant ego, but each should be explored and learned from, then well expressed. Religiously, this naturally led to a new psychological polytheism, which Hillman has articulated finely out of Greek mythology.[16]

Kenneth I. Pargament is a recent psychologist of religion who has emphasized less theoretical understandings of religion in psychological terms than the use of religion and spirituality in clinical settings. In a nonsectarian way, he has shown how psychotherapists can use spiritual dynamics, belief-based images, and spiritual concepts such as forgiveness and gratitude, to help clients deal with difficult issues, while avoiding negative evasive uses of religion. He represents a trend toward returning to William James' pragmatic view of religion.

Finally, a word must be said about attempts to find a neurological explanation of religion. From time to time one sees a news item about discovery of a "God gene," the idea that human beings can inherit a set of genes that predispose them to religious and mystical experience. Proponents of the idea are careful to point out that such research does not of itself prove or disprove God or religion, but only demonstrates the way belief and religious experience are articulated on the biological level, just as are all other emotions and subjective experiences. One researcher, Dean Hamer, claimed that spirituality can be quantified by psychometric measurements, and that spiritual individuals are favored by natural selection because of their innate sense of optimism.[17]

Andrew Newberg, using brain imaging to study Buddhist meditators and Franciscan nuns at prayer, suggesting apparent neurophysiological correlates with these states. These and other studies were eventually explored in several books.[18] While Newberg certainly expounds the neurophysiological side to religious experience, showing exactly where in the brain experience of God is located, in the later books especially he concludes positively that meditation, prayer, and other spiritual practices permanently strengthen neural functioning in specific parts of the brain. This in turn, whether it is called spiritual, psychological, or physiological, helps lower anxiety, wards off depression, and enhances our empathy with others. Reasonable spirituality, in other words, makes us think and interact better.

Is it God, God genes, or just nerves? That ultimate question remains open. It has been open for a long time. William James, to refer back to the patron of American psychology of religion, inveighed in the opening chapter of *The Varieties of Religious Experience* against what he called "simple-minded" "medical materialism," which "finishes up St. Paul by calling his vision on the road to Damascus a discharging lesion of the occipital cortex, he being an epileptic."[19] These kinds of notions, he said, are not necessarily wrong, but unhelpful, since (1) if the experiences of religionists can be so explained, so could the views of the medical materialists, who perhaps disbelieve in religion because of some anti-God gene; and (2) these notions do nothing to explain the whole complex influence, good and bad, of religion in millions of individuals and in society over innumerable years of history. All this calls for a much finer comb, which to be sure researchers such as Dean Hamer and Andrew Newberg are beginning to provide.

SUMMARY

Psychologically, religion is based on the self-evident fact that we experience varying, shifting states of consciousness, or of moving from one "subuniverse of meaning" to another. Religion accepts the reality of these states or subuniverses and evaluates some of them as better and truer—more expressive of the true self in right relationship with Ultimate Reality—than others.

The psychology of religion also focuses attention on how religion interacts with changes in life. First, there can be experiences that definitely point one in a particular direction spiritually: conversion and mystical experiences. These may apparently come spontaneously and may profoundly affect one's religion for life. Conversion may be either intellectual or emotional or a combination of both.

Second, structured rites of initiation or transition are designed to induce religious experiences that also have a lifelong effect.

Third, the ordinary stages of life—maturation, marriage, children, sickness, death—are marked in most religions with rites and teachings that bring out their spiritual implications. Finally, models can be devised for understanding how religion is experienced and what it is likely to mean to people in different ages of life, from early childhood to old age. We must also think of feelings or states of consciousness important to religion: meditation, liminality, guilt, dependency, inner freedom.

Religion has been understood differently by various important psychological thinkers. William James looked at it pragmatically. For Freud it meant basically an unrealistic desire to return to childish attitudes; for Jung, archetypal symbols for aspects of personality; for humanistic psychologists, names and techniques for the "peak experience" that is the highest state of consciousness. Hillman sees it in terms of the many separate archetypes or personalities. Pargament has revived a positive clinical understanding of spiritual dynamics in psychotherapy. Neurologists such as Hamer and Newberg have explored deep relationships between our expanding knowledge of the brain to locate and explore religious experience. The trend in psychology of religion seems to be toward a pragmatic rather than ideological view of religion's role in the individual and society.

KEY TERMS

conversion, p. 68

guilt, p. 71

liminal state, p. 70

meditation, p. 71

peak experience, p. 70

rebirth, p. 67

states of consciousness, p. 61

subuniverses, p. 62

CHAPTER

6

Inner Adventure:
The Way of Realization,
the Way of Faith

Pilgrims approaching the Lotus Temple in Delhi, India, a house of worship of the Bahai
Faith built in 1986   (Idris Ahmed/Dorling Kindersley)

LEARNING OBJECTIVES

After reading this chapter, you should be able to:

- Discuss spirituality as a journey, and the stages on that journey as understood by authorities such as Paul Ricoeur and Gordon Allport.
- Point to the relevance of the "peak experience," and the B-state and D-state, as described by Abraham Maslow.
- Present the Way of Realization of Evelyn Underhill, with its five stages: Awakening, Purgation, Illumination, the Dark Night of the Soul, the Unitive state. Show similarities in the way of enlightenment of Buddhism, and perhaps in other paths.
- Interpret the Way of Faith, as represented by Luther and Honen, as a very different approach. Explain its appeal to many troubled souls.
- Talk about whether you believe the Ways of Realization and Faith can be reconciled.

WAYS TO GO

Religion is almost always defined as going somewhere. Its great adventure is a journey of which earthly pilgrimages, whether to Mecca or Jerusalem or Rome, are but symbols. "Lead me from the unreal to the real. Lead me from darkness to light. Lead me from death to immortality," say the ancient Upanishads. "On our way rejoicing" and "Onward, Christian soldiers," sing the old Christian hymns. "Next year in Jerusalem," is recited at the end of the Jewish Yom Kippur and Passover Seder services, implying that wherever one abides in exile, the hope is for a sacred and final journey to the Holy City. In mystical lore Jerusalem is not only here below, important as that place is to Jewish identity, but also above, or inward, in its heavenly and eternal ideal form.

To see religion as a journey reminds one of images the Sufi (Islamic mystic) Hafez (1325–1389) liked to use. He said that the role of God in human life and death may be seen in two ways. One is to picture a courtroom, with guilty people and innocent people, a judge (God), a court stenographer, bailiffs, and the rest. The other is to see a caravanserai, or way-station for caravans, with expeditions coming and going, some travelers ahead of others, but all moving on.

The religious adventure, then, can be seen as a journey, like life itself.

The French philosopher and historian of religion Paul Ricoeur (1913–2005) described three stages of religious growth.[1] One starts out, probably either in the religion of their birth or of an early conversion, in a "First Naïveté," a literal and accepting belief in the concepts and values of the religion, often centering around what he called taboos and refuge. Tabooed are actions, and also ideas, inconsistent with the religion and therefore forbidden; refuge, the positive side of the equation, is the strength and comfort the faith provides in a power greater than oneself.

Then a time comes—not for all believers, but for some—when, on the basis of further education and life experience, or just an innate restlessness of spirit, the disciple begins to submit these beliefs to intellectual examination. They may not hold up, and if so, they may be abandoned, at least inwardly. This is the second stage, "Critical Distance." In it, in Ricoeur's phrase, the "immediacy of belief" is "irremediably lost."

Some spiritual travelers, however, may emerge from critical engagement into what Ricoeur called "Second Naïveté," attained "in and through criticism." Now, at best, the individual is able once again to accept the basic ideas and practices of the religion, but with a new dimension of depth and sophistication in his or her understanding of it. Perhaps faith now has a better philosophical foundation, having survived engagement with the broader world of ideas. Perhaps some of it is now understood as myth and symbol in the positive sense of the words—for philosophy also uses symbols— as representations of realities so profound as otherwise to be almost inexpressible. "Dissolution of the myth as explanation is the necessary way to the restoration of the myth as symbol," said Ricoeur.[2] It may even be that the journeyer has now attained a state of mystically realizing the presence of the divine at all times, in all places, and for that very reason the journeyer is uninterested in rejecting God's more everyday depictions, knowing that in religion it is often better to affirm where one is now than reject the signposts along the road by which one traveled thus far.

These stages may be compared to the account of the American psychologist Gordon Allport (1897–1967) in his influential *The Individual and His Religion*, of immature versus mature faith. Immature faith is unreflective and characterized by such traits as magical thinking ("If I act in such-and-such a way, God will do something, punish or reward me"), wish-fulfilling ("If I pray really hard, I will get an A"), fanaticism ("Unbelievers are totally wrong and bad"), literal mindedness ("My religious beliefs and scriptures are totally true, without shading or metaphor"), second-hand ("I believe what I was taught"). Mature faith, on the other hand, is able to ask questions, to accept some things and not others from a tradition, bases itself at least in part on individual experience, grounds morality in personal values rather than fear, integrates all of life with the faith, and is a doorway to further spiritual exploration.[3] Clearly, these qualities are related to a kind of theological liberalism not all may wish to endorse. However, let us see where this quest leads.

Something may seem to be left out of the religious psychologies of Ricoeur and Allport, the possibility that mature, adult faith may be not just a matter of right reason and ethics, but may also have its own kind of profound inner experience. Here is where the psychology of the American Abraham Maslow (1908–1970), presented in Chapter 5, may be mentioned again.

Maslow came to consider much of the conventional psychological view of spirituality to be flawed because it was based on clinical experience with persons holding neurotic and immature religious attitudes. Why not, he said, begin instead with the most creative and fulfilling experiences of happy, highly productive people instead? These hours he called "peak" experiences: The moments when one comes afire with an exciting new idea, when creativity in art, writing, engineering, business, or relationships engages and ideas surge out into manifestation, and one is in virtually a state of ecstasy. A peak for a musician might be when something clicks just right and the music flows out almost of itself better than ever; for an athlete, when getting into the "runner's high" or being "in the zone." These people are, for the duration, in what Maslow labeled the B (for "Being") state.

In the B-state, people are content in the here and now; nothing is required beyond it. One loses all sense of time, as one is not waiting for anything more to come later. One loses any sense of separateness because one is integrated dynamically with the world, functions effortlessly, is free of blocks and fears, is spontaneously creative, and is at the height of his or her powers. The peak experiencer expresses himself or herself freely in poetic and rhapsodic terms, has a playful nonstriving joy, and is most intensely himself or herself. Moreover, the peak experience is "self-validating": It is obviously valuable of itself and requires no outside justification.[4]

The peak experience includes creative, ecstatic moments in all areas of life, not excluding the raptures of love, but it shades into the religious. Maslow was well aware of many similarities between the peak experience and classic accounts of mystical experience and deliberately pointed them out. In both, there is that feeling of being in a timeless moment, of integration with one's deepest wellsprings of being and creativity, of immense joy, of *rightness* about how things now are. Above all, note in both secular and sacred peaks the quality of egolessness: One is free of the stifling, self-conscious, always-wanting-more-and-always-explaining ego with which we live so much.

That ego-bound person is in what Maslow called the D or deprivation state. In the D-state, some need outside the present always motivates the person: He or she is hungry or is working toward a future benefit or needs love or security, and being deprived makes you very aware of self, unlike the B-state in which the present is enough— indeed, is overflowing with plenitude.

What do Ricouer, Allport, and Maslow all have in common? Basically, the notion that most of us start off with, and perhaps feel most of the time, a negative state that is self-centered. We would like for good things to happen magically; if they don't, we probably feel anxiety, frustration, deprivation, perhaps even what Henry Thoreau meant when he said most men lead lives of quiet despair. Call it First Naïveté, immaturity, the D-state. This starting point applies as much to undeveloped religion as to childishness in any other area of life.

The point, as we will see in the work of explicitly mystical writers also, is that the spiritual journey can begin with intense but egocentric (focused on "this is how *I* feel") religious experience, accompanied by no less intense attachment to particular doctrines and practices associated with the experience. The trip advances toward deeper ego-free living in the presence of the divine—perhaps not even explicitly named. That ultimate would be Maslow's B-state, or the great medieval mystic Meister Eckhart's assertion that one is closest to God not in seeking him, but knowing him wordlessly like an infant, even an infant in the womb.

St. Teresa of Avila, with her usual subtle perceptiveness, writes of a union with God in which the soul is aware of union and "rejoicing in its captivity"—the typical high religious state. Then she describes an even higher state in which there is no sense of anything but enjoyment, without any knowledge of what is being enjoyed, and yet the soul now "enjoys incomparably more" in contemplative prayer, without any words or ideas coming between the mystic and complete union.[5]

Here is a more contemporary example from Maslow again. It took the final years of the psychologist's life for him to find something even better in some ways than the peak experience: what he called the "plateau experience." Though less intense than the peak, this state is steady, pervasive, and of great power to free one from all fear. A very serious heart attack 2 years before his death brought the psychologist to the plateau, which he also called his postmortem life, his life after death.

He said that life after this experience was like a gift, to be lived in a new way, without the anxiety about death which so often afflicts us.[6] Now, as it were on the other side of death, everything seemed doubly beautiful and precious. Everyday visions like flowers and babies, every acts like walking and dining and talking with friends, became marvelous, almost miracles.[7]

This is obviously a state in which the ego no longer gets in the way; it no longer matters what *I* think about flowers or babies, so one is free just to see their piercing importance in themselves. How does one get to that point in the journey we talked about at the beginning of this chapter? Two ways have dominated this issue down through the history of religion, what we call the Way of Realization and the Way of Faith.

THE WAY OF REALIZATION

Under this heading we consider spiritualities that view the path to the goal of salvation, enlightenment, or oneness with God as a series of stages. In order to get a picture of how this looks like, let us begin with five stages of the spiritual life presented in Evelyn Underhill's classic work, *Mysticism.* [8] Her study is based primarily on accounts of traditional Catholic mystics, though with some reference to other Christians and Islamic mystics. But as we will see the steps correlate remarkably well to those presented in other faiths, and to the psychological stages of development already discussed.

Underhill's stages include (1) Awakening, (2) Preparative or Purgative, (3) Illuminative, (4) the Dark Night of the Soul, and (5) Unitive. We will talk in a moment about what they each mean. First, however, we need to present a caveat. As Evelyn Underhill herself made clear, these stages are not intended to represent a rigid, lock-step hike up the trail to Oneness. Some aspirants may skip a step, do them out of order, find fulfillment without going all the way to Unitive, even go back and forth between two of them for a time.

It is not, then, a matter of going in one end of the process and coming out the other end a certified saint or mystic, or holder of a graduate degree in holiness. The spiritual life is far subtler a matter than that, more like an art than a science. The greatest artists or musicians can have good days and bad days, find some techniques difficult and others easy, struggle to the end of their days with fully expressing what is in them.

The stages' pattern should be thought of as like a road map. Different people taking the same trip between two cities may have quite different experiences, even though their maps look the same. Some may drive on a bright sunny day, some in a terrible storm; some may have smooth riding and keep right on course; others have a flat tire or get lost and wander off the road for a time. The value of the map is not that it means everyone's trip is the same, but that it shows travelers there is a way and a goal, and that many people have taken this journey before.

Philosophically, the schema offers a view of the spiritual way that sees it as a long process, like life itself, throughout which one psychological or spiritual experience builds on another to produce a final result not dissimilar from maturity, in

Meditators in a city park   (Tyler Olson/Shutterstock)

which one is able to live free of inner bondage to desires, feelings, and the "self" composed of them.

Awakening

The outward voyage commences with the Awakening. Characteristically, this can take many forms. For some it may seem like kind of call. A great Zen master was first stirred to seek enlightenment by hearing a crow caw in the middle of the night; St. Francis of Assisi heard the painted lips of Christ in a dilapidated chapel tell him to "Rebuild my church"—at first he took this order literally and started work; later he realized the command was meant spiritually as well.

Others may have a powerful conversion experience like Paul on the road to Damascus, or the many souls who have been saved at revival meetings. Sometimes this is a hard, powerful ordeal that begins with a strong conviction of sin, a realization of the emptiness and wrong in one's life as it is, and ends with the tremendous ecstasy of knowing God's forgiving grace. One feels reborn, a new person who can start off fresh from where he or she now is. Though the sins were as scarlet, one is now white as snow.

Still others may grow more quietly but surely toward a moment of realization that now it is time to begin a serious spiritual life, either in one's natal religion or another. Whatever form it takes, something happens that causes one to set foot on the path.

The Awakening ought to inspire in one at first a deep commitment to the moral values associated with the religion in which it occurred. Indeed, at first, as the full meaning of the change is being sorted out, the aspirant may for a time be excessively

St. Francis of Assisi   (Prisma Archivo/Alamy)

rigorous and condemnatory. However, traditional teachers insist that a good moral life is foundational to spiritual advancement, and they also hold that it must be expressed in a loving way.

Inevitably, though, problems arise. The Awakening is likely to be an intensely emotional experience, and intense emotions come and go. The day will come when the feelings are no longer there, and the aspirant may feel lost and abandoned by God, not understanding that the profoundest spirituality is more a deep inner peace than billowing emotionality.

Preparation

It is needful, then, to direct the newfound spiritual energy into proper channels, such as digging irrigation canals to calm surging floodwaters and shunt them toward thirsty growing plants at regular times and in the right amount. This is the task of the Preparative stage. At this time it is important to have a regular spiritual discipline, prayer or meditation or yoga or whatever, which one practices on schedule whether one feels like it or not. The spirit becomes an ingrained part of one's life, not subject to gusty moods and feelings, but a habitual part of life. Bad habits are also rooted out; this is the Purgative part of this stage.

Illumination

In time, the flowers planted, watered, and well cultivated in the Preparatory stage burst into bloom. The Illuminative stage is essentially a happy time of religious satisfaction: of prayers answered, blessings received, rich experience in worship, the presence of God near at hand. It may take different forms for different persons and in different traditions, but in all cases it is a divine consummation of the Awakening and Preparation. For many people, it is what religion is supposed to be all about and is enough.

Dark Night of Soul

There are some, however, who go on to something more. At first the next stage seems far more negative than rewarding. An unexpected, and very unpleasant, feeling of emptiness indwelling what had until now seemed spiritual fulfillment arises. Prayers and prostrations are mere hollow forms, and God in his true reality is hidden or withdrawn. Mantras or meditations are only dry springs, not the fountains of grace they once were. Some may assume at this point that religion was after all only an illusion, and give up.

This is the stage described by St. John of the Cross (1542–1591) in his monumental work, *The Dark Night of the Soul*. The Dark Night is actually another, higher level of Purgation, designed to prepare one for even greater fulfillment.[9] It is intended to cleanse the aspirant of attachment even to the fruits of religion itself.

For religion can itself become an addiction as surely as the pleasures of the table or the bottle. The music, the symbols, the ideas, and the inner experiences become something one feels one cannot live without, and the attachment is to them rather than to God. Therefore, according to masters such as St. John, God takes them away that he himself may be found in a new way. One finds oneself at midnight on a dark desert without a compass, only the cold stars far above for light or direction.

Unitive State

If one does not surrender to despair, one is now ready for the Unitive state, being joined with God deep within and so not dependent on outward means. It is not that one rejects customary religious practices; rather, they now have a different meaning, because the divine is nearer than hands and feet, and as St. Teresa noted, the divine is enjoyed without even necessarily being named. For this is the state of deep inward joy and peace of the greatest saints, the fulfillment of the promise of Awakening.

INSIGHT

Let us compare this model with that of Buddhism. Our specific example will be the way of vipassana, the meditation of insight, as presented in the fifth century CE *Visuddhimagga* or way of purification, by the monk Buddhaghosa.[10] (This sprawling work does not present vipassana as distinctively as more recent texts, but its outline is there, as well as the basic ideology; the *Visuddhimagga* is the foundation of Buddhist meditation traditions.)

Vipassana is the culminating form of meditation in Theravada, "The Way of the Elders," the Buddhism of southeast Asia (except Vietnam), though something similar is found under other names in the Mahayana Buddhism of Tibet, Vietnam, China, Korea, and Japan. In Theravada, it is usually paired with samatha, the meditation of tranquility, through which the practitioner can still the mind and raise consciousness to the most rarefied of heavens. Vipassana is superior because it leads to distinctively Buddhist insights, above all the wisdom by which one is liberated from the wheel of existence altogether and into **Nirvana**.

The distinctive insights are that existence is characterized by *anicca*, or imperma-nence; *dukkha*, or suffering; and *anatman*, or no selfhood. By mindfulness, watching one's actions, feelings, and above all one's thoughts rise and fall, come and go, one comes to realize that none of them last; for that reason if one tries to find happiness through any of them, the pleasure is brief and the suffering at its absence long; and in it all no real, solid "self" is to be located, only the congeries of ever-changing desires, feelings, and thoughts that keep blowing through the brain like clouds. (Is there really an *I*? If you say, "*I* want or like this," or "*I* hate that or the other," *who* or *what* exactly is that *I*?)

However, as one inwardly watches that passing panorama of moods, dreams, and memories—not just in reverie, but as the focused mindfulness meditation of vipassana—the day may come when one not only gets their emptiness, but also as it were in the nanosecond gap between one thought and the next, something else: like a golden instant, the first flicker of another kind of reality, light, free, unformed, unself-identified, peaceful beyond all imagining, a flash prevision of Nirvana. Gradually, over many meditations, perhaps over several lifetimes, this Nirvana reality is stabilized, and one becomes as Arhant, or one entirely liberated.

The classic Buddhist writings do not often give full details of the Awakening stage, different as it would be for each seeker, but assume an aspirant determined to follow the path, though in need of purification. (In traditional societies, the initial entry into the religious life may well have been almost perfunctory, but where one went with it was the journey. One example is Ajahn, or Achaan, Chah, 1918–1992, an influential Thai monk of the twentieth century who trained several important Western Buddhist teachers. Like most Thai boys, he was introduced to the monastic life as a youth, in his case at the age of 9, but returned to work on the family farm. However, the cloister had left its imprint. At the age of 20, following his heart, he went back to seek formal ordination as a monk. After several years of basic training—the prepara-tion or purification stage—he set out on his own to be a wandering mendicant and finally established himself in a forest hermitage. To it seekers and disciples came in growing numbers to benefit from his simple, direct, and wise instruction.[11])

Texts such as the *Visuddhimagga* commence with what is really essentially purification, starting with *sila* or basic morality. Without *sila*, other supposed spiritual attainment will get you nothing, unless possibly the powers of a black magician. (In Buddhism, the fundamental 10 precepts of *sila* include five that are general: Do not harm any living being, take what is not given, engage in sexual misconduct, lie, or lose control through alcohol or drugs; and five more specific to monks: Do not eat after midday, watch frivolous entertainment, wear perfumes and jewelry, sleep on a high or soft bed, or use money.)

As far as the mind is concerned, partly through training practice in *samatha*, the novice learns concentration to the extent of stilling the wandering mind, replacing that mind with "mindfulness"—ability to see all things, including one's own thoughts, feelings, and actions, as phenomena. They are each separate and distinct, though linked by endless chains of cause and effect (karma) going nowhere. One is then ready to reflect on those chains, too many of them wrapped around ourselves like those burdening Morley's ghost in *The Christmas Carol*: to see them, through vipassana, as neither pleasant nor reliable nor as somehow making up a self, but as dukkha, anicca, and indicative of anatman.

At this the purification stage may be said to flow into the illuminative. Because as one comes to see the chains for what they are, they increasing fade away before the gaze of insight, and around them one sees the brilliant light, rich feelings, peaceful energy, and floating joy of Nirvana. One feels one is getting there, and is aglow with the easy yet clear perception, and the sheer happiness, of realization.

But we are not there, though much has been attained. Yet, just as we in the West have had our Dark Nights of the Soul, when the joys of the Illuminative way seemed snatched away, so in Buddhism these first raptures are seen as Pseudonirvana. "For it is after illumination, etc., have appeared in one who has already begun insight [vipassana] that there comes to be knowledge of what is the path and what is not the path."[12] Still too much of ego, in the subtle sense of attachment to the bliss of spiritual exultation, affects the pilgrim. Finally she or he has to realize this too is unsatisfactory, being finally in the realm of physical and mental phenomena, of a very high order as they may be. These illuminations being seen for marsh-lights, the seeker knows it is night.

What remains is gradually to perceive all links in all chains, from the grossest physical urge to the most exquisite filament of thought, to be equally limited, suffering, passing away, devoid of ego nature. Finally the day comes when she or he no longer really sees them as more or less desirable. *This* is the true first-knowing of Nirvana, though it lasts less than a second. Gradually it will flourish, till the mystic is with it all the time.

Nirvana means "blown out," as in a fire extinguished. But the fire so dealt with is the fire of the senses, and the ego-self built up by them; liberation from these is not self-extinction unless in a lower sense, but rather freedom from all that brings suffering. It is joy, peace, and love beyond anything one not yet there can even understand. One may be no-self, but one is also one's real self in a way one never was before. Daniel Goleman writes of the Arhant:

The arhant is free from his former socially conditioned identity; he sees consensual concepts of reality as illusions. He is absolutely free from suffering and from acting in a way that would further his karma. Having no feelings of "self," his acts are purely functional, either for maintenance of his body or for the good of others. The arhant does everything with physical grace. Nothing in his past can cause thoughts of greed hatred, and the like to come to mind. . . He lives fully in the moment; all his actions bespeak spontaneity. The last vestiges of egoism the meditator relinquishes in his final stage include: his desire to seek worldly gain, fame, pleasure or praise; his desire for even the bliss of the material or formless [spiritual states]; mental stiffness or agitation; covetousness or of anything whatsoever. For the arhant, the least tendency toward an unvirtuous thought or deed is literally inconceivable. With the full extinction of "unwholesome" roots—lust, aggression, and pride—as motives in the meditator's behavior, loving-kindness, altruistic joy, compassion, and equanimity emerge as bases for his actions. . . His motives are totally pure.[13]

This writer goes on to comment that even the arhant's dreams change. He no longer has dreams due to his bodily state or mental impressions, to which he now has no clinging. But in his clarity he may have dreams indicative of future events. Most important, though, is the arhant's ability to live in love with all beings, practicing benevolence toward the whole world with no thought of self, and in accordance with the four "unlimited" virtues of Buddhism: unlimited friendliness, compassion, sympathetic joy, and equanimity of mind. This is certainly nothing other than the Unitive state.

Similar stages paralleling the way of realizing master plan, as found in Underhill's *Mysticism*, could also be illustrated for such sources as the Hindu Yoga Sutras of Patanjali, the manuals of Sufism or Islamic mysticism, the way of Kabbala in Judaism, and Christian mystics such as St. Teresa of Avila in her great work, *The Interior Castle*. Please investigate them on your own; we must now move on to another tack in the spiritual quest.

FAITH, AND MONKS WHO HATED GOD

The Way of Realization can sound wonderful, but what if you try it and it doesn't seem to work? What if you seem even to hit the Unitive state once or twice, but then on other days you find yourself just as nasty as ever? Then what is called for is bypassing such vain struggle by means of the Way of Faith.

Prince Arjuna, according to that great Hindu classic the Bhagavad Gita, had this problem. After listening to the divine Krishna's instruction, he made this plaintive query:

Suppose a man has faith, but does not struggle hard enough? His mind wanders away from the practice of yoga and he fails to reach perfection. What will become of him then?

When a man goes astray from the path to Brahman, he has missed both lives, the worldly and the spiritual. He has no support anywhere. Is he not lost, as a broken cloud is lost in the sky?[14]

In other words, this person is in truly a bad way, without either spiritual realization or a good rollicking worldly life. Krishna's response in the Gita was to recommend to Arjuna the path of *bhakti* or devotion. In this path, it doesn't matter whether one is high or low, learned or ignorant, a great yogi or mystic or meditator. More than mortification, more than following a path step by step, more than good works, more than right doctrine, who wins out is the one who loves the Lord in his or her heart. Devotion is something anyone can do, freely and spontaneously, at any time, only with the help of God's grace; God's love to us to which we respond, as one lover to another, with our love for God. This is the great Hindu path of *bhakti*, wherein God may be conceptualized in a form like that of Krishna, Vishnu, or the Great Mother.

> He gives me all his heart,
> He worships me in faith and love:
> That yogi, above every other,
>   I call my very own.[15]

The famous Protestant reformer Martin Luther (1483-1546) was in a somewhat similar fix. As a monk, he tried seriously—and Luther was nothing if not serious:

> I was a good monk, and I kept the rule of my order so strictly that I may say
> that if ever a monk got to heaven by his monkery it was I. All my brothers in
> the monastery who knew me will bear me out. If I had kept on any longer,
> I should have killed myself with vigils, prayers, reading, and other work.[16]

And again:

> I was myself more than once driven to the very abyss of despair so that I
> wished I had never been created. Love God? I hated him![17]

Then came the answer, as the desperate monk read the scriptures and came across the line, "He who is righteous by faith shall live" (Habakkuk 2:4, Romans 1:17):

> Then I grasped that the justice of God is that righteousness by which through
> grace and sheer mercy God justifies us through faith. Thereupon I felt myself
> to be reborn and to have gone through open doors into paradise. The whole
> of Scripture took on a new meaning, and whereas before the "justice of God"
> had filled me with hate, now it became to me inexpressibly sweet in greater
> love.[18]

Luther's answer was salvation through simple faith, or inward openness to God and his saving power—or more strictly—divine grace received through faith. This grace and faith is unearned, not the result of any effort on our part, or the reward of good works, or the end-product of assiduous prayer and meditation, or the final stage in a path of purification. Rather, it is based on quite a different understanding of religion and salvation.

Luther felt he could never find peace of mind by those other means, because how could he ever be sure if he had prayed enough, done enough good works, followed the rule strictly enough, or made meditations deep enough, to gain God's favor? Then, in

Martin Luther   (Library of Congress)

that scriptural verse, "He who is righteous by faith shall live," he found an entirely different approach: *sola fides*, "faith alone." And faith as a grace, a free gift (*gratis*), which one can receive even while a sinner.

This grace will also help one do good works and live in the right way. But it is not for good works themselves that one is rewarded or saved; rather works are the fruits and confirmation of salvation by faith. One who is profoundly grateful for salvation by faith and grace will do good works as it were naturally by the same grace. Grace may even bless one with deep experiences of oneness with God, but it is not through mystical experiences either that one is saved; they are freely given divine blessings. It is not even through fervor of devotion, as in bhakti, that one is saved and brought into oneness with God. Luther was well aware that it is as futile, and as subtly self-centered, to try to manufacture the "right" feelings as it is the right works of charity in the hope of thereby winning salvation, as you never know if they are exactly, precisely "right." Instead, just opening oneself by simple, pure faith—not "feelings of faith" but bare inward faith—was sufficient, and it was equally available to everyone.

A comparable development appeared in East Asian Buddhism, with particular sharpness in Japan. This is Pure Land (Japanese *Jodo*) Buddhism, the belief that Amida Buddha, a figure declared to have been enlightened in the far distant past, vowed out of compassion that all who call upon his name in faith will be brought into his "Pure Land" or Western Paradise, a sort of heaven from which entry into Nirvana is easy. The important point is that salvation is through faith, simple faith in Amida's vow, usually expressed by just reciting the *nembustu*, the phrase *Namu Amida Butsu*, "Hail Amida Buddha."

The real founder of Jodo in Japan as a separate school or denomination was Honen (1133–1212). A monk, he claimed to have read the texts of all other Buddhist schools five times over, but found no peace of mind until he read a book about Amida's vow. He then had a sudden realization that the only path to salvation was putting total faith in Amida, to the exclusion of all else. He devoted the rest of his long life to preaching this way.

There were, he said, two ways: the *shodo*, or path of holiness, and *jodo*, the way of Pure Land. The former was all right for those who could sufficiently purify themselves and follow all sorts of holy practices, so as to be saved by their own efforts. But this path is highly deceptive. If the idea of Buddhist liberation is to get rid of the ego, such labors can be subtle forms of reinforcing it; one can become proud of one's ego-lessness. Better the Pure Land way, in which one just gets rid of ego by putting faith in the power of another.

Honen put emphasis on *choosing* the *nembutsu*. Like Martin Luther, he was interested in breaking through religious anxiety by finding a single, simple, sure key to salvation, and for him faith in Amida's vow was it. Perhaps this is something to which many moderns can relate.

The complex world of religious "truth claims" is full of conflicting "facts," ideas, and arguments. At some point, it appears, one must simply make a decision. The Danish philosopher Søren Kierkegaard (1813–1855), called the father of **existentialism**, proposed that in the end arguments for and against the existence of God balance out, with as much to be said on one side as the other; one must finally just *choose* whether to believe or not—and this is the way God *wants* it, because God desires belief that is a freely given "leap of faith," compelled by nothing, not even human logic. Faith in Amida for Honen was something like this, as was faith in Christ for Luther.

Honen had a disciple named Shinran (1173–1263) who took the radical implications of Pure Land even farther. Called the Martin Luther of Japan, he recognized that if salvation really depends on faith and not on our own works, it made no difference whether one was a monk or not; like the German, he gave up the monastic robe, married, and had children. He said that the Pure Land was all the more the way

for sinners, who in their desperation can only have faith, than for the conventionally good. He said he did not really know whether the nembutsu would bring one
to heaven or hell, but he had made his choice, because he knew he was not capable
of attaining Buddhahood on his own; if he ended in hell, he could have no regrets,
because he knew he had made the only choice he could. . . the "leap of faith."

THE MEETING OF THE TWAIN

Therefore, it is that across the religious world these two ways, the Way of Holiness
and the Way of Faith, have been laid out under various names, and each has had its
devotees. Many factors are involved in defining them. Each has a particular view of
the psychology of religion, and perhaps even of God. One may well involve considerable separation from the world, as a mystic, monk, nun, or hermit; the other,
such as Protestant Christianity and Pure Land Buddhism, emphasizes the living of
the religious life through inward faith in the midst of the world. The way of the path
may involve a many-layered and many-faceted religious worldview; the Way of Faith
centers on a single, simple, sure key to salvation.

　　However, there may be ways in which realization and faith can be seen as intertwined. Try dissecting Luther's life in light of Underhill's stages. He first vowed to
enter the monastery when, while a university student, a tremendous lightning bolt
in a thunderstorm had knocked him to the ground: the Awakening. His scrupulously
exacting life as a monk was like the Purification, plus the Dark Night, and the final
liberation through faith like the final Unitive stage, though he would not have used
that term. For Luther saw himself as always a sinner separate from God though
always forgiven. The issue is that for Luther the purgative or purification stage
seems to have deepened directly into the Dark Night of the Soul—despair, hatred of
God—without any alleviating illumination—which would not come to him till after
his breakthrough.

　　Likewise, the *Visuddhamagga* expected faith in the path at the outset, in the sense
that the first of the Buddha's Eightfold Path, right views, can be taken as accepting the
basic Buddhist worldview—the Four Noble Truths and the like—as a kind of working
hypothesis which one is then willing to test through practice.

　　Perhaps, in the subtle world of personal spiritual life, there are times when both
ways have a place. What do you think?

　　However, now it is time to confront one of the most basic problems religion faces,
and a root cause of its existence: evil.

SUMMARY

The spiritual life is like a journey, with stages of growth that have been described by
writers like Pauyl Ricoeur and Gordon Allport as moving from less to more mature
stages. Abraham Maslow has added to the account the idea of the mature peak experience and B-state. All these models have in common starting with a negative state—
Maslow's D-state—then going elsewhere.

　　The Way of Realization is portrayed in Evelyn Underhill's five stages of the spiritual life: Awakening, Purgation, Illumination, the Dark Night of the Soul, and the

Unitive state. They are roughly paralleled in the Buddhist way to enlightenment, with the Unitive state like the realization of Nirvana.

In contrast, the Way of Faith, exemplified by Martin Luther, Hindu bhakti, and Pure Land Buddhism, says that liberation is not a "state" at the end of a long process, but can be found at any time through faith.

There may be ways in which realization and faith can be reconciled.

KEY TERMS

existentialism, p. 89   Nirvana, p. 84

CHAPTER

7

Why Evil?

Satan   (Dusan Kostic/Fotolia)

LEARNING OBJECTIVES

After reading this chapter, you should be able to:

- Present your own definition of evil.
- Phrase the "problem of evil" in your own terms.
- Tell and explain myths of the origin of evil and death.
- Discuss whether and how, in your view, religion can create evil.
- Describe dangers connected to initiation.
- Summarize how religious thought has dealt with evil, through polytheism, divine mystery, divine justice, and other ways.

WHAT EXACTLY IS EVIL?

We can all imagine things as they ought to be: a perfectly loving family; an ideal world without crime, poverty, cruelty, or even disease; oneself always feeling good and doing the right thing. We know all too well such a picture is very far from reality. Insofar as any religion portrays a world governed by an all-powerful and beneficent God, or ruled by inexorable laws that always work for good, it has a problem. The tremendous gap between what ought to be and what is has to be explained, and moreover religion needs to show how the gap can be bridged, both by individuals and the world as a whole. Evil is the most basic issue confronted by religion, and likewise the most difficult. More than one otherwise elegant philosophy or theology has floundered on inability to deal convincingly with the terrible, yet every day, face of bad: the "problem of evil."

Evil is the gaunt features of a child stunted by hunger, eyes empty from lack of love or opportunity. It is an animal unable to live the life for which its mind and body were clearly intended, by cruel act of nature or through human exploitation. It is the devastation of cities by war, and of a single household by selfishness and abuse. Evil is anything that cuts short or perverts the normal lifespan and life experience of any sentient creature, leaving frustration and often real suffering; on a deeper level it is that which destroys the joy of life we all ought to be able to feel. To be sure, one can learn from evil, toughen oneself from evil, even triumph over it, but can one say why it must be there—why there must be such a world—in the first place? Or why evil also happens to beings unable to learn or triumph as you and I might, but can only endure without knowing why?

In one sense, it may be impossible to give a logical, rational answer to why evil, since virtually by definition it is irrational, that which ought not to be, yet is. In the language of the New Testament, it is "The abomination of desolation. . . standing where it ought not" (Mark 13:14). In this respect, the language of myth and religion is well suited to the problem of evil, as it can present the issue in terms of story rather than philosophical propositions, and it is in our own lives as stories, and in all the stories of this globe, that we most forcefully encounter evil. Let us consider what some of these stories are.

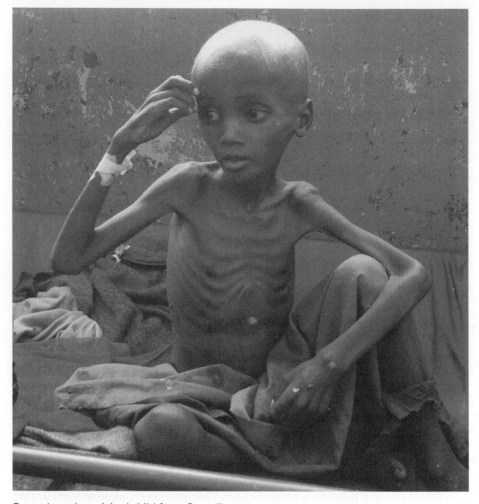

Severely malnourished child from Somalia   (Farah Abdi Warsameh/AP Images)

MYTHS OF THE ORIGIN OF EVIL

Let us go back to the myths of the Beginning. After the mighty days of creation have passed and life settles down to normal, so also does the pain and frustration arise, which is the ordinary lot of humankind that afflicts our lives. And those lives are short, for there comes also, as Coyote learned to his horror, the ending called death. Whence arrives evil and death to that once-beautiful creation?

The widely varied stories of the world's peoples on this all-important topic surely say much both by their content and their tone about the culture, and the attitude toward life, of the tellers. Take for example an African story offering a wryly amusing tale about evil and death.

This tale is from the Limba people of Sierra Leone. They noted that the snake could apparently avoid death just by changing his skin. Afterward, he looks bright and fresh as new. Why can't we do the same thing?

Here's how the story went. Kanu, the Limba creator and high God, had originally meant for both humans and animals not to die, and he mixed and brewed till he had made a medicine that would prevent death. The deity gave part of it to the snake, and it worked for him; all he had to do was shed his skin, and he was good as new. Kanu then handed that same immortal snake a bowl with the rest of the elixir splashing around in it. He told the serpent to carry the precious vessel over to the Limba people.

But the toad objected, saying the snake moved so fast he would spill the liquid of eternal life. Toad insisted on taking it himself, even though Kanu asked him not to. Nonetheless the amphibian put the vessel on his head. He then started hopping, and with the second hop the fluid all spilled. Disgusted at Toad's disobedience, Kanu refused to make more, and for that reason all people and animals die, except the snake, who dies only if someone kills him.[1]

One can imagine a story such as this being told to great comic effect by a master storyteller. Undoubtedly the point is not that it must be believed absolutely in the way the more rigorous advocates of some religions say their scriptures must be believed. Rather what it does is set a certain feeling-tone toward the coming of death. Hearing this tale, we feel wistful over what might have been, yet we also chuckle at the narrative's humorous lines. A good many of the blunders of our own human lives are like that, sad, yet funny when you see them in the right light.

The Limba tale seems to say, if we can't do anything about the human situation and its tragedies, why not just laugh instead of weep? Perhaps it is all a big joke, a big cosmic/comic mistake of some ridiculous kind. Even human birth defects, terrible as they are, can be subjected to the same kind of myth. Here is another African story. The Yoruba of Nigeria said that after the god Obatala came down from heaven and had labored long hours, making human beings out of clay, he became hot and thirsty. He drank deeply of palm wine, so that when he went back to the work, his fingers had become clumsy. His humans started coming out misshapen, bent, and twisted, as some still are today.[2]

Though it also involves a snake, far different in tone is the traditional Jewish and Christian account of the fall of humankind into sin, and the coming of death as a consequence, through the Satanic temptation and disobedience of Adam and Eve in the Garden of Eden. Outside the second and third chapters of the biblical Book of Genesis, the best-known telling of this tale, at least in the English-speaking world, is John Milton's splendid epic, *Paradise Lost* (1667). While other recountings of it, such as the medieval mystery plays, have varied in tone, Milton's great poem, grounded in England's Puritan movement, is overall serious and majestic.

Satan, originally the most magnificent of the angels, in his pride and resistance to submission turned against God, refusing to honor and serve the Divine Majesty. After war in heaven, Satan and his angels were cast out into hell, and the great antagonist declared, in Milton's words, "To reign is worth ambition though in hell: better to reign in hell than serve in heav'n." His rebel band became demons who continued their guerrilla subversion of the divine order through temptation, first of Eve, then Adam, then their progeny. Spoke the prince of darkness, again in Milton's language, "Farewell remorse: all good to me is lost; Evil, be thou my good."

Adam and Eve expelled from Eden: nineteenth century engraving   (imagebroker/Alamy)

Disguised as a serpent, the foe induced the primal pair to eat of the fruit of the one tree in the paradisaical garden forbidden them, the tree of the knowledge of good and evil; it was forbidden lest they become like gods, knowing both. The first parents were then thrown out of the Garden; hereafter Eve would bear children only in much pain, and Adam eat bread in the sweat of his face (Gen. 3: 16–19).

The poem's solemn tone rests on the foundation of the absolute sovereignty, justice, and goodness of God. Disobedience to him on the part of angel or human is therefore evil, or sin. Satan after his insurgency, knowing better but puffed up with pride, is absolutely wicked, God's eternal enemy. Adam and Eve, after succumbing to Satan's wiles, being human and fallible may not be totally bad, but they have sinned. For sin a price must always be paid, for God is just as well as good: Satan's fall from heaven, the couple's becoming outcasts from Eden, and their "original sin" remains to twist the lives of their progeny the world, which is why so much is still wrong in it, and in ourselves. According to Christianity, paying the price for that sin required the death of the Son of God.

Here, in this great Biblical and Miltonic drama, the characters are no folktale half-comic gods, animals, and people, but personae of high drama. The primal parents who threw those dark shadows from Eden down through the centuries remain no laughing matter, as we their kinfolk still survey the atrocity and suffering all around us. Whether we take Eden literally or metaphorically, in its willing disobedience, lies one answer to the question, Why evil?

Or, what if the origin of sin and death were a family matter, as it not seldom can be in our own lives? An example is the Egyptian myth of Seth and Osiris. The two were brothers, great-grandchildren of Re, or Atum-Re, the solar god and creator of the world. The family context is intensified when we realize that Osiris was married to his sister, Isis, just as the pharaoh customarily married his own sister. Osiris, beloved by all, was a god of fertility and giver of culture to humankind, but his older brother Seth embodied disorder and destruction, because he seems to have come out of the vast windy deserts on either side of the narrow green Valley of the Nile. The disparity between the siblings, and the barren lot given the elder one, seems to lie behind the beginnings of evil in Egypt, just as similar differences often surface as warped attitudes, even violence, in families. Seth's jealous rage, long simmering, broke loose one day, and he killed his benign younger brother. Not content with murder, according to one version, the wrathful sibling cut Osiris' body into pieces and scattered them across the land.

Osiris' sister-wife Isis, mistress of magic, was distraught. In her grief she searched and searched until she had found all the pieces of her mate, put them back together, and by her mystic arts animated the reassembled corpse just long enough for it to impregnate her with a son, Horus. Then Osiris, as spirit, departed to reign over the beautiful western Kingdom of the Dead. The story goes on to describe a protracted family fight between Horus and Seth, with many gods intervening. As both humans and gods will, in the heat of battle all displayed faults stemming from out-of-control anger, but Horus, representing order, finally prevailed to become ruler of Egypt. From now on the living pharaoh was always said to be Horus, the late deceased ruler Osiris. Seth retired to his eternal desert realm of storm and desolation.[3]

Here the origin of evil is understood in terms of family dynamics, which may be where many of us first became aware of it far back in childhood. Exaggerated here, perhaps, but the scenario is known to all of us: rivalry between brothers (compare Cain and Abel, and Jacob and Esau, in the Bible), the son replacing the father, the distraught mother endeavoring through it all to bring all together and maintain the family line.

In Hinduism and Buddhism, what is called evil in the West is often termed "suffering" instead, and is said to be caused less by sin and rebellion like that of Satan, and of ourselves as his apt pupils, than by ignorance. In the first of the Buddha's Four Noble Truths, often translated "All life is suffering," the term for "suffering" is *dukha*. This is a rather unusual word that may originally have meant wobbling like that of a wheel loose on its axle. It suggests not just excruciating pain, but the pervasive frustration, anxiety, and emptiness of so much ordinary life.

The reason for this morass of human unhappiness is ignorance, *avidya* in Sanskrit. The *vidya* part of it, related to English words like vision and video, means "seeing," so *avidya* is "not seeing," not seeing things as they really are. By not seeing that our grasping leads only to suffering in the end, and our self-centeredness to defeat in death if not before, we are the cause of our own suffering. The second of the Buddha's Four Noble Truths is, "Suffering [*dukha*] is caused by desire." It's homemade, not imported by Satan, though some of it may be carried over from the past by karma.

Yet the difference between the suffering/ignorance model and the evil/sin/rebellion model may not be in the end as great as first appears. How could one sin and rebel against God or the eternal order, unless through some sort of willful ignorance of the true nature of that reality? How could one be so ignorant as to make oneself suffer over and over—though we often do so—without in effect rebelling against the evidence before our eyes? In both cases there is pain, each individual has some responsibility for it, yet is also part of a larger bramble patch in which we are entangled, call it sin or karma. By all accounts the world is not as it ideally should be, and this is every religion's problem.

EVIL RITUAL, EVIL INITIATION: CAN RELIGION CREATE EVIL?

Conventional religion is part of that entanglement. It is well known that religion through the millenniums has embraced many attitudes and practices that most modern people find objectionable: human sacrifice, animal sacrifice, and rigid class, caste, and gender distinctions. To this must be added the economic practices of certain historic religious institutions, and their alliances with tyrannical political regimes. However, much of this was accepted by the culture of the time and place. We cannot think of these horrific abuses as religion *creating* evil so much as just going along with the assumptions of the day, though we might well contend that, if religion really has a higher perspective, it ought to have been in advance of the society in protesting them, as were, for example, some of the Hebrew prophets. Nonetheless, it was assumed in many archaic societies that there are circumstances in which a human sacrifice is necessary for the good of all. In that case, the religious professionals of the community cannot be too severely faulted for carrying it out, however bad the murderous act may look in the eyes of a very different time and place.

Rather, in looking for religion *creating* instead of just perpetuating evil, let us turn our gaze to situations in which a religious activity seems to prepare people to do what otherwise is regarded as evil even in their own society. We will now examine less religious ideas than the actual physical and emotional processes that change one's temperament so as to let the evil flow. Some religious practices, from intense prayer to sacred dance, such as a war dance or march, can let loose an alternative persona in which one feels governed by a greater force than ordinary right and wrong. In prayer it is possible to receive such a conviction of God's will that one will perform an action even if it seems contrary to usual morality, such as killing a person thought to be an enemy of God. In dance, or marching with an army, one develops a powerful sense of being not an individual but a disciplined member of a group, well able to participate freely in whatever the group action is. But the most powerful transformer of all may be rites of initiation. We have talked about initiation before. Now let us look at it in a new light.

What is an initiation? Formally, the word means a beginning. After the primary initiation of birth, an initiation is another new beginning in life, ideally becoming like another person, based on a real change of consciousness and of feeling. One now sees the world through new eyes and treats others according to new criteria. Are they initiated brothers and sisters, or outsiders? Are they like me or not?

This level of change cannot be just in the head. To make a person who truly sees and feels differently, who acts as though she or he were in another skin, that person must have been marked by very powerful implants on the planes of the senses, the emotions, even the physical body (for some traditional initiations have included physical mutilations) as well as in stories and ideas conveyed while the subject is under the extreme stress of the ordeal. All this together can truly make the individual a different person. One who has been ritually scarred or circumcised in an initiation will not easily forget the pain, and if one is ever inclined to do so, the bodily mark is there as a reminder.

The initiate knows, as well as he or she knows his or her own name (which may well be a new name given in the initiation as a sign of a new identity), that he or she is now a person forever different from others outside the initiatory circle, and no less different from whom he or she was before. One will never forget the initiation and will always know that only those who have been through the same life-changing trial are really like oneself deep within. Some things only they can understand, only they can be counted on to act in the same way, to share the same values, even to dream the same dreams. They are, it will often be said, brothers or sisters for life in a way even birth siblings are not.

However, is the outcome of initiation always a higher good? Some initiations have produced individuals molded into groups that caused everyone else far more fear than joy, and even seemed something other than human.

Take, for example, the berserkers of ancient northern Europe. Our expression "going berserk" comes from them. These were initiated warrior bands under the patronage of Wotan who fought in a kind of ecstatic fury (called *wut*) and animal ferocity. The name "berserker" probably means "bear-shirted" (though "bare-shirted," in the sense of without shield or armor, has also been suggested). Identified with the spirit of a bear, or it seems in some cases of a wolf (the werewolf?), in their fighting rapture they made the sounds of the enraged beast, they grappled without mercy like one; for all intents and purposes the berserker *was* a bear or wolf.

Wut has been described as "a mysterious, nonhuman, and irresistible force that his fighting effort and vigor summoned from the utmost depth of his being."[4] Summoning it up, learning to *become* a bear or wolf down to the deepest levels of feeling, must have required serious initiation. The full scenario is not completely understood and may not always have been identical. At least some candidates had to kill an enemy before he could cut his own hair or beard, or had to fight a bear to the death, or had to be able to fight unarmed. They may have had to enter a cave and there fight off no less than ten initiated berserkers before they could themselves join the ferocious order. The culminating rite of passage into berserkerdom came when the candidate was ritually clothed in the skin of a bear or wolf, clearly an act of imparting him with the consciousness and quasi-magical soul of that deadly beast of prey.[5]

An example from a very different milieu is reported in Peggy Sandy's book, *Fraternity Gang Rape.* This fascinating study spotlights an American college fraternity that had gotten into very serious trouble because of episodes of "gang rape" at its parties. The same underlying motif we have been referring to, initiation into a bonding and a state of consciousness that makes acceptable what would be morally unacceptable on an individual basis, clearly comes across here. Initiation can lead one to do what otherwise one would not do, and if that thing is evil, initiation is a source of evil.

The initiations of this fraternity were traumatic enough. An insider, identified as Sean, said, "We felt that salvation is achieved through brotherhood, and nothing else (certainly not our individuality) mattered at all." He confided that after the initiation the brethren all shared stories and laughed about their initiatory ordeal, about how they had "fallen apart," cried, and acted "foolishly," but that no longer mattered: "We were laughing together about our common weakness as individuals, because we were building bonds that were transforming us into something larger and, hopefully, stronger." The laughter was, he perceived, to put their separate selves at a distance. "We were collectively celebrating the death of our individuality." According to Sean, one symbol used in the initiation, the sun rising over a coffin, indicated one's rebirth as a perfect spiritual self after the former mortal self had "died" as the young man joined the society. Brethren in the fraternity, having survived "punishment," and undergone death to their past individualistic kind of being, were now living as another, more powerful brotherhood self.

The consequence was that now, according to Sean, they had no moral code except the brotherhood's. The fraternity was able to create a private society in which the initiated could see those outside its parameters as dark and terrified and, in a real sense, subhuman. As Sean again put it:

> Everyone and everything [outside the fraternity] was open to ridicule, all people and all standards became vulnerable, because we had powerfully felt our own vulnerability [in the initiation]. That was our deepest kept secret, the thing that really separated us from the world outside: we knew how insignificant people can feel when they are really up against the wall—how insignificant we felt during initiation. . . Our initiation experience and new knowledge constituted the deepest insight and a sacred revelation. . . Now we could be masters of life. . . we could toy with it and watch with amusement as everyone else staggered blindly through it.[6]

Ironically, in view of the fraternity's customary attitude toward women, as among those with whose lives they could "toy" and whose vulnerabilities they could exploit, the central figure in the myth behind their draconian initiation was an "astral goddess." The initiates claim that the secrets of the brotherhood were first given to them by a Greek goddess, and that it is to her astral plane that they ascend in initiation. However, it is not uncommon for males who vaunt superiority over "real" women here on earth to profess devotion to a divine female figure.

Clearly what happened in this initiation was to enable men who, alone, felt powerless, as youths, as students, subject to the authority of parents, teachers, and many others, to bond with a group that collectively felt all-powerful. But with this power they, like the berserkers, could work evil as well as good, because with the loss of their former selves, they felt themselves beyond good and evil as the outside world understood it and could toy with lives at their pleasure.

WHY DO BAD THINGS HAPPEN? RELIGIOUS THOUGHT AND EVIL

How can we deal with the problem of evil on an intellectual level? We will not here deal with those perspectives that, looking at religion from the outside, see it as part of the problem, but rather with ways in which those who assume the existence of a good, all-powerful God, or a supreme divine order of the universe, explain the existence nonetheless of evil as we have defined it: lives stunted, cut short, imbued with pain, and with countless frustrations and disappointments; a world that seems rife with injustice and undeserved suffering.

Here are five ways in which the religious response has presented itself.

First, polytheism like that of the ancient world postulates many gods, gods often in disharmony with one another or favoring one human faction against another, and none in absolute control. Such fickle and finite deities, as a by-product of their own often-conflicted lives and their favoritism, frequently leave human lives devastated.

In ancient Greek mythology, the world, as we know it, virtually began with battle between the Titans and Olympian gods. At the time of the Trojan War, Athena, Poseidon (the sea god), and Hera (oft-jealous wife of Zeus, Olympian king of the gods) favored the Greeks, while Aphrodite (goddess of love) and Ares (her lover and god of war) were on the Trojan side. Human warriors fought, and were sometimes like pawns, in the hands of these heavenly players, immortal and more powerful, but no more moral, than mortals.

In the ancient India of the Rig Veda, the oldest Vedic scripture, rivalry raged between the asuras, originally good deities who presided over the social order, while devas ruled the world of nature. Later the asuras declined to the level of demons, or at least power-hungry spirits, raging against the gods, but the asuras could still acquire power over the world, and even the gods, through great asceticism and divine energy.

Polytheism has sometimes been reduced, in effect, to dualism, a belief in two sides, one good and one evil, in eternal warfare against each other, with humans caught in the middle. Explicit dualism was the view of some forms of Zoroastrianism, of the Manichaean religion derived in part from it, and in practice represents the outlook of many Christians who see religion as a long-term battle between God and Satan, though as in Zoroastrianism God will win in the end.

Second, a stance represented by the Book of Job in the Hebrew Scriptures and some schools of Islamic theology, acknowledges one supreme God but insists that the ways of this God are so far beyond human understanding that we can simply never comprehend why things are the way they are, or penetrate the problem of what to us looks like evil.

Job, in the book of that name, was a righteous, God-fearing man of means who suddenly suffered the loss of all that he had, including his seven sons and three daughters, plus breaking out in loathsome sores from head to foot. His misfortune was the result of a sort of bet between God and Satan as to whether, under such affliction, the just man would finally curse God for his injustice. Yet he did not, but said, "The Lord gave, and the Lord has taken away; blessed be the name of the Lord" (Job 1:21). But he did curse the day he was born.

Then came friends who tried to convince the sufferer that all his suffering was just. He must, that said, have committed some secret sin that brought down God's wrath. But Job refused such dishonesty; he refused to save God's reputation by lying about himself, because he knew that he had done nothing proportionate to the calamity he had undergone. Something was very wrong.

Finally God spoke to Job out of the whirlwind, pointing to the wonders of creation beyond his comprehension, from the song of the stars to the marvelous creatures of earth and sea. Job could only reply to God:

> I know that thou canst do all things,
> and that no purpose of thine can be thwarted. . .
> Therefore I have uttered what I did not understand,
> things too wonderful for me, which I did not know. (Job 42:2–3)

This righteous person's suffering was intended not to show God's justice but rather God's mystery, not to reveal the limits of God's power but its extent, beyond even this world and the mind of man, and its purposes going back to the Beginning and that will not be fully unveiled until the End. In the process we may suffer, seemingly unjustly, but our souls will be deepened.

The highly influential school of theology in Islam called Ash'arism, based on the writings of Abu-l-Hasan al-Ash'ari (873–935), taught that God, as absolute power and grace, is mysterious rather than reasonable on the human level. We mere humans can only adore and obey; we cannot presume to understand the reasons behind his decrees and his love.

Then, three ways argue for divine justice, holding that even if we cannot fathom all, we can understand that God or universal law balances things out, so that in the end there is no problem of the unrighteous prospering and the righteous unfairly suffering. A reason exists for everything, and that reason will ultimately show apparent evil to be good, or at least just, or will lead to just recompense for the innocent sufferer. But behind each of these "ways" stands a mode of explaining evil that is related to the way divine justice is understood in that tradition, and this we will try to comprehend. The ways include karma and reincarnation; heaven, hell, or purgatory right after death; and eschatology, or judgment and a new heaven and earth at the end of history.

The first divine justice way, karma and reincarnation, means reward and punishment in this world, or sometimes through a temporary reincarnation in another world or plane of existence, as a way of balancing the scales.

Karma here refers to cause and effect, continual action and reaction, as the motive force for life and the universe. For every thought, words, and deed there is a response from universal law. What is distinctive when this idea is associated with reincarnation is belief that one's next lifetime is the consequence, good or bad, of one's actions in the present. (Of course, karma can come back to one in this present life as well.) Karma, as the law of moral cause and effect, has caught up humans, animals, gods, and all other entities in its wheel of *samsara*, or birth, suffering, and death. Of this immense cycle we humans are only a part.

Crude ideas of karma are on the level of saying that if you are greedy, you will be reborn as a pig, or if excessively angry and violent, as a warrior destined to never-ending battle until the bad karma is exhausted. More sophisticated views see rebirth as educational, teaching lessons over and over until they are absorbed, or dealing with unfinished business or relationships. Either way, karma and reincarnation are meant to rectify divine justice, seemingly so often lacking in this world.

These beliefs are particularly associated with Hinduism and Buddhism today. In them, evil, as we have seen, is understood mainly as a consequence of ignorance, *avidya* ("not seeing") in Sanskrit, above all ignorance, willful or otherwise, of karma and the rest of the principles by which the universe works, as well as of the divine nature in all beings. But ignorance can always be corrected by experience and proper education. It is no doubt suitable, then, that recompense for evil thoughts, words, and deeds should not be eternal, but last only as long as it takes for the lesson to be truly learned. It is simply a way of understanding the consequence of our actions, and an opportunity to learn and do better in another lifetime.

The second divine justice way, life after death in another world, such as heaven, hell, or purgatory, will be discussed more extensively in Chapter 13. Here the stakes may be even higher, because the reward in heaven or punishment in hell may be eternal. Probably that is because in these traditions, above all Christianity and Islam, evil is the result not of mere ignorance but of rebellion against God. Rebellion suggests an active act of the will defying God and the good. Intentional faith or rejection toward God is infinite in significance as God is infinite. Our attitude toward God cannot therefore be measured out as though we were only dealing with merits or demerits, or repeating a class in school.

The prototype is the myth of the rebellion of the archangel Lucifer (Satan; Iblis in Islam) presented earlier in this chapter, followed with the story of the "fall" of Adam and Eve in the Garden of Eden. That story explains why the world as a whole is tarnished with evil, not just humans with moral responsibility. Satan, as lord of this world, has left the whole planet fallen, all seriously imperfect, not just humankind.

Purgatory is a Roman Catholic doctrine of medieval background that teaches some sins can be purged away in the afterlife; the penalty for them, called venial in contrast to mortal sins, is temporary rather than infinite and eternal.

The third divine justice way, eschatology, means a new heaven and earth at the Last Day. It will also be discussed in Chapter 13. Although this doctrine usually coexists with belief in heaven and hell as immediate after-death states, in principle it defers the absolute establishment of divine justice until the drama of world history has been played out and the curtain rings down. This divine justice way adds to the picture a strong vision of evil as historic and cosmic, but it is also personal, because it presents a view of the world from creation to culmination as a mighty drama, in which we are all actors, and everyone's part is important. In this play the end is like a return to the beginning, because the new heaven and earth resemble a return to Eden before the fall, the world this time ready to do right what went wrong before. The dead are raised from out of earth and sea on that last day, all primed to stand before the throne of judgment. After the wicked have been sent off to hell, the polluted old earth is destroyed, and even the old heaven goes, to make way for a pristine new heaven and earth for the righteous to enjoy eternally.

A few other beliefs about the cause of evil and its relation to divine justice have presented themselves. Vedanta Hinduism sees the world with its evils as maya, illusion or, more accurately, seeing things as other than what they are, like the man who proverbially sees a rope but mistakes it for a snake and jumps back in fright. Evil has no more real existence than that illusory snake, but because we are drawn to the illusions of this world, created ultimately by our own ignorance, desires, and fears, so likewise do we entrap ourselves in the suffering that goes with them.

   Similarly, the basic text of Christian Science, *Science and Health, With Key to the Scriptures*, by Mary Baker Eddy, speaks for many traditions that base evil on mind, thoughts, or states of consciousness rather than external realities, when it says, "The notion that both evil and good are real is a delusion of material sense, which Science annihilates. Evil is nothing, no thing, mind, nor power. . . it stands for a lie, nothing claiming to be something."[7] Evil, in short, is the product of wrong thinking, of seeing something else when nothing but God exists at all.

   Or it may be that evil is a result of creation itself. The great Kabbalistic Jewish mystical philosopher, Issac Luria (1534–1572), said that the universe was made possible by a sort of withdrawal or shrinkage of God, to leave space for the worlds, which

Job and his friends, engraving by Gustave Doré, 1870   (Album/quintlox/Album/SuperStock)

are like remaining fragments reflecting the light of the retreating deity. Creation, in other words, was a kind of divine pulling back.

In all views wherein the creation is a breaking up of primordial unity into many parts, evil is likely to arise simply from the way these parts are each finite, limited, and likely to jar each other, or be in competition with each other, as they blindly seek their way back to union with the One. In Lurianic thought, the separation and dispersal call for *tikkun*, the healing of the universe by seeking out lost and strayed fragments containing the light, and through goodness bringing the many back together into divine unity, a task in which we humans now have a part.[8]

This teaching is undoubtedly related to the myths of the ancient Gnostic Jews and Christians. They said that the world was created not by the supreme deity dwelling in the halls of light above, but by a lower and flawed god or angel who arrogated the creation to himself. He (or sometimes she) bungled the job, which is why the planet is such a mess. (However, bits of the higher light are entrapped in the imperfect creatures themselves entrapped in that world—ourselves. In Christian Gnosticism, Christ was sent to call that light back to its true home.)

On a more philosophical level, religion has dealt with much the same issues in terms of intellectual analysis. Much Western religious thought on the problem of evil derives from Augustine (354–430). The North African bishop was a convert to Christianity from Manichaeanism, rejecting its view of an external power of evil in favor of the Neoplatonist Plotinus' view that evil is privative, that is, simply the deprivation, corruption or absence, of good. God made everything wholly good; therefore nothing is evil of itself, but it can be twisted and deprived of good to make it bad. Augustine and Plotinus also taught what has been called the aesthetic concept of evil, that some of what appears evil in isolation may actually be a necessary part of a larger context which is good, as death may be a part of a larger perspective on life, or a dark patch part of the larger harmony of a painting.

The issue of free will has been a no less important concern over the centuries. How can we choose the good and to what extent are our wills truly free? Augustine believe that we do have free will, but inevitably, especially in consequence of the "fall" of Adam and Eve, we turn away from the good in our choices to respond to lower, but more pressing, desires. Yet if we truly perceive the good, we desire it, as it is far more desirable than the other. When that happens, it was God's grace that presented the good to us as a choice, and our freedom—now used rightly—which made that choice.

These issues are still very much with us, whether we put them in traditional theological language or some other way. Much modern psychology can make us wonder whether we actually have free will or not, because even decisions that "feel like" free choices can be attributed to various "unconscious" desires over which we seemingly have little control. And as for the problem of evil, even if we accept the full scientific view of the origin of the universe and the evolution of humanity, with its picture of what we call evil as simply embedded in cosmic and animal nature, we still have no explanation of why it had to be this kind of universe in the first place.

Evil is a great mystery to religion, the mystery of iniquity. But religion can offer world-level explanations for it, often expressed in the language of myth, and more important, it shows vividly the consequences of evil and its remedies.

SUMMARY

Evil is that which, in a perfect world, ought not to be, yet is.

Myths of the origin of evil, and of death, which is closely associated with evil, are very widespread. Their tone, from humorous to highly solemn, give clues to the temperament of the people reciting them.

Religion can sometimes lead to evil through its legitimating of behavior that otherwise would be wrong, just as it sometimes inspires persons to the noblest behavior. In particular, initiations can have both these effects.

Religious thought deals with the problem of evil in a variety of ways, through concepts of polytheism, karma, divine mystery, reincarnation, reward and punishment after death, eschatology. Philosophical views, such as those of Augustine, can see evil as privative, having no existence of its own, or as part of a larger pattern of universal good. Or it may hold that evil is within the mind.

CHAPTER

8

Faith Through Form: Religion and Art

Stained glass rose window of Notre Dame cathedral, Paris   (Circumnavigation/Fotolia)

LEARNING OBJECTIVES

After reading this chapter, you should be able to:

- Give reasons why art is important to religion.
- Trace the story of painting from the earliest examples in cave art on, noting the role of animals, nature, and the human form in religious art.
- Tell how sculpture can differ from painting in its treatment of religious subjects.
- Speculate about how and why religious images became more anthropomorphic, especially at the time of the rise of the great religions.
- Summarize the role of music in religion, mentioning why it has sometimes been seen as dangerous, but more often as helpful in the creation of religious sentiments.
- Discuss poetry as expressive of feelings and responses to religion, sometimes in a complex way. Select a favorite religious poem and analyze it in terms of its combination of words, pictures, and feelings.
- Describe how drama can create archetypal divine or human images, and also present human beings with all of their flaws.
- Summarize the role of religion in literature, and tell how novels and stories can present profound images of human nature with which religion can work and how they can also chronicle human experience in all its fullness. Give examples from stories you have read.

STAINED-GLASS WINDOWS

Many older churches have windows of stained glass in which the white light of the sun is colored and shaped to take on the form of haloed saints and conventional symbols of faith. In a real sense that is what all of religion does. We have noted the difference religions make between sacred and profane realities. Now let us go a step farther back and see what lies behind this distinction by using a set of relatively neutral terms from the Buddhist tradition: *unconditioned* and *conditioned reality*.

Conditioned reality is what most of us know most of the time. Conditions mean limitations. We are, first of all, conditioned or limited in space and time. If we are, say, in a city in the United States, we are not also situated in Hong Kong or on the planet Neptune. If we are living in the early twenty-first century, we are not also in the ninth century with Charlemagne or in the twenty-third or twenty-fourth century with *Star Trek*. Our minds are also of limited capacity. Most of us cannot think of more than one thing at a time or multiply more than 2 two-digit numbers in our heads, and we forget far more than we remember. Further, we have observed that this conditioning is the state of all ordinary reality around us.

But what if another reality existed, which was the opposite of all this and which was equally present in all times and places, unlimited in mind, all-seeing and all-knowing, as unconditioned as we are conditioned? This reality would, in a word, be what religions ordinarily postulate as God, Brahman, or Nirvana—however Ultimate Reality is named.[1]

All religions, one way or another, think that there is a different kind of reality, made up of gods and spirits, transcendent over the ordinary conditioned reality plane. The great religions generally go on to think of a "split-level" universe, made up of unconditioned and conditioned reality, of God or the Absolute on the one side, and the human realm on the other.

One could, of course, deny that there is any such thing as unconditioned reality, or say that if there is, it could not be known by conditioned beings such as ourselves, so we might as well just live in the world we know. Religions, however, believe that both sides can be known and that the borderline between the two is, so to speak, filled with doors and windows. Indeed, this porous boundary is the realm in which religion works.

In the eyes of traditional religion, visitors from the other side—gods, saviors, saints, angels, spirits—have entered and may continually enter our conditioned homeland. Messages in the form of revelations and spiritual gifts are regularly sent. The symbols and worship forms of religion say significant things about the nature of unconditioned reality, as do its doctrines. Conversely, persons from the conditioned level such as ourselves can inwardly enter, or taste something of, unconditioned reality through rite, prayer, and mystical experience.

This borderland is also the territory of religious art. The term *art* used here in the broad sense, to include painting, sculpture, architecture, music, poetry, drama, and fiction—and even such "minor" arts as garden landscaping and jewelry making. Art, therefore, is obviously congruent with symbolism as presented in Chapter 4, though our emphasis here is not on core religious expression such as official scriptures and major forms of worship. We look rather at how great artists in all these visual, audio, and literary forms have dealt with themes drawn from religion.

Sometimes great artists have portrayed the splendor of unconditioned reality as transmitted through the window of a particular faith; sometimes they have voiced the anguish of guilt or doubt through which a religious quest can lead. But in any case, the virtue of great art is that it expresses feelings or visions that many have had, but have not been able to put into form or word; in its presence we may find ourselves saying, "This experience of seeing, hearing, or reading has clarified something important for me; now I understand both myself and reality better."

The poet Shelley wrote that "Life, like a dome of many-colored glass/Stains the white radiance of eternity." So should great art, reflecting life, refract the light of unconditioned reality into hues and forms that bring it closer to home yet still make it seem like something from another world. Like a stained-glass window, it should be an inviting portal between two worlds.

Art also connects parts of our own human selves. The one thing that unites all the art media, whether painting, sculpture, architecture, music, poetry, or prose, is that they are things made by humans and not solely to meet practical needs. Rather, like religion, they also meet a different kind of need, in this case to express something specifically human, indeed specific to the artist however well the artwork also expresses what others feel. Art says in ways *humans* understand things seen, heard, and felt. It helps us know feelings of beauty, awe, or dread enhanced through the power of art to the point where they are strong and clear.

Art may draw themes from nature, or from human society, but it does not leave them just as they are, pure and simple. Rather, it filters them through the artist's own human nature, to come out in ways that show us how people can see, hear, and emotionally respond to what is around them. Or, art may draw from themes that seem more inward, from the realm of dreams, or of symbols, or of moods and feelings and mental images. Art too can create forms that can suggest our innermost thoughts and fancies, and help us see and respond spiritually to them. Art, in other words, is a mysterious process that links three vitally important human arenas: nature, the subjectivity of the artist, and the audience of the art in human society.

When an artist works with religion, she or he is not just presenting the images and symbols of the religion in some untouched form. To be sure, religious art has a very important role in preserving the myths, history, and symbols of the faith, generation after generation. When closely associated with worship, it also has the role of helping create the *expected* spiritual world and our reaction to it, that is, of facilitating faith by taking part in worship's *orchestration of symbols*.

Yet if it is great art, it will also have something of the artist in it, and that artist will in some sense be a great person, full of texture and complexity. Religious art will say things superbly about the objects of faith and the varied human ways of responding to them. We know that being a human is not easy. Great religious art can lead us into hours of tremendous spiritual exaltation, and also into times of despair—of faith lost and faith found, of shallow faith and deep faith.

PAINTING

Religious painting probably goes back as far as the paleolithic cave pictures, and certainly as far as painting from ancient Egypt depicting divine figures with human bodies and animal heads. These strange combinations surely reveal something about the deities not seen in any ordinary creature, but which for an artist could express something about the human and divine through the freedom and imagination of art, as though the god combined something of animal, human, and superhuman. That freedom has made paint and brush particularly fluid vehicles for making statements about the divine beyond sober visual realism, yet profoundly important to religious understanding.

For example, the **icons** used in Eastern Orthodox churches are vivid examples of the painting as a window to the transcendent world. These portraits of saints, the Blessed Virgin, Christ, and even the Trinity are done in a highly stylized, traditional way that emphasizes the spiritual nature of the subject: large soulful eyes, conventional gestures, halos to show the inner radiance of a holy person, a golden or starry background indicating eternity. To believers, the icon shows the subject as he or she is now in heaven, and these pictures are treated with the profoundest reverence whether in churches or a prayer corner in the home.

The traditional Christian religious painting of Western Europe is more flexible in subject matter and style, often developing themes from biblical stories or the legends of saints. Yet, at least in medieval or early modern examples, the picture is certainly also intended to be an entry into another world of wonder, miracle, and supernatural reality.

For example, the treatment of the baptism of Christ by the Florentine master Giotto (1266?–1337) makes Jesus, standing nearly naked in the water of the Jordan river, a quite human young man of about 30. No less manly is John the Baptist, in his camel's hair tunic and rose-colored cape, reaching out to his messiah in a natural way

Greek icon of Madonna and Child   (Koufax73/Fotolia)

from the shore. Yet both have a nimbus or halo, and above the two, reaching down from heaven, his finger pointing at Christ, is God the Father. On the two banks of the river are saints and winged angels watching the scene intently. The typically Western European attention to physical detail, especially of the human form, and to the drama of events, is thus combined with features making it clear that, in these bodies and this happening, nature and supernature are united.[2]

Sometimes it is nature itself that conveys that which is behind or within ordinary nature. This is especially true of Chinese and Japanese landscape paintings in the **Zen** tradition, such as those of Sesshu (1420–1506), widely regarded as the greatest of all Japanese artists. In Zen, everything, even the humblest bird or leaf, seen just as it is, reveals the Buddha nature, the essence of the universe as perceived by a Buddha in his enlightenment.

The point of all the famous Zen arts, whether rock gardens or flower arrangement or **Chanoyu** (the "tea ceremony"), is to bring out that hidden nature by letting things reveal the whole universe down to its innermost heart through being just what they are. A rock in a rock garden is not just a rock, but also a rock that is an outcropping of the universe as a whole in one particular time and space, a rock in Nirvana as well as in conditioned reality. A tea-ceremony cup of tea is a cup of tea enjoyed as nothing but a cup of tea, yet is no less the universe in one's hand. All the attention of an adept of this rite is to be on nothing but its aroma and flavor, just as a saint's might be on nothing but God. But because the tea is simply Nirvana in disguise, the tea adept is no less liberated than any other devotee who is in harmony with unconditioned reality.

This is why much of the great Zen *suiboku,* ink-wash painting, is of the ordinary but grand things of nature: mountains, trees, water. Yet they reveal something else as well, something even older and deeper, from the Buddhist point of view. For these landscape paintings can be seen as divided into three layers from bottom to top, each corresponding to one of the three great bodies, or forms of manifestation of the Buddha nature according to **Mahayana**: in the plain outer world of physical manifestation and conditioned reality where we usually dwell; in the heavenly worlds, no different from the intrapsychic realms where dreams and visions come from; and in the *dharmakaya,* essence of the universe itself, where the whole is seen as the Void, and the dance of molecules and galaxies takes place.

Thus at the bottom of a Sesshu painting will be something like a lake and a beached boat, and perhaps a humble figure in straw raincoat, at the foot of a mighty cliff and mountain. Halfway up the mountain will be a jewellike, or dreamlike, temple, perchance the dwelling of a wizardly hermit. Still higher up, the peaks will disappear into mists and empty skies, washing into the formlessness of timeless eternity.

Yet another perspective is given by those painters who represent religious subjects or moods in abstract or symbolist forms. For meditation purposes, Hindu deities can be presented as **yantras**, diagrams. For example, Shiva as universal essence and his Shakti, or consort—earth and manifested reality—can become a series of interlocking triangles, those pointing upward representing Shakti, those pointing downward, Shiva. In certain Tibetan meditation paintings, the tokens and body parts of a powerful Buddha or bodhisattva or consort-goddess are scattered randomly; it is the exercise of the meditator to bring them together by the force of his concentration.

Marc Chagall (1887–1985), artistic chronicler of Jewish life in the villages of old Russia, in his unforgettable "Fiddler on the Roof" studies, presents what seems at first to be the rather bizarre image of a musician playing on, indeed almost floating above, the ridgepole of a peasant cabin. Yet after a few moments of letting our conscious and subconscious minds absorb the spirit of the painting, we understand how the player's music, and sheer joy of life, soars above the squalor of his earth-plane existence.

Many other modern artists, adherents of such schools as impressionism, surrealism, or cubism, have also clearly been on a spiritual quest through the medium of paint. Their rejection of ordinary realism, in fact, arises from a passionate desire to see and reveal realities beneath the surface that often converge with spiritual lines of perception. Van Gogh's superluminous starry night shows the heavens with a splendor perceived by no ordinary eyes, but true to the divine glory behind them—behind both the eye and the star. Piet Mondrian's straight lines and blocks in his cubist period hint at the saying attributed to Plato, "God geometrizes." Many, if not most, of such artists have not been believers in any conventionally orthodox sense, but they have shown anew how art can be a reflection of nature, the artist's own subjectivity and that of a human audience—and Ultimate Reality or windows and doors thereto.[3]

SCULPTURE

Alongside of paintings and other two-dimensional (or bas-relief) representations of religious subjects, one sees the full-figure forms of wood, metal, or stone known as statues or sculpture. Indeed, when a physical object of human construction is a visible focus of religious worship, whether the image of a god or Buddha, or the cross or crucifix of a Christian altar, it is—with the notable exception of the Eastern Orthodox icons already mentioned—most likely to be a three-dimensional sculpture of some kind. Paintings of religious figures or stories are commonly found on the walls of churches, temples, abbeys, or pious private homes, but statues may be the focal point of worship on the altars and in the shrines themselves.

For this reason, human-form statues are suspect in some great religious traditions. They are not usually found in Eastern Orthodox or Protestant Christianity, Judaism, Islam, Shinto, or Confucianism, unless in a purely ornamental or memorial capacity. For these religionists, devotion directed toward such a physical form comes too close to idolatry, or the worship of something other than the true God. (Three-dimensional symbols, though, such as the Protestant cross or the Confucian tablet bearing the name and title of the Great Sage, may be acceptable.)

For other faiths—Buddhism, Hinduism, Taoism, Roman Catholic Christianity—however, the artistry of statues can interact with worship. The carved form, though strictly speaking not worshiped for its own sake, serves to align the worshiper's thoughts and feelings. It becomes a focus of prayer, an aid to devout visualization, and sometimes is seen as an outward repository of divine energies.

Our concern now, however, is not with the religious use of sculpture but simply with it as a form of religious art. Here we may first of all observe that statues are particularly good at capturing the archetypal meaning of a religious figure or symbol. A statue usually tells less of a story than many paintings, but may do even more to freeze its subject in a single timeless gesture that sums up its meaning as a window to unconditioned reality. The subject, in other words, becomes an **archetype**, embodiment of a great universal theme, like those of which Carl Jung wrote. She or he is just the Great Mother, the Hero, the Sage, the King, captured in a single gesture of compassion or fortitude. While paintings, of course, can do this also, statues do it especially well, facilitating concentration without distraction on just that one aspect of the sacred in rounded form. Great religious sculpture, as it combines a single significant gesture by an eternal being with the solid durability of a medium such as marble or metal, powerfully bespeaks the transcendence of religious reality over ordinary time and of divinity over corruptible human flesh.

In much devotional religious sculpture, the archetypal significance swallows up any serious realism. The figure may display only fertility, as apparently does the "Venus of Willendorf" and many similar round, faceless, sometimes multiple-breasted female forms from early Europe. Or they may be only stern guardians, such as the famous giant stone Easter Island heads, or ancestral eyes quick to anger, or the sly trickster (crafty mythological gods such as Coyote, sometimes helpful but unpredictable) with his crooked smile. Whatever it is, these images show no human complexity of personality, but are limited to a single function.

The archetypal function undoubtedly controls another great wing of religious sculpture, the **theriomorphic** (animal-shaped) form. Divine animals, or animals with a divine mission, are exceedingly plentiful in religious myth and folklore, and there are examples in religious sculpture: Hanuman the Hindu monkey-god, Bast the sacred Egyptian cat, Quetzalcoatl the feathered serpent of Mayan lore. An animal can clearly present an archetype very well.

But animal-god statues are somewhat less common than those of deities with animal heads and human bodies. In them, the archetypal and the human are significantly joined. Examples include many of the ancient Egyptian gods: the jackal-headed Anubis, the mortuary god; ibis-headed Thoth, god of wisdom; the lion-headed goddess Sekhmet. There is also the Hindu Ganesha, the elephant-headed remover of obstacles. Still another variation is the animal companion of an anthropomorphic (human-shaped) or abstract deity. Many of the Hindu deities have such a follower: Nandi the bull stands before Shiva, the owl consorts with the wisdom-bearing goddess Saraswati.

Then there are **anthropomorphic** statues as such. Many of them also possess "unnatural" features suggesting archetypal functions, such as those Hindu gods and Buddhist bodhisattvas with multiple arms and faces. These indicate supernatural capacity to do many works of mercy in many worlds simultaneously, or to see in all directions—that is, with infinite omniscience—at once.

Other sculpted gods simply possess artful human form. The ancient Greeks developed this type of expression to its greatest glory. To them, it was the natural but ideally beautiful human form that best mediated divinity. Their Aphrodite, Ares, Athena, Poseidon, and Zeus were women and men of normal attributes, perfectly proportioned for their age and gender.

The Greek ideal has had a wide influence, particularly in the sculptured art of the great religions that arose in the wake of the Axial Age. The influence of Greek models on indigenous trends cannot always be measured exactly. But it is of interest that Greek influence at its most far-reaching coincided, broadly speaking, with the rise of new, artistically and devotionally more human-centered religions, especially Buddhism, Christianity, and emergent forms of Hinduism.

In the East, the Greek ideal of human-form gods spread through the conquests of Alexander the Great, culminating about 326 BCE in India, and in the West, through Greek cultural influence on Rome and its empire. These new religions gave fresh and

The famous statue of Miroku (Maitreya), the coming future Buddha, in the Koryuji temple of Kyoto, Japan (Christophe Boisvieux/Corbis)

central roles to the sanctified human, the saint, Buddha, bodhisattva, savior, and avatar (Hindu god who has come into the world in human form), as well as to anthropomorphic gods and angels. For them, the Greek ideal was well suited, and, though with considerable adaptation, its reflection can be seen from the Buddhas of Kyoto's famous temples to the saints in medieval European cathedrals.

ARCHITECTURE

Those temples and cathedrals call to mind the next important religious art form, architecture, the construction of great buildings in the name of faith. Religion's buildings, its temples, shrines, churches, and mosques, can be edifices of great beauty in themselves, by virtue of their materials and proportions, and so reflect the beauty most believe to be latent in unconditioned reality. Their arrangements also make important statements about the nature of the religion.

Religious buildings have two possible roles in relation to their religious purpose. They can serve, either symbolically or concretely, as the home of the deity, the *House of God.* They also can serve as a place of worship, an assembly place for the *People of God* as they gather for worship and visibly become a religious community. And, of course, religious buildings can be both simultaneously.

Shinto shrines, Hindu temples, and many others are primarily houses of the deity. They are built as one would, in that culture, build the home of a great person, even a king, who is venerated and honored. They boast courts where visitors may come to pay respects, offer gifts, and submit petitions, as if in audience before such a kingly personage. Food and other services may be offered regularly with all the ceremony of a royal repast. But there is no room for an entire congregation or community to be inside at once. That is not the purpose of what is essentially the private house of a deity. At major festivals, when the assembly is large, people may pass before the honored deity in a steady stream or gather in a courtyard or foreground.

The Brihadeeswarar temple of south India, indicating the ornateness and architectural richness of the Hindu temple   (Jayakumar/Shutterstock/Pearson)

Muslim mosques, Protestant churches, Jewish synagogues, and some other religious buildings are today primarily places of congregational worship. They may also be politely called the *House of God*, and treated with due respect, but that epithet is not taken as literally as in the courtly sort of temple. The architectural emphasis is instead on providing an adequate facility for large gatherings, with good acoustics for music and sermons, and an inspirational atmosphere for the corporate worship experience.

Roman Catholic churches, some Buddhist temples, and a few others are really both. Their altars are sanctified by the presence of the Blessed Sacrament incarnating divine presence, or by venerated Buddhist images, yet they are also places for both services and individual prayers.

Thus religious buildings may, first of all, be divided into those that are divine houses or palaces, those that are essentially auditoria, and those that are both. The auditorium-type structures are likely to be quite large. Indeed, the interior open spaces and vistas they require pose difficult architectural problems. These were met in some places by the development of the dome and the vaulted roofs of Gothic cathedrals.

Then there are various architectural styles of sacred buildings, each bearing its own message through the layout of the structure as well as through the religion it serves. It would not be possible here to present all the religious architectural styles in the world, but an example, the traditional Western Christian church, may be of help. They have passed through several stages of dominant styles.

The first large-scale church, appearing with the fourth-century liberation of Christianity, was the basilica, an oblong building with a central nave or passageway, based on the Roman court of law. It suggested the church as a place of important meetings and proclamations, where a community could be gathered, and the gathering presided over by duly authorized officials at the front.

The next development was the Romanesque church, a squarish domed building, often with high narrow windows, which appeared in the early Middle Ages. In those troubled times, it strongly suggested the church as a fortress, a place of refuge and security. One variation often found in England and the United States is the square-towered Norman church. But as the medieval period advanced, the Romanesque bastion of faith was succeeded by Gothic churches and cathedrals, with their high-pitched ceilings, soaring steeples, and larger stained-glass windows, frequently including round rose windows. Such edifices seemed to speak not only of security but also of human aspiration toward the heights and the heavens.

The Baroque church of about 1600 to 1750 is represented in the United States by Spanish missions and other buildings in that style. The Baroque style is characterized by graceful curving lines, a sense of proportion and perspective, and above all by elaborate ornamentation. Nothing could be left plain; Baroque columns were twisted and creased, altars gilded, and the walls behind them featured cascades of carved foliage, scallops, and polychrome saints. This fashion obviously reflects the new wealth, artistic creativity, technical advances, and exuberant self-confidence of Europe in the Renaissance and subsequent Baroque eras. While often criticized by later generations as pretentious and overdone, Baroque at its best communicates a sense of the overflowing richness and color of sacred reality, and the divinely playful joy of artistic creativity.

At around the same time, the simpler Georgian or Palladian style, represented in many Colonial American churches, took hold in England. It is characterized by proportioned steeples, arched clear windows, simple but elegant lines, and much use of plain white woodwork in both the interior and the exterior. These churches seem somehow to reflect both Protestant restraint and the clarity of thought that was the ideal of the Age of Reason in which they flourished.

The nineteenth century, though a great age of church building, brought Romanesque, Gothic, and other revivals, but little that was truly innovative. In the twentieth century, in contrast, new styles of religious architecture commenced. On the one hand, economic changes effectively sealed off the past. Costs, plus a dearth of tra-ditionally trained craftspersons, made it now nearly impossible to build new medieval-type Gothic cathedrals, although the National Cathedral in Washington, D.C., and St. John the Divine in New York were ambitious and attractive, though controversial, attempts.

On the other hand, new techniques in glass, poured cement, and construction, combined with new inspiration from various schools of streamlined modern architec-ture, made a fresh plasticity available to churches. They were now shaped like ships, tents, or skyscrapers, were elevated or half-sunken, were built in the round with the altar or pulpit at the center, and sent out numerous novel messages about churches to the world around them. We cannot decode all these communiqués here; perhaps you could study one or more of the contemporary church, temple, or synagogue buildings in your area, and decide what they are saying through the architecture of the edifices themselves.

MUSIC

Churches, temples, synagogues—all evoke not only sights but also sounds, above all perhaps the sound of music. From the stomps and drums of tribal dances to the strains of a mighty pipe organ, from the haunting sound of the shofar, or ram's horn, at the Jewish high holy days to the gravelly chants of Tibetan Buddhist monks, music has been religion's constant companion. Melody has elevated the spirit, made sacred words memorable, and galvanized individuals toward conversion and assemblies toward action.

To be sure, the very power of music has caused some to suspect it, at least in public religion. They have feared with Plato its appeal to feeling rather than to rea-son or to the still, small inward voice, and have viewed with apprehension the way the hypnotic rhythm of drums, say, can reportedly counterfeit true mystical states. A few Christians, such as the Quakers, have given music only a minor religious role. Unless one counts the rhythmic recitation of the Qur'an or the muezzin's call from the minaret, melody is not heard in Muslim mosques, though many **Sufi** Islamic mystical orders use hymns, chants, and dances in their fervent devotionalism.

For most of the rest, though, music is inseparably part of religion. In the Confucianism of traditional China, music was seen as an important indicator of the spiritual constitution of a society. A militaristic state would have martial music, and a peaceful one idyllic music. Music was also important as an instrument of education and social control. Good music promoted virtue, and as Arthur Waley commented in his translation of the Analects of Confucius, such good music "is an intrinsic part of the Way that causes gentlemen to love other gentlemen and makes small men easy to rule."[4] We have spoken in Chapter 4 about the role of religious music as audio symbol. Now it remains to distinguish different kinds of religious music.

In many tribal societies, music is closely connected to dance. These are both communal, community-creating dances, and performances of specialist shamans. Both entail heavy rhythm and percussion, and may also include chants or melodies uttered by shamans and shamanesses when in a trance or when calling spirits. This music survives not only in remaining tribal societies, but also in such forms as the music of sacred dance.

Chants, or the rhythmic, repetitious, monotone, or quasi-monotone singing of religious words or texts, undoubtedly had their origin in the recitation of tribal myths and lore before the invention of writing. In those days, as in many folk cultures to this day, remarkably long pieces of song and story were committed to memory by the wise and presented on solemn occasions. Rhythm and a clear chanting tone of voice were aids to memorization, hearing, and creating the special atmosphere called for by the reverent recounting of the past. Chanting of magical formulae was also done, as in those Vedic chants called **mantras**, their peculiar tone adding to the sense of a different use of language than the ordinary; in these cases the very sound—vibrations—of the words themselves was part of the power.

In later religions, chanting of both mantras and longer texts became the particular province of such specialists as Brahmin priests, nuns, and monks. Sometimes the words and their meanings became obscure to all but scholars, because they were often in a nonvernacular language, Sanskrit in the East or Latin in much of the Christian West. But literal meanings are superseded by other religious meanings of chants: the symbolic creation of a monastic community singing in common, the creation of a religious aura, and the channeling of prayerful feeling through haunting sacred melodies.

In this connection, it is interesting to contrast the sounds of chants in different traditions. The chant of Zen monks in Japan, for example, is a deep monotone that has been compared to the drone of a pond full of frogs; it may even be reminiscent of a Japanese tradition that compares the Buddha seated in meditation to an old bullfrog. In any case, the Zen sense of spiritual closeness to nature is evoked. Much Roman Catholic monastic recitation, on the other hand, is in what is called Gregorian chant, or plainsong. Its elegant but simple and repetitious melodies are somewhat farther from nature than those of Zen, somewhat closer to a purely human concept of sweetness and beauty.

That brings us to another form of religious music, what may be called liturgical. It is intended for use in the services of faiths with a formal **liturgy**, as the Roman Catholic, Anglican, Lutheran, or Eastern Orthodox. Jewish service music led by a cantor has a comparable role. This music is just a setting for regular parts of the service, though often sung by choirs and musically much more elaborate than chants.

Hymns are also sung in services—though of course they may be at other times as well—but are more variable and occasional than liturgical music. Hymns are often devotional in intent, and so express tender feelings in their words and melodies (e.g., "Jesus, The Very Thought of Thee, With Sweetness Fills the Breast," and similar Hindu **bhakti**, devotional hymns to Krishna and other gods), although they may also be martial, such as "Onward, Christian Soldiers."

Finally, there is religious performance music: oratorios (e.g., Handel's "Messiah"), spiritual songs, organ voluntaries, and the like. They are based on religious themes and create a religious mood, though they may not be strictly parts of worship and its orchestration of symbols, and may well be performed separately from formal worship, at concerts and festivals.

POETRY

We come now to religious artistry in words. Poetry, of course, is not too far removed from religious music in that the words sung to the latter are generally poetic. But now we look at poetry with emphasis on the words. Poetry may have originally been intended to be sung or recited, especially in a religious setting, and one may argue that it is still best appreciated that way. But today, more often than not, it is just read, or spoken silently in the mind from memory.

Poetry is above all an arrangement of words, vocal rhythms, and sometimes rhymes that create powerful, abiding images in the mind to make a picture, a mood, or a story resonate with one's deepest feelings. It is not intended primarily to impart information or argue a case dialectically, though there are poems that do those tasks more effectively than a hundred books by the force of feeling and/or images they associate with the information or argument. But chiefly, poetry ties together pictures and emotions, and in so doing it is ultimately close to religion and its roots in myth and symbol.

Poetry is truly religious when the pictures and feelings it calls forth move into the areas of the doors and windows between conditioned and unconditioned reality, of what the theologian Paul Tillich called *ultimate concern*, not just when the theme is explicitly religious. Indeed, there is much bad poetry on religious topics, which may not really move us in that way. And some very good poetry that, though free of religious language, does so move us through its ability to stir up deep thoughts and forcefully ask the ultimate questions about the origin, purpose, and end of our lives. (However, we should bear in mind also that, as was the case with religious painting, sculpture, and music, not all sacred poetry has to be truly great; some religious examples that are merely serviceable do have the valuable function of keeping alive traditions with their symbols and stories.)

We have mentioned the Japanese identification of the Buddha with a frog—sitting as though in meditation—on the banks, or atop a lotus, in one of the innumerable temple ponds of the island nation. That image is reminiscent of a well-known *haiku,* or concise 17-syllable (in Japanese) poem focusing on a single significant image, though perhaps with a "spring" or change in the middle. This *haiku* by the great Zen poet Basho (1644–1694) is perhaps the most famous of all and has been said to sum up the whole of Buddhism in three lines, as it speaks of the Buddha's entry into the world, or into Nirvana from the world, and the spreading out from that entry of the *dharma,* Buddhist Gospel.

An old pond—
A frog jumps in—
The sound of water.

Like a Zen painting or the tea ceremony or a Zen garden, this verse says what has to be said in veiled, simple, concise language.

In a real sense, the English poet William Blake (1757–1827) attained the same end in poems such as "The Tiger." Without directly mentioning God, he raises the problem of evil—why is there evil in the world, why are there tigers that eat lambs?—as boldly as it has ever been presented in literature, as he asks whether the same hand that made the lamb also made the tiger. And if not, whence came the tiger?

> The Tiger
> *Tiger! Tiger! burning bright*
> *In the forests of the night,*
> *What immortal hand or eye*
> *Could frame thy fearful symmetry?*
> *In what distant deeps or skies*
> *Burned the fire of thine eyes? . . .*
> *Did he who made the Lamb make thee?*
> *Tiger! Tiger! burning bright*
> *In the forests of the night,*
> *What immortal hand or eye*
> *Dare frame thy fearful symmetry?*

Blake was influenced by the ancient Gnostic school of Christianity, which, as we have seen, believed the present world was created not by the high God, but by a lower deity who bungled the job. This explains why there is so much evil where, one might think, an omnipotent creator could have done better—why there are carnivorous animals, and humans; why limitation after limitation is built into the realms of conditioned reality.

But Blake's poetry is subtle and not dogmatic. He does not sermonize but points to evils from the victimized lamb to victimized human children like the chimney sweeps and prostitutes of his day—and no less the abused or abandoned children of our own—and simply asks, straightforwardly and unavoidably, what hand framed all this?

And moreover, claiming the usual religious separation of soul and body to be an idea from the devil, Blake affirmed, "Energy is the only life, and is from the Body; and. . . Energy is Eternal Delight."[5] It is the "mind-forged manacles," not the flesh and its innocent desires, that truly bring us under the hammer and chain of whoever could frame this world of tigers and weeping children.

Gerard Manley Hopkins (1844–1889), Jesuit and celebrated religious poet of the Victorian era (like Blake more appreciated in the twentieth century than in his own time), presents here, in "God's Grandeur," a more affirmative view of God's subtle presence in the world.

> *The world is charged with the grandeur of God.*
> *It will flame out, like shining from shook foil;*
> *It gathers to a greatness, like the ooze of oil*
> *Crushed. Why do men then now not reck his rod?*
> *Generations have trod, have trod, have trod;*
> *And all is seared with trade; bleared, smeared with toil*
> *And wears man's smudge and shares man's smell: the soil*

Is bare now, nor can foot feel, being shod.
And for all this, nature is never spent;
There lives the dearest freshness deep down things. . .
Because the Holy Ghost over the bent
World broods with warm breast and with ah! bright wings.

Perhaps this divine vision benefits Hopkins' vocation as a priest, though despite this calling, his spiritual path was often difficult, and the ecstatic consciousness of God's omnipresence in poems such as this not easily won. We, however, can appreciate how he is saying what Blake in his own way also tried to say: that despite all that the humans who infest this world have done to obscure it, there is nonetheless a deep splendor beneath the surface, or in the flash of a bright wing, that connects to unconditioned reality. Hopkins could see that smudged radiance as none other than the hidden God of orthodox Catholic Christianity. For Blake, the glory was the fleshly "eternal delight" represented by the energies of Jesus and the human world in which Christ was embodied, and was not at all from tyrannical old Nobodaddy, the bungling "spiritual" Father-God of this suffering planet in the poet's personal mythology.

But in both cases, the visionary religious poet sees with distaste a smeared and smudged outer world, stained by tears and greed, and peeking out from behind it almost invisible realms of glory.

DRAMA

Like many other art forms, drama has its ultimate roots in religion. The first plays were probably little different from rituals, the acted-out or danced-out myths and services of people, connected with times of festival. Remnants of this background remain in some places. In the No drama of Japan, among the most sophisticated of all dramatic performances in the world, the backdrop inevitably features a pine tree, sacred in Shinto. The oldest and still most commonly performed of all No dramas is *Okina*, "The Old Man," said to derive from an occasion when an old man was observed dancing under a spreading evergreen at the Kasuga Shrine in Nara; the ancient one turned out to be the god of that shrine.

Traditional drama, such as that of No, or the classic Greek theater and Shakespeare in the West, commonly uses verse in its lines and so has an important connection with poetry. On the other hand, the plot has features to be considered in a moment in connection with stories and novels. What is distinctive about drama is that it is to novels as sculpture is to painting. The drama enhances the story in its ability to "freeze-frame" its high, archetypal moments in memory.

At the same time, drama, whether tragedy or comedy, is also particularly good at bringing out the flaws in characters. Greek and Shakespearean tragedy depends on the tragic flaw, the fatal weakness in even the most heroic-seeming personalities that brings them down in the end. And the very essence of comedy is the laughable contrast between human pretension and reality, suggested in the pompous personage who slips on a banana peel, or the public figure trying to explain his private life.

A No work such as Zeami's *Tsunemasa* and English dramas such as Shakespeare's *Hamlet* or Shaw's *Saint Joan* raise spiritual questions on stage that are made all the more provocative and powerful by a play's ability to depict slow dramatic movement and vivid confrontations.

Tsunemasa gets underway as a ghostly voice from offstage begins to chant over the shrill tones of flutes, the complex rhythm of hand drums, and the eerie atonal chants of a chorus. The unearthly words are those of a slain warrior returning from the Other World. He laments that he could find no rest there, and has slipped like a shadow back to the realm of his former life, yearning for something he had left there.

The singer now progresses down the runway toward the stage. We see him in the brilliant court dress of a samurai, his face frozen by a small white mask bearing a subtle smile. As the play advances, we learn that this is the spirit of Tsunemasa, a warrior who also had a great love of music and the lute. Because he died in battle, he was condemned to the Buddhist realm of asuras, continually battling titans or demons, but now, having heard a lute struck at a service in his memory, he is able to return for a few moments to his first love, before having to return, wailing, to his torments in the other world. The staged drama of his slow, precise steps, his music, and his hauntingly sad song uttered in low, slow syllables is a triumph of the actor's art. No mere reading of the story could have quite the same effect.

So it is with Shakespeare's Hamlet, after having seen his father's ghost, when he utters his famous "To be or not to be" soliloquy, and later, as he confronts his mother in her supposed sins. The look in the eyes, the actor's gestures, the cutting turn of the head—how can these be the same on the printed page, however well crafted the words? Or Saint Joan, in George Bernard Shaw's great play about her, facing in tears her tormentors and even her supposed friends at her trial. Religious plays can ask all the unforgettable religious questions, the *what ifs?*—and can act out not one but several speculative answers.

What if something one especially loved can call one back for a few moments even from the dead? Would this be a boon, or only a curse if it made leaving the light, and then the rest of one's purgatorial sentence, all the worse? How much should a son, like Hamlet, heed the ghost of his tormented father and judge the sins of his mother? What if, like Joan, one hears voices supposedly from God? Should one follow those monitions unreservedly, bloodying one's own sword and in the end perhaps tasting blood, or the flames, oneself? Or is it better to ignore them?

If drama raises religious questions, so do cinema and television stories. These newest and liveliest arts, probably those most familiar to many of us, claim many of the characteristics of stage drama, and even more in the way of both close-up intimacy and special effects. Some, in the adventure mode, are like hero-myth stories. Others are more subtly psychological, in the mode of plays like those just cited, and raise religious queries as profound. Perhaps you can take one of your own favorite movies, think it over in your mind, and decide what religious *what if* it is really asking, and how it answers the query—not only in terms of a final verbal answer but in terms of how the drama and the characters develop. Is it convincing, or not?

NOVELS AND STORIES

Fiction, the telling of stories, no doubt has its ultimate origin in myth and so in religion. The first stories, in other words, may have been tales having to do with themes covered by religion: the origin and destiny of the world, the meaning and purpose of human life, even the significance of those humorous, anomalous, trivial pains and pleasures that beset human life but make good anecdotes.

All significant stories also have the use of symbols in common with religion. The theologian Paul Tillich once said, "Faith has no other language than symbols," and the same could be said of literature, for in the end, all the characters and incidents of memorable writing are such because they stand not only as themselves but also as symbols of something greater that remains unspoken. Thus they resonate with that which is otherwise unspoken within ourselves as they present human moods, aspirations, and desperations we know are there, but can scarcely name until the story or novel identifies them for us and helps us to say, "I have felt that way too, but hardly realized it until I read such and such a story."

Religiously oriented literature may present explicitly religious symbols. A character may be a Christ figure, embodying redemptive suffering as in Morris West's *The Devil's Advocate*, a Buddha, as in Hermann Hesse's *Siddhartha*. The theme may be presented only obliquely, and it is up to the reader to make what connections he or she finds meaningful.

Some religious literature, then, continues in the vein of traditional mythology, particularly the myth of the hero, one who embarks on a great quest, overcomes obstacles, endures suffering, and finally triumphs. The major heroes of religion past, such as Rama, the Buddha, or Jesus, are essentially in that pattern. They have set out, have been tempted and suffered like Jesus on the cross, and prevailed not only for their own benefit but that of all humankind.

As we saw in Chapter 3, in *The Hero With a Thousand Faces* Joseph Campbell outlined fundamental features of this mythic paradigm. These may again be summarized by saying that the hero undertakes an important quest, undergoes important suffering, receives important help, and finally, in attaining victory, experiences important transformation. The hero paradigm is particularly significant in many modern adventure, science-fiction, and fantasy works. One thinks of J.R.R. Tolkien's *The Lord of the Rings*, Ursula LeGuin's *The Wizard of Earthsea*, and Westerns such as Zane Gray's *Riders of the Purple Sage*. Though sometimes dismissed by literati, such novels should not be discounted by those attuned to the religious dimension in literature. They represent modern perpetuations of the hero myth, a very important component of religion. Some would say that moderns neglect it, and many other traditional aspects of spirituality, at their own peril. If the hero and the spiritual quest are not acknowledged freely and appropriately—let in through the door—he and it may come back in through the windows in far less desirable guises. One recalls the well-known cults of heroism and pseudo-spirituality in fascist and other totalitarian regimes.

Yet religious sensibility in literature does not stop here either. It can also be indirect. Some works regarded as the most monumental parables of the spirit, heroism, spirituality, and archetypalism are made indirect so the characters have room to be fully human, not merely ciphers for religious values.

In serious literature, the fundamental point is to create and embody a human image, a picture of what a human being is in all the species' diversity. The image may be crafted in the form of a character's experience. But great works of literature will turn the camera on inner experience just as much as outer, and flash the lights into the subbasements as well as the attics of its protagonists' minds. The wildest science fiction or fantasy stories that humans can imagine are as significant a part of this literary documentation as the most down-to-earth realism.

This documentation of the widest possible human experience, in the depths, in the heights, and in the outward world of action and relationships, is important for religion because it shows what religion has to work with. If religion is to do its job, it needs to know real humans, real human life, and the innermost thoughts of real humans. In the end, it cannot operate out of just a "theologically correct" view of humankind, but needs a real, authentic human image based on everything in humans. Constructing such images is what great novelists are about.

But as Lynn Ross-Bryant has pointed out in *Imagination and the Life of the Spirit*, religion and literature may interact, but they are two different things and cannot just be equated.[6] A fundamental reason is that while religion, in a way like logic or science, deals with what is presumed, at least, to be definitely true, literature can deal with possibilities. Literature, says Ross-Bryant, following Giles Gunn, can present a hypothetical creation. It can ask us "to suspend our ordinary categories of judgment," and say, in the words of Giles Gunn, "If you will grant me my initial premise, or set of conditions, then such and such would, or at least could, follow from them."[7]

This kind of freedom clearly can go much beyond the framework of a collective, or "official," myth. Yet literature can also say, of myth or of any other hypothetical religious reality, "What is this supposed reality, and how does it—or might it—work itself out in the lives of different kinds of people? Here are some who believe in this religious story easily, over there are some who believe only with difficulty if at all. There are those for whom it smooths the path of life, and those for whom it presents very hard choices. Let's work up stories about each as a way of understanding their quite different lives in depth."

If a writer really wants to do this honestly and well, the characters and their settings must be totally true to real life in all its complexities. Innumerable well-meaning but second-rate religious novelists have failed, making us say, "It sounds nice but I just can't connect with the religion presented in that story, because I can't believe the characters who espouse it are real."

Let us take a few examples of excellent religious literature. These are novels whose principal characters are, on the face of it, unedifying figures though in religious roles. But in spite of that—or because of it, as their very imperfection helps us identify with them—their narratives raise important religious issues. Graham Greene's *The Power and the Glory* is set in Mexico at the time of the fervently anticlerical revolution of the 1920s, when the Roman Catholic church was harshly persecuted. In this novel we meet a bungling, alcoholic priest who despite being, as he well knows, a poor exemplar of his calling, nonetheless takes serious risks and remains somehow true to God or to something in himself by continuing to say Mass in a string of isolated rural churches.

The question asked is, suppose you were a priest like this in such a situation. Maybe you know you are being persecuted unjustly on a personal level, though you also know you are unworthy, and moreover you know the revolution had some valid criticisms to make of the role of the church in that society. How would you live? And what would that say about the positives and negatives of religion?

In *Kinkakuji*, (translated as *The Temple of the Golden Pavilion*), the Japanese novelist Yukio Mishima (pseudonym for Hiraoka Mikitake, 1925–1970), we have the story of a disturbed, stuttering novice at a famous Zen temple in Kyoto who finally attains a strange kind of release from his inner torment by setting fire to the supremely beautiful edifice. The story is based on fact. In 1950, an unbalanced young monk actually torched this fabled golden dream of a temple out of jealous anger at its uncompromising perfection. (It has since been rebuilt.) Mishima's fictional re-creation of the character and the event is a profound study of abnormal religious psychology.

The young monk-arsonist, Mizoguchi, goes to study at that temple upon the death of his uncomprehending, well-meaning father, a country priest. The younger man is there under the rule of the abbot, a plump, worldly cleric. But Mizoguchi is far more at the mercy of dark forces within himself that he only dimly understands, and can only express through violent rage, locked as he is in a festering inner world by his ugliness, his stammering, and his limited intellect. The temple itself finally becomes the victim, though its only sin is that of being sublimely beautiful and so the opposite of all that Mizoguchi feels himself to be.[8]

There are superficial similarities between *The Temple of the Golden Pavilion* and the book often considered to be the greatest of all religious novels, *The Brothers Karamazov* by Fyodor Dostoyevsky. The story, set in a small town in nineteenth-century Russia, goes like this. Fyodor Karamazov, a well-to-do but drunken and dissipated old man, has three legitimate sons, Dmitri, Ivan, and Alyosha. The three represent three distinct psychological and spiritual types.

Dmitri, a vital, immoderate, hard-living (and perennially in debt) army officer, full of romantic passion and few principles, represents an essentially physical/emotional life, but one lived to the hilt.

Ivan is an intellectual, a religious skeptic full of the "advanced" Western European scientific and philosophical ideas that Dostoyevsky, like many Russians of his day, found fascinating but also profoundly ominous. Ivan represents an essentially mental life, a person who often seems to have his head in the clouds, but who shows that even seemingly quite abstract ideas—"mere theories"—can have very sharp consequences indeed.

Alyosha, the real heart of the novel, is very spiritual, a mystic when it comes to nature and love. He is a novice in a monastery and a disciple of Father Zossima, a Russian holy man of the old school. Alyosha is no plaster saint, however, because he is sometimes given to doubts and temptations, and is deeply involved in the complex and sordid affairs of his family—but by his temperament and approach, he represents in this context an essentially spiritual life.

Then there is the fourth, Smerdyakov. He is the keen-eyed but unschooled illegitimate son of the old man, and lives in the house as an ill-treated servant; he sees no need for moral scruples in a world that has shown him little pity or concern.

The Brothers Karamazov is a most intricate story, and we cannot trace all of its characters and subplots here. Of most interest are some of the religious discussions in this novel of ideas. Ivan argues to Alyosha that he does not reject God but, on the other hand, cannot put trust in God because he cannot accept the world God has made—and gives horrifying examples of the abuse of innocent children in this world, cruelty that can in no way be reconciled with divine justice. Ivan tells his brother, "It's not that I don't accept God, Alyosha, only I most respectfully return Him the ticket."

Ivan recites to Alyosha a prose-poem he says he wrote several years before, the story of the Grand Inquisitor, the most famous passage in this novel. This narrative tells us that during the sixteenth-century Inquisition in Spain, when numerous people were being arrested and terribly tortured for alleged heresy, Christ or someone resembling him appeared in the streets. He took up again his work of healing the sick and lame, and crowds began to flock around him as of old. But the Grand Inquisitor recognized him and had him arrested, just as he was in the first century, and brought to a cell in the Inquisition dungeons.

That night, the Inquisitor himself came to the cell to visit the unexpected captive. Knowing full well to whom he was speaking, the Grand Inquisitor told Christ that because the Savior had rejected Satan's three temptations (to turn stones into bread, to cast himself down unharmed from the pinnacle of the temple, to accept rule over all the kingdoms of the earth), Jesus had thereby rejected miracle, mystery, and worldly power. In so doing, he who was the supposed Redeemer of humankind had placed a burden of freedom on humanity too great for most men and women to bear.

It was necessary for the Church to correct those errors, claimed the Inquisitor—to give people the security of bread, to offer them something miraculous to worship, and to take worldly power unabashedly and use it for human benefit. For these boons most people willingly gave up spiritual freedom, and the Church should help them do so. In following this course, the Grand Inquisitor acknowledged, he was rejecting the purity of Christ and following something of Satan instead, but he was doing so for the good of the great mass of ordinary people whom Christ in that purity could never save.

During all this discourse, Christ remained silent. Then, still silent, he approached the dry-lipped churchman and kissed him. The Grand Inquisitor suddenly freed Christ and told him never to come that way again.

Then the novel climaxes. Smerdyakov had heard and grasped just enough of Ivan's freethinking talk to take to heart the idea that now, if God is gone, all is permitted, and one may, like the Grand Inquisitor, deny God to do good. He, therefore, murdered the old Karamazov, whom he, like many others, hated. He covered himself well, however, and Dmitri was instead arrested, tried in pages packed with colorful courtroom drama, and to everyone's surprise was convicted by his jury of town residents and peasants.

But then Dmitri, with his animal passions, and his well-known differences with his father over women and money, should have been the murderer. In fact he was not; the homicide was, Dostoyevsky seems to tell us, instead committed by a combination of too lofty rational ideas and the dark, abusive, and cruel side of human life. Yet, on another level, all four brothers were guilty, for three of them had in their own way killed their unworthy father in their hearts; and even Alyosha, by omission, had prepared a path for Smerdyakov's crime. Neither God nor reason come off very well, only faith and love, or rather faith in love, for sinners, for animals, for the earth itself. This was the Gospel of Father Zossima, and of Alyosha when he, for all his purity, connives and bribes officials to allow Dmitri to escape the country rather than serve an unjust sentence for a murder he did not, legally, commit.[9]

As we read the end of *The Brothers Karamazov*, when we finished *The Temple of the Golden Pavilion*, we probably feel, as the author intended, a disturbing awareness of inchoate depths in men and women out of which wrath beyond reason—in a word, sheer evil—can flow. Yet because these characters are drawn nonetheless as fellow humans, they also evoke in us deep, poignant understanding and perhaps even compassion. "I too," we say with a smile and a shudder, "in that time and place, and that body, could have been Mizoguchi, or Ivan, or even Smerdyakov." In that light we can assess their religious significance. This is what religious art can do: Make us aware both of human life and of spiritual traditions, and so press us to put the two together.

SUMMARY

We begin an understanding of religious art by thinking of a distinction between unconditioned and conditioned reality. Conditioned reality is the realm of time and space and limits in which we live; unconditioned reality is the opposite of this, and is what religions call by such names as God, Brahman, or Nirvana.

Religious art can be thought of as doors and windows between the two, enabling us to see, hear, or think about something of the other side and its interaction with human life.

Religious painting can take as its subject either nature, showing it as a manifestation or creation of God or Ultimate Reality, or the human form, revealing that reality in the form of gods, Buddhas, saviors, saints, or spiritual scenes.

Abstract or surrealistic religious art can reveal religious symbols and forms on subconscious levels. Sculpture, often used in making figures that are the focus of worship, is particularly good at depicting religious archetypal meaning.

Around the time of the origin of the great religions, religious figures often became less theriomorphic and more anthropomorphic in conception, in part under Greek influence, in part because new religions arose with human founders and central figures.

Religious architecture has also gone through many stages. It basically has two roles, either being a House of God or a place of the assembly for worship of a People of God; some buildings, of course, may be both. Religious music, though sometimes regarded with suspicion, generally helps evoke and channel religious feelings and has an important place in worship. Its forms vary greatly from chants to devotional hymns.

Religious poetry can convey religious ideas and express feelings and responses to them through combinations of words, pictures in the mind, and emotion; often the feelings are challenging and complex.

Drama and fiction, both stories and novels, may be read religiously, particularly in terms of how they create an image of human nature in all its complexity, its nobility and flaws alike, because it is this that religion has to work with. Stories with a religious theme, such as Dostoyevsky's *The Brothers Karamazov*, also ask very important questions about religious meaning, about good and evil in the world, and about the reality of God.

KEY TERMS

anthropomorphism, p. 114
archetype, p. 113
bhakti, p. 119
chanoyu, p. 112
icons, p. 110
liturgy, p. 119

Mahayana, p. 112
mantras, p. 119
Sufi, p. 118
theriomorphic, p. 114
yantras, p. 112
Zen, p. 112

CHAPTER

9

Ghost Marriages and Country Music: Popular Religion

Grave of Elvis Presley at Graceland, Memphis, Tennessee   (David Caton/Alamy)

LEARNING OBJECTIVES

After reading this chapter, you should be able to:

- Explain what is meant by "two kinds of religion."
- Offer some examples, perhaps based on your own observation, of a traditional religion being understood and practiced in a popular religion way.
- Explain how "Great Tradition" and folk or popular religion differ.
- Give some characteristics of folk or popular religion.
- Present pro and con on the issue of whether such ostensibly nonreligious places as Disneyland, or a popular culture phenomenon such as Elvis or a movie based on the hero myth, can be considered religious, and in what sense. Be sure to start with a good working definition of religion.
- Discuss the "postmodern" changes some observers believe are taking place in religion. What is new and what is old in the religious scene today, especially among young people?

TWO KINDS OF RELIGION

We have, in this book, visited great cathedrals with their soaring spires, and famous temples adorned with the treasured artifacts and memories of many generations. We have gazed at religious paintings and statues that draw throngs of tourists and are rightly said to represent the noblest aspirations of their cultures. We have looked at, and will examine in more detail later, religious philosophies and doctrines able to hold their own in the marketplace of ideas along with other world-class articulations of human thought about the Ultimate.

But what about the religious devotion poured out in cement-block and storefront buildings, at crude wayside shrines, or by mass media preachers over the airwaves? How is it different from the religion of the "higher" side of the tradition, or is it different at all? Is one side better than the other? Some people hold to the "high" culture side, and scarcely hide their contempt for simplistic common-people faith, while others think it is simple folk religion that is most authentic.

And what about songs, theme parks, and cinema epics? Take, for example, the role of superheroes in popular culture, comic books, and movies? Are they gods, all-powerful, dealing out justice in extralegal ways, in their own terms, or just imagination in the "nothing but" sense? And is there as much religion in country-western or "gospel" music as in Handel's *Messiah*?

All this is part of what is commonly called popular culture, as over against the "high" culture of, say, Shakespeare and Handel. Popular religion can be considered a sector—and a very important sector—of popular culture. Two forms of popular religion present themselves: the mainstream religion as it is understood and practiced on the popular level, and religious meaning embedded in ostensibly nonreligious popular culture, such as making pop culture entertainers or cinematic heroes into religious icons. We will examine first mainstream religion on the popular level.

POPULAR EXPRESSIONS OF MAINSTREAM RELIGION

One place to begin the first form would be with artistic representations of religious figures. In the United States, an obvious example is the head of Christ by Warner Sallman, painted in 1935 and published for wide distribution from 1940 on.[1] By the 1960s it was said to have been reproduced over a billion times, and was ubiquitous in Protestant churches and homes—a classic example of the point to be referenced a

The famous Head of Christ by Warner Sallman   (Head of Christ Â© 1941 Warner Press, Inc., Anderson, Indiana. Used with permission.)

little later, that while "high" culture arises out of original individual creation, popular culture, religious or otherwise, is disseminated through mass production.

Critics faulted the painting's posed look, pious tone, and alleged soft feminization of the Savior (despite the beard), but millions found Sallman's conceptualization of Jesus what they needed for prayer and commitment. One Louisiana woman put it this way: "It is the softness of the eyes and the face. I picture what it would be like to talk to this person. I feel he would understand anything you would say to him and would answer in kindness & understanding. . . I study this picture many times when I am troubled."[2]

Clearly this is not the Jesus who, according to various academic theories, was a revolutionary, a gnarled peasant, or a subversive trouble maker, but rather a Jesus the comfort of those who are themselves rebelled against, overworked, and troubled. Similar comments could be made about popular Catholic images of Jesus, such as the Sacred Heart, and above all of the Blessed Virgin Mary, the wise compassionate mother, arms outstretched to embrace her erring yet faithful children. Indeed, in some cases, such as Our Lady of La Salette, the immaculate mother herself must defend those children against the heavy arm of her Son—in that conception, a Jesus rather different from Sallman's.

Does it really matter what you believe so long as you live a good life? Nancy T. Ammerman has studied what she calls "Golden Rule Christianity"—an attitude, very often heard expressed on Main Street, U.S.A., that it doesn't matter what you believe or to what church or faith-tradition you belong, so long as you live in accordance with the Golden Rule: "Do unto others as you would have others do unto you."[3] Undoubtedly focusing on this precept is in part a popular response to the extensive pluralism of contemporary American and world culture. Now, regardless of with whom one worships on the weekend, one must meet, and work with as equals, people from a broad diversity of faiths the other 6 days of the week. Popular religion always has to find ways to help often-prickly **Great Traditions** get along in the workaday world of ordinary people.

On the other hand, in some situations a single religion, held tenaciously, is itself the popular response to the social situation. Wladyslaw Piwowarski has written of Polish Catholicism as "the guarantor of national identity" in Poland; such affirmation is particularly the case when, as in Poland under the weight of Russian domination, or Catholic Ireland in the days of British rule, a culture feels itself under alien repression and holds to its religion as its most powerful vehicle of self-expression.[4]

We could find such colorful examples of popular adaptations of the prevailing faith across the religious world. In Japan, where pilgrimage—travel ostensibly for the sake of religion—is immensely popular, millions make the ascent of the nation's iconic Mt. Fuji every year. This is despite the fact that the Shinto goddess of flowering trees said to sanctify the spectacular peak is, by most accounts, relatively unimportant, though devotees expand her significance to make her like the spirit of Nature. Some Buddhists have said the mountain embodies Dainichi, the "Sun Buddha" who is the essence of the universe. But for most pilgrims it is the act of climbing itself, and reaching various stages that are seen as steps in self-transformation, which is the real heart of the experience—doing, not thinking.

Would you marry a ghost? In traditional China, a popular accommodation of Confucian values regarding family lineage, in combination with folk concepts of ghosts and spirits, made such unlikely nuptials advantageous. A girl who died unmarried was in an unfortunate position, as it would have been through marriage that she obtained her true lasting identity, and it would be at the household shrine of her husband's family that her own ancestral tablet would be honored. Moreover, the offerings presented at a spirit's enshrined tablet not only kept alive her memory but also sustained her own life and vitality in the world of ghosts. Therefore, sometimes the spirit of such a deceased girl would appear to members of her own family, and ask to be married.

But how does one find a groom for a ghost-bride? One trick was to place "bait," in the form of the red envelope customarily used for gifts of money, on a road down which a likely young man was proceeding. Family members of the distressed spirit-girl would conceal themselves along the wayside. When the prospective husband arrived and, curious, picked up the envelope, the prospective in-laws would spring out and inform him he was the mate selected by a bride in the spirit world. If he refused, they would tell him that therefore his life would not go well, for he would suffer the vengeance of a scorned lover possessed of supernatural powers. But if he accepted, he would receive his invisible mate's quite this-worldly dowry, which, if generous, might go far to alleviate his reluctance. The wedding would be like any other wedding, except that the bride was represented only by her ancestral tablet. The groom's family was then obliged to place ongoing offerings before it as though she had been a daughter-in-law in life before dying.[5]

It is worth noting that funerals, memorials for the deceased, and concepts of the afterlife tend to play a much larger role in popular religion than in the Great Tradition, except as the latter accommodates the ordinary peoples' needs and desire for assurance in this regard. In several traditionally Buddhist countries, priests and monks find much of their time is spent conducting funerals and requisite periodic memorial services—and much of their income obtained from the customary donations that support these rites—despite the way the highest Buddhist philosophy would call for nonattachment to life or death.

In Hinduism, persons come to die in the holy city of Varanasi (Benares). Bodies are cremated on the burning ghats there by the sacred Ganges and the ashes thrown into that stream. Prayers and rituals called Shradh are offered on behalf of the deceased to Yama, king and judge of the dead, that the departed soul may obtain moksha or liberation, or at least a good rebirth; the holy cities of Ujjain and Gaya, the latter virtually a capital of the dead, are especially auspicious places for this worship.

More philosophical Hindu traditions emphasize nondualist meditation on our timeless oneness with the eternal as the way to transcend birth and death. In more popular Hinduism, though, *bhakti*, devotion toward beautiful saving deities, brings us across to the other shore of life. Opulent pictures of the idyllic paradise of Krishna, his eternal Vrindaban, in which it is unspeakable bliss for a devotee to be reborn even as a blade of grass, continually awaken dreams of endless love and joy in the souls of devotees. In that heaven Krishna fills the air with the unearthly music of his flute to which his gopis or milkmaids dance, and it is said that without Krishna there is no song.

In the Christian west too, in spite of a long tradition of the religion's prominent teaching about the importance of salvation, usually meaning going to heaven rather than hell after death through faith in Christ, some preachers and theologians have wanted to downplay what they see as excessive otherworldliness, not to mention too exclusive an idea of who will be saved, in favor of ethics, liberation from evil systems in this world, and affirmation of living with God here and now.[6] Yet at the time of writing no fewer than two books on U.S. bestseller lists are reports of visions of heaven received in near-death experiences.[7] The experience of Dr. Eben Alexander, a neurosurgeon who said he has previously been skeptical of such accounts, but who reported that in coma he perceived beautiful clouds, heard transcendent music, met a radiantly lovely guide, and was told "You have nothing to fear," was featured on the cover of *Newsweek* and in a book.[8]

Clearly, the very popular near-death experience accounts answer to a real religious need. First, they provide assurance of life after death in a way that corresponds to the increasing desire for belief based on direct experience rather than traditional dogma or philosophical reason. Reliance on experience or reports of experience is a characteristic of popular religion. Most importantly, all direct experience is egalitarian, since anyone can have an experience as good as any other even if they are not credentialed authorities or trained philosophers. Indeed, the experiencer in one of those bestseller books was a small child at the time.[9]

Second, the recent accounts of near-death experiences fit into society that remains deeply interested in spirituality but less attached than before to religious institutions or rigid doctrinal systems. To be sure, many near-death experiences reported in the United States are in a broadly Christian theological context, like the two cited (which indeed presuppose an evangelical perspective), and a few have disclosed experiences of hell as well as heaven.[10] But usually the accounts are nondenominational, bespeaking a basically sanguine, almost universalistic outlook. Unlike comparable medieval stories, which suggest that whether ordinary people will be saved is a very close thing at best, the modern narratives proclaim the good tidings that most will enter into the Light, though they may need to face a review of their life first, which in some instances is quite grueling.

THE DEVIL'S SHARE

Another facet of much popular religion is a very concrete belief in powers of evil. In many traditional societies, misfortune was commonly ascribed not to chance or natural forces but to witchcraft or evil spirits; people, it seems, would usually rather believe in a world permeated with malevolent entities than one in which things happen that are simply meaningless or impersonal, and no one is to blame. This is very much the case in much of traditional religion. Evil is often thought to be caused by witches living on this plane or in the spirit world, or by ancestral spirits displeased with the lives of their living progeny.

Witches (who in this usage may be persons of both genders) acquire their craft by being initiated into it, which sinister empowerment can be given even to a fetus in the womb: by receiving and eating food given by a witch, or by a strong will to power. Response to the witch's dark art calls for the skills of a "witch doctor," the popular term for a specialist able to detect and counter the power of witchcraft.

Native American Navajo lore often identified witches with "skin walkers," malevolent were-persons believed capable of turning themselves into wolves, coyotes, bears, birds, or some other animal. Sometimes the skin walker, in magical mood, may have just worn the skin of the animal, but in others was thought actually able to make the transformation. The story is told of a young Navajo man who, driving his pickup down a highway just before sunrise, noticed a young woman he knew by the road, so he stopped to offer her a ride. As she came near the truck, though, he noticed her face was painted white and she had a wolf skin over her shoulders. Realizing she was a skin walker, he gunned the engine and sped off. But the woman then ran beside him, keeping up however fast he went for at least a mile.

Later the girl's family offered him money if he would keep quiet about what he saw, but he declined, knowing he would die if he held this sinister secret to himself. Soon it was whispered everywhere in the community that she was a witch. Not long after that sorceress herself sickened and died, of no cause doctors could diagnose.[11]

The devil's share in popular religion is not necessarily limited to traditional societies, but may in fact reemerge as an apparent challenge to modernity. In the 1980s, remarkable rumors swept across the United States, Britain, and other "advanced" societies, followed by articles and TV specials in the popular media: the "Satanic panic." It was said that numerous underground covens of Satanists, involving many thousands of persons, were performing "ritual abuse," including the use of Satanic symbols and the sacrifice of animals and even infants. Often, these obscenities took place in daycare centers, according to the accounts of children who told parents and counselors of dubious "games" in which they had to take part, involving sodomy, "devil" masks and robes, and animal or human body parts. On the basis of these tales, arrests were made, and some teachers and others brought to trial. In the end, although certain unfortunate individuals had their careers and lives ruined, it became clear to all sensible persons that the charges were entirely spurious. No concrete evidence of crime was ever found, no bodies or even symbols, and most authorities agreed the children had been interrogated in far too leading a way.

One can only speculate as to why the rumor took hold at the time it did. Certainly it had some roots in the resurgent evangelical Christianity of the day, which had revived belief in a literal Satan and his cohort demons, and which often seems to need enemies against which to showcase its spiritual power. The occult-suffused late 1960s and the 70s saw an upsurge of tremendously popular films with Satanic themes, such as *Rosemary's Baby* (1968) and *The Exorcist* (1973). It may also be significant, so far as the preschool part of it was concerned, that this was about the first generation of families in which both husband and wife went out to work, leaving young children in the hands of a rapidly growing world of daycare centers and preschools. Deep half-conscious anxiety as to whether this was right, and about what kind of care their precious young ones would receive, might have projected itself into fantasies about satanic goings-on in those places to which they had been entrusted.[12]

GLOBAL CHRISTIANITY

Now a word about the position of evangelical and Pentecostal Christianity around the world as popular religion. These forms of the world's largest religion display robustness in North America and even Europe, as well as explosive growth in Asia, Africa, and Latin America. Both stress a personal relationship on the part of the believer to Christ, and in Pentecostalism emphasize manifestation of the gifts of the Holy Spirit through speaking in "tongues," the interpretation of tongues, and spiritual healing. The structure of the church and of worship is relatively informal, though enthusiastic, compared to the older denominations, and unlike the "state churches" of old independent of government, though needless to say politicians often find it desirable to befriend these socially powerful groups.

Such styles of Christianity show many features of popular religion, and this certainly is connected to their appeal. Ours in an age when the Great Tradition, from monarchy and social class to an established "canon" of great literature in education, no longer has the authority it once possessed, and in much of the world everything, from tribalism and the family to movement from peasant life in the countryside to urbanization, seems in flux and change. Religion is changing in synch: State churches, socially prestigious denominations, and religious conformity are fast fading in importance.

Martin Marty has shown that far from being an outdated version of the religion, evangelicalism, Pentecostalism, and even **fundamentalism** (in all faiths) actually fit in well with the conditions of contemporary life for many people.[13] In a time when social and even family networks are shifting and frayed, these styles of faith offer themselves as intensely personal rather than merely societal religions. They fit with the compartmentalization of modern life, in which more than ever home, work, friends (including Facebook friends), and religion are quite separate spheres, and may involve quite different sets of associates—very different from the traditional village or home-above-the-shop arrangement of generations ago, when these four venues could well be rolled into one.

The institutions of evangelical and Pentecostal Christianity, based on congregationalism and charismatic preachers, are prepared to flourish in the "free enterprise" religious life left after the withering away of state church and cultural religion. Moreover, they have been particularly adept at the use of modern technology—radio, television, videos, websites, and the like—despite their allegedly unscientific, miracle-based message. For of course technology, and scientific theory about life and the universe, are two quite different things for many people; they are quite willing to use the former, with thanks to God, to advance a gospel stemming from before the scientific age.

Indeed, that gospel may be particularly welcome in a scientific age, for not a few folk find our complex world, so much governed by technology and assorted "experts," in which many of us can do little more than listen and act out a role, decidedly ambivalent. Improved health and various conveniences such as cars and telephones might be appreciated. But on the other hand, the workday compartment of life, which perhaps means sitting all day dealing with names and numbers on a computer screen (whose technology we hardly begin to understand), or doing endless tests in a lab, or selling mass-produced products, may leave us yearning for something else: some bit of magic, myth, and wonder, above all something that makes our own inner life and feelings important—that says you are not just a cog in the machine, but a beloved child of God, a vessel filled with the Holy Ghost, a member of God's Forever Family.

Now let us back up a little, and with these examples in mind, think about some general features of popular religion.

THEORIES OF POPULAR RELIGION

John Storey, in *Cultural Theory and Popular Culture*, offers several possible characteristics of popular culture: Quantitatively we find more of it than of "high" culture; it is what is "left over" after high culture (i.e., in religion, "orthodox" doctrine and proper liturgy) has been separated out; it is universally communicated, for example through mass media. As we have seen, Storey further observes, in an interesting point, that popular culture is also mass produced in contrast to the individual, personal works of art honored by "high" culture.

A political point likewise presents itself to Storey: Popular culture is often a symbol of resistance to what ordinary people see as attempted hegemony by an educated, well-connected elite. Note the mutual disdain, and often political opposition, between popular evangelical or "fundamentalist" religions on the one hand, and the kind of ideas current in major universities, the "establishment" media, and "mainline" to liberal churches on the other.[14]

(In traditional Russia, modernization was seen as a threat to faith, perhaps something that would even provoke the dread apocalypse. It is reported that when railways first cut across that vast land, peasants sometimes set up sacred icons by the tracks to try to stop the trains.[15])

How can we understand these two worlds of religion; the "high culture" side and the popular? Robert Redfield, an anthropologist who studied Mayan religion in the Yucatan, has written about Great and **Little Traditions**.[16]

The Great Tradition refers to the religion of a land as it is understood and practiced by the elite: the well educated among priests, monks, scholars, and rulers. The Great Tradition is highly literate and based on careful, though no doubt highly traditional and orthodox, learning. In the past, it controlled the major religious institutions, from cathedrals and temples to universities and publications, and probably exercised considerable economic and political power. It also patronized great music and art and encouraged philanthropy, consistent with its tradition. The Great Tradition is still with us today doing much the same things, though its power is more limited in the modern wide-open marketplace of ideas and spiritualities; some, like the postmodernists, as we shall see, do not hold that, just because a tradition was dominant in the past, it should now be more weighty than anything else.

The Little Tradition is the same religion as understood and practiced by the ordinary people. In premodern societies they would be mainly peasants, mostly illiterate, and it would be called **folk religion**. In contemporary society the Little Tradition would be urban as well as rural, and though not illiterate, may be functionally so, as far as the Great Tradition kind of books about the religion are concerned. It is called popular religion.

What is distinct about folk and popular religion? They center on devotion and experience more than theory; they focus more on "cosmic" religion—the turn of the seasons, seasonal festivals, and sacred places in nature or pilgrimage sites—than on formal history; they are transmitted mainly in myth and story told by family and community, or by a few sacred texts revered, as we have seen, as sacred symbols in themselves; and leadership is likely to be through charismatic figures—shamans, "holy men," wise women, or today's television evangelists—as well as by local priestly or ministerial representatives of the Great Tradition. The last often find it wise to accept without too much scruple the practical outlook on the religion of the populists, or even partly share it themselves. Indeed, there have been persons, from ancient prophets to John Wesley, who have mediated well between the two "worlds."

So it is that in folk or popular religion saints and bodhisattvas become timeless semidivine entities, able to answer prayers, rather than historical figures; the cross or star and crescent become signs of sacred space, as on a church or mosque, as much as memorials of a historical event. Festivals, such as Christmas, Easter, Passover, or the Buddhist Wesak become seasonal, with overtones of winter or spring, as in cosmic religion, as well as quasi-historical commemorations.

Redfield points out that Little Tradition practices can continue long after the corresponding Great Tradition has faltered, or been replaced by another. In the Yucatan he studied, the Great Tradition in his time was Roman Catholicism, but the Little Tradition included many usages persisting from the religion of the long-gone Mayan empire. "The shaman-priests of the villages," he said, "carried on rituals and recited prayers that would have their full explanation only if we knew what was the ritual and the related body of thought at Chichen Itza or Coba."[17] By the same token, celebrating Christmas on December 25, just after the Winter Solstice, is based on the pre-Christian Saturnalia and the festival of Sol Invictus, the Unconquerable Sun, of ancient Rome; the very name Easter is derived from an Anglo-Saxon goddess of Spring.

Popular religion and folk religion can be very conservative, little concerned with the latest vogues in philosophy or theology. On the other hand, it can sometimes sanctify, albeit in traditional ways, current vogues in entertainment and celebrity worship. Let us summarize a few common features of popular religion.[18]

1. Transmission through person-to-person or popular means. Today, this would mean religion passed on through family and community talk, local preachers, radio and television, the Internet, or popular pamphlets, magazines, and books usually not considered "literary" by the Great Tradition—not the kind you study in college. You hear religious stories at home, listen to radio preachers, or turn to odd corners of the World Wide Web.

2. A personal and experiential quality. Religion transmitted this way does not deliver intellectual ideas so much as trigger religious experience. It says praying with faith in this or that way, or loving the Lord in your heart, is better than much learning.

3. Renewal movements. Popular religion is sometimes given to revivals, or political crusades, usually on behalf of single issues important to the ideology, or to oppose those considered enemies of the faith.

4. Permanent, visible objects such as amulets, holy pictures, and scriptural books, regarded signs and triggers of religious reality. Popular religion makes much of such objects, from keychain or dashboard amulets to sacred books such as the Bible or Lotus Sutra, regarded more as objects to venerate or swear by than as prose or poetry actually to be read like any other book. These objects all function to symbolize and concentrate the power of the faith.

5. Relation to nature and the cycles of nature, or to pilgrimage sites. We have already mentioned the importance in folk and popular religion of seasonal festivals and, often, sacred places such as the trees, mountains, and pilgrimage sites of Shinto, or of Catholic apparitions of the Blessed Virgin Mary.

6. Importance of women. Great Tradition religion is often dominated by males, but as though in compensation popular religion frequently gives greater place to the informal wisdom and leadership of women. Nineteenth-century Spiritualism, for example, gave women roles as mediums and lecturers they would hardly have had in the major religious institutions of the time.[19]

Regarding these points, let us again take evangelicalism and Pentecostalism as an example. They meet most of the criteria for popular religion as listed previously. True, they do not make much of amulets, but pictures such as Sallman's head of Christ, already mentioned, have an almost comparable part. The Bible itself, not only as authoritative text but an object sacred in it own right, carried about, held up, placed on pulpits and altars, can have something of the same symbolic role. Being dissociated from cosmic religion, these Christian faiths are not oriented to the cycles of nature in the way of some folk religion, but it might be mentioned that the main seasonal Christian festivals, Christmas and Easter, despite earlier doubts have come to loom very important in evangelical culture. In Pentecostalism, women often have importance as preachers and speakers or interpreters of "tongues" to an extent not found in most other conservative forms of Christianity.

Peter Williams has emphasized the interplay of two forces in popular religion: the resources of the culture's major religious institutions or denominations and supplements from other venues.[20] Popular religionists may well participate in mainstream religion, yet also receive religiosity from sources outside its control: TV, books, popular preachers, and, of course, local tradition.

The interplay can be playful. Tom Beaudoin, writing of how popular culture continually intertwines the sacred and the secular in daring ways, examples music videos by the pop star Madonna, not usually considered an icon of spirituality. In "Like a Virgin" she dances on a gondola wearing a long rosary with a crucifix. In "Like a Prayer" she enters a Catholic church and kisses the feet of a statued saint, apparently Martín de Porres, bringing him to life; the holy man then embraces the entertainer and kisses her on the forehead.[21]

Whatever meaning one assigns to these winsome scenes, calling them irreverent yet spiritual, or just irreverent, or just spiritual in a new way for our times, one is reminded of a point made by Quentin J. Schultze, a professor of communication arts and science. He says there is often a "love-hate" relation between religion and popular culture.[22] Popular culture can help religion gain a "public voice," even find a way of access into common values, yet purists are likely to find their faith diluted if not seriously distorted in its populist packaging. This debate is likely to go on for a long time.

Now we may turn to another side of popular religion: making things that are not part of any traditional religion, and may seem to be entirely secular, into what some would call religious.

CAMOUFLAGES OF THE SACRED

Are Disneyland and Disney World religious? Or is an epic based on the hero myth such as *Star Wars* religious? Does Nashville-type country music convey religious themes beneath the surface? What about brand names? (An article entitled "Apple Is a Religion" makes the point that, according to neuroscientists, favorite brands and religion both trigger the same reaction in the brain; this author compares Apple stores to cathedrals in the response they evoke from devotees.[23]) The sacred hidden in the secular is the aspect of popular religion to which we shall now turn.

The heading of this section comes from the historian of religion Mircea Eliade, who in *The Sacred and the Profane* wrote that, "[T]he modern man who feels and

Mickey's Toontown at Disneyland, California   (Mark Bassett/Alamy)

claims that he is nonreligious still retains a large stock of camouflaged myths and degenerated rituals."[24] He alluded to the festivities of New Years, which however secularized have a very long sacred history; and to the mythologies produced over and over by Hollywood, the "dream factory," as those dreams follow mythic models of "the fight between hero and monster, initiatory combats and ordeals, paradigmatic figures and images (the maiden, the hero, the paradisal landscape, hell, and so on.)"[25]

Take, for example, Disneyland, or Disney World, as sacred space and time, two of the basic categories in Eliade's work. Eric Michael Mazur and Tara K. Koda, in "The Happiest Place on Earth," point out that these sites are, first of all, "bordered, demarcated space in which something out of the ordinary occurs."[26] One soon perceives man-made mountains, recalling Eliade's sacred mountains that are each an *axis mundi*, a meeting place of earth and heaven, or manicured vistas alongside sparkling lakes, all like a paradise positioned away from the noisy, dirty profane world outside the Magic Kingdom's gates. Not only that, but this happy realm commences with Main Street, U.S.A., a space embodying an American mythic past, then opens up into a panorama of adventures—Fantasyland, Frontierland, Tomorrowland, Toontown, and others—suggesting an ability to travel freely in enchanted time and space to worlds of wonder once and future, near and far, as though one was possessed of the skill of a sorcerer or shaman.

To be sure, Mazur and Koda point out flaws in this picture: the commercialization in Disney's Magic Kingdom, the idealization and distortion in its portrayal of history and nature, with negative elements of the American past "programmed out" and the mechanically animated animals all harmless and generally cute. But religions do the same. The point is that Disneyland, like pilgrimage sites from Lourdes to Mt. Fuji, presents a demarcated space wherein one can enter the mythic past or future, the world of fairy tales, or a paradise of clean lawns and friendly animals, just as in pilgrimages of the feet or of the spirit one can enter set-apart places where the religion's mythic world becomes true. Here, as at many a pilgrimage center, miracles of a sort can happen, life can be at least temporarily transformed, and the world can seem more welcoming here than outside. Whether this is religion, pseudo-religion, or what is a matter of definition, the experience is there nonetheless.

Disneyland is a matter of space and time; what about feelings? Does popular music sometimes camouflage the sacred? Take the style of country music for which Nashville is famous. It's mostly girlfriends and boyfriends, wives and husbands, breakups and barroom brawls, loneliness and drinking, trucking and hearing the distant whistle of trains. Class rings and even wedding rings are left behind as one's mate, or oneself, falls into the arms of another, or a rambling man feels the exaltation and then the emptiness of endless roads, or of days in the jailhouse, or of the false sacraments of fists and the bottle. We sense life hell-bound toward hopelessness, Kierkegaard's "sickness unto death," in the putative story behind the words of many a song.

Then, next over the radio, we may hear explicitly religious ballads, largely retelling biblical stories—myths in the positive sense of the word—in lyrics with flowing melody. Or we may simply hear about a style of love and loyalty, between lovers, between parent and child, that goes in an opposite direction than descent into despair. One hears not only the singing of the blues but also redemption through song.

An exceedingly popular apostle of song in the twentieth century was Elvis Presley (1935–1977), the King of Rock and Roll. One of the most interesting discussions surrounding popular religion is whether he has himself become a religious figure, even the messiah of a new religion, after death.

The heart of that cult is Graceland, Elvis' home and place of interment in Memphis, Tennessee. There, in the Meditation Garden containing the entertainer's grave and those of his immediate family, fresh flowers and soulful mourners are usually found. I myself, on a visit to Graceland, was struck by the virtually sacred atmosphere of this place. The high point is the week in August marking the anniversary of the King's death. Many thousands of fans arrive to take part in meetings and festivities, and above all in a candlelight vigil and procession to the Meditation Garden, now thick with floral displays and teddy bears presented by fan clubs around the world.[27]

Some writers, such as Ted Harrison and John Strausbaugh, have argued that the Elvis cult has characteristics of a real religion, and could become such one day.[28] Comparing the sect to Christianity, it is noted that Elvis, like Jesus, is referred to as "the King"; fans recount his life and good works even as those of the earlier savior were told in the gospels; they collect souvenirs as though they were relics; Elvis impersonators function like priests of the faith; fans do charitable works in his name (including, perhaps significantly, donating blood to the Elvis Presley Trauma Center); and much is made of Elvis' own serious interest in religion, theosophy, occultism, and mysticism: At Graceland one can see a display of the impressive collection of books of this sort the King insisted on taking with him in a special trunk on his frequent concert tours, a side of him about which many may not have been aware. Most significantly of all, it is claimed that Elvis is still alive, either in an earthly sense (his death and funeral are widely rumored to have been faked), or as a mythic, supernatural King who continues to watch over his fans from above, intervenes on their behalf through visions and miracles, and will some day return or meet his followers in heaven.[29]

Raymond A. Moody, in *Elvis After Life*, reports alleged after-death sightings of the singer. One remarkable incident involved a woman he calls Hilda Weaver, unmarried, a successful clinical psychologist in her late thirties, who had an unexpected visitor in her office some 3 months after Elvis' death. Although she had seen the King once before as a child and had fantasized about him for a time afterward, she now regarded herself as well educated and sophisticated. She did not count herself a fan, nor had she thought much about him since.

But this day, when she believed she was alone in her office, she looked up and to her amazement saw him sitting in the chair facing her. She said, "I sensed the overwhelming kindness that just lingered in the atmosphere around the man." As they talked, he gradually and tactfully led her to face certain aspects of her life she had denied before, and when the session was over she "understood that there is much more to the mind and the spirit of the human being than I had allowed up to then, and that if I was going to be a full human being to the point where I could be helpful to others, I had to realize this and let it affect me fully from within."[30]

However one regards this experience psychologically, it is clear that a figure out of popular culture had worked his way deeply into the spiritual life of another, to the point he was able to be the catalyst of a real inner transformation. Nor is Hilda's experience unique.

Could a new god for our times first be met on the pages of a comic book? Here is another possible camouflage of the sacred: the myths of comic book, and now movie, superheroes: Superman, Batman, Spiderman, any number of "Captains" this and that. Though clearly in some sense human, and though certainly not God Almighty, these beings have powers such as those attributed to the lesser gods of ancient myth, and to the shamans, saints, bodhisattvas, and immortals of religions still living: the ability to fly, to see what is unknown to most ("x-ray vision"), and above all superhuman strength.

Is it significant that, also like gods, saints, and bodhisattvas, they became what they are in different ways, but always in a manner reminiscent of divine beings dwelling among men and women of old? Superman came down from another world, like an avatar or incarnation, and as Clark Kent has an "ordinary life" in which his otherworldly identity is disguised. Batman achieved his ability through ascetic training and tireless development of his physical and mental abilities, like a yogi or desert saint of old, as he prepared to enliven the life of grim, corrupt, and impersonal Metropolis. Spiderman, on the other hand, was a troubled adolescent who got his powers from a bite by a radioactive spider, that is, by accident; Eliade, in his classic work on shamanism, tells us many of these adepts first gained their powers after a chance encounter with a divine being or a serious injury, whether accidental or provoked.[31] Are these new myths as real as any out the past, and what do they tell us about the state of religion and life today?[32]

Superheroes bring to mind other heroes in cinema, as indicated by Eliade's remark that movies replay over and over the eternal story of the hero's battle against monsters and evil, his or her initiation, and the triumphant one's ultimate return bearing gifts. As we have indicated, it is well known that the career of the hero in George Lucas' *Star Wars* saga is based on Joseph Campbell's schematization of the heroic archetype in his *The Hero With a Thousand Faces*. I recall opening night of one of the episodes in this drama. The large, cavernous theater was packed, but as the titles began to appear on the screen, the house fell oddly quiet; one sensed hushed, almost reverent expectation, as though a congregation was awaiting the commencement of a mighty liturgy. Then, as the drama proceeded, few vocal comments broke the quiet awe save the occasional gasp of wonder or excitement as we vicariously entered the world of the mythic hero, as alive today as ever. (In countries such as Britain and Australia, where a religious query is part of the census, a number of young people have listed their religion as Jedi, after the heroic knights of *Star Wars*.)

ARE THEY RELIGION?

But is all this religion? Does it matter what you call it? Obviously the "religions" of Elvis and *Star Wars*, or of country music and Disneyland, are not religions in the sense in which the term would be applied to the historical "great" religions, or even of some new sect with a regular creed and worship service. But are they religions in the sense of evoking, like a brand name, feelings virtually indistinguishable from those others might bring to worship in the past, or at least (as no one can really know someone else's inner feelings) express themselves in ways that suggest such feelings? Or is it more like play religion?

Scholars have devoted much attention to these intriguing topics. Gordon Lynch, starting with Eliade's concept of the sacred and the profane, suggests we need to go beyond outward sacred space and time to focus on "sacred objects," the sight or sound (as of a song) of which evoke a particular quality of thought, usually connected to important memories in a person. Those sensations in turn call forth certain feelings and behavior, ultimately linked to one's grounding or source of power. Thus, presumably, for an Elvis or *Star Wars* devotee, posters recalling the King or the cinematic epic might dial up the same strong feelings of joy and wonderment that the "object's" presence and power, then bright and fresh, had presented the first time around. As that connection replays them now, they bring a rush that makes one feel rightly placed and fitted out for life in, to use words from Shakespeare's *The Tempest*, one's own personal "brave new world, that has such people in't!" as Elvis or Luke Skywalker.

If this is religion, it is so thanks to a shift in recent theories of religion away from emphasizing faith as a relationship to the transcendent, and toward seeing it as a way of understanding and experiencing the self.[33] Whether you call the Buddhist Samgha or a Holy Apostolic Faith, or Elvis or the Jedi, religion—in this light the nomenclature is less a matter of ideas or activities than of how it seems from the perspective of the *self*. In other words, does it "feel like" religion, and does it make one act as though it were religion?

So it is that, according to the sociologist Paul Heelas, the new religious environment can be characterized as "expressive individualism." This means that the exclusivist religious barriers of the past have broken down to make for a system in which seemingly religious feelings and behavior can be activated by many different traditions, as well as nontraditional means. The spiritual world is "de-regulated and un-policed. . . The distinction between the high and the low fades away."[34]

Increasingly, both sociological and journalist observations confirm the same. A 2011 *Washington Post* article by Cathy Lynn Grossman of Religion News Service was significantly entitled, "More Americans Designing a Make-Your-Own Religion."[35] The point, based also on George Barna's book, *Futurecast*,[36] is that denominational or religious lineage labels means less and less, as people appropriate for themselves whatever seems good from this tradition and that. Barna said, with only a wry hint of exaggeration, American is headed for "310 million people with 310 million religions."

No doubt many people, including conservative Catholics and the evangelicals, Pentecostalists, and fundamentalists mentioned earlier, would object that such a dictum hardly applies to them. They know the truth, and it is not just what anyone wants to think it is. Nonetheless, inclusiveness is also a very widespread mentality in the modern world, often so pervasive as to be almost unconscious, and sometimes even coexisting with exclusive sides of the same person's religious character. (Don't we sometimes meet people who attend very conservative forms of worship, yet also do yoga, follow astrology, and are "extreme" fans of Elvis or *Star Wars*?) It is all part of what has been called postmodernism: In a postmodern world, things are not privileged just because they are the latest thing (the rejected "myth of progress") or the oldest thing (authoritarian traditionalism) but only from what they evoke in an individual person. If religion is to find a place in such a world, clearly it needs to be flexibly understood.

Sociologist Wade Clark Roof has called us "spiritual omnivores," and says a "considerable recasting" is going on in religion: In this situation, religion is "commodified" (sold like a product, promoted in effect by the mass media, in which anything from Elvis to a new god in India is instantly world news), and all sorts of images, symbols, personalities, feelings, and ideas are mixed together, to be sorted out and made into a unity, insofar as they are, in the individual rather than any particular institution. Ours is a "deregulated and de-monopolized world."[37] Meredith McGuire adds that religion is something that changes over time as a person makes and remakes her or his sense of self in relation to the sacred, and we're now looking again at the self, not the abstract sacred, as the real locus of religion. "At the level of individual, religion is not fixed, unitary, or even coherent," but is changing and growing its stories, symbols, attitudes.[38]

All this may help us realize how, even if we do not fully accept the notion, it is not as absurd as one might have initially thought to say that Disneyland or Elvis could be a religion, or part of a religion, or at least have religious meaning, for a postmodern person. Indeed, John Caputo has raised the possibility of what he calls "religion without religion" today. The religious impulse is there, alive and strong, but traditional formal religions cannot entirely contain it. Thus religious drives and phenomena are being relocated in other places outside them. He explicitly uses the example of *Star Wars*. This series, Caputo says, "offers many young people today a high tech religious mythology, a fairly explicit 'repetition' or appropriation of elemental religious structures outside the confines of the institutional religious faiths."[39]

Whether as folk religion or today's popular religion, religion outside the box, but responding to the immediate need of individuals and communities for symbols that help empower their lives, has always been with us. (One could, for example, compare the *Star Wars* or superhero phenomena to the impact of Richard Wagner's mythic dramas in nineteenth-century Germany, the No plays of medieval Japan, or the quasi-sacred dramas of ancient Greece.) But today the swirl of available symbols, swashed around the world by the media, has given us more than ever to work with and talk about. In the twenty-first century, looking at popular religion is as good a starting point as any for understanding what religion really means and doesn't mean, in our times.

SUMMARY

A religious Great Tradition differs considerably from folk or popular religion. The former is the way the religion is seen and practiced by learned professionals, the latter by ordinary folk, peasants in premodern time ("folk religion"), the general run of people today ("popular religion").

Examples of the popular adaptation of traditional religion include the vogue for Sallman's Head of Christ, "Golden Rule" Christianity, ghost marriages in China, a great interest in death and survival of death including near-death experiences, emphasis on the power of witchcraft and Satanism. Global Christianity also has many popular-religion features in its evangelical and Pentecostal forms, which are actually especially well adapted to contemporary life.

If we look at features of popular religion, we find an emphasis on personal transmission, on experience, on seasonal festivals, on the role of women, and of course on the religion's local base.

Popular religion can also take forms not related to any traditional religion, but which some observers see as essentially religious: Disneyland, the cult of Elvis, comic-book superheroes, cinematic mythological dramas. All of this indicates to some ways in which religion today is becoming more flexible and adapted to personal styles.

KEY TERMS

folk religion, p. 138

Little Traditions, p. 138

Great Traditions, p. 133

CHAPTER

10

Infinite Information, Worlds Without End: The Internet, Religion, and Virtual Realities

Student using laptop in the library   (cristovao/Shutterstock)

LEARNING OBJECTIVES

After reading this chapter, you should be able to:

- Discuss how the Internet is related to religion in the following ways:
  - As a source of practical and academic information
  - As a forum for religious discussion
  - As a way to participate in a religion
  - As a way to play games that reflect mythic scenarios
  - As a medium that opens up philosophical questions about virtual and "real" reality
  - As a medium for creating new "virtual" religions, or greatly changing old one
  - As, speculatively, a vehicle for ultimately creating a radically new kind of human, or post-human, life, in which the meaning of religion would also be radically changed.
- Talk about what the religious meaning of artificial intelligence might be.
- Survey the religious and ethical implications, positive and negative, of video games.
- Say what you think the future of the Internet in respect to religion might be.

THE WAY WE LIVE NOW

A twenty-first century family is sitting around the table just finishing dinner. The mother says she plans to go to a religious service that evening but is not sure what time it is; she'll check on the group's website.

Dad says he needs to write his partner about a new business development that has just come up. He'll use email, of course, and hopes the partner isn't too busy arguing religion on a favorite blog of his to get back to him soon. Dad mutters something under his breath about how some people can be sharp in business and everything else but have really crackpot ideas on subjects like religion and politics. No doubt, they had such notions in the old days too, but they kept them at home or only held forth down at the local coffee shop or bar. Now with the Internet anybody can shout anything to the world (using caps and exclamation points), and people can argue it in front of the whole world, on and on till it's nauseating. That's what dad said.

The older sister, who's in college, nods slightly as though in agreement and says she has to write a paper about a certain new religion. But she's like confused by all the online information she's getting up. Some say this religion is evil, of the devil, and a menace to humanity. Others say it's a true, divinely revealed faith. Still others take an academic approach, just relating objectively its founding, doctrines, practices, and so forth. Somehow, she believes, all this has to be taken into account to give her paper flesh and blood. But she's not quite sure how. She's tempted to bring down and buy a prewritten paper on the topic but knows that isn't really ethical, or educational.

The older sister chatted on. Today I ran into Debbie, she said, you know that girl who's always seemed kind of lonely, like she didn't quite fit in anywhere. She told me she's really gotten into an online Pagan group, like it's called Starlight Coven I think, and there are people like her there she'd never have met any other way. She said they'd just done an online ritual. The circle is cast, the quarters are called, that's how they talk, and this ritual had someone online in the far north, south, east, and west of the country, so the circle was drawn all around the land to make it the Place between the Worlds for a moment and with the goddess arising in the center. And when they ended, they all typed in "Merry meet, merry part. . . and merry meet again," just the way they say it. I guess it means something to a person like Debbie to be able to do this.[1]

Her younger brother, in high school, eyes dancing, declares he's going to spend the evening in the virtual reality of an immense video game he's involved with. In fact, out there in this particular cyber universe he's lord of a whole planet, one of thousands managed by human avatars such as himself. He's busy developing the politics and religion of this world. The religion, he says to anyone who'll listen, will honor gods sometimes seen in the many-colored clouds continually streaming across the purple sky of this world. They are gods who stand for justice, but who also give quasi-magical powers to its citizens in their endless battles against the space pirates (other players) always griefing those who labor for peace in the galaxy. Tonight he will try to construct splendid temples and imposing rituals for these deities, all as grand and lofty as imagination alone can make them.

Why quarrel so much or study so much about the old religions of this little old planet, he adds with a glance at the others, when you can go online and make your own, then give the new faith a whole world in which to grow and evolve? The day is coming, he proclaims with a certain visionary look on his face, when the line between virtual reality and what we call "real" reality will fade away. So will the line between artificial and human intelligence. Then computer-generated religions will take over the earth, and after that the galaxy.

The others look back at him a little skeptically. But only a little; they know ours is a day in which visionary computer nerds like younger brother have come into their own, leaving the "practical" types far behind.

LEVELS AND LIFE

This vignette may provide some idea of ways computers and the Internet are interacting with religion in this new age of the cybernetic revolution. These ways exist on several levels.

First, the computer can provide everyday information on times of services, addresses, leadership, and even basic teachings of mainline (and alternative) churches and temples. These might first of all be for the benefit of persons already involved in the religion. But they would also be of use to seekers looking for a religious place to visit, or just curious to learn more about.

The next level uses the Internet as a source of information on a religion for purposes of study, or just out of personal interest. Like the older sister in the story above, the investigator is likely to find all sorts of material under that heading: negative, promotional, and just factually informative in the manner of an encyclopedia article. It requires some intuitive skill to navigate through these postings, taking what is useful and recognizing that which is partisan propaganda pro or con for what it is. (One hint: Acknowledging that virtually every religion has lines in its basic texts which, if taken out of context, can make it look bad, and others that make it only good, regard with caution those sites that seem to just "cherry pick" such sentences, and go with those

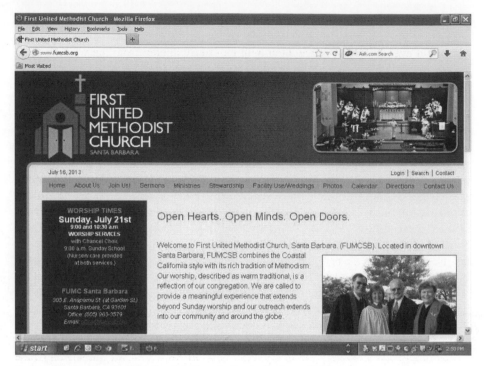

Online Site for the First Methodist Church, Santa Barbara, California (Courtesy of First United Methodist Church-Santa Barbara)

that calmly try to develop the overall message of the scriptures and the religion as a whole throughout its writings and its history.)

Going on to a level beyond this, the seeker or the member can become involved in the religion more and more, indeed almost entirely, through the Internet. On many sites one can ask questions and have them personally answered, get into discussion groups or follow blogs, as much as one wishes. Not a few people have been converted to a religion, taken part in prayers and rituals as did "Debbie" above, and even become a minister or teacher, while sitting alone in front of a monitor. For such persons, the computer becomes church and one's e-correspondents the congregation.

Then, ascending to a still loftier level, we rise to the issues surrounding "virtual reality" and the philosophical queries behind video and Internet "games," including the magic and the making of worlds, heroes, even religions, that underlies them. Why do these games so often seem to have European quasi-medieval (though apparently pre-Christian) settings complete with wizards and heroes? Or an interplanetary science fiction venue, or (like *Star Wars*) an odd combination of the two? Are such numinous realms camouflages of the sacred? What does it mean for religion that players act out quasi-religious roles, working sorcery and even wielding divine powers, creating worlds with their own cultures and religions, as they take their part in dramas playing out across Middle Earth or across the galaxy?

And what comes next? Computerized artificial intelligence? As though replaying in technological terms the eschatological or apocalyptic scenarios of traditional religions, some techno-philosophers predict that, much sooner than we may think, computers will give us a world, or universe, in which the very nature of life, mind, and spirit, and even time, space, and God, will be utterly altered from the way we think about them now. By the middle of the twenty-first century, so they say, a "Singularity" will occur as artificial intelligence excels the natural human mind, and in a real sense the planet becomes theirs, not ours. But we could hold our own with implanted bio-computers though which information can be directly downloaded into our brains, or as we augment our puny minds with the massive intellects of world-class computers.

This will, for all intents and purposes, make us a different species from humans as we now know them, and for good measure we may no longer even need a physical body, a computerized mind in far more durable wrappings than flesh and blood having taken its place. Cyborgs. (An article in the *New York Times* on Singularity thought was entitled, "Merely Human? That's so Yesterday."[2]) Speech, even words except perhaps as thought-symbols, not to mention books, will be obsolete. Plugged literally into a World Wide Web, we will all be able to communicate directly mind to mind.

Needless to say, the beings of such a brave new world would be able to play around with the indeterminate quantum substratum of the cosmos, as well as the ground of consciousness that is ultimately one with that substratum. They will, so to speak, log into the great cosmic computer behind the universe as they demolish any distinction between virtual and "out there" reality. The future drama of souls and worlds will be ours to write, and for this video games were only novice practice sessions.

All this may sound like science fiction. But the proponents of this vision of the future say that our own grandparents, when young, would scarcely have been able to imagine the world in which we now live. The pace of change, they add, is only accel-erating every decade. Any present imagining of what computers will be, and will make us, in a century or two is probably actually too modest.

There are of course plenty of skeptics who doubt that so much will happen so fast, or that some of it will happen at all. There are likewise alarmists who say that if it does happen, the result will be the destruction of the human spirit rather than its enhance-ment. Ability to process information a millionfold or even to make virtual worlds is not wisdom, they submit, nor is a mind-to-mind network a community of love.

In any case, the computer revolution is here. For good or ill or both, its ultimate meaning can now be perceived only very dimly. But undoubtedly it will so reshape human life that in the end screen and keyboard will have at least a great an effect on religion as, say, the agricultural revolution of 12,000 ago. Will this be your world? What do you think?

That's a preview of the computer and religion story. We will now survey its levels in more detail.

INFORMATION PLEASE

The information side of the Internet may seem rather prosaic compared to these futur-istic speculations. Yet it is already affecting the way religious groups operate, and the way people practice, and seek to spread, their faith. A 2004 Pew Report said that even then 64 percent of web users reported going online regarding their faith. Forty percent said they have sent or received messages with spiritual content, sent online greetings for religious holidays, or sought out news about religious affairs.[3] Seventeen percent looked for information about where they could attend religious services, and 7 percent have made donations online to religious organizations or charities.

Typical uses would be to send out notices of classes, download hymns and sermons, or talk about religious beliefs in discussion groups or blog responses. The younger the person, the more likely she or he is to use the Internet rather than other modes of communication. That means young people are most likely to have received whatever religious information they possess from Internet sources, or perhaps from religious institutions first located and accessed online.

What kind of information is this, and what does it mean that more and more people are getting religious information via the Internet, rather than mailers or word of mouth, or even the ringing of church bells or the muezzin's call? (Of course, those media are still there, often encrusted with sacred tradition. But at the same time, that fact reminds us that religion is rooted in another era, and its antique modes of formal communication—including formal preaching and reading of scriptures in worship—are not *really* where we are today when it comes to getting most of our information.)

First of all, note that information and the alleged changing nature of information in the Internet age are themselves major topics of discussion. First, what some authors see as the bad news. James Glieck, in *The Information*, claims that, in large part due to the Internet, we've gone from seeing information as the expression of human thought and emotion to looking on it as a commodity, as data.[4] Not only that, but the data has become a flood, far more than any one person can truly process or understand in human terms. But it keeps coming, and almost of itself generates more and more information, till we're not so much informed as just swamped.

Nicholas Carr, in *The Shallows*—a book significantly subtitled *What the Internet Is Doing to Our Brains*—makes the case that the "information age" is indeed changing the way we think, with profound implications for philosophy and religion. We have already noted how literacy, the transition from oral to written communication, involved movement from myth and story to abstract ideas—all eventually the burden of books rather than speech—as carriers of major ideas. Carr explains that, however, the printed page serves to focus our attention, and promote deep and creative thought. In contrast, the Internet fosters the rapid mining of small bits of information, as it encourages an ethic of speed and efficiency. You can never have all the information, it seems to say, so all you need to do is get enough together to finish a particular job, then go on to the next. You don't have to think profoundly about it the way a philosopher of old might.

How would this apply to religious life? Lisa Miller, in an article entitled, "My Take: How Technology Could Bring Down the Church," commemorates the 400th anniversary of the King James Bible, but notes that undoubtedly numerous fine leather-bound Bibles lie gathering dust in contemporary homes, while their denizens get their real information, including the Bible itself, via iPads and iPhones.[5] There is, for example, the "almost-insane popularity" of a free digital Bible called Youversion, through which users can "'consume' their spirituality the way they do their news or their music. . . dip and dabble, the way they browse Facebook." They can go on to share thoughts about it through a community component.

Anything wrong with this? Nothing, if one assumes that religion should be a direct, spontaneous, noninstitutional experience, in which you get what you need right this instant and no more than you need, perhaps while on the run to some other job. You get the Bible verse for right now like a consumer, without having to go to church or listen to a sermon in which you might hear something from the Bible you don't want to hear at that moment, much less read the whole Bible through in a way that would give you the overall picture of its grand narratives, and its many challenges. Of course, so far as sermons go, you can also download them, naturally the ones you want to hear from a preacher you like. This is why Lisa Miller says that technology could bring down the church—if we look at the church, or any other religious institution, simply in consumerist terms, as purveyors of a product that may now be more cheaply and easily available elsewhere, in an age of instantaneous information and on-call experience without depth or commitment to go with it. Sociological evidence is coming in that churches are getting increasing numbers of younger attenders who visit in the same spirit, declining to join but sitting in a pew as they feel a particular need, perhaps having received information about that church online. They may enter the doors of several churches in the same way, without staying long.[6] Clearly something significant is going on in religious consciousness—we noticed much the same thing in relation to popular religion in Chapter 9, and one could go on to mention fast-changing jobs and relationships or marriages—and it would be easy to relate it all to the ubiquitous screen, with its easy-going religious sites, job markets, and dating services.

Ubiquitous? Everywhere? Another issue is that the Internet is not in fact available everywhere. In the twenty-first century the screen also cuts an economic gash across the world, for there are millions who cannot afford computers or even cyber cafes. The information, blogs, Bible verses, and all the rest of it are now shaping the spiritual world of part of the human race, not all. The Internet has yet to fulfill its promise of uniting humanity in a single conversation. Until it gets there, it is also making for a deep divide between privileged and non-privileged. What are the ramifications of this?

These are some of the issues that have been raised about the Internet and religious information. How important are they? It can be argued that little of this is truly new. In the long-ago pre-Internet era, not everyone read deep and creative books either, and no doubt then as now many approached the spiritual marketplace with a consumerist mentality, or with an eye to a church's social status. Religion has always had its elites; not too long ago, religious professionals were among the few in most communities who were well educated, or even able to read.

Nonetheless, something cybernetic certainly is going on, and it will profoundly affect religious structures, both intellectual and institutional, in the near future. Will its ways of thinking be shallower, or just different, from now? Are the past's great bookish edifices of philosophy and theology the only way spiritual truth can be accessed? There are those who counter that technology is so going to change the very nature of truth, and of reality itself, as to render what we used to think of as deep only the surface of the pond, even meaningless. But first, let's go on to the next stage past information, two-way talk.

ALONE TOGETHER: RELIGIOUS TALK ONLINE

Here is a true example of religion at work online. Patricia, a young woman deeply upset by a friend's cancer, wanted to pray but felt she did not know how, or even if she believed in a personal God, so she went to the Internet, starting with the search engine AskJeeves.com. She went through several links, and in time came to Everystudent. com, a site operated by Campus Crusade for Christ, the conservative evangelical student group. Everystudent presented itself as "a safe place to explore questions about who God is and what it might be like to know God." This seemed right to her; she read the articles and prayed a prayer put up on the screen in a heartfelt way. Then she submitted a query by email: "I think I'm a Christian, now what do I do?"

The response came the very next day, with an encouraging letter and then a book and Bible by regular mail. (She had said to the Campus Crusade worker that she did not want to go out and buy a Bible because her mother, who had dropped out of church long before, might become hostile if she thought her daughter was getting religion.) A month later, when she started at a university, she was directed by email to the local Campus Crusade chapter. She has since become an active spokesperson for her kind of Christianity on her blog and *Facebook* page. She says, "The internet has become an extension of who I am, it is a tool I use to present what I am all about. The way I talk about my faith on my blog or on my *Facebook* provides a reflection of who I am as a Christian."[7]

Moving to a different religious venue, Helen Berger and Douglas Ezzy, writing about teen witches, describe several who first became interested in Wicca (a term used today for witchcraft as a religion) through their peers' interest in the occult, or simply by coming across the word Wicca in a fantasy book a friend of hers was reading. The puzzling term led these curious youngsters to scan the Web, which characteristically led them through Satanism and Paganism to Wiccan sites. One young man said that, "Well, somehow in middle school I got this reputation of sort of being. . . weird and a lot of people thought I was into black magic right off the bat, when I really wasn't. . . So basically, just out of curiosity. . . I went on the Internet and checked out some Web pages on magic and that is how I sort of got introduced into Wicca. . ." He goes on to add that he soon learned that Wicca as a religion is not about black magic.[8]

What can we make of this? Both the new Christian and the Wiccans coming to their chosen religion via the Internet. . .

First, as a way of access to religion, the Internet provides a particularly useful tool to the sort of seeker, most likely young, who is bright, curious, open-minded, but perhaps not too social nor comfortable with family, and doesn't want his or her household to know about the religious seeking. That individual spends quite a bit of time in front of the computer, exploring strange and arcane lore, or looking for urgently needed answers. She or he is certainly not the only kind of person who investigates religion on the Internet, but let's pursue the quest a little further. What does the seeker find?

Much information plus encouraging voices reaching out in response to the search. If you query a particular religion online, posing a question or entering a discussion, like Patricia you will meet a virtual community ready to welcome and guide you. The medium may be *Facebook*, personal blogs, or discussion sites. The invisible congregation embraces all sorts of virtual presences, from lurkers and inquirers to chatty middle-level participants, to those who are, or see themselves as, senior authorities.

Though the nature of the conversation will vary, depending on personalities involved, it is bound to deal with basic questions about the religion, accounts of personal experience with it, and debate over ritual and other practices. Sometimes one may encounter strongly worded opinions on the politics and leadership of the group, tendentious views of what is happening in the world from its perspective, and much else. Open discussion groups, even if limited to registered, that is, insider, participants, can be quite free-wheeling, giving voice to remarkably unorthodox or skeptical angles as well as stock answers.

And don't forget: There are also religious dating sites.

Naturally, religious sites are also of great value to the researcher just interested in doing a general study of a religious group. For if a paper is to deal with real-life religion as it is, it must rise to the challenge of supplying not only a few historical and doctrinal facts but also a feel for what one might call its culture: the kind of people it seems to attract, how they think and live, what they talk about among themselves in reference to the religion, what are their hopes and doubts.

Researchers will find much of this sort of material online now that would have been far harder to obtain before the ubiquitous keyboard and screen—not just the statements of leaders, but also voices less heard before the Internet: the spiritual strongholds and misgivings of more ordinary members, the "public opinion" of a religion. (I recently glanced at an easily accessible discussion site on a prominent and sometimes controversial American religion. Most of the discussants were members, probably birthright, but some of them were clearly questioning key points of this faith in talk with others also raised in the tradition. I was immediately hit by inside stuff it might have taken me, as an outsider, weeks or years of confidence winning to get from wary members face to face. But now I was able to listen in.)

It is important always to keep in mind that this kind of discussion is as worldwide as the World Wide Web itself. These parleys are going on in Hindu India, Buddhist and Shinto Japan, everywhere. A recent book by Mohammed el-Nawawy and Sahar Khamis, *Islam Dot Com*, explores contemporary Islamic blogs and discussion online.[9] The study makes clear how many Muslim voices are out there, not just those of prominent "clerics" or scholars, nor those of militant radicals. Many younger voices are radical in other ways than they, advocating peaceful reform and new ways of looking at an ancient faith in a changed world.

It's possible to go on from religious talk to religious worship online. It is not hard to find examples, from churches that merely offer online videos of their regular services—though if people wanted just to worship by means of this virtual rite rather than actually attending in person, nothing stops them—to churches that are entirely online and finally to whole online religions. In the middle are numerous sites offering the opportunity to submit online prayer requests. Like many online sites, they are often couched in cyber versions of the old and familiar. One displays a picture of an old-fashioned doorbell, saying, "Need someone to pray with? Ring the doorbell. A prayer team member will logon within a min., if available." The applicant is given a place to "sit" in the meantime.

Brenda E. Brasher, writing of how the Internet can create sacred space in cyberspace, describes a site called Cyberheaven, where users can leave memorials to departed loved ones.[10] One could also mention online spiritual counseling, guidance in such practices as religious fasting and pilgrimage, and much else. The Roman

Catholic church has, despite proposals and attempts to set it up, ruled out online confession and absolution as a substitute for the actual sacrament of reconciliation.

However, there is a website for the Sanctuary of Our Lady of Lourdes, the famous Roman Catholic healing shrine in France, at which sick, confined, and poor people unable to visit the grotto in person can make a virtual tour of the sacred site and send a personal prayer to it. Prayers sent by email are burned onto a CD and put into Mary's "mailbox" at the shrine. Some are read daily by a priest celebrating mass at the holy place.[11]

Far less familiar are some of the virtual religions out there: The Church of the Subgenius, The Church of Virus, Electric Messiah, First Church of Jesus Christ Elvis, Technosophy, The Church of the Blind Chihuahua. Many of these look like parodies, a teenage geek's idea of humor. Sometimes, however, there is a certain poignancy to their virtual witness. The Church of the Blind Chihuahua professes to be based on an actual dog that lived in Austin, TX, in the late 1970s, and though unseeing was so loving, forgiving, and faithful as to become a "totem," not of God but of humans as we are in our spiritual blindness, and as we should be at our best, hence the name, and the logo that shows a chihuahua wearing a pair of dark glasses.

What about religion online? As Morten T. Højsgaard has pointed out, most religious communication online is not cyber religion in the sense of being about these virtual "churches" but is about "real people, actual places, established institutions, and so forth."[12]

It is not new religion, just a new means of religious communication, he says. Nonetheless, Højsgaard like others suggests that online religion, from conventional sites to the new cyber-religions, represents one aspect of an evolving human consciousness, in which distances are shrinking to "virtual" immediacy, whether geographical or social or between the secular and sacred. But this does not mean we are suddenly being changed into something other than human.

Arianna Huffington, in an interesting article, proposed that the Internet has now gone beyond its adolescence and into a kind of maturity. "Its adolescence was, like most formative years, filled with late nights, video games, loud music, junk food, and trying to figure out exactly what it wanted to be when it grew up." But now, in adulthood, it is not—as some thought—turning us into machines, but rather has become a machine to help us be more human, through enabling community and connections; it is a tool, not a life.[13] Religiously, this would mean that the Internet as an enabling tool would help us find religious communities, but finding them we would not stop with the Internet and its solitary quests. We could go on to what the screen can never provide, real grown-up face-to-face talk, real hugs and handshakes, real religious buildings and shrines, real feasts and fasts and sacraments.

But does everyone want to go on to face-to-face? Is there really anything lacking in strictly online religion? Is there anything lacking in off-line religion? What do you think?

Certainly there are those who still think, whether it's adolescence or true vision, that the Internet and its virtual reality has hardly left infancy, much less reached maturity, and that as this marvelous child grows bigger and bigger, he will change our reality so much that religion and everything else can hardly help but change unimaginably from what it is now.

To enter this reality, as far as one now can, let us begin with the world of gaming.

GAMESMANSHIP

What happens in a video game? Two basic principles are there. First, there is the original narrative: a backstory that explains how the situation of the game arose, and lays out the task to be accomplished. Second, you start playing, and there are several directions and levels you can reach depending on how well it is played.

Lists of the most popular video games vary, but certainly among the top examples at the time of writing are *World of Warcraft*, *Halo*, *Diablo*, and *Mortal Kombat*, as well as *Grand Theft Auto* and NCAA football and basketball games.

Looking at the first four named, what do we see? A science fiction kind of setting, combined with medieval-style swordplay and fantasy creatures. *Warcraft* began with only humans and orcs (obviously borrowed from Tolkien), but *Warcraft III* and *Warcraft III Reign of Chaos* added more: Night Elves, the Undead, the Draenei and Nagas, together with new units called Heroes. The game takes place on a large maplike terrain, with rivers, mountains, seas, and cliffs, which the player—in the form of his in-game impersonation or avatar—must explore and thereby uncover, in the process establishing settlements, gaining resources, and attacking the grisly enemies of his endeavors. Generally these games can be either single or multiple player programs; in the latter players take the roles of human or other combatants, striving against each other just as they may do in sports simulation play.

In *Halo*, it is the twenty-sixth century, and humans have colonized numerous worlds. A colony on a distant planet has been devastated by alien races who consider human presence an affront to their gods, the Forerunners. The Forerunners themselves seem to have been a wise and noble race who built a ringworld, called the *Halo*, but their misguided worshipers oppose the arrival of another intelligent species.

Mortal Kombat also takes place in a science-fictional universe that includes six kingdoms created by the Elder Gods. These vividly realized realms, each ruled by a sub-deity of its own nature, are worth mentioning for their mythological resonance: Earthrealm, home to heroes; Netherrealm, abode of the most vile demons; Outworld, a land of constant strife; Seido, the Realm of Order, whose dwellers value propriety and precedent; the Realm of Chaos, whose inhabitants conversely observe no law and in which continual turmoil and change are worshiped; and Edenia, land of beauty and artistic expression. The structure of the game was established by the rule, imposed by the Elder Gods, that the folk of one realm can only conquer another by defeating the other's greatest warriors in 10 consecutive *Mortal Kombat* tournaments.

As in the case of many an ancient myth, the appeal of the game's basic worldview, and its artistic and technical mastery, is matched only by its violence and gore. *Mortal Kombat* became famous—or notorious—for the splattered blood and body parts of its warrior confrontations and its spectacular death scenes, which in the United States led to government intervention in the form of rating games as safe for children, teens, or only adults.

On the other hand, mention should be made of a recent game from Poland, *The Witcher 2: Assassins of Kings*, which is also brutal and in which innocent people perish, but in which the mystical warrior, the Witcher, must make moral choices among possible actions, included some involving dwarves and elves, persecuted minorities not unlike Jews in the Poland of the past.[14]

Playing a video game   (MENDIL/BSIP SA/Alamy)

Another popular game, unusual in that it contains no physical violence, but rather exploration of a mystical, magical island, is *Myst*. The player, identified as the Stranger, is brought to the island of Myst through the last page of a marvelous book. He explores this land and its several sub-realms, called *Ages*; in the process he must solve various puzzles and move from one Age to another by means of further enchanted volumes. Clearly, this game opens up the potential of the genre for simulation of mystical, consciousness-expanding adventure instead of the warrior-hero's quest.

Increasingly, games are going beyond the primitive video-game screen to become 3D, and also to include simulation elements. In play like that of *Grand Theft Auto*, *EVE Online*, or Nintendo's new Wii consoles, one can construct one's avatar character (oneself in the game), down to dress and hairstyle, as well as some aspects of the environment. Play can lead into nongame virtual reality activities, like *Gaia Online* or *Second Life*, in which the whole point is to create a persona and world after your dreams, including interaction between your avatar and those of other players, in performances from business dealings to flirtation.

What about the religious significance of the games just mentioned? Good, bad, or mixed?

The first reference must be to the obvious mythological elements in the background of these stories. While the "myths" may be contrived in many cases, obviously they reflect the timeless mythological themes of the battle of heroes and monsters, and of worlds full of spiritual powers visible and invisible, including the common archaic concept of a hierarchy of gods or angels above humans. In *Mortal Kombat*'s Gnostic-type myth, for example, the One Being is said to be the origin of the six realms, whose Elder Gods have divided up the consciousness of the One Being and feed off his essence.

It can be argued that some players probably don't pay too much attention to the backstory mythology; it's basically just a "shooter"-type game they would play the same whatever the characters and their supposed story. I'm not so sure. If we play any game enough, its spirit becomes part of our spirituality, its characters and imaginative vision part of our arsenal of mythic models to set over life. The real myths of any individual, the ones that seep into deep levels of mind and often unconsciously affect attitudes or decisions, can come as well from Internet games as anywhere else.

Our own real and personal myths are not necessarily those ancient myths carefully studied in school, not those *called* myths, but the models and ideals, with stories attached, that are just there in everyday life, in the personal fantasies that lie behind who we like in sports and entertainment, in the unspoken dreams that help determine who we want to be, in what we look for in relationships. If you yearn to be a scientist, do you see before your mind's eye images of an accomplished experimenter making a major discovery? If you dream of a wholly satisfying love affair, do you hear inwardly the story of a great love, whether from myth or modern movie, telling you what it ought to be like? All this is living myth today.

Then there are the remembered older myths that lend language to the otherwise unmythical doings of business, politics, or the laboratory, as when we say a suspected intruder is a Trojan Horse, or we vote for the candidate who resonates best with our personal myths about our country, or we call a desired result the Holy Grail of a particular project.

Myth old and new is essentially religion in story and symbol form. As such, it sets our own stories against timeless and transcendent stories that give them larger significance: This is not just *my* battle against evil; fighting the evil in front of me makes me a part of the battle of all heroes, on this and all other worlds, against evil and the monsters or demons that embody it.

Obviously problems come with this territory. A fundamental issue is that myth, like its video game enactments, tends to reduce characters, including ourselves and our foes, into one-dimensional figures that are just one virtue or one vice. In the real world, where we are all far more complex mixtures of good and bad, such stereotypes can lead to terrible results if not handled very carefully. Nonetheless, all religion is based on some such worldview, and we steel ourselves for moral combat by conjoining ourselves with the heroic perfection of Christ, or Krishna, or a bodhisattva, or the near perfection of a prophet or king of old. If the game helps us move in and out of mythic reality, perhaps it helps, or perhaps it wants to make our world more black and white than it ought to be.

Another aspect of mythic gamesmanship that might be mentioned is the way their settings help create a sense of wonder. If not overdone to the point of obsessive escapism, that is a good thing: It always helps have an inner retreat from the drabness, and the tension, of ordinary everyday life. The fabulous venues of some games, whether outer space or the romanticized Middle Ages, is as good as any so far as evoking wonder is concerned.

It is interesting to reflect on why these two venues, incidentally, seem to be so heavily favored. The worlds of science fiction, of course, have been a dominant modern myth for some time, one that some of us dream of actually entering sometime in the future. In the other direction, we may not literally want to go back to the Middle Ages, but at least since the Gothic novel and the romances of Sir Walter Scott, medievalism has seemed a colorful and adventurous alternative to the present, one in which individual heroism combined with knightly splendor to create a world where one could be a very effective avatar.[15]

It has also been claimed that games represent an idealization of play, and hence of light-hearted attitudes, including ideas that even killing is not serious—one just gets another life. But play can be many things, both in children and adults: trivial and serious, fair and unfair, innocent and mean-spirited, even degrading to certain players. Yet it is rightly said to be, for children and in some situations also for adults, an essential tool for learning the game of life.[16]

Jane McGonigal, countering the frequent assumption that gamers are lazy and unambitious, says that in fact they are working hard to achieve goals whether in the game or out of it and that striving to get to higher levels in the game inspires hard work, learning from failure, and setting ambitious objectives on the job and in one's life.[17] It is said they also heighten hand-eye coordination and visuo-motor skills, such as resistance to distraction—all no doubt important for jobs in today's computerized office, rocket science, and military.

McGonigal also asserts that video games aid in socializing, especially when we play with friends. It's better to play with real-life friends and family, she says, and better to play face-to-face with them than just online. In this case, presumably playing an up-to-date video game with friends is no different than playing old-fashioned checkers or cards with the same friends.

But even distant online playmates can have relationships. Stephanie Rosenbloom begins an article entitled "It's Love at First Kill," like this:

> This is a love story. It began on a hot summer night in Santa Barbara, Calif., when Tamara Langman helped kill the yellow-eyed demon known as Prince Malcheszaar. She was logged into World of Warcraft, the multiplayer fantasy game, and her avatar—Arixi Fizzlebolt, a busty gnome with three blond pigtails—had also managed to pique the interest of John Bentley, a.k.a. Weulfgar McDoal.[18]

Needless to say, more followed. First their two avatars found a quiet place to sit. Eventually, after talking about everything in their lives, "Ms. Langman realized that while she was in the fictional world of Azeroth, she was also on a date." After a couple of more months on online talk, they decided to meet in real as well as virtual reality and were together in both realities from then on out. This is far from the only case in which a game functioned as an online dating service as well as escapism.

Such inspiring accounts are not likely to quiet all alarms about the negative effects of video gaming. Elias Aboujaoude, in *Virtually You*, has explored those dangers as a psychiatrist at some length, and certainly demonstrates that games can be addictive, and in those so caught up in their sorcery can produce delusions of grandeur and illusions of power. After all, in a game you can destroy a whole planet with the flick of a switch. Impulsiveness and indifference to the consequences of one's actions can result too—one gets used to the idea that death is just part of play; one can easily go on to another game or another life.[19]

All this sounds like nothing more or less than what happens to people who get involved in the dark side of the force, or with demonic reality, or in Hinduism with the tantra of the left hand. Such twisted energies, whether articulated in psychiatric or mythological language, are certainly real. Yet it could be argued that video games, like the mythic and horror genres generally, themselves talk us through the bad, and so go some ways to denature it. We might give the last word on this to that contemporary master of horror, Stephen King.

King has stated that the horror story, beneath its surface suggestion of a world full of terror and monsters out of control, is really as conservative as any right-wing preacher or politician in its values. It shows what happens when taboos are broken and people—or other beings—wander beyond the limits of the moral code. They see things out there to make them scream like hell-beings or shake in sheer fright at the margins of madness. In actuality, the modern horror tale or flick is no different from the medieval morality play, which showed Satan and his demons in all their grotesquery, but ended up with God and righteousness on top.[20]

And opening up in back of the video game with all its worlds of wonder and woe is another level, ready to expand the moral, religious, and spiritual awareness in ways guaranteed truly to astound those who have so far only dabbled at the edges of virtual reality.

GATEWAYS TO WONDER

Moving on to that next plane, we might begin with the witness of Jennifer J. Cobb, in *CyberGrace: The Search for God in the Digital World*.[21] As a high-tech public relations consultant also fascinated by the sacred wisdom she sensed embedded in the ancient Celtic sites of Britain and France, she initially felt deeply split between these two worlds. Then one day, realization opened up within her that those two realms, cyber and Celtic, seemingly so different, were somehow linked in worlds of wisdom as they were in her own soul.

She understood that both operated on the level of religious experience, of the sacred and of pilgrimage, because cyberspace is not just dead matter, energy or information linking mind to mind. In surfing the World Wide Web, one moves through an infinite network of pathways that are connected, not in a hierarchical or linear manner, but simply because they are parts of the larger whole of cyberspace. As in understanding Plato's image of the cave, in which we learn that the world as we see it is only shadows, so do the computational webworks challenge earlier views of the universe.[22] For when we enter this quasi-infinite realm of cyberspace encircling the globe, we find ourselves in a place not so much on the material plane as a pure energy continuum of images and symbols like Plato's cave-shadows, bearing information but hinting at still more.

The ancient Greek had argued that we are caught in a cave of matter and can see the real world of ideas only as shadows. He urged the philosopher to emerge from the dark secondhand shadow/matter realm and live in the clear sunlight of pure ideas and their symbols.[23] In a comparable way, cyberspace unites the subjective and the objective at a point where matter becomes pure energy, like thought—consciousness is just quantum phenomena in a higher sphere—and the universe resolves into a single unified, but unimaginably intricate, dance of information moving at the speed of light and thought.

A great deal of cybernetic science is going on in India. That ancient land's Hindu philosophy provides its newest accomplishments with accessible thought tools. An Indian scientist designing a new computer chip told a Western reporter that at the initial stage, "You can simulate a chip. . . but none of it is real. . . in Hindu philosophy the reality is in the ultimate concept: the Brahman. In the Advaita system. . . you are taught there is no duality between you and the Brahman, and that what you believe is physical and hence 'real' is really all maya. So designing a chip can be a bit like maya." Another Indian told him "it was impossible to design or build pages on the Internet if you thought in a linear way, since it changed constantly and was of infinite size. A web page might look like a page but really held a complex web of links. The Internet seemed to be a Hindu concept, a deity with many arms. . ."[24]

Such meditations show the mysterious, sacred meaning of the Internet going well beyond mere postings on religious activities, or games with mythical resonances. For these devotees, it seems now of itself to be a new holy home of life and thought, a new mediating realm between heaven and humanity, like the gods of Olympus or the bodhisattvas of Buddhism, and we are part of it, even the makers of it.

Avatar activities like *Second Life*, in which you enter a world that fulfills your fantasies, and where you can interact in this your alternative home with the avatars of others, whether for ordinary commerce, adventure, or romance, can also put you in destinations made for spiritual adventure and romance. Sites available on *Second Life* include a Zen meditation center; a replica of "St. Mary Abbotts Church" in Kensington, England, where visitors "can take in the stained glass and enjoy the peace and solitude as they search for religious inspiration"; an "ecumenical center for Contemplative Christianity"; and a Unitarian Universalist sanctuary. While these offerings may seem a bit thin so far, no doubt they are only a foretaste of spiritual destinations to come.[25]

To manufacture a whole sacred realm wholesale might seem rather ambitious, if not presumptuous, for us mere humans, even though Cobb does contend that the religious is really within. However, other writers, such as David Noble in *The Religion of Technology* and Erik Davis in *TechGnosis*, have pointed out that in fact human invention and technological development were initially usually accompanied by millennialist hopes that the new tech would be the means to transform the world, a key to the gates of utopia.[26] Whether it was steam power or electricity, communication at the speed of light or flight at the speed of sound, or even atomic energy, idealists have dreamed, and often proclaimed, that this was the discovery that would finally emancipate humankind from slavery to toil, freeing the race for a brave new world of peace, leisure, and noble ideas. All laborious tasks now done by machines, ours could be a society wholly devoted to the pursuit of happiness, in the forms of sport, art, love, and creativity. Though such hopes have never been entirely realized, the dream remains, now computerized.

We are not surprised, then, to find that, as these writers point out, beliefs surrounding this latest and perhaps most provocative technological innovation of all, the Internet, show no small similarity to the scenarios of myth, magic, and millennialism in past ages of faith. Though it came out of the human mind rather than descending down from heaven, might the coming cybernetic city not be at last the prophesied new Jerusalem? Might life in cyberspace, as beings transmuted into cyborgs, be the new resurrection of the body, and the life everlasting?

CYBER APOCALYPTIC

Take, for example, Ray Kurzweil's bestselling books, such as *The Singularity Is Near* and *The Age of Spiritual Machines*.[27] Using the principle known as Moore's Law, that technological innovation accelerates exponentially, Kurzweil postulates that within the twenty-first century, within many of our lifetimes, the cybernetic revolution, above all in its creation of artificial intelligence (AI), will so radically change our lives as to make everything, including of course our spirituality, utterly and unimaginably ahead of where we are now.

Thus, in about 2029, AI will exceed human intelligence, and in about 2045 we will come what he calls the Singularity, the point at which AI achieves the ability to replicate and improve itself at its own accelerating rate. At this point one might think that mere humans would be ready for the trash bin of history, having been suddenly superseded by a far superior, indeed virtually invincible and immortal, intelligence in the machines we once thought were merely our tools. However, as it were on the principle of "if you can't beat 'em, join 'em," Kurzweil predicts that at the same time, nanotechnology will be able to put minicomputers the size of blood cells into our bloodstreams. These tiny allies will both enhance our mental ability, enabling us to download computerized information and calculating ability directly into our brains, connect wirelessly with computers outside ourselves, that is, with the entire sovereign Internet. We will in fact be cyborgs, mixture of man and machine, alloys of our own minds and the mystical universal www.mind. In the process—this seems very important to Kurzweil—we will learn how to defeat death, and these hybrid trans-human beings will not die.

Stephan D. O'Leary, looking at the prospect of cyborgs and their new utopia of deathless hybrids, inquires, "What will we have lost when the transition to the cyborg self is completed? What will we gain, and what will we give up, as we allow ourselves to be implanted with chips that will improve vision, enable hearing, and ultimately allow unprecedented extensions of the human lifespan?" Would we in fact be human, or is humanity necessarily related to the experience of suffering and the knowledge of death? Could such a creature have anything such as human feeling and wisdom?[28]

And would we agree with Stephan O'Leary as he goes on to say, "If acceptance of a wired connection directly into the brain is the price we will have to pay for experiencing 'virtual' reality as indistinct from the 'real,' then I for one will opt out of this future. I don't want to live beyond a normal human lifespan. . . and I'd rather maintain the distinction between the world of sensual experience and the virtual world"[29]?

Whether on as short a timeline as Kurzweil's or not, many cyber prophets predict some such destiny as the ultimate product of the computer revolution. The distinguished physicist Freeman Dyson, in *Imagined Worlds*, predicts that in time, perhaps by the end of the twenty-first century, the emergent technologies of computerized automata or robot-like machines, and that of genetic engineering, will merge. This marriage of the future will birth bio-computers made up of both genes and integrated circuits, both enzymes and electric motors. "In the end, physical and biological components will be so intimately entangled that we will be unable to say where one begins and the other ends."[30]

These remarkable beings, more trans-human than human as we now understand the term, may also profit from what Dyson calls radiotelepathy, the ability of one mind directly to read another, not by "psychic" telepathy, but through the quite scientific implantation of transmitters capable of sending and receiving brain activity in the form of radio signals. Radioneurology is already used in brain research, and the technology is developing apace. Sufficiently enhanced along the lines of Dyson's speculations, it could ultimately become a World Wide Web of consciousness. Humanity could then quickly evolve into a single supermind, a planetary brain no doubt heavily reinforced by direct links to supercomputers—no more need for books, screens, or perhaps even words. Needless to say, this being would be immortal, because even if a single unit like yourself perished, it would be no worse for the whole than the loss of a single cell in your body, and the universal mind would go on with hardly a pause.[31]

The religious and spiritual implications of such a cyber-apocalypse are as staggering as would be its meaning as the culmination—and end—of history and personal life as we know it. Would this be the final judgment and the new heaven and earth, or the reign of Antichrist? Would we be making God out of ourselves and our tech, or a demonic simulacrum of God? Would the planetary consciousness use its immense power for good or evil? What would good and evil even mean in such a world?

Dyson, well aware of the ethical implications of radiotelepathy, points out that Olaf Stapleton, in his 1931 science fiction novel *Last and First Men*, had Martians use it for evil, to marshal their forces into a totalitarian war machine, but for us earthlings, after we acquired it from them, "it becomes a force for good, allowing humans to understand one another better and settle their differences peacefully."[32]But what would it do next?

We will leave such questions, because they are questions for the next generation. By then, in your lifetime, they may be all too real.

And a further question arises: Could we prevent, or opt out of, such a world transformation even if we wanted to? Or is Moore's law of exponential technological acceleration irreversible? Would this be an ultimate test, one way or the other, of humanity's spiritual nature?

SUMMARY

The Internet is affecting religion substantially in a diversity of ways: as a source of religious information both practical and academic; as a forum for religious discussion; and as a way to participate in religion through online worship sites, and even entire "virtual" religions.

On another level, many computer games reflect mythic scenarios, enabling players to imbibe something of the atmosphere of mythic heroism and conflict. Critics wonder if too much game playing leads to detachment from real life, an overly black-and-white mythic view of good and evil, and the idea that problems are solved by firing a shot or getting a "second life."

Going even farther, there are techno-philosophers who speculate that the computer revolution may ultimately lead to a radically new kind of human, or post-human, life that would radically change the meaning of religion as well. Critics ask whether becoming a cyborg or part of a universal database would diminish or destroy the human spirit.

CHAPTER

11

Traveling Together: The Sociology of Religion

Worship in a Protestant church   (James Steidl/Fotolia)

LEARNING OBJECTIVES

After reading this chapter, you should be able to:

- Discuss whether it is true to say that all religion is social.
- Tell how the nature and structure of a religious group itself gives messages about the meaning and experience of the group, by whether it is close-knit or loose, has authoritarian or democratic leadership, and so forth.
- Present the various ways in which a religious group can relate to the surrounding society.
- Discuss the meaning for the sociology of religion of Redfield's concept of great and little traditions.
- Distinguish between established and emergent religion. Describe major forms of each: international, national, and denominational for established; intensive and expansive for emergent.
- Describe the circumstances out of which emergent religion typically derives and some of its fundamental characteristics, such as selection of one central symbol and practice, future orientation, and central, charismatic prophet.
- Briefly describe major types of religious personality.
- Define some leading ways in which religion transforms the society around it.
- Tell how religion interprets history.

ALL RELIGION IS SOCIAL

Think of any religious group of which you have been a part, or have known about, or can imagine being part of. How much does the way others in the group talk about the religion support your own belief in it, and your participation? How much do you find yourself using the same language as they when you are around them and in the religious context? Indeed, can you imagine yourself as having come to this religion totally on your own, without a social context of family or friends, without encountering its words whether spoken or in printed texts?

Religion as we know it is always social, inseparable from the fact that we humans live in societies, in a network of interpersonal relationships, and use language. Therefore, for every religious concept, experience, or practice there is a social form of expression—a group formed, words spoken, a book published. Religious language of itself tells us that religion is social, for language obviously derives from the interpersonal context of human life, even though it can also be used to think within oneself, and to privately name one's experiences, whether of God or pain. A truly private religion would be one in which no words were used, even in one's own mind to interpret it. (Books may be read alone, and thoughts thought alone, but they obviously depend on language, a social construct and tool, and that tells us religion, as we know it, is always social in origin.)

True, people may have subjective yearnings and intuitions and even ecstasies like those of religion independent of any dealings with other people. If our understanding of religion is valid, however, these remain only subjective feelings or musings or even ritualized gestures, unless they are given symbolic completion through words and the experience is related to the social environment.

Think of it like this. Suppose you had feelings while walking in the woods that seemed to you religious. But how could you even think of them as religious, or about God, without using words like religion and God in your own mind? These words, like all words, derive from language, and language is a social thing. We learned it from our parents, friends, school, and community. We give these words meanings that were first given to us by society, and so likewise the divine meanings that lie behind them. (The social background would be all the more the case if our religious feelings came in a religious setting, like a church or temple, where we were surrounded by socially created sacred stimuli.)

We use words and ideas, then, to understand things about ourselves in our own minds as well as to explain them to others. Try thinking through to yourself some half-way complex thought without using words in your mind, the way an animal or prever-bal infant would have to, with only pictures and feelings on the brain, but no words. You will quickly realize that language is just as important as an essential tool for think-ing, as it is for communicating with others. Conceptualization and reasoning—even our most inward thoughts—are products of society, since they are products of language like books. Religious thought and consciousness, of any sort of which we can possibly conceive, are results of our living in societies, though the separate individual has an innate biological potential for them.

RELIGIOUS GROUPS

Religion then is bound up with the way we live, talk, and learn in groups. A *religious group* is a set of people whose interpersonal relations complete for one another the symbolic expression of religious experience. In such a group, we say to ourselves in effect, this religion must be all right, because all these other people think so too. Since the group of itself is a religious symbol, of the *idea* of a church or movement, it also stimulates further experience.

Say you have been converted to a particular religion. You may soon find a group within it made up of like-minded people from that religion. It is a congenial fellowship that completes the initial experience by supporting it, and shows that what you felt is, after all, a shared experience. No doubt, soon enough group and setting will stimulate more experiences along the same line as the initial one.

On the other hand, it is hard to maintain a really different religious belief solely by oneself, without anyone else to talk with about it, or even the knowledge there is anyone else in the whole world who shares it. To put it bluntly, many a widely accepted religion would sound quite bizarre, if not the mutterings of a lunatic, if sud-denly declared by just one person and no one else had ever heard of it. But let even one other person share the beliefs, and you have not a monomania, but the beginnings of a group, perhaps the seeds of a worldwide faith, shared eventually by families and communities over centuries. Then what once was odd becomes sane, acceptable, and socially important. The group is all-important in making belief into religion.

The group also establishes a sense of religious power in the individuals within it. Religion helps one believe she or he can make oneself and the world better through prayer, right ritual, good behavior, and contact with the divine. Through religion the average person can feel effective and important, close to power and ways of changing things the nonreligious world knows not.

The Chinese peasant prayed in temples to gods who were deified high Mandarin officials. In the flesh she or he would hardly have approached such an exalted personage with a peasant's humble requests, but now that they are elevated to temple gods they are, paradoxically, more accessible to the common person. Though she may not have been heard by earthly officials, she could be heard in heaven.

Ordinary churchgoers, troubled by news of hunger and revolution in other areas of the world, mention these places in prayer groups and contribute to missionaries. They believe these gestures help. Religion creates a human-sized, individual-sized world and universe in which, through the religious group, people not only can find meaning for themselves but also may be effective in the larger world and universe.

Let us now examine some styles of religious sociological activity. These range from vast international religions numbering hundreds of millions to private visions shared with one or two others. We'll start with the most common form.

ESTABLISHED RELIGION

That form is the familiar, well-established kind of religion of family and community which has probably long been part of a culture.

Although religion is never really changeless, it does have a side that likes to think of itself as unchanging and that is closely related to the most deeply rooted structures of the society: the churches or temples that were built a long time ago and, ideally, are still thronged with people happy in the faith of their forebears. This kind of religion may be called **established religion**. (The other kind we will call **emergent religion**.)

Established religion comes in many shapes and sizes. We cannot mention every kind of sociological expression it takes, but only a few representative categories.[1] First, there are the **international** and intercultural religions. The major faiths that are truly intercultural are Buddhism, Christianity, and Islam; within Christianity, the Roman Catholic church stands as a unique example of a very large religious institution that is highly international yet centrally administered. Each of these religions has been a bearer of culture to many lands and so has generated in them a particular cultural tone, usually working its way down from the religion's great tradition, which is more international and intercultural than most aspects of the little tradition, described in Chapter 9. They have also appeared in each place as a new religion that has come into that culture within historical time. Thus, each exhibits a degree of tension with the earlier indigenous religion, like Buddhism and Shinto in Japan or Christianity and remains of the previous pagan culture in Europe, or Native American religion in the Americas.

The message of large established religions is that to be in rapport with the Divine, it is better to be aligned with a culturally rich and very numerous movement. Truth is not just for a handful, and is not even just the possession of one nation or one culture. One should not say one's own land or way of life is the greatest, beyond criticism; for the international and intercultural religion says there is an even higher perspective from which that land and that way can be judged.

These faiths are overwhelming majorities in most places where they are found, though minorities in some—as is Christianity in Japan and Buddhism in America. They have the experience of being both broad-based religions and tiny withdrawal groups, depending on circumstances. Where they are greatly preponderant, they are examples of established religion.

Besides such international institutions, established religion can also be manifested as **national religions** when embraced by the majority of the population, whether predominant churches, such as the Church of England or Lutheran churches in northern Germany and Scandinavia, or Roman Catholicism in Spain, or largely one-culture religions, such as Hinduism in India or the traditional religious complexes of China, Japan, and some African societies.

Finally, established religion can be expressed through denominationalism. A **denomination** is a particular institutional and sociological organization within a larger religious tradition. In effect, it ministers mostly to the spiritual needs of its members, probably a minority of the total society. In what has been called a denominational society, of which the preeminent example is the United States, a number of parallel denominations include the great majority of practicing religionists. They are considered legally and sociologically equal, though they may differ in belief and in one's personal opinion of their social standing. In America, long prominent denominations of colonial background were often considered more socially respectable than newer movements like Pentecostalism, though this is changing. In effect, the denominations all together collectively represent the society's established religion.

The United States is a denominational society in a special way, because of its immigrant and slavery background—indeed it is worth noting that it is the only large society in which a majority of citizens traditionally belong to religious bodies which were not established, and often oppressed, in their immigrant forebears' country of origin, whether "dissenter" groups like Puritans (Congregationalists, now United Church of Christ), Baptists, and Quakers from England, Roman Catholics in Ireland or Poland, or Jews in most parts of Europe.[2] Denominational society characteristics are also shared by some British Commonwealth nations and, in many respects, Japanese Buddhism. Indeed, in today's **pluralistic** world, in which established religion in the traditional sense is fading rapidly, and as we have seen independent Christian and other movements are spreading in force to the ends of the earth, the whole planet is becoming more of a denominational society.

At the same time, denominations also seem to be losing the importance they once had as primary centers of religious identity and loyalty in the United States and Europe. While the majority of churches in the United States still have a denominational brand, and denominational headquarters still handle much of the administrative work connected with religious institutions, ordinary laypeople increasingly select churches with much less of a sense of denomination than their grandparents did. About half the Protestant churchgoing population now attends a church denominationally different from the one in which they were raised. Moreover, a growing number of independent churches are arising, above all the so-called megachurches, churches with many thousands of members and elaborate programs, which tend to be either completely independent or very tenuously connected with a denomination. By 2012 about one-fifth of Protestants were attending independent, nondenominational churches, and denominational headquarters were cutting budgets and staff.[3]

Conversely, it is mainly in connection with denominational societies that another manifestation of established religion, called **civil religion**, has been discussed.[4] This name pertains to a belief that society as a whole has a sacred meaning apart from individual religious groups. In the United States, for example, it is the "religion" (cutting across many denominations of a pluralistic society) of patriotic holidays, such as the Fourth of July and Thanksgiving, and the belief that the nation as a whole has a calling from God and a divine destiny. It has been argued, in fact, that there is a civil religious interpretation of American history that parallels biblical history—the coming of the Pilgrims corresponding to the call of Abraham, the Revolutionary War comparable to the Exodus, Washington like Moses, the Civil War the redemptive suffering of this new Israel, and Lincoln—murdered on Good Friday—like Christ in his wisdom and sorrows.[5] Whether one goes this far or not, there is something spiritually American yet nondenominational that many people feel and that expresses itself in certain attitudes, holy days, and places like the Arlington National Cemetery.

Whether international, national, or denominational, a church connected with established religion tends to have certain characteristics. Because it has a long tradition and an institutionalized structure, in theory it generally has strict, clearly defined doctrinal and moral positions. In practice it has to be fairly tolerant as long as the integrity of the institution is maintained. Since it is the nominal religion of the great majority of the people—of those who have not made a self-conscious, deliberate choice to be something else—it must find ways to accept people in all stages of spirituality. It has ways of incorporating infants into its symbolic network through baptism or comparable **sacraments**; has a conspicuous role in traditional festivals and community celebrations; its architecture is old and monumental; its leaders are spokespersons for and to the community on moral, and perhaps political, issues of general concern.

The established religion enforces, probably through some pattern of constraint and reward, the normative values of the community. While offering paths to sainthood for those called to follow them, it provides ways for those of more modest ambition to pursue meaningful spiritual lives in some hope of commensurate reward. In predominantly Buddhist countries, the Buddhist institution offers monks opportunity to make the ultimate meditations that lead to Nirvana and laypeople opportunities to gain merit through good deeds and devotional practices that will result in a desirable reincarnation.

Structures of the established religion tend to parallel those of society as a whole, especially on the national and denominational religious level. In America they have democratic parliamentary forms, in Japan they have hereditary leadership, and in India they center around the charisma of saints.

Every kind of religion has its own message about human nature and the way to transcendence. Established religion says that one can find ultimate meaning through living within the religious traditions of one's community. It says that sufficient religious truth can be known by most people, not just an elite. Referring back to the great and little tradition idea introduced in Chapter 9 on Popular Religion, established religion indicates that even though the great tradition of such a religion may be more ample, the way it is practiced by the little tradition—that is, as popular religion—is adequate and perhaps even more devout, so this religion operates alike in universities and peasant communities. Although popular forms of the faith may superficially appear superstitious, they still represent what has been called implicit faith in the central religious truths. Established religion, then, says it is better to participate in the normative religion of one's relatives, neighbors, and friends than to break with them for the sake of some individual calling.

One could ask whether established religion as a concept still has the meaning today that it did in the past. Modern secularism, loss of belief or interest in religion, and revolutionary changes like those in China have greatly altered the meaning of such a notion as the normative religion of a society. But it still helps in understanding a society to know what its traditional established religion was.

Three Kinds of Religion

Now let's conclude these observations by considering three ways of being religious that can all be found in established religion, and often also appear in the emergent. These are the **traditionalist style**, the **liberal style**, and **conservative style**.

Traditionalism maintains religion basically as it has been known, particularly by people who grew up with it and have not yet been exposed to anything else—a rapidly dwindling number in today's world. But there are groups sometimes called neo-traditionalist who, in full knowledge of other options, choose to maintain the religion in its traditional form, sometimes adopting attitudes similar to those of the fundamentalist, below.

Religious liberalism is another reaction to the exposure of traditional religion to the world outside the tradition: to other cultures, philosophies, and scientific knowledge. It takes the new worldviews seriously, and says that real truth, including religious truth, must be consistent with real truth in all other areas of knowledge. Religious doctrine, therefore, must be interpreted in a way that is in harmony with the best philosophical, scientific, and social thought of the times, though seeking to add to them a transcendent and ethical dimension. Liberals usually see religious truth as important but always partial and developing; it is therefore to be held in a way that preserves large areas of inner and outer freedom.

Conservative, sometimes called fundamentalist, religious responses to change go the other way. It says the important thing is that religious doctrine be consistent with itself and with its sources, such as scripture, and if that puts it at odds with the current intellectual and scientific world, then it's just doing its job. For true religion is not supposed to be harmonious with the present age, but to stand over it, in judgment and as a summons to a greater truth. Authentic religion's beliefs are parts of highly consistent systems based on scriptural or ecclesiastical authority. Conservative or fundamentalist religionists hold that absolute truth and absolute authority are real and available. The view that human nature needs absolute truth and authority may be reflected in family and social values as well.

EMERGENT RELIGION

Emergent religion contrasts with established religion, but has roots in it. If established religion in a culture is a pervasive sea, emergent religion is a volcanic island breaking through its surface and roiling the waters around it.

The definitions of the word **emergent** suggest several salient characteristics of the sort of religion of which we are now speaking. As an adjective, <u>emergent</u> means something arising out of a fluid which heretofore has covered or concealed it, or suddenly appearing, or coming as a natural or logical outcome of a situation of change, or arising as novel in a process of evolution. The word can also indicate an entity that stands out, as a tree above the forest.

These definitions really apply quite well to the counterpart of established religion. New religions emerge out of the fluid sea of popular religion, perhaps suddenly, perhaps in response to situations that impel change such as wars or conquest or new cultural contacts, perhaps as a result, like a mutation, of a process of evolution. They are likely to be recent, for the tendency is for an emergent religion to become a new established religion, or a part of an ongoing complex that makes up established religion, within a few generations—unless the novel faith disappears. A few emergent religions, like the Amish, remain emergent in the sense of maintaining a distinctive visibility indefinitely; they do not mix and never really become part of the establishment.

An example of emergent religion is Tenrikyo, one of the new religions of Japan, although it is now over a century old. Tenrikyo traces its inception back to 1838, in the last decades of old Japan before its phenomenal modernization that began in 1868 under the Emperor Meiji. The final years prior to the end of the old regime were times of increasing economic trouble and civil unrest. The traditional popular religion persisted, but popular frenzies of dancing and pilgrimage swept through from time to time, more and more associated with prophecies of immense change.

A church of Tenrikyo, one of the "new religions" of Japan   (CulturalEyes-AusGS2/Alamy)

In 1838, the son of a prosperous farmer near Nara suffered intense pain in his leg, but a series of shamanistic healing sessions seemed to give him temporary relief. The shaman's female assistant would go into trance and be possessed by a god, whom the shaman would then worship for healing. On one occasion the shaman's usual assistant was not available, and Miki Nakayama, the farmer's wife, substituted for her. When she went into trance, however, a very unexpected thing happened: a voice spoke through her lips saying "I am the true and original God" and declared that he would use Miki as his residence in this world.

From then on, according to Tenrikyo belief, Miki Nakayama was the instrument and shrine of God. She lived a busy and holy life; she healed and gave forth words and writings that are believed to be messages of God. Above all, she taught a sacred dance that reenacts the creation of the world by the one God and indicates the sacred spot where the creation of humankind began. A fundamental Tenrikyo belief is that by knowing and dancing out the creation of the world by God the Parent, as the Creator is called, humanity can be brought back into original harmony with God.

Now, as Miki instructed, a pillar stands over the creation-spot, and it is the heart of a vast temple, which in turn is the hub of Tenri City, a religious center with administrative headquarters of the faith, pilgrimage hostels, training schools, and a university. Pilgrims come from all over the world to this site, and the sacred dance is performed around the pillar.

Thus, belief in the revelation of God through Miki Nakayama has grown and prospered. Tenrikyo began as a small and often-persecuted band around the foundress. Since her death in 1887, it has become a fairly large and well-organized institution, with an ample structure of classes, churches, and services, as well as missionary zeal.

Other emergent religions could be cited, from the twentieth-century **cargo cults** of some colonial areas—typically centering on a prophet who says that if the native people will show enough faith, ships like those of the white men will bring them rich goods— to a number of well-known religious movements in modern Europe and America. Nevertheless, the story of Tenrikyo adequately illustrates several of the most important features of emergent religion.

First, it emerges at a time of change, when many people feel that traditional values are being shaken and the future is uncertain. (This is not too much of a qualification, since most periods are experienced as times of transition and uncertain future to the people actually living in them, becoming eras of calm and stability only in the retrospective vision of later generations caught up in their own times of change.) In times of change, some classes of society feel left behind or want ways to comprehend and relate to the changes. Emergent religion usually first takes root among groups of people who are relatively powerless within society or not at the center of change— peasants in Japan, colonial peoples, minorities, the young, women. It provides them, as an elect who are in on a divine secret, with a compensatory, even greater power.

The emergent religion says that God is doing something in the changes that only they know about, or else that he is doing something even greater than what is happening in the outer world and that this will climax in the near future. This teaching enables the believers to accept change by understanding it in the religious language familiar to them from the older popular and established religion, but with a new twist. As the institution grows, it enables believers to take part in an activity with a new and modern feel, similar to that of the modern government and business to which they may be outsiders. But the new religion represents modernity in a form they can understand. Today new religions may be more efficiently organized, and use more up-to-date media of communication effectively, than older faiths.

Second, the emergent religion typically makes the jump from established religion to the new by selecting from out of the amorphous sea of tradition *one* God, place, teaching, practice, and group as its focus, to give it a new, crisp, distinct shape.

While established religion tends, without saying so, toward many objects of veneration—a number of saints and heroes as sacred personalities, of charismatic preachers, of possible institutional affiliations, of sacred churches and places—when emergent religion breaks through in that scene, this tendency goes into reverse. As in the case of Miki Nakayama, emergent religion singles out and absolutizes particular examples of these manifold forms. It selects one shaman or spiritual person out of many candidates, one God out of many polytheistic candidates, one sacred place out of many shrines of established religion, one religious practice or rite out of many possibilities. This selectivity gives it a unique identity within the prevailing religious complex but at the same time sets up the likelihood of conflict. Conflict, however, is the stuff of life for emergent religion, since it enhances the distinctiveness that it craves.

Another characteristic of emergent religion is that it is likely to emphasize a future orientation. It will probably teach that in the near future a utopian kingdom, or a divine judgment that will vindicate its claims, will occur. This sort of prediction can only enhance the new creed's appeal to people caught in a time of rapid change when the future is unsure. Religions offering a wonderful prediction of the future should find their niche.

Eschatology, or religious teaching about future events, suggests that what the God can do in the future is greater than what any human changes (about which one may in any case feel anxious) can bring about. It says that what you have already seen is nothing compared to what God or the gods will bring to pass.

Emergent religion usually centers around a charismatic personality—an individual who by the radiance of his or her own personality and the appeal of what he or she is, rather than any structural authority, draws people. The centrality of the charismatic person, rather than the institutional appeal of the faith, is very important. Unlike established religion, which can depend on the allegiance of all those not sufficiently moved to protest against it to make a self-conscious adult choice to be something else, emergent religion is mainly made up of converts who *have* such a choice—which gives it a reservoir of highly committed persons but also means that it must maintain a level of intensity sufficient to counteract the natural pressures of family, community, and inertia that keep people within the established religion at their particular place.

In terms of practice, emergent religion generally displays not the wide variety of prayer, rituals, and kinds of services catering to many kinds of people of large established faiths, but focuses on a single, simple, sure practice—a particular chant, rite, method of meditation—done with the intensity that, like other aspects of the convert's choice, compensates for all that is given up and undoubtedly produces initial results. But all intensity tends to wear down over time.

The upshot is, in fact, that after two or three generations most emergent religions become established religions or, at least, a part of whatever established religion is prevalent. This is a result of the process called by the sociologist Max Weber "routinization of charisma"—when the grace and teachings communicated in unexpected ways by the religious founder come to be channeled, or are said to be channeled, through an institution in particular times and places. What he or she did spontaneously now comes through sacraments; the original chosen disciples are succeeded by professional leaders legitimated by ordination in a lineage from the founder; what that founder said on odd occasions now comes through preaching at regularly scheduled services.

Two basic kinds of emergent religion should be distinguished, **intensive** and **expansive**. The pair corresponds with what some sociologists of religion have called respectively *sect* and *cult*. But those terms no longer have appropriate connotations.

Intensive emergent religious groups withdraw from ordinary society in favor of a more intense and rigorous commitment to major symbols of the established religion. Within American Christianity, they would be groups such as Seventh-Day Adventists and Jehovah's Witnesses; within Judaism, distinctive Hasidic groups. They tend to be legalistic, feeling ordinary followers of the same religion are lukewarm or hypocritical and not really serious about the religion in which, for cultural reasons, they find themselves. Sometimes, as in the case of the Amish or Hutterites, intensive religionists are communal. More often they are not, but their members tend to have a high involvement with the group and relatively little relationship, except perhaps for evangelistic purposes, with the society outside of the intensive circle. The intensive religion communicates a message that apart from a very high level of group involvement and intensity of commitment, the full realization of religion's ability to make one feel like a real self and have access to infinite life cannot be realized.

Expansive emergent religion, on the other hand, withdraws from ordinary society in order to found what is, in its adherents' eyes, a more broadly based experience than that of the monochrome religion of the society. It seeks to combine elements of the established religion with new ideas and teachings from science, from far-away places, and from inner vision. In America, examples would be movements such as Spiritualism, Scientology, and various meditation and devotional movements brought in from India or Japan. Expansive religion is generally centered more on mystical experience than on the truth of particular rules or tenets. It is, however, just as likely as **intensive emergent religion** to be centered around loyalty to a particular charismatic leader and some simple, sure technique for spiritual transformation. It may also be just as much a withdrawal group. Expansive groups, though, are more likely to have outer, diffuse circles of followers of milder fervor, since it is possible to study the teachers and practice the meditation or whatever with a greater or lesser degree of separation from the ordinary world.

It should be emphasized that no specific religion is established or emergent per se; these categories are dependent not on the nature of the religion but on its role. A religion can be emergent in one place and established in another, or it can be one at one point in its history and the other at another. Buddhist faith is established in Thailand and Japan but apt to be emergent in America, just as Christianity is emergent in missionized countries. Buddhism and Christianity were both emergent at the time of their inception but became established within a few generations. As has been indicated, most religions that survive become established within two or three generations because of routinization of the original charisma and because more and more of their members are born within the faith rather than converted.

RELIGIOUS PERSONALITIES AND ROLES

Intertwined with different kinds of religious groups are the different sorts of religious personalities that go with them, sometimes as their founders.[6] Each of these, in his or her own way, communicates a message about what it means to be religious. The number of conceivable types of religious personality is very great; perhaps every religious person is in the last analysis his or her own type. Several that are largely shaped by distinctive and well-known roles within religious history are listed here. These are not so much psychological types as role types, created as much by the times as by the person. They each also imply a particular kind of religious group interactive with their kind of religiousness. The groups will also be described here if they have not been elsewhere. Here they are:

The Shaman. The shaman is an individual in primitive or archaic religion who, having become master of spirits that initially seemed likely to drive him or her mad, now uses them in public and private séances to heal, divine, and perhaps guide him or her to the worlds of the dead and the gods. The shaman's performances, which will follow traditional patterns, are centers of the experience of transcendence for the community and reinforce the sacred view of the universe. The shaman is typically the spiritual leader or activist in a particular tribe or community, in which she or he has a definite role. This community often sees itself as a definite spiritual as well as social organization, with its own gods, myths, and rites, and their shaman, together with the chief in other roles, is their mediator.

In later societies, many persons have exercised a shaman-like vocation, whether called guru, adept, mystic, evangelist, or something else, insofar as they have depended on their own independent charisma more than a social role to attract followers and influence spiritual life.

The Priest. This category includes other religious titles, such as bishop, minister, or rabbi. It embraces religious specialists, commonly professional, who hold office through heredity or training and whose primary function is to perform customary religious rites or services in expected ways. While he or she may be personally devout and have had a personal call, it is the priest's position that assures his or her status. This would ordinarily be obtained through a recognized process of education, selection by appointment or election, and formal ordination. The priest mediates the sacred, without necessarily internalizing it, objectively through rite and word and thus grants the community the necessary ongoing symbol of its presence afforded by institutions and their reliable custodians. Some religious specialists combine attributes of shaman and priest, fervor being a part of their role. The priest of course has a religious community, though it may vary greatly from a traditional faith to a modern voluntary church.

A Taoist priest or monk on a sacred mountain in China   (BOISVIEUX Christophe/Hemis/Alamy)

The Monk and Nun. This category includes many sorts of holy people as well, such as the sadhus of India and some Sufi mystics of Islam. Unofficial approximations of its way can be found in the lives of some Protestant missionaries and members of contemporary religious communes. Not all approximations of the **monk and nun** type are even celibate, but the point of the type is to live a life outside the ordinary structures of society (yet in reality accepted and provided for by the religion) that exemplifies the ideal spiritual life as understood by that tradition. The way of the monk and nun has three goals: to save one's own soul; to exemplify the ideal way of perfection; and to support the tradition through prayer, teaching, and service. It is often (though not always) lived communally for mutual help in this difficult way and to exemplify the ideal social as well as the individual model of perfection. Because its ideal is total dedication, this way may have (when well lived) an aura of poverty, abstinence, and inward holiness about it. Organizations are characteristically monasteries or convents where all live the life together under the rule of a superior, sometimes called an abbot or abbess. Lives are closely regulated, all rising, praying, dining, and working at the same time, following the rule or directions even in small matters, owning no personal possessions, and wearing distinctive and identical garb. All this witnesses to the totality of religious commitment.

The Layperson. The **layperson** is one who lives in a community and participates in its religious usages but is in no way a specialist or professional. He or she may be a farmer, fisherman, or townsperson who is an ordinary worshiper. His or her place in the religion is not to be defined only negatively, by what he or she is not. Rather, it is a definite and distinctive role, with its own pattern, and is structurally essential to the religion as a whole. His or her religious life has, in practice, different goals and self-interpretation from that of the priest or monk. It is more related to supporting family, community, and ethics and to prayer and receiving limited but specific benefits from the deities, as well as ultimate transformation or salvation. In the total life of the religion, the layperson's role is to provide its material support, to make its rites and teachings practically possible by serving as their recipient, and to show the universality of the religion's worldview by manifesting how it structures society and how it can have some kind of effect on the life of everyone.

The Philosopher and Theologian. These are likely to be priests or monks, but some have been laypersons. Their special role is to interpret the religion in terms of the intellectual tradition of their culture. Often they are in seminaries (schools devoted to the training of clergy) or universities.

More subjective and spontaneous religious types appear out of a person's inner need rather than out of a wish to fill (even if on the basis of a deeply felt calling) a role or niche already existent in the tradition. The following are some subjective types:

The Founder. This very important religious type, the founder of a major religion, like the Buddha, Jesus, or the Prophet Muhammad, together with his disciples, have been presented in the Chapter 2 of this book. His, of course, is a particularly comprehensive and influential role.

The Prophet. The word "prophet" literally means to "speak out," and contrary to popular usage great religious prophets like those of the Hebrew Scriptures have not been primarily predictors of the future, but persons who "spoke out" about issues of their own times. (They may, however, have predicted an often dire or unexpected future as a consequence of how things were now.) The earliest prophets seem to have been persons who spoke in trance, not unlike shamans, but in course of time became more like orators and then writers. The message often centered around righteousness as then understood, whether as ritual purity, true worship, moral rectitude, or social justice. The prophet has sometimes been contrasted with the priest. Not all prophets were opposed to formal worship, but whereas the priest is typically concerned primarily with proper worship, and therefore with the social-cohesion role of religion, the prophet is more an individualist, and more concerned with inner attitude and outward ethical behavior.

The Mystic. The mystic is usually within a particular religious tradition, although sometimes, like Kabir in late medieval India, he or she is on the borderline of two and occasionally may seem genuinely independent. The mystic's emphasis is on attaining special states of consciousness considered direct, unmediated experience of the religious reality. Understandably, to the mystic these states are more important than religious structures or rites, although their attainment is not necessarily inconsistent with the latter. Within the religion, the mystic has a role as an exemplar of its spiritual reality. He or she may be a teacher and writer, though of course many mystics have not been literary. Many mystics have attracted a small, often informal, group of followers around them. Sometimes, like the early followers of St. Francis of Assisi, or of many Sufi mystics in Islam, they have evolved in time into important religious orders.

The Reformer. The **reformer** works within a tradition rather than starting a new one but shares with the founder some sense of a new historical situation that requires a new application of the tradition, particularly in relation to the structures of the social order and the religious institution's own structures. Although the reformer feels these structures ought to be changed, he or she does not believe that the essential doctrines of the faith need to be altered. Rather, the reformer has the tradition highly internalized; he or she does not need to depend on its outward forms and so can urge their extensive modification. In internalization, the reformer may be like the mystic, but unlike the mystic the reformer is critically aware of outward structures and wants to make them conform to the internalization.

The Denominational Founder. We have talked about the denomination as a religious group, especially important in America, situated between the major religion, like Christianity or Buddhism, and its local expressions. The founders of these denominations, then, have had a significant role. Typically, they are the kind of persons able to link Great and Little traditions; we have mentioned John Wesley, founder of Methodism, in this position. The denominational founder is also typically a reformer within the greater religion who emphasizes a particular aspect of it—salvation by faith, believer's baptism, trust in Amida Buddha—as key to rightly living the whole, and has the organizational ability to effect changes, not in the whole faith, but on a segment of it—his or her own following.

The Popularizer. This category applies to a wide gamut of effective and charismatic preachers, Sufi saints, Buddhist missionaries, and Christian evangelists. The **popularizer** is not particularly a reformer or necessarily a mystic (though some have been these, too) but is a dynamic and attractive person able to appeal to the masses as well or even better than the founder. He or she makes no pretense of being original but is a transmitter of faith from out of his or her inner and contagious fervor, chiefly through rhetorical performance. The popularizer may well be an important link between great and little traditions.

Other types of religious personalities could be cited—saint, seer, convert, penitent, and mystagogue are among those that have been used in lists similar to this. But these should be sufficient to give us a sense of the wide variety of persons who make up the religious world.

Note the kinds of religious organizations these imply: the tribe, the temple, the monastery or convent, the founder of prophet with a small informal band of disciples, the great church with its internal reformers, the denomination as a crystallization of that reform, the informal religious or spiritual movement of a popular teacher.

THE TRANSFORMATION OF SOCIETY BY RELIGION

Having considered the effect of historical situations and surrounding society on religion, the reverse, which is equally important, must be noted. That is the transformative impact of religion on society. Religion and other social factors work both together and in reaction against each other to produce spirals of change. Here are some ways religions have effected change in society.

Image of the Normative Nature of Society

All religions contain an image of the normative nature of society, a picture that says, "This is how it ought to be." It is not always explicit but is implied in the fundamental myths and symbols of the religion itself, especially in the life of the founder and his or her relationship with disciples. But the scriptures, and all the literature of a spiritual tradition—novels, poems, plays, pictures—give us images of an ideal social order, looked at rightly. For they honor persons living rightly according to the ideals of the religion; we need to only extrapolate to envision what a society would be like if everyone lived this way, like the saints and heroes.

Worship and Sociology of Religion

The worship and sociology of a religion also offer models of how it conceptualizes the ideal community, and such models work on deep levels in the minds of people. Whether the worship and the style of leadership imply highly structured forms or mystical freedom, charismatic or routinized leadership, egalitarian or hierarchical patterns; whether worship has mainly verbal or nonverbal symbolism; whether participation is passive or active for most—all these deeply affect the social and political values of the community as well. One can see how Hinduism with its ideal of the holy man prepared India for a leader like Mohandas Gandhi. Denominationalism in America with its models of routinized, egalitarian, and democratic leadership, together with the charismatic styles of leadership that emerge especially in revivalistic evangelicalism and Pentecostalism, help explain American social and political styles.

Historical Impact of Religion

There is also the direct historical impact of religion, especially of the international religions that have conveyed cultures, literary heritages, and political systems across continents. Buddhism, Christianity, Islam, and Confucianism have influenced cultures outside the one in which they began, and not only through formal doctrine. They have come into new lands as models of a different and often seemingly more advanced style of civilization. Commonly they have either come together with new imperial rule from outside or been catalysts in major political changes internally. At the least, the new religion offers a sense of history, maybe even a discovery of history, that implies the possibility of change in many areas of life by showing that values can be revamped.

Prophetic Teaching and Religious Demands for Justice

Religions have also produced leaders across the centuries who have directly demanded change and justice from those in political and economic power, from the Hebrew prophets to Gandhi in India. In modern America, a good example would be a religious figure like Martin Luther King, with his dream of a land of racial equality, in which his children and everyone's would "one day live in a nation where they will not be judged by the color of their skin, but by the content of their character." Such great persons, speaking boldly out of a moral vision shaped by religious teachings, have had a vast if sometimes indefinable influence on history.

Religion has always had two sides socially, the conservative side in which it is a support for the traditional way of doing things, and the radical, in which speaking from outside and above the existing order, it says there are abuses which must be righted and ways that do not please God or the gods. Both must be kept in mind in assessing religion.

RELIGION AND THE INTERPRETATION OF HISTORY

Finally, religions affect history because they affect the way history is interpreted, understood, and even remembered. Thus they affect the way history is written and the way we come to know it. Confucian historians in China, for example, taught their sense of morality through the medium of history by making good things occur during the reigns of virtuous sovereigns and bad things under evil ones. In the Hebrew Scriptures, a comparable pattern is discernible, often emphasized by the prophets, of God's favoring faithful rulers and passing negative judgment on unrighteous rulers and people alike. The Hebrew Scriptures also offer an emergent overall historical pattern of God's leading his people into the Promised Land and forward in life in a covenant with God.

Many religious groups have understood history in terms of major religious institutions remaining true, or falling away from the true faith and in need of reform. This is the Protestant view of Christian history, or more recently the Mormon. Often secular history is likewise interpreted in light of such large-scale religious historical periods. The great sociologist Max Weber, for example, associated the rise of modern capitalism with the Protestant Reformation, and its focus on the righteous living a good life in this world rather than a monastery, on families rather than celibacy, and on nationalism rather than a universal church. All these qualities, he said, tended to favor modern capitalist rather than medieval feudal organization of economics and society.

How is the religious understanding of history changing today?

RELIGION TODAY

We might end this chapter with a look at the sociological status of religion today, particularly among younger people. In *After the Baby Boomers: How Twenty- and Thirty-Somethings Are Shaping the Future of American Religion*, the sociologist Robert Wuthnow presents several findings.[7] Taking three major segments of American religiosity, mainline Protestantism, evangelicalism, and Roman Catholicism, over the years 1972–2002, he found his cohort's affiliation to mainline Protestantism declined by about half. In the other two groups, evangelicals and Roman Catholics, affiliation was marginally decreasing or increasing. The number of the religiously affiliated declined in this age range by 20 percent, and actual attendance at services by 6 percent. Only about a quarter were regular churchgoers. Between 1998 and 2008, another poll reported that the number of 18–39 year olds saying they were "spiritual but not religious" grew from 11 to 18 percent.[8] No doubt this can be fitted in with the do-it-yourself attitude toward religion mentioned previously in connection with popular religion.

A 2012 Pew Research Center poll found religious decline in the United States, especially among young people, to be continuing. For the first time, less than half of Americans, 48 percent, identified themselves as Protestant. The percentage of "nones," those who said they were atheist, agnostic, or "nothing in particular," claiming no religious identity, had jumped from 8 to 20 percent in two decades. About a third, 32 percent, of people under 30 were in this category. Many of them, however, professed to be "spiritual but not religious," to believe in God and spirituality in some

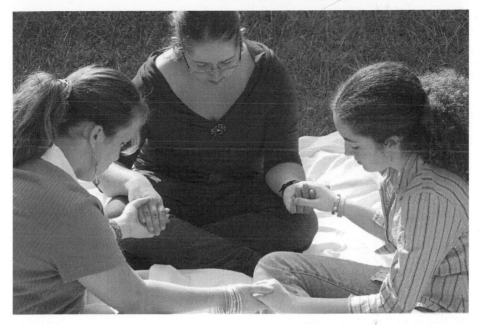

Young people in a small informal prayer group   (Lisa F. Young/Fotolia)

way, but outside of organized religion. Speculation as to reasons for this shift ranged from backlash against excessive involvement of religion in politics to a broader trend away from formal organizational involvement, evident in the recent decline of many clubs and societies whether religious or not.[9] The major 2012 figures broke down to 48 percent Protestant, made up of 19 percent white evangelical, 15 percent white mainline, 8 percent black Protestant; 22 percent Catholic; and 19.6 percent unaffiliated.[10]

What lies behind this data? As a sociologist, Wuthnow in *After the Baby Boomers* did not attribute the appeal of his three religious strands to their inherent theological appeal so much as demographic factors. Evangelical Protestantism has the advantage of being rooted in rural culture in which people marry younger and have larger families than in mainstream or liberal Protestantism. (Nonetheless, as evangelical Protestantism has become more middle-class, its younger adherents have begun to adopt more "liberal" lifestyles if not beliefs, and membership has recently stabilized or even started to decline, as the 2012 Pew Report suggested.) Marriage, Wuthnow says, is the most consistent indicator of religious participation, and today's general trend in urban and relatively liberal sectors of society toward later and later marriage and childbearing—if there is marriage and childbearing at all—clearly has had a negative effect on church attendance among these influential classes.

Here are a few more sociological observations, these from the overall U.S. population, not just youth, reported in another source, Mark Chaves' book *American Religion: Contemporary Trends.*[11] The data is largely based on polls taken between the years 1972 and 2008. In this period, the stability of American religion was generally impressive, as was the way the United States is far more religious than most other comparable nations. There were certain areas of notable change: a decline in belief that the Bible is the inerrant word of God; a rise in what this author calls "diffuse spirituality," especially among young people, who say they are "spiritual but not religious"; a rise in the growth of those who say they are not religious at all, to nearly 20 percent by 2008; and decline in the appeal of religious professions as a vocational choice, especially for young people; increasingly the ministry, priesthood, or rabbinate is a midlife career change rather than an early decision.

One could go on to mention other factors in the culture affecting religion, from the changing role of women to the pervasive presence, already discussed, of the Internet, which undoubtedly influences religious participation directly or indirectly. But this should be enough to give an impression of how sociologists think of about religion. They recognize, above all, that people take part, or don't take part, in religion for many reasons other than formal belief, and all this can be measured and charted— not precisely, but enough to give an idea of trends that will shape the spiritual future.

Indicators like these, of course, keep changing. Perhaps by the time you read this, other data and trends will be in. But these examples are suggestive of the kind of work sociologists of religion do. That work is very important for seeing religion as it is, "on the ground," not just in the realm of ideas.

There are those, however, who would say that religious truth ought to be determined by criteria other than what are the current trends, or the beliefs of one's family, ethnic heritage, or peer group. In Chapter 12 we will look at some of the means proposed by philosophers for determining truth in religion.

SUMMARY

All religion is really social, deriving from the social nature of human beings. Even private religious experiences are conditioned by our social nature through the use of language to interpret the experience to ourselves as religious; without such words and concepts as *God, sacred power,* so forth, religion as we know it would be unimaginable, and language stems from society.

The great importance of society to religion is also seen in the role of religious groups. Those with religious visions typically try to form groups based on them, for a group gives the vision legitimacy and an accepted role in society. Religious experience becomes more real as it is shared, and the structure of the group itself tells much about its nature and message.

Important messages are also conveyed by the way the group interacts with surrounding society. A large, deeply rooted religion virtually coterminous with the society tells us that truth is broadly based; a small withdrawal group, that it is best found in a small, intense group.

An important distinction is that between established and emergent religion. Established religion embraces both great and little traditions insofar as they together are the stable, dominant religion of society. It may be expressed as a great international religion like Buddhism or Christianity, as a national religion like Hinduism, or as a denomination like Methodism or baptism.

Emergent religion refers to new religious movements which emerge out of established religion. It may be intensive, striving to practice the dominant religion more strictly and devoutly; or expansive, bringing in new ideas and practices, perhaps combining them with local ones. Emergent religion frequently arises in times of uncertainty and rapid social change. It tends to focus on one central symbol and practice, to be future oriented, and to be built on the authority of a charismatic prophet.

Religion produces distinctive types of personality and personal roles. Those that are basically structural include the shaman, priest, monk or nun, layperson, and philosopher or theologian; those more subjective or spontaneous are the founder, mystic, reformer, and popularizer. They are defined in the word list later.

Religion serves to transform the society around it through the image of the normative or proper nature of society its stories and ideas suggest, through its moral commandments and literature (even though these may not always be followed literally), through the social message embedded in its worship and organization, through prophetic teachers who call for justice, and through the impact it has on the history of society when it arrives, often bearing an outside culture as well as faith.

Religion also affects societies by interpreting their histories, describing historical events as divine judgments, redemptive suffering, calls for crusades, or meaningless illusion. All these ideas affect the behavior of individuals and societies in the present.

Religion today is in flux, as it often is, with much stability but some apparent softening of religious commitment and participation.

KEY TERMS

cargo cults, p. 174

civil religion, p. 171

conservative style, p. 172

denomination, p. 170

emergent religion, p. 169

established religion, p. 169

expansive emergent religion, p. 176

intensive emergent religion, p. 176

international religion, p. 169

layperson, p. 178

liberal style, p. 172

monk and nun, p. 178

national religions, p. 170

pluralistic, p. 170

popularizer, p. 180

reformer, p. 179

sacraments, p. 171

traditionalist style, p. 172

CHAPTER

12 Truth Messages: The Conceptual Expression of Religion

Traditional image of God the Father, painted 1885–1896 by Victor Vasnetsov   (Vasnetsov, Victor Mikhailovich (1848–1926)/Tretyakov Gallery, Moscow, Russia/The Bridgeman Art Library)

WAYS OF THINKING ABOUT GOD

As a transition from psychology and sociology of religion to philosophy, let us look at another recent American demographic study, one concerning different ways of thinking about God.

A 2006 survey by researchers from Baylor University concluded that Americans tended to have one of four different concepts of God: the authoritarian God, the critical God, the distant God, the benevolent God.[1] (5 percent said they were atheists.)

The 32 percent who embraced the authoritarian God believe that God has strict rules, is angry at those who violate them and willing to punish those who do so, even through seeming natural disasters like floods and earthquakes. Fifty-one percent of these people attend church weekly, and nearly half believe in the literal truth of the Bible; they also want government to be based on religious values.

Another 16 percent affirmed a "critical" God, one who has values and an unfavorable view of society, but does not intervene in this world to punish ill-doers, though he will subject them to judgment in the afterlife. Only 10 percent of these went to church weekly, and few felt it was necessary to convert others or make government conform to religious values.

The 24 percent holding to a distant God sees God as uninvolved; it is up to us to decide what is right or wrong. God is, in fact, essentially impersonal and more like a cosmic force. About half of them never go to church, are open-minded on questions like gay rights and abortion, and have a higher average income than the other groups.

Finally, on the other hand, the 23 percent who see God as benevolent—gentle, forgiving, helpful—see God as active in their lives, answering prayers, caring about their suffering. About half of them strongly advocate Christian values for the rest of the country and world, while the other half support tolerance above all.

No doubt many of us have feelings, perhaps strong feelings, about which of these "Gods" we prefer, if we believe in God at all. But how do we decide, apart from our own feelings, which one is *right*? Indeed, how do we decide if a God exists at all—or if there is a divine reality, does he/she/it correspond to the traditional Western concept of a sovereign personal God that seems to be presupposed by this survey?

First let us look at various ideas of the divine, then to the issue of determining truth among them.

GOD

Virtually all **religion** affirms the reality of being, knowledge, and bliss greater than the human, and power to go with these attributes. Generally, this belief is expressed in belief in a **God** or gods—self-conscious centers of being, knowledge, and power superior to humanity, upon which ordinary humans must depend and make prayer and offering for their well-being. Even when this ultimate being is not personified, as the Dao, Nirvana, and Brahman of Daoism, Buddhism, and some expressions of Hinduism, respectively, there are personal gods and Buddhas between the ultimate and ourselves who refract its power and so are symbolic personal manifestations of it. Significantly, however, in Daoism and Buddhism the superior beings who now personify ultimate being were once human.

Three basic understandings of divinity can, in fact, be specified. They may be understood in light of H. Richard Niebuhr's understanding of God as *center of value*—that which, as the touchstone of meaning, one cannot go beyond.[2] **But such a center of value could be personal or impersonal, and expressed as one or many.**

First, God can be thought of as an **impersonal absolute**. To those who believe that God must be impersonal, personality such as you and I have is seen essentially as a limitation. Because we can think about only one thing at a time, there are always millions of things we are not thinking about. This shows how small and circumscribed our personality-based consciousness is.

Furthermore, personalities such as ours are really constructed out of various human desires, anxieties, defenses, and cosmic ignorance. Think how much who you are, in your own mind, is based on what you want, what you like, what your dreams and ambitions are. Such a consciousness provides a poor model for God. Better, according to impersonalists, to understand God as pure being and consciousness without the hindrance of personality—let the Absolute be like an unstained mirror in which all things rise and fall, itself untouched by their vicissitudes. The human correlate is that it is those moments when individual personality is most subdued—in deep meditation, in scientific contemplation—that we best know, or realize, the divine.

We might add that the God of impersonal absolutism is often thought of, like the Brahman of Vedanta Hinduism or the Dharmakaya (body of dharma or, roughly, the form of universal truth or reality) of Mahayana Buddhism, to be one with the universe and all that is. This view is often called **monism**, or oneness. Vedantins actually prefer the term nondualism (advaita; not two), saying even oneness is a concept and this God is beyond all concepts, and Mahayana Buddhists say emptiness (sunyata) in the sense that it is a realm of no beginning, end, or place of attachment, but always changing. Instead of perceiving the oneness, though, we see the world as many different things because of our ignorance of its true nature as One, and our "superimposition" of our ideas based on attractions and distractions in our limited minds.

Some western philosophers, such as the ancient Stoics and Baruch Spinoza, have been unqualifiedly monistic.

Second, God can be thought of in terms of **personal monotheism**. In the Judaeo-Christian-Islamic tradition, this belief considers the absolute power of the universe to be personal, but personality far beyond human limitations. God is personal, but personality at its best. Personal monotheism, therefore, can speak of God as having a sense of purpose, as loving, as being the eternal friend. Its best argument is this: although God may be infinitely greater than personality as we know it, personal existence is the highest form of existence we do know, so we can do no better than to start by thinking of God as personal on the model of our own personalities and then try to expand this idea to infinity.

The God of personal monotheism is often seen as transcendent, that is, standing outside the universe though its Creator, having a relation with it not of identity or oneness but of love, and also of judgment and guidance. It is natural, therefore, that this God has often been spoken of as universal Father, Lord, or King.

Finally there is **polytheism**, belief in many gods. Polytheism, as Paul Tillich sagely observed, is really a matter of quality rather than quantity—the point is that multiplicity of gods creates a cosmos of very different tone from belief in one center of value. It suggests that every old tree, golden grove, rushing stream, and ponderous mountain may have its gods of independent mood, as does every fertile field and city, and every changing human occasion, from love to war or business to contemplation. At best they may belong to some hierarchy; otherwise they may seem, as often does human life itself, to be running off in several directions at once. In any case, polytheism presents religion not as forcing all of life around a single center of value, but as reflecting our usual fragmentary experience of life and the world. But it sees all these many fragments opening up in back, so to speak, toward transcendence. The apparent polytheism of Hinduism, Buddhism, and Daoism, as we have seen, often goes together with belief in an impersonal absolute underlying all the gods and immortals.

DETERMINING TRUTH IN RELIGION

But again, in all this, what is true? Some people, in fact, may reject the word *true* and only ask what in religion has *meaning*—*what*, other words, would provide a workable symbol system for the individual concerned. I have had vehement discussions with students about whether truth in religion can be ascertained, or has only meaning or value for the individual.

Nevertheless, let us keep the word *truth;* I cannot quite persuade myself that there could be real meaning or value in a religious experience or symbol one was not convinced was founded on some sort of truth, though it may be far beyond the apparent, superficial "truth" of the experience or symbol. The means for determining what is true in religion are diverse, however, though not as varied as the beliefs themselves. Yet it is fair to note that different sorts of beliefs carry with them distinctive styles of verification. Belief in a sovereign creator God is likely to include an appeal to reason; belief in salvation and afterlife is likely to include appeals to personal experience and teachings accepted on **authority**. The following are some major approaches to determining truth in religion.

Reason

This approach is based on the presupposition that the mind can know truth through the honest and unbiased use of its capacities to work through logical process from pure premises to their consequences; and the presupposition that fundamentally the universe is orderly and works by cause and effect. If these presuppositions are granted, it seems justifiable to assume that a logical process can parallel the way things are when it starts from accurate data and is procedurally flawless. It would then yield up real truth, even to knowledge of the God who is the source of all other truth.

The most famous example of an approach based on **reason** is that of Thomas Aquinas, the great philosopher and theologian of the thirteenth century, noted for his five proofs of the existence of God. These are, first, the cosmological argument, as it is often called, from the motion of all things in the universe, which requires an unmoved First Mover; the second, similar to it, that the chain of causation we see all around demands a First Cause; the third, that the fact of existence ("Why is there something rather than nothing?") calls for a Necessary Being; the fourth is an argument from comparatives—if we say something is better or more beautiful than something else, an absolute standard, the Best or Perfect Beauty, is indicated; the fifth, sometimes called the teleological (from Greek *telos*, "end" in the sense of "ultimate purpose") argument, and sometimes the argument from design, says that things in this world are clearly designed for a purpose, and therefore indicates a Designer.

Other commonly invoked arguments of the same rational type, but involving observation of human society as well as of nature, include the moral argument,

St. Thomas Aquinas   (St. Thomas Aquinas Reading, c.1510–11 (fresco), Bartolommeo, Fra (Baccio della Porta) (1472-1517)/Museo di San Marco dell'Angelico, Florence, Italy/The Bridgeman Art Library)

which says that all human societies have standards of morality, often broadly similar (i.e., sanctions against murder and theft), thus there must be a divine Lawgiver who implanted these ideas in our consciences; and the argument from general consent, pointing to the fact that all traditional human societies have had some kind of religion, hence the probability there is something real behind it.

Most interesting of all, perhaps, is the so-called **ontological argument**, advanced in the Middle Ages by Anselm of Canterbury (1033–1109). As Anselm puts it, it goes roughly like this: God is said to be the greatest possible being. A being that exists is greater than one who does not exist. Therefore God must exist.

This argument has been often supposedly refuted and dismissed as simply ridiculous wordplay. Thomas Aquinas argued against it, even though it obviously has some kinship with his third and fourth arguments above. Yet philosophers have never quite been able to let it go, and down to the present have wrestled with it and sometimes defended it in a modern form. The eminent twentieth-century theologian Charles Hartshorne argued with Anselm that if God is possible, then he must exist, since the opposite—a God that was possible but did not exist—would be absurd. Therefore, the real task of theistic philosophy is to show that God is not impossible.[3]

Alvin Plantinga, in a similar move, advanced a form of the argument which acknowledges it is impossible to prove or disprove the existence of God flat-out, but a philosopher can demonstrate that it would be rational to accept his existence. Using controversial formal logic, he goes on to argue, in his so-called "Victorious" argument, that if God's existence is necessarily possible, then such a being necessarily exists. Plantinga also makes a case that the knowledge of God is comparable to our knowledge of other persons; we cannot absolutely prove that a certain other person exists (she or he might be just a fantasy or "projection" on my part), but if the other acts like a person, and it is possible for him or her to exist, it is reasonable to conclude that the existence is real.[4]

On the critical side, other philosophers, such as the Mahayana Buddhist Nagarjuna, of approximately the first century CE, and David Hume (1711–1776) in Britain, as well as more recent "analytic" philosophers, have used reasoning processes to show the limitations of reason, of cause-and-effect thinking, and of language itself. They would say that most reasoning, including traditional proofs of God, is really circular and proves no more than what is implicit in the way the original premises are put, which in turn is based on our human modes of perception. To say the need for a First Cause proves God only works if we equate the words God and First Cause—but what if the First Cause is something other than God as traditionally understood, or if there is no First Cause, or if not everything has to have a cause?

(Perhaps it is the mind, not nature itself, in which everything is intricately interrelated, that sets up the neat patterns of cause and effect from which we extrapolate a First Cause, or that isolates out of infinite variety phenomena we call evidence of purpose because they happen to parallel what we as humans can understand as purposeful. It is this kind of quagmire that the modern revivers of the ontological argument have been trying to avoid; by saying the issue is not whether God can be proven, but whether he is possible.)

Reason as a means of determining truth in religion has the advantage of seeming to be as independent as possible from emotion or bias. Critics point out that this is not so much the case as practitioners of reason may assume; a façade of reason can mask decisions made on quite different grounds or be based on premises themselves assumed on nonrational bases. You want something, so you set up reasons to justify your wants. As true of wanting to believe in God as anything else, so they say.

Furthermore, reason is said to be cold and even inhuman—a poor basis for determining something as warmly human as religious commitment. Reason is not especially in fashion today as a way to determine truth in religion. Many people are suspicious of it and prefer to follow the late twentieth-century emphasis on experience as the royal road to spirituality and personal growth. If you have experienced something, we tend to say, that is better than merely deducing it (or criticizing it) from the high plane of reason alone. Perhaps we need to have a chastened rebirth of confidence in reason; although it can easily go awry, it does affirm a precious human capacity, the power of the mind to think.

Experience

This is the great alternative that stands against reason in the minds of many. Whether in conversion, mysticism, or simply gradual growth through worship and reflection to subjective religious surety, felt **experience** of religious reality convinces in its own way. It seems beyond doubt or at least adequate for the individual. Its advantages are that it is accessible to all regardless of intelligence or education, it has immediacy, it is something that involves the whole person, and above all it provides religious motivation at the same time that it gives conviction. As we have seen, experience, from the ethos of do-it-yourself religion to the near-death experience, seems to be particularly in vogue in the postmodern late twentieth and early twenty-first century, as faith in traditional institutions and their classic philosophies fades.

Weighty objections, however, can be made against depending on experience alone as a religious guide. One can never be sure whether or not some psychological explanation is possible. Furthermore, intense and convincing experience can be found in all religion; one does not find that it points to any particular truth. If one tried to determine what is religious truth from religious experience in general, rather than just one's own "truth," one would quickly be very confused about everything except that there *are* such experiences. (One may even be confused by personal experiences; those of one person are often far from consistent, and in following them exclusively one can be swept far out to sea on tides of emotion and subjective imaginings.)

Usually one's religious culture does much to explain the content of a religious experience. The experience itself, say a sense of the numinous or transcendent, is not the same as its interpretation. As we have seen, if you say you had an experience of God or Christ or a bodhisattva or of a certain god, *that* interpretation was certainly based on the religious language available to you, and so came out of a tradition.

It would perhaps be safest to say that although certainly religious experience is real and significant *as experience,* we need to think deeply about what the experience is saying and from whence it comes. There may be important guides to truth and meaning in it, but we must be aware of where the interpretation came from.

Empiricism

This method bases claims to truth on direct observation of external things, rather than on inward experience or reason. It is the method usually favored by science. A number of possible **empirical** tests of religious truth have been advanced by religionists. Eighteenth- and nineteenth-century philosophers such as William Paley, making much of the teleological argument, drew from alleged evidences of design in nature to support the existence of a Designer.

Others set store in claims of prayers answered, lives changed, and the beneficent effects of religion on human history to support its truth. Still others show that data of the sort produced by psychical research—telepathy, cases suggesting reincarnation or survival of physical death, nonphysical movement of matter—tend to affirm the religious world at least by demonstrating invisible forces and realities.

Some go further to say that the existence of miracles, the soul, and life after death can be affirmed in this way, and so validate much of traditional religion empirically. We cannot assess the many empirical arguments for religious truth here. We can point out, however, that in an age when science, in which empirical data and testing are of crucial importance, has such great prestige and use, it is natural that empirical arguments in religion should become increasingly used, even as they have always (in prescientific or nonscientific forms) been central to popular religious advocacy. Whether they have much of a future in philosophical religious thought will depend on whether religion comes to parallel the sciences in method and kind of knowledge sought or whether it is essentially perceived as something very different—perhaps more akin to the poet's way of "knowing"—for which such quasi-scientific proofs are peripheral.

Authority

For millions the real touchstone of religious determination of truth is an authority—scriptures, tradition, church, pope, guru, and so on. Arguments from authority, of course, are finally dependent on other arguments, those by which the authority is established. These are often arguments from reason, experience, and empiricism, the last often generalizing from ways the authority can be shown to be correct. To say something is true because the Bible or the pope (or Vedas or sutras or a guru) says it is true is meaningful only within a context in which that authority is accepted. Arguments from authority not only deliver a **content message** by affirming the point in question, but also deliver a structural message by reinforcing belief in the authority.

Related to authority is the argument from Testimony, that is, from the reported experience of others prepared to testify to what religious faith has done for them. The testifiers may be figures from the past, or contemporary persons speaking directly. In some churches and religions, such testimonials are an important part of religious practice. Of course, the testimony of others, and its interpretation, should be assessed in the same way as other arguments from authority, or from experience, in this case another's rather than one's own.

Immersion baptism, reflecting personal experience, biblical and testimonial authority, and the sociological expression of religion   (Design Pics Inc./Alamy)

Sociological Factors in Religious Preference

Sociological considerations, such as we discussed in Chapter 11, do not precisely argue for truth but for meaning and value, although they may be virtually a form of an argument from authority as general consent. For many people sociological criteria are immensely important. The operative determinant for them in affirming religious statements is that the statements are affirmed by a group important to them—given groups, such as family or ethnic tradition; or peer groups, activity groups, and other groups they want to feel a part of. Usually when people use such grounds to decide on religious belief, ultimate truth is not an issue; it is either taken for granted or handled relativistically ("This is our way; it's all we know. We follow our way and others can follow theirs") or pragmatically ("This must be true because it works for us"). Sociology does not answer all the questions that a highly philosophical mind might raise, but it indicates one of the main things a religion ought to fulfill—a sense of group coherence.

Existential Choice

This approach is based on the premise that religious truth *cannot* be proved by means extraneous to the real nature of religion, which is belief or commitment. Means such as reason, empiricism, sociology, and the like are really distractions that only lead to false sorts of religion since they set up something less than God, or the absolute, as the real object of worship, be it the human mind, scientific method, or society. True religion can only be seized by faith, meaning a choice *not* based on such secondary support, but made totally freely— out of a free choice of what kind of person you want to be and how you want to live your life and expressed through what you affirm is ultimate.

The approach of **existential choice** was classically stated by Søren Kierkegaard (1813–1855) as mentioned in chapter 6. He said that the evidence for and against the existence of God in the philosophical arguments are equally balanced; from the vantage of the human mind, as much can be said on one side as the other. Therefore, whether one believes in God or not is pure choice and that is the way God *wants* it. God wants belief based entirely on faith freely given, the "leap of faith," not conditioned even by the pressure of logic.

Søren Kierkegaard   (akg-images/Newscom)

One must decide and one gets what one decides for. You can choose no God, or perhaps a "God" who is merely a God of reason or of social convention, and live a fairly comfortable life, quite possibly a church-going life, devoted to aesthetic gratification—including fine music in church—or even admirable ethical goals. Deep down, however, one feels in these ways of life alone a kind of emptiness. Aesthetic and ethical religion were, for Kierkegaard, lesser than the religion of real faith.

You can also choose a truly religious life of faith and commitment to the ultimate God, who may be neither the God of the philosophers nor the God of society, and whose way may be hard, but who embodies the highest meaning given to humanity. It is through choice that one comes to this truth, but it is not choice that makes it true; rather, religious truth is a special kind of truth accessible not to reason or the other means but only truly discoverable in a decision for that which is greater than oneself.

ARE RELIGIOUS BELIEFS IRREFUTABLE?

The advantage of an existential choice is that it cannot be refuted. If you believe something simply because you choose to believe it, there is really nothing anyone else can say. Some would suggest, however, that all religious beliefs are actually of this character; although supportive arguments from reason, experience, consent, and so forth can be brought in, religionists easily shift from one to the other. After lengthy argument, one sometimes wonders if it is possible to prove that any beliefs are *untrue* as long as they are held as religion.

According to certain rules of modern logic, however, a statement must be falsifiable (i.e., one must be able to show how it could be proved wrong) or it cannot really be considered verified as a newly deduced truth. Without falsifiability, it is only a tautology (i.e., something that says in different words what you started out with). Ask the person you are arguing with what it would take to prove to him or her that a strongly held belief is *false*.

An example is the affirmation "God is Creator," as in the God-as-First-Cause argument above. One can support belief in a Creator through arguments such as the cosmological, but it is hard to think of an equal argument that would prove God is *not Creator* if one is thinking in terms of God and creation at all. This is because the two terms really imply each other by definition, at least in mainstream western religious thought. What is God if not a Creator, and what is a Creator if not God? So just saying "God is Creator" doesn't really add anything to just saying "God."[5]

The same goes for the kind of experiences many cite as proof of a religion's truth. A mystical vision has a religious meaning for practitioners of a religion—though particulars may vary with religions. Hindus have visions of Krishna and Roman Catholics of the Blessed Virgin Mary. Many religions cite other miracles. Nonreligious people easily deal with visions as psychologically explicable projections, and miracles as overly credulous accounts of random occurrences.

As the great philosopher David Hume said, miracles may happen, but there could never be *reasonable* cause for believing in them since by definition they go against reason. It also seems to be the case that there is no religious phenomena for which reasonable (i.e., nonreligious or at least nonsupernatural) explanations could not be adduced by nonbelievers.

One could argue, with the philosopher Ludwig Wittgenstein at one stage in his philosophical career, that religious statements are "language games" with only internal reference within the circle using them. If you have ever been part of a fairly intense religious group, or any kind of club or profession with its own jargon, you know how much words are used in special ways that have a special meaning for the group. This is partly because knowing the lingo is itself a sign of belonging, being in the inner circle. That can be a good feeling.

The downside is the way this game cuts you off from equally intimate dialogue with people outside the circle. You can't really talk or argue with people who don't share the insider words, you can only preach at them—that is, try to bring them through conversion into the circle where that language pattern is meaningful because one has associated it with important experiences. Language game religion, then, can neither be proven nor disproven because there is really no outside umpire to rule one way or the other.

But can anything be proven—or disproven? The philosophical theologian Charles Hartshorne, already mentioned, argued that a valid "proof" of God's existence would not actually prove God, which may not be possible, but what it *would* do is to show the intellectual price paid by rejecting God.[6] This is apparently the way existential choice is made. Making or not making the "leap of faith" is an issue of what you gained or gave up.

A supposed proof of God, then, actually just shows what one gives up if one elects to live in a universe in which God is not. Without God, you can do anything but it is all finally meaningless, and intellectually you have to give up on a lot of big questions, like why does anything exist at all, and why am I who I am and not someone else.

With God, you give up much on the worldly side, if you then go on to live a life consistent with a divine reality, but you get to see yourself part of a much bigger pattern than yourself alone. Going back to the language game circles, you see that, whatever circle you are in, the price to be paid for staying in the charmed circle of one religion or another, or of nonreligion, is denying the others: other circles, other games, other lives as real as our own.

ESSENTIALISM AND DECONSTRUCTIONISM

But is there anything special about religion and "God-talk" at all?

The use of terms like transcendence, the supernatural, and the sacred, not to mention God, has come under considerable criticism in recent decades. The philosopher Richard Rorty (1931–2007) has charged such terminology with **essentialism**, that is, believing that the subject, in this case religious reality, has a definite independent nature. We should "fight free of the old Greek distinction between the apparent and the real," instead looking at the pragmatic meaning that a symbol of, say, a supposedly transcendent, supernatural, or sacred reality actually has in the particular situation. Perhaps it is in fact nothing more than a social convention, or a relic whose former meaning is practically forgotten. In any case, Rorty claims many people are, in Max Weber's words, "religiously unmusical." They just don't get it, and their perspective deserves as much credence as that of the devout. This philosopher thereby rejects the notion we could use reason, religious experience, or any other such path "to reach an ahistorical, God's-eye overview of the relations between all human practices."[7] Be content with living the life set before us.

As we saw earlier, "essentialism" has been much criticized in religious studies by scholars like Jonathon Z. Smith and Russell McCutcheon. They hold that we should not presuppose any unique, special, *sui generis* (of its own type) character in religion, but approach its study through many disciplines as we would anything else. Nonetheless, most ordinary people probably assume that religion, whether you like it or not, has a special quality because of its relation to the invisible realities and the "unseen order" of which William James spoke.

Certainly religion should be approached through several disciplines—psychology, sociology, philosophy, etc. as we have tried to do in this book. In that respect, religious studies is like other interdisciplinary studies on some campuses, such as Women's Studies and Black Studies. In them too one could ask whether or not there is something "essential," some essential nature, to being a woman, or an African. Or is such an idea only constructed by scholars, or students, writing papers?

When it comes to religion, as we have seen the use of the word ranges from very narrow meanings to include such phenomena as Elvis and Disneyland. The very use of the word "religion" often stems from some kind of belief about religion. Certain people insist theirs is the only real religion, while others like to say their faith is "not a religion," using that term for the "man-made" faiths of others. How do you think the term religion is best used?

The related philosophical movement called Deconstructionism, associated particularly with the French thinker Jacques Derrida (1930–2004) has broadly attempted a similar critical task. This line of thinking is also labeled post-structuralist, in that it takes issue with precisely those kinds of patterns or structures, such as sacred and profane space and time, that a historian of religion like Mircea Eliade sought to place over the phenomena of the religious world to make sense of them.

Structuralism, following the linguist Ferdinand de Saussure and the anthropologist Claude Lévi-Strauss, teaches that structures declare their meaning through binary oppositions: good/evil, day/night, and of course Eliade's sacred and profane. But Derrida insisted that in each case we must look at text and context, that is, the meaning of those "structures" in their particular setting. We need also to look at the meaning in terms of participants', or believers', individual life-story, consciousness, and total situation, as in family and community. To put it briefly, one person's sacred may not be the same for another person.

Derrida's deconstructionism of such concepts as reason, tradition, religion, even God, was severely criticized for its alleged trashing of much that is sacred and vital to the maintenance of a stable society. Yet he contended all he was trying to do was help people think clearly, understanding how slippery even the most sacred words are as they are used in different texts and contexts. He wanted to show that such words from God on down have no simple meaning, but are an interweaving of many voices and many arguments. He himself professed a love of what he called the "undeconstructible," a vital reality beyond all the shifting words and concepts, but for that very reason inexpressible in them.[8] Derrida was willing to call the attitude one has toward this reality "faith," not faith in any particular belief, but what he called "faith without religion," a universal attitude necessary to life itself, and what is necessary after everything else has been deconstructed.[9]

What philosophy of religion works for you?

THE NEW ATHEISTS

Or perhaps no philosophy of religion works for you. Lately there has been much talk about the new atheists: bestselling authors and book like Richard Dawkins, *The God Delusion*; Victor J. Stenger, *God: The Failed Hypothesis*; Christian Hitchens, *God Is Not Great*; and Sam Harris, *The End of Faith*.[10]

Little impressed by fine-tuned arguments out of technical philosophy such as those we have just rehearsed, they have come at God mainly with a tough-minded scientific mindset, arguing that God is not needed to explain the universe or human consciousness.

Here is what they say.

Plain naturalism is sufficient to deal with the natural world, and what other world is there? Science can do the job well enough on its own; the questions it leaves unanswered are also unanswered by religion.

Scientific cosmology, for example, does not need to postulate, as did Thomas Aquinas, creation *ex nihilo*, out of nothing; the argument from a first cause or prime mover is pointless since today's cosmology, like most ancient philosophies and religions outside the western monotheisms, sees the universe as beginningless and endless. Jim Holt, in *Why Does the World Exist?*, records conversations on the great philosophical question, "Why is there something when there might have been nothing?" with a set of colorful, brilliant philosophers, physicists, and cosmologists on the cutting edge of a new era of computers, quantum theory, and multiverses that may be leaving traditional theology and metaphysics behind.

The Russian physicist Anrei Linde suggested, half-facetiously, that our universe could have been created by a computer hacker in a previous universe with some knowledge of physics. The German-American philosopher of science, Adolf Grünbaum, contended vigorously against the validity of the question, "Why is there something . . . " on the grounds that it presupposes that the "natural" or prior state of affairs would be for there to be nothing, in which it is the appearance of "something" that needs to be explained. But since we see and feel "something" all around us, why should it not be the other way around? "Something" is just be the ways things are, needing no special reason—which is indeed the way it was and still is except where the Christian doctrine that creation must be *ex nihilo*, out of nothing, has had its baleful influence. And there is always the question bright children like to ask when told God made the world, "Then who made God?"

Then there were those savants who affirmed that quantum logic and mathematics requires every possible universe, down to the last subatomic variable, to exist out there somewhere in unbounded space and time, a dazzling concept . . . worlds without end, literally, and on many worlds no doubt every imaginable or unimaginable dream, and nightmare, is realized. Even the "Big Bang" at the start of our particular universe was nothing special, only one among many, no doubt an infinite number, of Big Bangs.[11] (One could also mention that, despite the *ex nihilo* tradition, the first chapter of Genesis could be interpreted as saying that the dark waters over which the Spirit of God moved at the beginning, though representing chaos, were nonetheless preexistent matter out of which our world was made, as in most other ancient myths and philosophies of the Beginning.)

Evolution does not require a Designer, the new atheists say, and in fact if there were one he did not do a very good job of it since much in nature, and even in human anatomy, doesn't really work all that well, if you're honest about it. (Humans do not seem planned as well as could be to resist sickness and suffering, not to mention the occasional genetic defect, but only to live long enough to reproduce, nurture offspring, and perpetuate the species, which is more important than the individual; Dawkins was also the author of *The Selfish Gene.*[12])

Nor does the human mind need cosmic consciousness; our consciousness is no more nor less an evolutionary adaptation than legs or eyes. Indeed, the mind and body as they are leave plenty of occasion for suffering from both physical and mental pain, and as with most antireligious writers, their most forceful argument is really the problem of evil: if God is both all-powerful and all-good, why is there so much suffering in the world?

Much of the passion of these writers, however, is left for their blasts against the ill-effects of religion and religious institutions on society. Much is made of the all-too-frequent historic opposition of religion to science, free education, and democracy, and its role in fomenting war and oppression. We will return to that argument again in Chapter 15.

Just as few of the new atheist arguments are really new, so is the response of religious philosophers down through the centuries. Science can tell how, but not why; it can give method but not purpose, and just to say there is no why, or purpose, does not respond to every instinct to which religion—or human nature itself—gives rise. Moreover, critics allege the new atheists hold to a shallow belief in progress and rationalism, as though bigger and better science could solve all problems, despite the ambiguous nature of much technological and scientific development. Better minds and machines often cause as many new problems as they alleviate old ones.

Then religious critics come along to insist, like the existentialists, that, whatever may be said on behalf of atheism from the strictly scientific or rational point of view, it leaves one with a pointless existence in a mostly dead universe, living a life without meaning or hope, ending only in the eternal silence of the grave. The other side responds that, much to the contrary, life without the burden of God can be joyous, free, and loving in a way those in thrall to faith can hardly imagine.[13]

The debate is far from over, and one good result is that all sides will have to do a lot of explaining.

Religions, of course, have teachings that go far beyond just the existence of God, and the creation. They also canvass concepts of human nature, reasons for evil, salvation, the end of the world, and the life after death. It is beyond the scope of this book to lay out all of them in the various religions. However, by way of example, in Chapter 13 we will look at various perspectives on the afterlife.

SUMMARY

God may be thought about in several ways, as authoritarian, critical, distant, or benevolent.

The divine nature may be seen in impersonal, monistic, personal, or polytheistic terms.

Conceptual beliefs—what religions think and say about such great issues as God, the soul, or the afterlife—are not the whole of religion, but they constitute a very important part of the spiritual life.

A basic religious concept, of course, is that of God or gods. God or a god may be defined as a conscious center of being, knowledge, and power superior to the human, upon which ordinarily humans must depend or have relations of prayer and offering for their well-being.

Ways of determining truth in religion are reason, including the First Cause and Ontological arguments; experience; empiricism; authority; and existential choice. There are also sociological reasons why people adhere to particular religions. Each of these ways has strengths and weaknesses that must be critically assessed.

Finally, the question must be addressed of whether religious truth can actually be determined convincingly or whether it can only remain a "game" whose arguments have meaning only within a circle of believers. To a large extent this may be the case, but some philosophers and theologians argue that religious statements at least show what one is giving up if one does not accept them.

Recent philosophical debate on religion has centered on criticism of "essentialism," or belief that something like religion has a definite independent nature, and "deconstructionism," contention that binary (two-sided) structures of thought, such as the sacred and the profane in religion, too much oversimplify actual human life and experience.

The "new atheists" have raised many critical issues about religion. Their arguments need to be understood by those dealing with religious questions today.

KEY TERMS

authority, p. 189
content message, p. 193
empiricism, p. 193
essentialism, p. 197
existential choice, p. 195
experience, p. 192
God, p. 188

impersonal absolute, p. 188
ontological argument, p. 191
personal monotheism, p. 189
polytheism, p. 189
reason, p. 190
religion, p. 188

CHAPTER

13

Worlds to Come:
Religious Eschatology
and the Afterlife

Scene of heaven: Painting of the Holy Trinity in the cupola of the cathedral of Jaca, Spain
(Cro Magnon/Alamy)

LEARNING OBJECTIVES

After reading this chapter, you should be able to:

- Distinguish religions in which the afterlife is important, and those for which it is not.
- Tell what the attitude of the Hebrew Scriptures is toward the afterlife, and that of the ancient Greeks and other peoples.
- Discuss the issue of whether the afterlife begins at death, or a later Final Judgment is important.
- Describe views of the afterlife of Zoroastrianism, Islam, Christianity, and Buddhism, especially in regard to a final judgment versus eternal repetition or recurrence.
- Talk about an otherworldly afterlife, in heaven, hell, or another place, versus reincarnation.
- Interpret recent interest in reincarnation, and in the near-death experience.
- Compare theocentric and anthropocentric views of heaven.

ON THE ONE HAND, ON THE OTHER . . .

For many people, what happens after you die seems to be the most important thing about religion. Whether you go to heaven or hell, or have a good or bad reincarnation, is said to be the one really effective motivation for proper morality and right faith in us recalcitrant human beings.

It might surprise many of these people, then, to learn that some important religions have had, and still have, only a very dim view of the afterlife, or virtually none at all. The Hebrew Scriptures, the Old Testament of Christians, for example, offers very little about an afterlife; God's rewards and punishments are in this world.

This divide, between religions for which the afterlife is important and those for which it is not, is only the beginning of two-way issues regarding the ultimate question. Here are a couple others:

- Judgment and the afterlife commencing right after death versus a future Final Judgment and recompense at the End of Days, the end of life on earth as we know it.
- Eternal life in another place—heaven, hell, and perhaps an intermediate state—versus reincarnation here on earth in a state which amounts to reward or penalty.

Let us look at these options in more detail.

HOW IMPORTANT IS IT?

For some primal and ancient people, the afterlife was at best vague and unappealing. In a famous scene in in Homer's *Odyssey,* Odysseus went to the underworld in order to consult the soul of Teiresias, a great seer, as to what he must do in order to return home.

First the hero had to get the dead to hold still long enough to talk with them, for without their bodies they normally seem to be just flitting about aimlessly. A taste of blood will ground them; it took two sacrificial sheep for Odysseus to galvanize those he wished to interrogate. Odysseus was thus able to converse with Teiresias, and also with such former comrades in the Trojan War as Achilles and Agamemnon. One can well understand the eagerness of a visitor from our world to depart that dark and ghostly realm once he had gotten the information he needed. Of it Achilles went so far as to say that he would rather be a poor man's slave in the land of the living than king over all the dead.

The Hebrew Scriptures (the Christian Old Testament) are generally just about God's actions in this world. The deceased are either simply gone, or consigned to a shadowy Sheol without distinction of persons, rather like Homer's underworld. No doubt, it was from this realm of dust that the Witch of Endor called up the ghost of Samuel (I Sam. 28: 7–19). Sheol, mentioned 66 times in the Hebrew Scriptures, is generally portrayed as a place whose inhabitants are weak and unimportant; the Prophet Isaiah had dwellers in that dim realm say to the once-mighty King of Babylon upon his fall: "You too have become as weak as we! You have become like us! Your pomp is brought down to Sheol. . . ." (Is. 14: 10–11).

Rather, the blessing of God in these writings is manifested in victory, a comfortable life (the promise of "a land of milk and honey"), and above all in descendants, as in God's promise to Abraham: "I have made you the father of a multitude of nations." There are peoples today of the same perspective. The anthropologist Godfrey Lienardt said of the Dinka, in Africa, "Dinka fear to die without male issue, in whom the

Odysseus questioning the seer Teiresias in the Underworld, from the Odyssey. Watercolor by Peter Connolly, 1986   (akg-images/Peter Connolly/The Image Works)

survival of their names—the only kind of immortality they know—will be assured." And a Dinka chief said, "When a man works, he does not work for his own sake; he works for a child he has created."[1]

However, in the very latest of the Hebrew Scriptures, as in Daniel 12, we find references to resurrection of the dead, perhaps out of Sheol, possibly influenced by Zoroastrianism, in the end-time: "And many of those who sleep in the dust of the earth shall awake, some to everlasting life, and some to shame and everlasting contempt. And those who are wise shall shine like the brightness of the firmament; and those who turn many to righteousness, like the stars for ever and ever." Perhaps Enoch and Elijah, taken directly by God before death, enjoyed a similar glory.

The ancient Israelites' Semitic cousins, the Babylonians and Canaanites, held a similarly bleak view of the afterlife, again with rare exceptions. The dead in their ghostly underworld realm require offerings of remembrance from the living lest they rise above ground to work harm. *The Epic of Gilgamesh*, the most famous example of Sumerian and Babylonian literature, and perhaps the oldest extant written story in the world, relates the hero's attempt to obtain immortality in this life rather than abide in the "house of dust." He sought help from Utnapishtim, the Babylonian Noah who, surviving the Flood, uniquely attained deathlessness for himself and his wife. That worthy eventually told Gilgamesh of a plant able to renew youth. But when, through great effort, the seeker found and plucked this medicine of immortality, the sacred herb was seized from him by a snake. Sorrowfully, Gilgamesh realized that immortality is reserved for divine beings alone, plus serpents, and accepted the hard truth that mortals must die.[2]

Other ancient cultures had a much more robust image of life after death. The Egyptians are well known for their interest in postmortem states, though at first they may have regarded immortality reserved for the Pharaoh, who as we have seen was Horus during life and resuscitated as Osiris after death. According to the very early Pyramid Texts, the ruler's spirit joined the sun god Re in his solar ship to sail with him over daylight skies, and pass through the dark underworld at night. Later, as his identity with Osiris became more firm, and the afterlife was opened first to priests and courtiers, and finally to all Pharaoh's subjects. The former sovereign, as Osiris, was judge of the dead. The deceased had to pass through various tests to get to their reward. First was fending off demons, which necessitated knowing their secret names, information helpfully supplied on funeral texts. Then, at the dread throne of Osiris, the soul was weighed against a feather. If successful, the soul could then share the life of the gods, often portrayed as an endless round of delightful, sensual partying and lovemaking in a land quite similar to Egypt, with a great river running down its center. In a somewhat more exalted view, the spirit, like Pharaoh, united with Osiris, eternal lord of life.[3]

The ancient Celts, especially the Irish, likewise had a lively view of the Other World. Their beautiful and enchanted fairyland is preserved in countless legends. There food and wine are plentiful, and with these mainstays of life go feasting and dancing under a magical moon; there days and nights are always spring-like, and no sickness or death intrudes upon endless pleasure. This realm is accessible through holy wells, caves, and the barrow-like tombs of the dead. Many are the tales of a mortal who, by happenstance or intent, found the way there, often to learn that a day in the otherworld could count for many years in ours, or the other way around, and that the gold of that elfin realm could turn to dry leaves when eagerly brought back to our world of dust and decay.

The Celtic Other World was also to be found in the land of immortals at the Uttermost West, reached in legend by such intrepid sailors toward the sunset as Bran the Blessed or the Christian St. Brendan. In the Christian-influenced folklore of which we have documentation, the Other World was a fairyland parallel to this world, but not officially the abode of the dead. It seems probable, though, that this blessed realm far overseas—the Irish Tir nan Og or "Land of Youth" and the Welsh Annwn—as well as its underground equivalent, is more or less continuous with the pagan abodes of both gods and departed spirits.[4] Tir nan Og is an example of what is called horizontal cosmology, the sacred realm far across land or sea but on the same plane as our land, in contrast to vertical cosmology, the now more common imaging of heaven as above earth and the underworld beneath.

By and large, as time advanced, the vision of the afterlife became increasingly positive in ancient times. The Greeks added to Homer's grim underworld the western Isles of the Blest, Gardens of the Hesperides, or Elysian Fields, where heroes and others of the happy dead could dwell, though at first this site—horizontal cosmology again—was reserved for only a few. Still later, perhaps under Egyptian influence, Orphism and other Mystery Religions provided means by which a wide range of believers could attain immortality.

NOW OR LATER

The great religions of the Axial Age were likewise to share in the growing ancient emphasis on the afterlife as important and available to everyone. As we saw in Chapter 2, the Axial Age and its new founder religions developed the distinctiveness and responsibility of the individual, and stressed that we live in irreversible historical time. These led to two models, not entirely compatible, of the afterlife: a robust picture of individual judgment, and reward or punishment, assumed to be at the hour of death; and an equally imposing picture of the Last Judgment at the end of history, summing it up and settling its accounts, as well as those of all individuals then brought before the divine throne.

Both prospects were developed in the first, and prototype, Axial Age religion: Zoroastrianism. According to the great Persian faith, after a 3-day waiting period the soul of the deceased is brought to angels of judgment, who place it on the scales of heaven. If good outweighs sin, the anxious newcomer to the divine court perceives a beautiful maiden, who represents a good conscience. But if the judgment goes the other way, he is confronted by a hideous visage instead, the face of a twisted mind.

Then there is another test. All spirits are then led across the Chinvat Bridge, which leads to heaven over the abyss of hell. For the righteous, its span is a broad highway over which they proceed joyously into the realms of light. But for the wicked, the bridge shrinks down narrow as a razor, and they fall down into the dread place of punishment below.

That personal fate is not the final scene in this great drama, though, because next comes the end of history part. As we have seen, the new Axial Age style in religion was fundamentally conditioned by the discovery that we live in historical time, which is irreversible and presumably had a starting point and an ending (though some religions encompassed both within larger cyclical patterns). Probably this discovery was ultimately dependent on the invention of writing, which enabled the keeping of chronicles. But history taken raw is pretty depressing. Too often, for most ordinary people, and even for kings, the times in which we live are just one death and disaster after another with a few good years thrown in. Historical time cries out for some endpoint at which the dying will stop, the meaning of history's horrors be interpreted, and the scene shifted to something better.

The larger drama, in which for the Zoroastrian individual life and death was but a play within a play, was the mighty universal war between light and dark, good and evil. The hosts of Ahura Mazda, Lord of Light, are set against the high lord's eternal foe, Angra Mainyu, Lord of the Lie, and his demons of darkness. In this battle, human beings are like bait, for the evil one tries to turn us to his side through seductive temptations. But every time we resist, his power is weakened by so much, and Ahura Mazda's enhanced.

The end of this war is not in doubt. When it is about time to ring the curtain down on the last act, a savior sent by the Lord of Light, Saoshyant, will appear. His heroic task is to defeat evil once and for all, and restore creation to its original pure and pristine state. Even hell will be emptied and its inhabitants purified, for unlike traditional Christianity, Zoroastrianism does not postulate eternal damnation. The dead will be resurrected, all humanity will be given a wonderful drink of immortality, and all will live forever in joy and peace in a beautiful world.

ISLAMIC END-TIME

A similar two-level salvation, individual and world-scale, can be found in the other western monotheistic religions, which were probably influenced at some point by Zoroastrianism: Judaism, Christianity, and Islam. We have noted the late appearance of resurrection in the Jewish Book of Daniel, after Jews had had contact with the Persian faith in Mesopotamia. In mainstream Islam, the righteous first of all entered a paradise after death. One might have expected a desert people, as were the first Muslims, to envision paradise as a well-watered garden, like the oases for which they yearned, and so it was. God provided those winning paradise with male and female companions; the famous houris or female attendants are said by stricter commentators to symbolize spiritual states of rapture.

As for hell, although pictures of fire are used, the chief image is of chaos, the chaotic mind and soul of one in denial of God, which amounts to denying oneself as a child of God. Whether the penal state is necessarily eternal is a matter of interpretation; some *hadith* or sayings of the Prophet suggest that any denizen of hell who truly finds faith and wishes to leave the land of the lost may do so at any time. The trouble no doubt is, as many of us know from experience, that we can actually become attached to our sins, our familiar forms of chaos, and our states of denial; like some addicts today, we would rather stay in a familiar hell than try to break free.

Islam, like Zoroastrianism and the other **Abrahamic religions**, complements individual salvation at the hour of death with a final Day of Judgment, Yawm ad-Din, also called the Day of Resurrection. It is a familiar theme in the Qur'an. Several events indicate the coming of the Last Day. First chaos and disorder, symbolized by Gog and Magog, will devastate the world. Then the Mahdi, "Rightly Guided One," a sort of Messiah, will set the world aright for a brief period of moral clarity. But his benign reign is broken by another destructive intruder, al-Masih ad-Dajjal, literally "impostor messiah," a deceiver who promises true revelation but instead delivers only lies and tribulation. It is as though at the end of historical time as we know it, the pendulum of good and evil swings more and more rapidly, and to greater and greater extremes both ways. But next the clock itself is stopped by the true Yawm ad-Din, the day when God himself appears. A trumpet sounds; the dead rise from their graves; God's judgment sends the righteous to paradise, the unrighteous to hell.

What do we make of this distinction, and subtle tension, between individual-at-death and final judgment-at-the-end-of-history scenario, in several of the world's most important religions? Clearly, these two scenarios have two foci, the moral meaning of an individual life, and the wrapping up of history as a whole.

They can be fitted together only with some difficulty; many attempts to do so have been made. Some say the faithful individual simply rests in peace until the Last Day. Some speak of a temporary state in which, as in a kind of Purgatory, remaining evil can be worn away. Some say souls may function as ghosts between death and resurrection.

In any event, the case remains open until the Last Day, though the true believer who has acted according to his beliefs can face it with confidence.

CHRISTIAN JUDGMENT

The same issue arises in Christianity. Most Christians, after the funeral of a loved one is over, say that person is with God and Jesus in heaven. Hell, and in some traditions Purgatory, of course are also possibilities; in any case, according to very widespread folklore and belief, the assignment has been made at the moment of dying. (An old Irish saying: "May your soul be in heaven before the devil knows you're dead.")

Nonetheless, the Christian Scriptures and creeds forcefully emphasize the Last Days scenario, depicted in much great Christian art: the bodily resurrection of all; the Final Judgment, when some are sent to blessed life eternal and others to perdition; the creation of a new heaven and earth. The traditional Nicene Creed says, "And he [Jesus Christ] shall come again, with glory, to judge both the quick [the living] and the dead; Whose kingdom shall have no end . . . And I look for the Resurrection of the dead, And the Life of the world to come. Amen."

These two visions in part represent two sources of Christian thought: the Jewish, which emphasized life as life in the physical body, and God's working in history, in this rendering bodily resurrection at the end of time is a natural climax; and the Greek or Hellenistic, with its view of the soul as itself an eternal life, separable from the body at death, and upon death the soul could fly directly to a separate destiny from that of the mortal remains.

This is really the dilemma of all Axial Age religions, as they endeavor to reconcile very old but still potent ideas of the afterlife, perhaps even Paleolithic or Neolithic ideas of the dead transiting to a heavenly sacred mountain or Dreamtime or a ghost-like condition, or the ancient Hades or Hesperides, with the new discovery of history and the notion it should culminate in a grand review of all lives and verdict on them.

Both sides held important truths and experiences in the eyes of the new faiths, but were not always easy to fit together. In Christianity, as in the others, teachers spoke of sleep to await the resurrection of the Last Day, or Purgatory, or a spirit-life or heaven or elsewhere till one was rejoined with the body in the resurrection. Lately, in some evangelical circles, the idea of the Rapture, when true believers will be taken bodily into heaven at the beginning of the End Times and so avoid its tribulations, has gained currency; it was a theme of the very popular "Left Behind" series of novels by Tim LaHaye and Jerry Jenkins.[5]

Those books and others like them reflect the way of reading the "end-times" known as **apocalyptic**. Versions of apocalyptic are found in most major religions, though with varying importance. In the Hebrew Scriptures, Daniel Ch. 7–12 and several of the prophets reveal apocalyptic themes. In the New Testament, apocalyptic is reflected in the Book of Revelation, sometimes called the Apocalypse, and the so-called "Little Apocalypses" of the Gospels (Matt. Ch. 24, Mark 13, Luke 21). In essence, apocalyptic teaches that a sudden, dramatic divine intervention ending the world as we know it and beginning a new heaven and earth is coming, probably very soon. Until it arrives, conditions on earth will probably get worse and worse till, in a tremendous reversal, God and his kingdom break through to set all ill to right, and punish the wicked. Leading up to this End, various signs appear to hearten believers in the days of tribulation. Sometimes apocalyptic appeals particularly to people who feel left behind by the changing and secularizing world around them, but who hold to the traditional faith. They may be bit players and extras in the superficial scenarios of the world, but because of their indomitable faith may have starring roles in the Last Days.[6]

To give something of the flavor of recent evangelical apocalyptic, here is an account of the Rapture, put in the mouth of a college religious studies professor. It is from Hal Lindsay's *The Late Great Planet Earth,* a runaway bestseller after its publication in 1970, and a book that did much to spark the popular apocalyptic vogue of the late twentieth century.

> "It was puzzling   very puzzling. I was teaching my course in the Philosophy of Religion when all of a sudden three of my students vanished. They simply vanished! They were quite argumentative—always trying to prove their point from the Bible. No great loss to the class. However, I do find this disappearance very difficult to explain"[7]

In regard to the afterlife, as of religion generally, perhaps it is well to bear in mind the saying attributed to the philosopher John Stuart Mill, that people are usually right in what they affirm and wrong in what they deny—at least in religion that would be because what we affirm comes out of our experience, whereas what we deny, and say is false doctrine, is someone else's experience.

ONE DEATH OR MANY: HEAVEN AND HELL VERSUS REINCARNATION

Is life just being born, living, dying, and then going to an eternal life in another place? Or is it rather that we have had not one but many, perhaps an almost infinite number of births, lives, and deaths? The second proposition is the perspective of a significant

portion of humanity: some primal religionists, Hindus and Buddhists, as well as followers of certain schools of western Neoplatonist philosophy and Jewish Kabbalistic
mysticism, and strands of esoteric Islam.

Perhaps at some point in our lives we have all wondered why we happened to
be born in the time and place that we were, to a certain set of parents, in circumstances high or low, rich or poor, easy or hard, rather than some other setting. For
these reincarnationist spiritual traditions, it was not happenstance that brought us to
that childbed, but rather our birth, like every other, was the last link in a very long
chain of cause and effect. In the East the chain may be called karma, action, or cause
and effect, which says that all our thoughts, words, and deeds have a lingering result,
like the ripples going out from a stone cast into a pond, and these finally will create
the conditions of the next life in one's chain. We do not generally remember our previous lives—that would be too much to bear—but they fix issues with which we are
born: character traits, unresolved relationships, problems to be faced, and lessons to
be learned. Karma deals us our hand at birth; how we play it is up to us.

Reincarnation need not necessarily be in this particular world. Buddhism has a
especially interesting picture of six lokas, or places of rebirth based on one's karma.
Starting at the bottom, they are the hells, the realm of the hungry ghosts, the animal
realm, the land of the asuras or fighting demons, the human, and the heavens.

The Buddhist hells are fearsome enough, even if not eternal, lasting only until one's
bad karma is exhausted; that may be a very long time indeed, but the karma, good or
bad, accumulated in one lifetime can only be finite. Some hells are of fire and some
of ice. Both no doubt reflect the inner state of a person who has isolated himself from
everyone else, and above all from the great Buddhist virtue of compassion, or "feeling
with" another. Sometimes we cut ourselves off through anger and abusiveness—
fire; sometimes through unfeeling coldness—ice. Either way, the hell-being would be
the "me-alone" type who always drives away those who try to befriend him/her, and
no less rebuffs those who seek help from him/her.

What these hateful actions bespeak is really destructive self-hatred, and fiery or
icy self-hatred is the real punishment of hell, and it is self-inflicted. No god sends one
to hell, one sends oneself to that terrible place by what one is within.

The hungry ghosts are beings with huge bellies and tiny mouths, and incarnation
in this pitiful form suits those who are continually desiring and never satisfied, including those who "have it all" yet always want more.

The animal plane is the only one of the lokas other than the human ordinarily visible to human sight. It is the natural end of a life marked mainly by stupidity and the
indulgence of sensual appetites. One who, in common parlance, acts like a pig or a
wolf or a tomcat becomes one.

On the other hand, persons whose lives are controlled by anger and violence are
likely candidates for the land of the asuras, who fight one another without end. Many
are the tales of implacable warriors, like the Japanese samurai, who ended up in this
realm. We mentioned one such unfortunate warrior, the music-loving Tsunemasa, earlier as the subject of a famous No play.

Above the human, good karma could instead bring one to the heavens of the gods,
or devas. Imagine a life of floating indolently on perfumed seas, as hours become days,
days become years, and years centuries, all the while listening to the most glorious

Buddhist hell, from Nechuns monastery, near Lhasa, Tibet   (Bjorn Svensson/Alamy)

music as your mind drifts lazily from one engaging reverie to another, or you talk delightedly with your most beloved friends. Or you might wander with them through fabulous gardens, meeting along the way fairies and elves of fantasy, now real. These would be among the lower heavens; higher ones, rising above form altogether, are like the timeless raptures of exalted mystical states.

So wonderful are these heavens that you may well barely remember that they will not last forever. But in fact all the lokas, from the hells to the heavens, are governed by karma. As we have seen, karma is always a finite quantity, since no finite life could generate infinite karma, and eventually that karmic energy will run out. Then you will be released from hell, strike your last blow as an asura, or drop down from a heavenly paradise to the grime of earth. The chances are you will then be given human birth again.

For human life is rather like a central station on the wheel of rebirth. Here, in our mixture of day and night, good and evil, and our ability to analyze the human condition, we are able to understand the wheel and decide if we wish to get off it. In the heavens too much continual delight keeps us from thinking much about the wheel and when all this will end; in the lower states too much pain and numbness of mind.

But here, in the ordinary human world, if we wish, we can do those meditations that enable us to understand, and to stop spinning around the lokas so as to move into Nirvana, unconditioned reality, unending bliss to which the best of heaven is but like a candle to the sun. Or, according to some Mahayana Buddhist traditions, we can at least enter one of the Pure Lands which surround the consciousness of a great Buddha like an aura; they are fabulous in themselves, and from them entry into Nirvana is easy.

Reincarnation is coming West too. A 2009 poll by the Pew Research Center found that 24 percent of Americans, including many Christians, claim to believe in reincarnation.[8] These numbers seem to be increasing, and certainly were given an impetus by the new religious involvements of the 1960s. But credit should also be given to a 1956 book, *The Search for Bridey Murphy*, by Morey Berstein.[9]

The story is this. In 1952 Morey Bernstein, a Colorado businessman and hypnotist, conducted deep hypnotic regression with a neighbor, Virginia Burns Tighe (called Ruth Simmons in the book). The young housewife described in much detail a previous life in Ireland as Bridey (Bridget) Murphy, born 1798, died 1864. She had been born in Cork, married a barrister and moved to Belfast; Virginia was able tell much about her house and way of life, and finally her death and burial.

When the book came out it was a sensation in an America for which such an idea of past lives was new to many people. Reporters rushed to Ireland. They were unable to verify the existence of anyone of Bridey's name and dates. On the other hand, the hypnotic accounts did contain accurate and detailed information about nineteenth-century Ireland which would not normally be known to a nonscholarly person like Virginia Tighe. Debate went back and forth.

More remarkable was the cultural impact of Bridey Murphy in 1950s America. Suddenly reincarnation became fashionable in some circles. A movie version of the book came out. Popular recordings carried titles like, "Do You Believe in Reincarnation?," "The Loves of Bridey Murphy," and "The Bridey Murphy Rock and Roll." Countless invitations went out to "Come As You Were" parties. It was as though a new worldview was ready to break through, and unsophisticated as reincarnation undoubtedly was in many minds, like all such new ideas it shed a fresh light on important questions about life. People said things like, "I'm afraid of water because I drowned in my last life," or "Something about that person makes me very uneasy; I think I had a bad marriage with him last time."

ETERNAL RECURRENCE

One other option that is not quite reincarnation, but might be mentioned here, is eternal recurrence. This is the idea that, over immense aeons of time, the universe repeats itself, including your own life, over and over. Something like this concept is found in some ancient Greek writers, and also in Hindu thought. In both, each cycle begins with a Golden Age but deteriorates down to the Iron Age, or Kaliyuga, when life is brutish and short. But after the worst ends and the cosmos has rested, the process starts again.

The modern concept of Eternal Recurrence is mainly associated with the nineteenth-century German philosopher Friedrich Nietzsche. His basic premise was that, if the universe contains a finite amount of matter but is infinite in time, eventually in its random reshaping of itself it would take the same form again, not once but an infinite number of times. What you are now doing, and your entire life, has happened times beyond number, and will recur innumerable times in the future.

Nietzsche never said that he believed literally in this notion, nor did he deny that he did. Rather he asked how you would feel about it if it were true. It was a touchstone of his philosophy of meaning. Would the eternal recurrence of your present life be the most depressing or the most wonderful news you could hear? Suppose, he asked in *The Gay Science*, some demon were to tell you this your life was to be repeated again and again, with every pain and every joy just as it is, would you throw yourself down in despair, or would you say in rapture, "You are a god and never have I heard anything more divine?"[10]

How would you yourself feel about such a declaration? For this philosopher, it meant every moment of life, just as it is, to be infinitely deep, literally eternal, and so worth ultimate joy.

Nietzsche is also noted for proclaiming the death of God, in *Thus Spake Zarathustra* and elsewhere. If Eternal Recurrence is true then God's death must also actually be an eternally recurring death and rebirth. Would this also bring about the ever recurring death and birth of religion as we know it, as it becomes a faith focused on the affirmation of all life in every moment, eternally recurring?[11]

WHAT KIND OF HEAVEN?

Let us turn back now to the traditional heaven of the non-reincarnational religions. Here the issue is between theocentric, or God-centered, pictures of heaven, in which the saved are chiefly engaged in the worship of God; and the anthropocentric, or human-centered, image of a heaven given over to innocent human delights.

The first, heaven devoted to worship or high mystical states alone, sounds like the higher heavens of Buddhism, and also one tradition within Christianity informed by such mighty theological minds as Augustine, Thomas Aquinas, and the major Protestant reformers. They considered that the "Beatific Vision," seeing and worshiping God face to face, would be enough to exclude every other thought. This would not mean, however, as lesser souls might fear, that heaven would be like being in church for all eternity.

Augustine, in the fifth century CE, taught (like many modern physicists) that time is only an aspect of the created universe, that is, of the space-time continuum. Heaven, being outside time, has no duration, but is all at once. Therefore, if the saints worship God unceasingly for all eternity, those endless hymns never get boring, since the singing all takes place in one magnificent timeless moment, and nothing else sounds before, after, or beside that tremendous chord.

Thomas Aquinas in the Middle Ages went on to contend that heaven, being perfect, can allow for no activity except contemplation, and since God is infinite the contemplation of his divine depths takes all eternity. Carrying on the same theme, Martin Luther also emphasized that heaven would be without change, without eating or drinking or any other ordinary occupation. "But I think we will have enough to do with God," the German reformer insisted.[12]

Nonetheless ordinary believers wanted more. If heaven is indeed the perfect place, why is it not also be the perfect place for innocent human pleasures like eating, drinking, dancing, friendship, even lovemaking? The straightest of theologians found themselves bending somewhat, at least for the sake of the weaker brethren. Later in his life Augustine allowed that the deceased had physical bodies in heaven—after all, there was the resurrection of the dead—and so eating and drinking, and meeting friends and loved ones, were possible there above as here below. But the eating and drinking was not for the sake of necessary nourishment (since they needed none), but only for pleasure, and friends and family were all equal, without parents being above children or rulers above subjects.

Likewise, a student of Aquinas', Giles of Rome, modified his master's thought to the extent of postulating that the saints in heaven must become a perfect society as well as contemplatives. This meant their lives included friendship, and all normal human activities in ideal form.[13]

Whatever his deepest thoughts, when Marin Luther's beloved daughter Magdalene talked of heaven as a place where she could get "lots of apples, pears, sugar, plums, and so on," her father only encouraged her, and moreover told his son Hans that heaven would be "a pretty, beautiful, and delightful garden where there are many children wearing little golden coats. They pick up fine apples, pears, cherries, and yellow and blue plums under the trees. They sing, jump, and are merry. They also have nice ponies."[14] Luther also referred to the new earth as well as the new heaven promised in scripture, saying that while heaven would be our home, we could make excursions to our present world in its perfected state, giving God glory for the wonders he had wrought on the now-sorry planet.

Renaissance art likewise veered in the direction of the anthropocentric heaven, little able to resist the temptation to portray the world of the saints in all its glory and variety. Fra Angelico, in his *Last Judgment* (c. 1431), shows the blessed, once they have heard God's favorable decree, rejoicing with dance steps, meeting and greeting, pairing off. In this great work, one even perceives a presumably heretofore celibate monk being chastely but firmly embraced by a clearly female angel.

But then only a little earlier Dante, in his *Vita Nuova* and *Divine Comedy*, had gladly been guided through heaven by his beloved Beatrice, whom he loved with both human and sacred passion, and saw as means of grace: "Her least salutation bestows salvation on this favored one, and humbles him till he forgets all wrong," and "This too has God Almighty graced her with: whoever speaks with her shall speak with Him."[15]

More recent ideas of heaven in popular religion have certainly been influenced by the visions of the Swedish mystic Emanuel Swedenborg (1688–1772), who believed that he had met God face to face, and then been told by the Almighty he would be enabled to travel to heaven and hell, see what they were like, and then write about them, which he did, voluminously, in Latin. In brief, Swedenborg saw heaven and hell as states, not places, to which spirits are drawn by their own nature, forming communities and even contracting marriages with others congenial in temperament, able to rise to higher and higher states as they improve. Hell is simply the state of those who are uncomfortable living with any but those given to hatred and cruelty like themselves.

Although the presence of God is everywhere in Swedenborg's heaven, his paradise is anthropocentric in the sense that its inhabitants are engaged in their own delights, from discussing philosophy to practicing fine craftsmanship, rather than the direct worship of God. Church services are not required in this heaven; the Lord is content to be praised through the blessed souls' happy activities, and their love for one another.[16]

The Swedenborgian kind of heaven, educational rather than judgmental, anthropocentric in the best sense of the word, appealed to many in the modern age shaped by the Enlightenment, democracy, and the growth of widespread education. Nineteenth-century movements like Spiritualism and liberal Christianity popularized it.

A fine example is the novels of the New England feminist Elizabeth Stuart Phelps, especially *The Gates Ajar* (1868) and *Beyond the Gates* (1883). These books vividly portray heaven as a place of happy families reunited forever in beautiful homes, surrounded by gorgeous scenery and busy cities. There one could meet great figures from the past: hear a symphony conducted by Beethoven himself, or a sermon from the lips of none other than St. John, the Apostle. The first of these books is based on the conversation of women dealing with the loss of loved ones in the then-recent Civil War. In the second, a desperately ill women of about 40 is taken on a tour of heaven by her predeceased father, where among other delights she meets a one-time earthly lover. There is little about hell.[17]

It is clear that these appealing stories express the Victorian idealization of the family, aspirations to "high" culture, preoccupation with death and mourning, and concern with the woman's point of view. They remind us that ideas of the afterlife not seldom reflect the concerns and values of the prevailing culture.

NEAR-DEATH EXPERIENCES

Finally, let us look at a recent interest relevant to the afterlife, already mentioned in connection with popular religion, the near-death experience (NDE).

Many of us know people who have reported interesting experiences at moments when they have approached the gates of death, or at least have read about them in the extremely popular books on the subject that appeared in the late twentieth and early twenty-first centuries, beginning with Raymond Moody's *Life after Life*, published in 1975 and selling some 13 million copies to date. Perhaps you have had such an experience yourself, or know someone who has.

According to these relations, people who were "clinically dead" in a hospital or accident situation experienced a profound alteration of consciousness, and a sense of entering a new and strange world. Some have told of a soft golden light that is also a loving Presence. Many have encountered other greeters: relatives, friends, angels, religious figures.

A less welcome meeting may be with a life review, in which all of one's life, good and bad alike, passes in review. Occasionally it may even become an empathetic life review, not only seeing but reexperiencing one's life, including the effects one had on others as well as oneself: the ripple effect that extends from everything one does, loving, careless, or callous, as they touch many other lives.

Overall, near-death experiences frequently include tremendous peace, a sense of being separate from the body, moving through a dark space—sometimes the "tunnel" often mentioned in accounts, sometimes more like a mist—toward a welcoming light sometimes personified as a "Being of Light," an awareness of being in or just glimpsing a beautiful land, a panoramic life review, and a decision or command to return to the body in this case. Here is a woman's account from Raymond Moody's *Life After Life*:

> I had a heart attack, and I found myself in a black void, and I knew I had left my physical body behind. I knew I was dying, and I thought, "God, I did the best I knew how at the time I did it. Please help me." Immediately, I was moved out of that blackness, through a pale gray, and I just went on, gliding and moving swiftly, and in front of me, in the distance, I could see a gray mist, and I was rushing toward it. It seemed that I just couldn't get to it fast enough to satisfy me, and as I got closer to it I could see through it. Beyond the mist, I could

Light at the end of the tunnel   (dannywilde/Fotolia)

see people, and their forms were just like they are on the earth, and I could also see something which one could take to be buildings. The whole thing was permeated with the most gorgeous light—a living, golden yellow glow, a pale color, not like the harsh gold color we know on earth.

As I approached more closely, I felt certain that I was going through that mist. It was such a wonderful, joyous feeling; there are just no words in human language to describe it. Yet, it wasn't my time to go through the mist, because instantly from the other side appeared my Uncle Carl, who had died many years earlier. He blocked my path, saying, "Go back. Your work on earth has not been completed. Go back now." I didn't want to go back, but I had no choice, and immediately I was back in my body. I felt that horrible pain in my chest, and I heard my little boy crying, "God, bring my mommy back to me."[18]

In Chapter 9, we talked about how experiences like this seem to be shaping contemporary impressions of the afterlife. They are first-hand narrations of experiences accessible to all, an important consideration in an age of democratic consciousness; they are also individualized and take into account individual life-stories and attainment; they respect duties that must still be fulfilled; yet at the same time they are relatively nonjudgmental—if one must experience the results of one's bad actions, that seems more a matter of learning or self-inflicted punishment than punitive divine action. All this seems to fit our basically easy-going, therapy-oriented society, and the NDE accounts certainly have their appeal.

In conclusion, it seems clear that ideas of the afterlife generally reflect the mentality and values of the society as well as input from its traditional religions.

SUMMARY

Belief in an afterlife is important in some religions, less so in others. Many ancient peoples, including the Hebrews, Babylonians, and Homeric Greeks, saw it in dim and dismal terms; others, like the Celts and Egyptians, had a much brighter picture.

With the coming of the Axial Age religions, the view generally became important along with individual rewards and punishment, and enhanced belief in a Final Judgment in some. Zoroastrianism was a prototype of this kind of belief. Judaism, Christianity, and Islam also have individual rewards or punishment, and a final judgment. In Hinduism and Buddhism, reincarnation and a cyclical view of time is also emphasized.

The question of whether significant afterlife begins at death, or a later judgment, is important. So is that of whether it is in heaven, hell, or another place, or through reincarnation. In respect of heaven, some picture it in theocentric terms, emphasizing worship of God, others as anthropocentric, giving more value to human delights there.

Another possibility is eternal recurrence, proposed by some ancient philosophers and some modern such as Friedrich Nietzsche.

Reincarnation belief, and accounts of near-death experiences, have recently become prominent in the West as well as the East.

KEY TERMS

Abrahamic religions, p. 207   apocalyptic, p. 209

CHAPTER

14

How Shall We Live?
Religion and Ethics

Pro-life and pro-choice demonstrators together   (Marc macdonald/Alamy)

LEARNING OBJECTIVES

After reading this chapter, you should be able to:

- Define meanings of the terms *ethics* and *morality*.
- Talk about how ethics are grounded in a meta-ethics, or overall worldview.
- Distinguish between deontological and teleological, or consequentialist, ethics. What does each say? How can each be criticized? Are there any ways in which they can be combined? Are there any other possible bases for ethics besides these two concepts?
- Describe what is meant by natural law, and by utilitarianism. Discuss debate over the value of intentionalism.
- Analyze the roles of law and love in ethics. Are they necessarily at odds?
- Discuss similarities and differences in the ethics of the major religions. In what respects are they generally similar? Where do differences come about? Be sure to think in terms of concrete examples.
- Present and analyze the major issues and points of view in important contemporary arenas of ethical debate; medical ethics, including abortion and euthanasia; the rights of women in religion; ecological and animal issues; and others. You will probably need to do some outside reading concerning these and other questions, but the text should point you toward what the discussions are about.

TAKING IT TO THE STREETS

You have just attended a fine religious service in a beautiful temple or church. The music was wonderful, the words and rites inspiring, and you leave feeling very good. In fact, for you on this occasion, religion truly spoke to you. You think you have become who you really are in relation to human society and Ultimate Reality. Whatever you do now will be based on that faith. Your actions will be consistent with your innermost nature, and with God or however you best understand the supreme source and context of your life.

Then, on the street, you see a homeless person trying to keep warm over a heating grate, or living in a packing box in an alley. He indicates he would like money for food. How do you respond?

You could refuse, saying to yourself—or aloud to the homeless person—that if he had real faith, God would take care of him and he would not be in this situation.

You could refuse, saying that if he joined a true religious body, that organization would be like a second family and support group, and would take care of his needs. Or in any case, since you give to religious and other organized charities to help the homeless, you don't need to do it on an individual basis.

You could refuse, saying that individual acts of charity only make people dependent and may be scams anyway; they don't get at the real problem. But out of your religious faith you vow to redouble your efforts to work through political and religious institutions to eliminate the root causes of homelessness.

You could refuse, saying you would like to give but you have only so much money, and you have already promised to help another needy person nearer your home.

You could refuse to help on "tough love" grounds, but stay to talk with the person about self-help and getting a job. You might even offer to help him get a job, since your religion says you should help others.

You could give to him, finding that to be the easiest way to forget him and continue to enjoy your religious experience.

You could give to him as an expression of the religious experience, because your religion says that everyone is a child of God and deserves to be loved, and giving is an act of love whether the recipient deserves it or not.

Then, when you get home, you find members of your family embroiled in a hot and heavy argument about sexual morality. Is abortion ever justified? Is sex before— or outside of—marriage right? What about homosexuality?

And when you go to school or work the next day, there are more issues. Someone shows you a way you could cheat on an exam or a business deal and not get caught. How do you respond?

Your school or company has to reduce staff because of budget cuts. How do you think they should decide who gets the ax and who stays? Seniority? Competence? Gender? Race? Or any of these grounds but called something else?

Issues like these confront us almost every day of our lives. They are clearly related to religion. If religion has anything to do with real life, it should guide us in how we act in context of the practical issues of life as well as in worship. If religion deals, as it claims, with the Ultimate Reality underlying everything that is, it ought to have something to say about every kind of situation that arises in the real world.

ETHICS AND MORALITY

These issues are in the realm of ethics and morality. They have to do with what behavior is right, and on what basis one decides what is right.

The line between ethics and morality is somewhat fuzzy. But ethics is usually defined as a somewhat broader term, referring to the rules of conduct or the highest standards of a tradition or group (Jewish ethics, Christian ethics, medical ethics), especially regarding honesty or the legitimacy of particular procedures (as when someone in a profession says, "I could do that but it would be considered unethical"). Moreover, those branches of philosophy or theology that inquire into right behavior and the principles of logic underlying it are usually now called *ethics*. This term may represent an ideal rather than everyday practice. *Social ethics* refers to issues of what is ethical for society as a whole, whether through legislation or widespread changes of attitude, as in such questions as how to deal with the causes of poverty, or whether war is ever justified.

Morality now tends to speak more to the normal standards of conduct expected by a society, or to personal codes of conduct (as when one says, "To me that's immoral"), especially in such highly personal areas as sexual behavior or truth telling. As these terms are commonly used, morals spell out rules of behavior, while ethics articulate the justifications for those rules.

But, especially in a religious context, morals may also refer to the standard teaching of a religious institution on right personal conduct and, though they now may sound slightly dated, one may use such expressions as *moral theology* or *moral philosophy* for the systematic study of what is right behavior in light of the thinker's ultimate religious or philosophical views.

Thus the terms often overlap. We will here ordinarily use the term *ethics* as it is most commonly used today in religious studies. Yet it should be understood that ethics are not just a religious matter. Quite serious and demanding ethical systems can be, and have been, propounded entirely on philosophical grounds, by ancients such as Plato and Aristotle or the Stoics and Epicureans, down to modern, nontraditionally religious ethicists like Bertrand Russell or John Dewey. In Western civilization, in fact, some tension has been brought about by the fact that the predominant religious influences, Judaism and Christianity, have sources in a different world of thought— that of the ancient Hebrews—from the predominant philosophical tradition shaped by ancient Greek thought. This has been as much the case in ethics as anything else, and has led to issues that have to be sorted out between *divine command* and *rational ethics*, or between the ethics of *absolute commitment* and the ethics of the *golden mean.*

But in any case, ethical decision making is a constant requirement of life. We make ethical decisions—not always good ones—even by not making them. Religion, when a part of one's life, can help one decide.

DOWN FROM ON HIGH

Any thought-out ethical system has to begin with **meta-ethics**; that is an overarching worldview from which the ethical system derives. All religions, and secular philosophies too, have a view of God or Ultimate Reality and of how the universe came into being that connects with the ethical values of the society. If a personal God is held to be the creator of the world, that God is usually also thought of as the supreme lawgiver. If, as in Hinduism, the universe itself is simply a visible manifestation of God, the social order with its rules *(dharma)* is built into the deity's outer manifestation. Nonreligious philosophies, such as those of contemporary scientific humanists, like the "new atheists" presented in the Chapter 12, may present ethical views consistent with what (in the view of that philosopher) science shows the real nature and value of human life to be.

Then there is the question of how religious ethics embedded in meta-ethics are transmitted to society. Here, as in any aspect of religion, one may look at the role of revelation, of sacred texts, of exemplary human beings (e.g., saints and heroes of the faith) and of guidance exercised through religious institutions.

A further question for analysis is this: how then does the religion or philosophy *motivate* behavior? It may appeal to peer example in a sacred community, or activate an inner sense of guilt. Forceful talk of after-death rewards and punishment (or punishment in this life, as in the ancient Hebrew Scriptures) can be convincing, as can the offer of personal spiritual advancement and a sense of participation in sacred history. Religion or philosophy may simply point to the authority of its sacred scriptures or institution, if that authority is widely and unquestioningly accepted.

In thinking about the actual social enactment of ethics, one should also consider what values are primarily theoretical, and what values are actually put into practice. As is well known, not all ethical ideals are strictly upheld by the societies that hold to them. Some may count for more than others in practice. Some societies that wink at various forms of minor cheating would harshly condemn public nudity. Some have, in practice, different standards for men and women concerning marital faithfulness. Some ethical ideals (strict celibacy or marital faithfulness, nonconsumption of alcohol, relative simplicity of life) may be expected of religious professionals but are not, in practice, demanded so rigorously of the laity. Some, like not killing, are limited by all sorts of practical exceptions, as in war, self-defense, or capital punishment.

We also find that practical ethical expectations differ between social classes. (The prudish Victorian morality supposed to be characteristic of nineteenth-century England and America, for example, was actually most held to by the burgeoning middle class; the upper and lower classes generally were less demanding of themselves.) All societies have such seeming contradictions—much can be learned about the way a society works and what its most serious values are by examining them. Discussion of real-life ethical practice in a society or setting is sometimes called descriptive ethics. From now on, however, we shall talk chiefly about theoretical ethics, that is, the systems of ideal ethics promulgated by religions and philosophers.

KINDS OF ETHICAL THOUGHT

Ethical views are, first of all, divided into two broad types known by two words, **deontological ethics** (ethics as "oughts," i.e., coming from duties or obligations seen as givens, presumably by God or nature or reality itself) and **teleological ethics** (meaning dependent on the consequence, or end product, of the act).

Deontological ethics (from Greek meaning "out of being itself") are derived from a previously determined view of the nature of God, nature, or reality. They tend to hold that certain actions or behaviors are right or wrong in themselves, because they are or are not in accordance with the will of God, or the laws of nature. If God is love, then as a servant of God one should always act in a loving way. If God has forbidden murder, then one should not do it, both because it is contrary to love and is further prohibited by divine command.

Some would extend that command to such controversial issues as war or capital punishment, saying that if murder is wrong, the state has no more right to take life than an individual, regardless of consequence; some would extend the case to abortion, saying that one also has no right to take unborn life.

Many deontological ethicists—some religious, some not—also talk about **natural law**, that is, whether acts are or are not in accordance with nature. Thus, nature clearly intends humans—unlike, say, solitary animals like the leopard—to dwell in families and in larger communities, the clan, tribe, city, or nation. Thus, what upholds the welfare of these units, including obedience to the legitimate ordinances of legitimate authorities, is ethical. Many religious philosophers, most notably Thomas Aquinas, combine divine command and natural law, saying that God is the ultimate author of natural law.

For some, natural-law considerations can therefore legitimate killing, as in war or capital punishment, when authorized by legitimate authorities, though the individual has no right to kill, save in extreme cases of self-defense or in the defense of another who is helpless; justification in such cases is thought to derive from **natural rights**.

These are good examples of a further tension between divine command and rational ethics even within deontology. The question is whether we determine what behavior is consistent with the nature or will of Ultimate Reality just by the latter's revealed command, or whether we may also use reason to so determine God's will or what is truly natural. We also can use reason, rational ethicists would say, to determine what has validly been mediated through legitimate authority, whether the state (as in exercising its power to execute convicted criminals or declare) or religious (such as the Roman Catholic papacy, or a Muslim *mufti*, or spiritual authority)—and when claims of authority can be rightly questioned.

The divine command approach would say that one must obey what God has commanded regardless of circumstance, such obedience being most commendable when the risk or cost is great and the reasons least apparent. An example would be a lonely pacifist refusing to fight, at the cost of humiliation, imprisonment, or even being shot as a traitor, in a war that most consider just, simply because he believes that all fighting and all taking of human life is wrong and forbidden by the Bible's "Thou shalt not kill." Rational ethics, even if ultimately based on command, would say that one can and should take circumstances into account and balance one obligation against another. Even when conjoined with religion, natural-law considerations, being determined by reason and observation in the first place, are usually in the rational camp.

To give another example, natural-law theorists might also say that the arrangement of the human sexual organs is such that certain forms of sex, such as procreation and expression of marital love, are natural, and other forms, such as homosexuality or heterosexual intercourse when procreation is not wanted, or deliberately prevented, is therefore, by definition, unnatural, and so contrary to natural-law morality. This position has been taken, especially but by no means exclusively, by conservative Roman Catholic moral theologians, who argue that since God made nature and natural law in the first place, following it is a part of religion. Needless to say, these strictures have engendered much controversy about just what is natural, and to what extent humans need be bound by nature.

Deontological ethics have been criticized for making guidelines for behavior too rigorous, insisting that certain acts are always right, or always wrong, regardless of the particular situation. Natural-law theory has been criticized for taking too narrow a view of what nature "says" regardless of the fact that nature itself, and our scientific perceptions of it, are always evolving. Defenders of these positions say that we humans need some firm, unquestionable limits given by a higher authority. Or else, they argue, we are likely to find ways to justify anything we really want to do, however dubious.

Human ethics must always acknowledge its contingency on something greater than the merely human, deontologists contend; otherwise they demean humans by denying our chief glory, that we are free, decision-making children of God; or, that we are manifestations of nature at its best.

Teleological ethics (from Greek meaning "based on the end," in the sense of consequence), sometimes called **consequentialist**, says that the consequences of an action are what is really important. The crucial thing is not whether the act comes out of divine command or natural law, but whether it produces good results. The rightness or wrongness of, say, capital punishment or abortion, should be judged not by an *a priori* judgment about murder, but by whether those acts of killing produce good *consequences* for the persons involved and for society as a whole.

An important subdivision of consequentialism is **utilitarianism**, developed by nineteenth-century British thinkers such as Jeremy Bentham and John Stuart Mill. This school says that the ideal should be "the greatest good for the greatest number," what Bentham called his "hedonic calculus" (from *hedon,* Greek word for pleasure or happiness). Ethical principles and social policies, according to utilitarianism, should be judged on this basis. While admittedly it is not always easy to make such judgments, the utilitarian ideal has lain behind a large amount of the social reforms of the last century and a half. Its light can be seen behind such staples of contemporary American life as universal suffrage, civil rights, and social security. No longer can the idea that policies are acceptable if they explicitly benefit only a minority, however elite, be advanced without strident argument.

Jeremy Bentham worked out on an elaborate system by which one could calculate the relative amounts of pleasure and pain for oneself and others in particular actions, and J.S. Mill further refined utilitarianism by distinguishing between higher and lower pleasures. Bentham was one of the first of the modern ethicists to take seriously the suffering of animals as well as humans, and in large part utilitarianism was a response in terms of democratic values to the gross inequities of the early Industrial Revolution.

Yet teleological ethics, and utilitarianism, can also be criticized. Critics will say that without some deontological principles, we cannot even rightly decide which consequences are good and which are not. Is preserving life always good without regard to the quality of that life? Whether we are talking about the beginning of human life (the abortion controversy) or the end (the right-to-die issue), the matter of quality of life cannot be avoided. Is a human life continuing indefinitely as little more than a vegetable a good or bad outcome?

"The greatest good for the greatest number" can also be subjected to deontological critiques. The case of slavery is sometimes given as a hypothetical case, although Bentham and Mill would certainly not have used utilitarianism in its defense. If, in a given society, the quality of life of the majority could arguably be improved by their enslaving a minority of the population, could this justify the suffering and degradation that would impose on the slave minority? If not, this indicates that some limitations to utilitarianism must be imposed by deontological considerations about human nature in general, as well as about relative degrees of pleasure and suffering.

Those concerned with the treatment of animals, as was Bentham and more recently Peter Singer in *Animal Liberation,*[1] have pointed to very disturbing parallels in the human use of animals, asking on what moral grounds animals can be subjected to pain, frustration of natural instincts, and wholly unnatural living conditions solely for the supposed benefit of their human owners and masters, whether for labor, meat production, or medical experimentation. Marjorie Spiegel, in *The Dreaded Comparison,*[2] demonstrated many similarities between the past treatment of African slaves and present treatment of animals, and in the rationalizations given for the justification of this use. In the animal rights issue both ethical sources are profoundly challenged: deontology, inasmuch as the subordination of animals is frequently given divine-command justification, and teleology insofar as human and sometimes even animal benefits have been invoked by defenders of the current situation. If animal suffering is figured in, how do our customary uses of animals compute by Bentham's hedonic calculus? More pain or more pleasure?

Utilitarianism and teleological ethics, when honestly applied, have wrought much good and corrected the tendencies of deontology toward excessive dogmatism, as it has consequentialism's capacity to fall into excessive pragmatism. No doubt the ideal is some combination of the two, or (as the animal rights and other ecological issues show) some new philosophical source that places fresh emphasis on the inherent goodness of species and beings in themselves. We will come to this later.

But combinations have not always proved easy to work out, and the conundrum suggests the complexity of ethical thought. For religionists, belief in life after death may also be factored in, not just in a crude rewards-and-punishment sense, but also in terms of the added dimension given by an eternal and universal perspective.

A further complexity lies in the issue of **intentionalism**. Do we judge the *intentions* of an ethical actor, or the consequences alone? Not seldom—as most of us know from our own experience—we intend good, but the results of supposedly ethical actions turn out to be disastrous. Often, deontologists claim that consequentialists, though meaning well, assess less adequately than they the true nature of reality and the limitations of human nature, and botch the job by being excessively optimistic, or pessimistic, about what will work. Teleological ethicists will respond that deontology usually doesn't work much better, its abstractions being far too hidebound to fit the infinite variety of real human life. In sum, ethical thinking is crucially important, but is no place for someone who wants a 100 percent success record. Intentionalism is central to the great debate over whether ethics should follow clear and definite laws or rules, or whether the important thing is to do the loving thing in every instance, whether that is always consistent with other situations or not. Often that would be the way judged best by intentionalism, since love in the highest sense is commonly held to be the supreme value. But what if it turns out that approach was too permissive and applying a few hard-and-fast rules might have worked better?

Buddhism, for example, teaches *karuna,* compassion, as the great virtue, equal in value only to wisdom, that is, true insight—the two go together, for one does not effectively have one without the other. Yet Buddhism also presents a number of precepts for living in accordance with compassion and attaining Nirvana. There are many for monks, and five basic ones are often undertaken by laypersons: not to take life, steal, engage in sexual misconduct, lie, or take intoxicants. Mahayana Buddhism teaches that bodhisattvas, persons near to Buddhahood, may act in a way guided solely by wisdom and compassion even when that seems to contravene ordinary moral rules. Unencumbered by egotism, they can glance down at a situation of human or animal suffering, with true insight see the actual factors that led to it, and guided by pure love take the right steps, whatever the cost in redemptive suffering on their own part, to counteract it.

Most of us, however, are far too impure in our perceptions and motivations to risk such ventures; it is overwhelmingly likely, says normative Buddhism, that we would do much better to follow conventional morality as our guide. Only a truly wise and selfless bodhisattva can be guided by love alone and not mess up.

And that's the problem. We need guidance as to how love is to be put into practice, both in means and ends. Religions and their rules force us to ask such questions as the following: Are some acts almost always contrary to love by their very nature, so much so that the exceptions are negligible and it is wisest to make it a rule never to do them? Are there others that are almost always a sure expression of ethical love? Does it make a difference whether we look at the acts deontologically or teleologically?

In practice, all the major religions, in their conventional expression, believe there is more wisdom—and safety—in following the rules than not. Some ethicists, however, have not been so sure. Probably the best-known modern exponent of a more radical position is Joseph Fletcher, who was a professor at an Episcopal seminary when he wrote his controversial book, *Situation Ethics*.[3] The basic theme of this work is that ethical decisions should be based on whatever the application of love is in a particular situation, not prior rules or laws. In other words, consequentialism taken to an extreme degree.

Fletcher opens his book with a story: A friend of his had arrived in St. Louis just as a presidential campaign was ending, and took a taxi. The cabbie remarked that he, his father, and his grandfather had always been straight-ticket voters for one of the parties. "Ah," said Fletcher's friend, "then I take it you voted for so-and-so." "No," replied the driver, "there are times when a man has to push his principles aside and do the right thing." Fletcher concluded that this St. Louis cab driver was his book's hero.

Situation Ethics aroused passionate debate.[4] The clerical author was accused of "the most unstable and absurd relativism" and worse, but he made a strong case in his reply that he was simply saying what has, in fact, long been the Christian stance on issues ranging from marriage (e.g., it is in principle indissoluble, but there are situations open to divorce) to war (it is evil, but there are situations that permit "just" war).

Try to think of how the situation-ethics principle could be applied to difficult problems like abortion, suicide, and the right to die. And whether situationalism really makes these hard decisions any easier or better in practice.

SIMILARITIES AND DIFFERENCES IN RELIGIOUS ETHICAL TRADITIONS

The major religions are broadly agreed on certain great principles of religious ethics, as they are in the practical juxtaposition of law and love. Such sources as the Ten Commandments, the Sermon on the Mount, the Five Precepts of Buddhism, the Qur'an (e.g., the "Islamic Decalogue" in 17:22–39), and the Analects of Confucius point to the evil of killing, inflicting injury, lying, the violation of property, and the breaking of oaths. All are concerned about the poor and the powerless, calling for justice toward them and commending the giving of alms and tithes for the assistance of those without means.

Increasingly, especially in the great religions as they emerged in the Axial Age, the era of religious founders(see Chapter 2), awareness of the worth and moral responsibility of the individual became more and more apparent. Doctrines such as karma, personal judgment leading to individual salvation or damnation, or the obligations of the Hebrew prophet or Confucian sage to stand alone if need be in denouncing evil emphasized—as did the founders themselves—that ethical religion is a personal as well as a collective duty.

At the same time, it must be recognized that there are significant differences in the ethics of the major religions. Generally, these are in the areas of application rather than of fundamental principle.

All recognize the essential wrongness of killing. One religion, Jainism, extends that principle to forbid strictly the killing of animal as well as human life; so to a large extent do the much more numerous Buddhist and Hindu faiths, though practice on this matter varies considerably among different social and religious classes, as does the concomitant practice of vegetarianism. Other religions, including Christianity, have generally condoned the killing of animals but have embraced minorities, such as Quakers and Mennonites, who have traditionally rejected any taking of human life and so have refused to take part in war and have opposed capital punishment, though the great majority of Christians have accepted "just war" theory, as we will see in the Chapter 15.

In the same way, all religions have recognized that marriage and sexual activity require some regulation for the well-being of society as a whole and to prevent exploitation of individuals, but have differed on the parameters of what is acceptable or to be recommended. Some endorse polygamy; others do not. Some hold up celibacy as an ideal, at least for religious professionals; others present marriage and the procreation of children as incumbent upon all. Some have taken premarital or extramarital sex much more lightly than others. As we have already noted, this is also an area in which much discrepancy between theory and practice has occurred, with a double standard not seldom obtaining between men and women. It must be further observed that traditional sex and marriage policies in most religions have worked toward the subordination of women.

CONTEMPORARY ISSUES IN RELIGIOUS ETHICS

Ethics is not merely concerned with theories or hypothetical issues, or with objective descriptions of the positions of various religions. It is, instead, the place where religion most frequently meets the real world in which it lives, engaging in issues that are often quite literally matters of life and death for real people. The ethics of medicine, and no less those of war and peace, clearly involve their real-life practitioners in stark decisions about who lives and who dies, much as they might wish it otherwise. Questions of who receives the use of scarce medical equipment, when life-support systems may be withdrawn from a terminal patient, or whether a city should be bombed, can hardly be construed in any other way. Many of these issues involve one's real view of human life. What is it really worth in extreme situations and in the face of very difficult choices, whether medical or of war or over against the preservation of nature? Let us examine some of these areas in practice.

Medicine is, as always and by its very nature, one important area in which science is creating new problems in defining and valuing human life. Many old and new issues involving ethics and, ultimately, philosophical or spiritual ideas about what it means to be a human person cluster about the practice of medicine today. Even old issues that were known and discussed as far back as ancient Greece, such as artificial birth control, abortion, voluntary euthanasia or the right to die, and experimentation on humans, are revamped today because of immense advances in medical research that have vastly expanded the possibilities as well as intensified the moral problems.

Physicians and society make life-or-death decisions when only so many transplants or artificial kidney machines are available, and their allocation must be determined by a hospital "God committee." Questions such as abortion and human experimentation provide

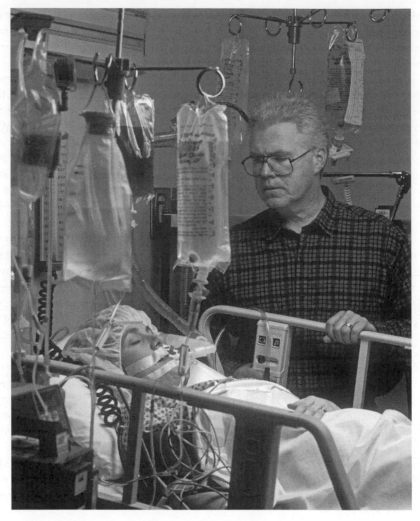

Concerned spouse watches over wife in hospital intensive care unit   (Mira/Alamy)

current foci for the kind of issues raised here. Society also decides on the biological life and death of individuals when it decides how to allocate resources for preventive medicine, what medical facilities it provides or fails to provide for the underprivileged, and for what issues it will dispose of human life in war. Let us look at a couple of examples of medical controversy, then go on to some other issues.

The Abortion Controversy

Since the 1960s and 1970s, one of the most bitter of all public ethics controversies swirled around abortion, the medical termination of a pregnancy by the removal or destruction of the unborn fetus. Lines are drawn between the *pro-life* faction, which sees nearly all abortion as nothing less than murder and favors laws narrowly restricting or prohibiting it; and the *pro-choice* side, which believes that in some cases the procedure can be morally justified. Pro-choice advocates therefore oppose most legislation against abortion, contending that the woman concerned is the only person who can morally make the decision. Let us look at the history and the issues.

In the United States until the 1860s, abortion was generally legal until the time of "quickening," that is, until the fetus began to move in the womb. The practice was then widely criminalized, largely under pressure from the rising medical profession. Laws against abortion were accepted without too much open dissent until the mid-twentieth century, when pressure mounted to once again legalize it. In the tumultuous 1960s, rising feminism and movements toward sexual and personal lifestyle freedom combined to convince many that whether or not to have an abortion should be an individual decision rather than a criminal matter. (It is no coincidence but characteristic of the times that, in the same period, sex of any sort between consenting adults was widely decriminalized and also made a matter of personal choice.)

A number of states repealed antiabortion laws. Finally, in 1973, the U.S. Supreme Court, in the famous *Roe v. Wade* case, declared laws banning abortion in the first two trimesters, that is, the first six months of pregnancy, to be generally unconstitutional. The Court said, "The right of privacy . . . is broad enough to encompass a woman's decision whether or not to terminate her pregnancy." But the right is not absolute, and in the last three months of development it can become a "compelling" interest of the state to protect the unborn life, and abortion may then be forbidden except when the life or health of the mother is at stake.

By now, however, religious groups were getting seriously involved. It is easy to see why. Abortion is an ethical issue with profound religious ramifications. It concerns the origin and meaning of human personhood, life and death, male and female roles, individual priorities, moral values—all to a very high degree and in a very provocative way. But churches and other religious organizations found themselves as deeply divided as the population at large.

Statements by religious groups range from those that hold abortion a denial of the "right to life" and so wrong in its very nature, to those that emphasize freedom of choice. It should be pointed out, though, that the range does not, in fact, cover all theoretical possibilities.

Groups on the pro-life side, such as Roman Catholics, Eastern Orthodox, and the more conservative Baptist and Lutheran denominations, have indeed condemned all abortion as murder, or at the most made concessions only in cases of rape, incest, or to save the life of the mother. They contend that some acts are simply inherently wrong, and so should be condemned as such by ethicists and forbidden by law, and that the taking of innocent human life—whether before birth or after birth—is one of them.

The more pro-choice religious bodies—even the most liberal, such as the Unitarian Universalists—do not, however, necessarily take the opposite position of condoning any abortion for any reason. They do not suggest that there is no moral problem with abortion on demand or abortion just for reasons of convenience. While some totally secular proabortionists may hold that an aborted fetus is nothing more than tissue, few religionists of any stripe would deny it is important to recognize it as a human being or a potential human being, and therefore to view the question of its life with appropriate gravity.

But—note here that they are at least partly consequentialist while the antiabortionists are almost entirely deontological, starting with rules and "oughts"—prochoice religionists believe other issues than the life of the fetus must be taken into account too: the physical and mental welfare of the mother, the prospect of the child's postnatal neglect or abuse, the kind of family (if any) there is. For them, the question of who decides—church, state, doctor, or mother—is also important. Thus, though they may hold that the recriminalization of abortion is not the answer, liberal religionists recognize the moral complexity of the issue and urge that decisions about it in any particular case not be made lightly.[5]

What are the issues? Here are some, as summarized in Edward Batchelor, Jr., ed. *Abortion: The Moral Issues.*[6] I have added some queries and comments in parentheses.

Is abortion a religious issue at all? (We have shown, I think, that it touches on some of the gravest and most central issues usually associated with religion: the person, life and death, men and women, moral choice.)

If so, how can the religious ethicist clarify the moral issues? (She or he can ask: What is life? When does it begin? When does human life become a separate person? How much does quality of life count when we have reason to think a baby will be deformed, neglected, abused, or contribute to the physical or mental pathology of the mother? What are the priorities? Who decides?)

Is preserving and protecting innocent human life an absolute value? (If so, what about war? Modern war almost inevitably entails the bombing or shelling of cities, in which babies and other innocents are slaughtered. If one is antiabortion, should one also be a pacifist, and also opposed to capital punishment, since all evidence indicates that innocents are sometimes executed?)

Are the rights of the mother or the embryo foremost?

Is an unborn child a human being with full rights?

If so, at which stage of its development? (The issue of *hominization,* when an embryo became a human being in the full moral sense of the term, was one which concerned premodern as well as contemporary theologians. Many classical thinkers held such views as that it was not ensouled and so truly human until 40 days after conception, or until after a full, though miniature, human body had formed. Modern thinking, as we have seen in the case of *Roe v. Wade,* also made some distinction between stages of pregnancy, often in terms of trimesters, or periods of 3 months. For antiabortionists ancient and modern, though, this periodization does not affect the moral case; to them, the unformed fetus must be seen as incipiently or potentially human, and so subject to moral treatment as a human.)

What is the proper place and function of religious, judicial, and legislative institutions in public-policy decision making on this issue? (Again, the question is: who decides?)

Even one who holds that abortion is always morally wrong still must deal with the question of whether it should be a state or an individual decision. These are separate issues, for not everything that is immoral is necessarily an appropriate subject for legislation and police intervention. The example of overeating has sometimes been cited. Although most moralists hold that gluttony is a sin, it has rarely, if ever, been suggested that excessive consumption of food should be made a criminal offense, unless in the context of something like times of war or famine.

On the other hand, such parallels seem fatuous and demeaning of life to those for whom abortion is simply direct, premeditated murder, hardly on the same plane as having an extra piece of cake one doesn't need. They point out that in all societies the violent and illegitimate taking of life is plainly criminal. It may not be possible to enforce laws against it in every instance, and offenders may sometimes be able to plead extenuating circumstances. But criminal life-taking is nonetheless a very serious denial of values most people hold sacred. Thus the state's visible, public, legal banning of it is a crucially important symbol of moral consensus, and that is why the statutes are on the books.

Needless to say, the antiabortionists' estimate of contemporary society, in which life as an unqualified value no longer appears to have consensus at least in the case of abortion, is not very high. The next step, they suggest, will be the "scientific" elimination of superfluous postnatal humans, which would be only an extension of what is now the fate of inconvenient prenatal persons.

Abortion is clearly a difficult and painful issue. It may be fair to say that no simple response is totally just to all the questions, points of view, and doubts that can be raised. It is probably no less right to suggest that discussion of the issue is immensely important today, not only because it is a major and divisive political question, but also because it raises extremely basic and crucial religious issues about human lives and souls.

The Right to Die

The next medical-ethics issue, involving euthanasia, or mercy killing, and the right to die, involves many of the same questions about the limits of human life and is, I am afraid, no less tangled.

We may take as an example the case of Karen Quinlan.[7] In April of 1975, this young New Jersey woman of 21, a few days after moving out of her parents' house in order to be on her own, consumed several alcoholic drinks in a bar along with friends to celebrate a friend's birthday. She had apparently also taken tranquilizers and/or barbiturates the same day, and had reportedly been dieting, maybe fasting, as well. All a bad combination. Suddenly she passed out, and never regained consciousness. She was taken home and then to a hospital. Her life was sustained, but without credible hope that she would recover mentally, talk, or ever be in more than a passive state.

She moved, showed various facial expressions, and even seemed sometimes to laugh or cry, but was never able to show any sign of clear intelligence or of being able to survive independently. Her family finally petitioned a court for permission to make Karen's father her guardian, with the expressed intent to withdraw life support from her, which the hospital would not do without legal consent. To Karen's loved ones, it was a matter of mercy, of the conclusion of a life that could never find further fulfillment, and of the right allocation of the family's limited emotional and financial resources. The New Jersey attorney general opposed the petition, saying that such a course was "death at will" and would "open the way for euthanasia." That is, it would set a precedent for allowing others, whether family or the state, to decide if such a patient shall live or die. Lawyers for the two attending physicians, who also opposed the petition, spoke of "Nazi atrocities" and implied that approval would move society in the direction of the Third Reich's euthanasia practices.

The petition for guardianship was denied by a lower court, but the New Jersey Supreme Court finally ruled in the family's favor. However, by then, the case was complicated for the Quinlans by ambiguous signals from the Roman Catholic church, of which they were devout members. Karen remained in a vegetative state for another 10 years, then died of pneumonia in June, 1986. The family had at that time asked that no antibiotics or blood-pressure medication be given, that is, that no special measures be taken to keep this patient alive.

Were they right or wrong?

Many of us have had the sad occasion to see a once lively and lovely friend or loved one fall into an apparently irreversible comatose state, with little or no flicker of consciousness, kept alive by various tubes and other "miracles" of modern medicine, perhaps—if and when aware—in pain or intense discomfort, and we have wondered if it would not be better just to "let her go" or "let him go."

Yet we, like the physicians involved, have also had to confront the awesomeness of any decision involving life or death, for oneself or another. When does one have the right—if ever—to unilaterally decide death for another? For a Karen Quinlan? For a grandmother obviously dying a hard and painful death of cancer? For a young friend suffering and despondent from AIDS? If one believes in a spiritual dimension to life, is pain, or even unconsciousness, necessarily the worst that can happen to one and death necessarily better? Who decides?

And what about making that decision for oneself? For while patients may sometimes be totally unconscious or mentally incompetent, in many other cases it is not so easy to say—they may speak but not rationally, or drift in and out of rationality, and one may be at a loss just how to assess their poignant pleas to be allowed to die—or to be kept alive at all costs.

Often the issue can be put in terms of not directly letting a patient die by "pulling the plug," that is, withdrawing life-support systems including even nourishment, but of simply not taking *extraordinary measures* to sustain life beyond what could be seen as its natural termination. Here too, the ethicist must face hard questions. Is there any real difference? Should financial cost—since extraordinary measures are usually very expensive—be a factor in such a decision? What about the allocation of perhaps scarce medical talents and resources? Should a patient's likelihood of long-term survival in any case be part of the decision?

And again, who decides? In some cases, people have made prior legally recognized declarations, often called a *living will,* defining just what medical care they want and do not want if they are unable to make a decision at the time. In other cases, the decision must fall to family and physicians, and the latter may well be heavily influenced by legislative guidelines and the prospect of malpractice suits.

And there is the other end of life. What about infants who are born seriously defective? Should they be kept alive by extraordinary measures, or allowed to slip away through "benign neglect?"[8]

Then there is the different—but comparable—case of Elizabeth Bouvia, terminally ill, who sought *voluntary death,* that is, suicide for medical reasons, in another widely publicized case.[9]

This saga commenced in 1983. Elizabeth, then only 25, had cerebral palsy and was almost totally paralyzed. Her life had been unhappy. She tried to starve herself to death. Her doctor determined to force-feed her, saying she would someday change her mind and be grateful to him. A local court was asked to enjoin him from doing this. But in December of 1983, it ruled in favor of the doctor and the hospital keeping the young woman alive even against her will. Later courts, however, upheld Elizabeth on the grounds that any patient has the right to refuse medical services. (Nonetheless, she did in fact appear to feel the point had been made and, after being allowed to decline nourishment, continued eating enough to sustain life. At the time of writing she was still alive.)

Undoubtedly, there are many unofficial suicides by seriously if not terminally ill patients who see no more point to their lives and just want to end the pain. Is this morally justified, whether done by a patient directly or with the help of a sympathetic physician? Joseph Fletcher wrote some time ago that there is no "real moral difference between self-administered euthanasia and the medically administered form when it is done at the patient's request," when the patient has become a "sedated, comatose, betubed object, manipulated and subconscious, if not subhuman."[10]

Those who favor euthanasia at a patient's request often cite the example of the Netherlands, where since 1985, the state has agreed not to prosecute physicians who administer euthanasia under guidelines adopted by the Dutch medical association.[11] These are:

Only a physician may implement requests for mercy killing.

The request must be made by a competent patient.

The patient's request must be free of doubt, well-documented, and repeated.

The attending physician must consult another physician before proceeding.

A determination must be made that no one pressured the patient toward the request.

Further, the patient must be in "unbearable pain," with no relief considered medically possible.

Within these parameters, in theory, even children could request to die and have the request implemented without their parents' consent, since it was thought that parents might have extraneous motives in acting or not acting on their children's behalf, though at the time of writing no such case has actually occurred. The Dutch provisions do not, in fact, cover euthanasia requested for someone else judged incompetent; they deal only with self-requests made by competent patients.

Can these standards be morally justified? They were opposed in the Netherlands by certain conservative religious groups, which held that medically assisted suicide is only another form of suicide, which in turn is simply self-inflicted violent homicide. Only God or nature, opponents say, have the right to take life whether one's own or another's. (You will note a sharp conflict here between deontological ethics, which put the rules first, and consequentialist ethics, which are willing to bend the rules for the sake of a presumably overwhelmingly benign objective, the ending of hopeless "unbearable pain.")

Many Dutch citizens also recalled uneasily the Nazi occupation of their country in World War II, when it was the scene of some of the acts of involuntary euthanasia performed by that unholy regime. Altogether, the Nazis put to death "humanely" some 90,000 people judged deformed, mentally defective, or otherwise useless—a figure that looks small only when set beside the 6 million Jews and other unwanted persons liqui-dated in the "final solution." In Holland as in the United States, fear was expressed that opening the euthanasia door even a crack could lead in the end to public callousness toward all sorts of state-supervised "convenience," or public-policy deaths, perhaps ulti-mately even on the Nazi scale. (You will recall the same argument made about abortion.)

No doubt because of that memory, the Dutch provisions emphasized the patient's own voluntary request made in a condition of mental competence. Defenders of the policy say that this makes the Dutch practice absolutely different from the Third Reich's involuntary euthanasia and liquidation programs. Quite unlike the unspeakably dehu-manized practices of the Nazis, defenders argue, the Dutch guidelines show extraordi-narily acute sensitivity to suffering and to individual rights, including the right to die.

To confuse the two quite different policies, the Nazi and the contemporary Dutch, they would say, is to give way to totally irrational fears and emotions in a situation that calls instead for making hard, clear-headed distinctions and choices. These can only be made on a case-by-case basis, and that is what the policy permits.

Opponents of these practices contend that medically administered suicide and euthanasia are morally no different than murder, and say that no one has the right to prejudge the continuing worth of a human life, one's own or someone else's. Even a life in great pain, and seemingly close to natural death in any case, may be able to give and receive love, and experience spiritually important states. There are other values in human life than minimizing pain and maximizing comfort, even for one *in extremis.*

What do you think?

THE ROLE OF WOMEN IN RELIGION

A science fiction novel by Ursula LeGuin, *The Left Hand of Darkness,* presents a world in which all people are both male and female. They go through cycles in which they are first one sex, then the other, and the mentality, institutions, and customs of that society are permeated with the ramifications of this unearthly biology.

In our society, however, no fact is more basic than the division of humanity into people who are permanently female and those who are permanently male. This, together with the need to nurture children, affects everything from family structure to world politics and is profoundly reflected in the symbols and institutions of reli-gion, from the Madonna or mother and child as a transcendent symbol to the almost exclusively (until very recently) male control of most traditional religious institutions. Although occasionally religion may rise to the purport of Paul's dictum that "in Christ there is neither male nor female," it is also very conscious, even obsessively conscious, of the fact that humanity was created male and female, and that great meaning must lie behind this division. Religious myths, symbols, and roles (and society as sanctioned by religion) are shot through with images implying set male and female patterns of life. It is fair to say that most traditional religion has been patriarchal in that it has made men the source of authority and of correct teaching in both church and family.

Today, the idea of distinctive male-female roles, and the validity of religious sym-bols and lines of authority based on distinctive sexual biology, are being challenged as never before. Women in particular, aware that traditional symbols and structures in religion and society have usually served to put them in a secondary role, point-edly query whether women should be ordained ministers and priests or whether God should exclusively be called Father. These challenges have had a profoundly disruptive effect because they raise issues and feelings that go very deep. For some people, religion should sanction the hierarchy of heaven and earth, with the father head of the family on earth as God is in heaven. For others, God is beyond gender, can transform all social structures, and liberates each person to be what one is as an individual self rather than one who just has to follow a predetermined sexual or social role.

Bishop Barbara Harris after consecration as the first Episcopal woman bishop
(VIN CATANIA / Getty)

If the latter attitude prevails, religion in the future will be affected by paradigms of the human person much less categorized by sexual roles than in the past. A person will be one of either sex who can do and be virtually anything—and this capacity will need to be reflected in roles in religious institutions as well as in religious language and symbols. One of the greatest challenges Christianity and Judaism, together with other religions, will have to face in the next few centuries will not come from science, political revolution in the usual sense, or new vogues in philosophy or theology, but from the far-reaching implications of these changes in sexual images and roles. They touch deeply the structure and very language of these faiths, from God as Father on down. One could well ask how much change on such a deep level Judaism and Christianity could take without really becoming different religions. For some, such a transformation would be welcome; for others, tragic.

Feminist theologians have emphasized the immense significance of these challenges, and have outlined no less far-reaching changes to implement them. One example is the Roman Catholic Rosemary Radford Reuther, who in books like *Sexism and God-Talk: Toward a Feminist Theology*, advocated calling God both male and female, and ordination of both men and women.[12] Another example is Judith Plaskow, a Jewish theologian, in *Standing Again at Sinai* and other works, urged bringing-out and understanding of the full and equal role of women in scripture and religious life.[13]

Not all who urge equality of men and women in religion, of course, insist that male-female roles should be flatly identical, as though there were *no* differences between the sexes except some physiological details. Instead, they feel that both have distinct and equally valuable contributions to make to worship and theology—which in itself would mark a radical enough change, since heretofore perhaps 90 percent of theology has been written and worship conducted by males and undoubtedly reflected largely male experience.

Perhaps that is why orthodox, masculine religion favors the concepts of divine sovereignty and law. Teachings of feminine spiritual leaders, such as Mary Baker Eddy and Helena Blavatsky in the nineteenth century, favored ultimate unity and spiritual evolution on the analogy of, perhaps, the womb and nurture. In the same light, the image of a woman behind the altar, bringing forth bread and wine, might be congenial. I once attended an ordination ceremony in a tiny modern Gnostic church in which the practice was for a husband and wife to be ordained as priests together and thereafter to celebrate the Gnostic Mass jointly and equally, each performing parts of the service that especially emphasized the sacred meaning of his or her gender.

RELIGION AND ECOLOGY

What does religion say about our relationship as human beings to our natural environment? This is an issue which has become increasing urgent, with talk of global warming, extinction of species, pollution of land and sea, and possible exhaustion of nature's resources, which to many represents a terrible if not sinful abuse of God's creation. There is also the simple notion that nature in all its beauty is meant to lead our thoughts to the divine. The Iranian-American philosopher Seyyed Hossein Nasr wrote, "What is certain is that, first of all, the environmental crisis must be recognized

Dead fish on the surface of a polluted river   (overcrew/Shutterstock)

in its spiritual and religious depths as well as its outward effects."[14] But the world's religions do not speak with one voice on the subject.

On the one hand, there are those who reject any idea that we should have much concern about ecology and the environment. Too much of it leads to the idolatry of "nature worship" instead of the worship of God, and our real fate is tied up not with the natural world but with the life to come; some would add that the end of this world, and the final judgment, is coming soon, too soon for what we do to nature to make much difference. Moreover, humans are meant to have "dominion" over nature and all its creatures, which in these eyes means use it in terms of what is good for humans, not for the environment or for the other beings.

Then, in the middle, many hold that nature, as divine creation or manifestation of the divine, is worthy of respect and even reverence, though not exactly worship, and that moreover dominion means not just the right to exploit it, but also the responsibility to care for it.

Finally, on the opposite extreme from those who decry "nature worship" are those who freely bend the knee before tree and mountain, honoring nature for its own sake regardless of the human situation. At most, they say, humans are only a part of nature, and not its best-integrated or most responsible part; let us not demean nature in all her ancient glory for the sake of human folly.

Let us look at the matter briefly in terms of various faiths.

Buddhism affirms the interconnectedness of all things, and the great virtue of compassion. It also affirms that the root cause of suffering is attachment, which on one level means simply a materialist/consumer mentality: thinking you can find happiness by consuming as many goods as possible. But if all is interconnected, by harming nature through excessive consumption of its bounty we ultimately harm ourselves. By failing to show compassion for animals and all sentient beings we reject that fundamental virtue, and by living to consume we only bring about our own suffering.

The American Buddhist Stephanie Kaza has written that "The word *free*, as used in Western discourse, carries the assumption that anyone should be able to do whatever s/he needs to achieve economic success." "The implication," she says, "is that a person can be 'self-realized' or liberated *independent* of context and relationship. This concept of freedom often is interpreted as freedom *from* relationship."

But "The Buddhist view, in contrast, starts form the assumption of relationship, defining freedom within this context. Each person exists and acts in a web of relationships. . ."[15]

These include the webworks of our relationships with nature as well as one another. To think we can be free without acknowledging all our relationships, natural or human, is delusion that can only lead to suffering. Therefore nature should be loved and valued as we love and value ourselves. Needless to say, not all Buddhists or Buddhist countries have lived these values, and some have emphasized other aspects of the religion, like salvation or "living in the moment," but the big picture is there.

Jewish approaches to environmental ethics are often linked to the concept that "The earth is the Lord's and the fullness thereof." (Ps. 24:1) This, according to a scholar like Jonathan Helfand, counters any view that human "dominion" meant the right to exploit and destroy at will. Helfand points out that God's ownership of the world was not relinquished in the Law.[16] One could say this is evident in, for example, rules for the Sabbath and sabbatical year, where humans withdraw from manipulation of much of the planet and its resources on the Lord's day, in Orthodox Judaism not even turning on an electric light after Sabbath sundown. On the sabbatical year declared in Leviticus, God reasserts that "The land is mine." (Lev. 25:23)

In Jewish thought this perspective is in line with the view, implied in scripture and expressed in the Talmud (later commentaries) that everything God created is good and has its place; everything manifests some divine purpose. Therefore the natural order must be maintained and all its inhabitants respected as who they are. The strictures in the Law against intermingling or interbreeding different substances or creatures (e.g., Lev. 19:19), bizarre as they may sometimes look to moderns, bear witness to the same ultimate principle: the creation is meant to be used very cautiously and judiciously, disrupting the way things were made as little as possible.

Judaism and Christianity have sometimes been criticized for seeing the world in human-centered terms, especially for the "dominion" idea already mentioned, from Genesis 1:28. Yet Christian leaders too, ministers, popes, and patriarchs, have spoken out strongly on behalf of stewardship of the earth, that we are to keep it pristine on behalf of its actual "owner," God, and use it only in ways that are to his glory. The encyclical *Centesimus Annus* (1991), of Pope John Paul II, for example, refers to "the irrational destruction of the natural environment." It adds:

> Although people are rightly worried—though much less than they should be—about preserving the natural habitats of the various animal species threatened with extinction, because they realize that each of these species makes its particular contribution to the balance of nature in general. Too little

effort is made to safeguard the moral conditions for an authentic 'human ecology'. Not only has God given the earth to man, who must use it with respect for the original purpose for which it was given to him, but Man too is God's gift to man. He must therefore respect the natural and moral structure with which he has been endowed.

Protestant leaders and denominations have also expressed environmental concerns. A report prepared at a World Council of Churches (the WCC includes Eastern Orthodox churches, but is predominantly Protestant) gathering in Rio de Janeiro in 1992, on the theme of "Searching for the New Heavens and the New Earth," included lines like these:

> We affirm the goodness of God's creation and the intrinsic worth of all beings. Anthropocentric, hierarchical and patriarchal understandings of creation lead to the alienation of human beings from each other, from nature, and from God. The current ecological crisis calls us to move towards an eco-centered theology of creation which emphasizes God's Spirit in creation (Genesis 1:2, Ps. 104), and human beings as an integral part of nature. Instead of dominating nature, men and women have the responsibility to preserve, cultivate the earth, and to work with God for sustainability of the planet.[17]

Further Protestant discourse on the environment has tended toward two directions. Heirs of traditional liberal Protestantism, with its emphasis on nature and nature's God, and its relatively benign view of human nature as a whole, do not minimize the present ecological problems, but hold out hope and affirmation of our ability to change. Liberal Protestantism is now sometimes identified with what is called Process Theology, a school based on the philosophy of Alfred North Whitehead. Declining to give precedence to being over becoming in God, it emphasizes that the universe, including creative divine nature, is in continual process of development, dependent on the free will of God and all beings. John Cobb, Jr., one of the leading process theologians, wrote that Christians believe in the power of God and God's grace, and "we can place no limits on the extent to which grace can make us into new men and new women."[18]

As for evangelical Christians, the place of humans has involved something of a paradox for many of them who are also environmentalists. They have been uneasy with the way some nonreligious environmentalists seem to have an affection for all species but the human, almost implying the earth would have been better off without us. This attitude is much at odds with the biblical position, as they see it, that humanity is the crown of creation on earth, meant to be its steward.

On the other hand, evangelicals are also very much aware of human sin, indeed often taking liberals to task for not regarding it seriously enough. Those who destroy all around irresponsibly have cut themselves off from God and God's plan. Yet humans themselves are also God's creations, with capacity for conversion and change.[19] The evangelical answer to see both the glory and the fallenness of humanity together, and this is no where more obvious than in the human relation to the natural environment, toward which we can be both profoundly appreciative and wantonly destructive.[20]

Moving East, the Ecumenical Patriarch Bartholomew (pictured on p. 55), leader of the Eastern Orthodox Churches, said in an encyclical of 2006:

We are treating our planet in an inhuman, godless manner precisely because we fail to see it as a gift inherited from above. Our original sin with regard to the natural environment lies in our refusal to accept the world as a sacrament of communion, as a way of sharing with God and neighbor on a global scale. It is our humble conviction that divine and human meet in the slightest detail contained in the seamless garment of God's creation, in the last speck of dust.[21]

Hinduism, with its view of the entire cosmos, natural and human, as a manifestation of Brahman or a divine creation, has a firm basis for honoring all nature as among the veils of God. It might also be mentioned that the example of Mohandas K. Gandhi, is his practice of nonviolent resistance, has been an inspiration to many in the environmental movement. Nonviolence seems especially appropriate to those who want to save rather than destroy. Setting themselves as ordinary individuals against powerful corporations and governments, their best strategy, like his, has often been simple noncooperation or just getting in the way: they have sat in trees rather than let them be felled, or sailed between whaling ships and their prey.

In Islam, one finds the same idea as in the other monotheistic religions, that the environment is sacred because it is a creation of God. This tradition particularly likes to emphasize that the environment is also sacred because it is a reflection of divine truth. Many passages in the Qur'an, including the headings of such chapters as "The Sun," "The Dawn," and "Morning Hours," reflect a sense of this loveliness mirroring the supreme source of beauty. That which opens a way to God must certainly not be destroyed.[22] Seyyed Nasr commented that ". . . all the creatures in the natural world sing the praises of God. In destroying a species, we are in reality silencing a whole class of God's worshipers."[23]

Finally, moving toward the radical side of nature-religion, let us mention a book by Bron Taylor, *Dark Green Religion*.[24] Taylor distinguishes between "Green Religion," which affirms that environmental friendliness is a religious duty, in more or less the way most of those advocates just cited have contended, and "Dark Green Religion," which goes farther. In this new creed, which he sees emerging in the environmental movement, nature itself, not just nature's God, is sacred. Therefore mountains and trees themselves have intrinsic value, as much as any god or God, and are due supreme reverence. Dark Green Religion, he declares, is often in tension with merely Green Religion, since the latter is usually only part of a traditional faith in which the transcendent is preeminent over nature.

Dark Green Religion, on the other hand, unapologetically claims for itself what has been labeled "nature worship," animism, pantheism, reverence for Gaia, and the like. Its Holy is not transcendent, "up there," but immanent, "out there" in nature, or rather is nature itself. And, its present-day prophets proclaim, the hour has now come for Dark Green Religion to reveal itself as the coming faith of the future.

Like it or not, the issue of environmentalism and religion is upon us. How do you feel about it? Should these concerns just be ignored, or denied, in favor of other aspects of religion? Should we take a middle-of-the-road tack of doing what we can so long as human needs, and wants, are met as well? Or is it time for a radical move toward saving nature whatever the cost? It's your world, and you will have to decide. If we don't, nature may decide for us.

SUMMARY

Virtually every day of one's life, one is faced with the need to make decisions involving ethics and morality. Although the line between them is often fuzzy, morality tends to deal with standards or practices in areas of personal life, while ethics deals with the philosophical reasons behind them, or with the practices of larger groups, such as professions or societies. Today, the intellectual analysis of proper human behavior is generally called ethics.

Ethical thought has been given two sources, deontology, or the "ought" approach—duty and obligation—probably derived from a greater power than the individual; and teleological, or consequentialist, which judges ethics by results. Both have been vigorously defended and criticized, and attempts have also been made to combine them or to bring in other considerations. Utilitarianism, the "greatest good to the greatest number," is a kind of consequentialism.

Most major religions in some way combine law and love—love or compassion as the supreme ideal, rules and norms showing how it is ordinarily to be implemented. Most religions also are fundamentally united in basic ethical values, such as opposing murder, theft, or sexual irregularity, and favoring honesty and justice. But differences can be found on some specifics of how these values are to be construed in practice.

Current areas of intensive ethical debate include abortion, euthanasia, and other aspects of medical ethics; the role of women; and environmental ethics. All these involve difficult, often painful, decisions about priorities and religious values. As a further example, we will choose a topic perhaps even more difficult and painful: war.

KEY TERMS

consequentalist ethics, p. 223
deontological ethics, p. 222
intentionalism, p. 225
meta-ethics, p. 221
mufti, p. 223

natural law, p. 222
natural rights, p. 222
teleological ethics, p. 222
utilitarianism, p. 224

CHAPTER

15

Horror and Glory:
Religion Confronting War

Civil War battle, painting by F.C. Yohn (1875–1933)   (Library of Congress prints and
photographic division [LC-USZ62-61636]/Yohn, F.C. [Frederick Coffay], 1875–1933)

LEARNING OBJECTIVES

After reading this chapter, you should be able to:

- Give your definition of war.
- Discuss the question of when and how war began.
- Describe what it means to be in the midst of battle.
- Present just war theory and alternative views on war and morality.
- Talk about the myth of the hero in relation to war, and the traditional warrior's code.
- Say whether you agree it is possible to enjoy war and desire it, or that war could ever be good for its own sake.
- Describe also the horror of war.
- Discuss the concept of "a moral equivalent to war." What do you think it might be?

INTRODUCING WAR

Most people today would probably agree that war is among the worst things, indeed on a large scale probably *the* worst thing, that humans can inflict on themselves. Not only is combat itself, the deliberate maiming or killing of humans by one another, and the destruction of property, unspeakably terrible—and contrary to any moral code in almost any other situation—but war requires for its execution many more acts otherwise immoral: deception (in propaganda and espionage), terror, and the treatment of human beings instrumentally as objects to be manipulated. Not only that, but war usually brings in its wake still other evils: pillage, rape, hunger, torture, disease.

Nonetheless, those who fight in wars, though committing acts that outside a state defined as war would be criminal and despicable, are honored and called heroes. After what they have been through, many feel they have earned honor

Humans fight wars repeatedly—not all humans at all times. Though the matter has been disputed, most evidence indicates that organized warfare rarely, if ever, occurred in Paleolithic times, that is, among hunting and gathering societies before the discovery of agriculture. Societies at that level until European contact, such as the Inuit (Eskimo) or the Australian aboriginals, did not fight wars between different tribes or communities. Violent quarrels between individuals and small groups no doubt occurred, but not organized warfare. Some peoples remain like this.

Anthropological evidence suggests that some 5–10 percent of traditional human societies are non-warring. These include, according to a recent list, not only the aforementioned Inuit and Australians but also groups ranging from the Saami or "Lapps" and the !Kung or "Bushmen" to the Andaman Islanders and such Native Americans as the Shoshone.[1] Some of these live in isolated environments; some practice the tactic of fleeing when danger approaches. (As Douglas P. Fry observes, "In Western thinking, it may be cowardly to flee from danger, but not all peoples think like Westerners. Fleeing is often seen as simply sensible.")[2] The nonviolent mentality can be deeply ingrained. Kirk Endicott once asked a Batak (of Sumatra) why his forefathers had not

not shot the poisoned blowpipe darts they used for hunting at the Malay slavers who formerly raided them. The Bataks' shocked answer was: "Because it would kill them!"[3]

But with the coming of agriculture came permanent communities that engaged in trade and in which goods, sometimes great treasures, could amass. The idea of raiding occurred to those first kingdoms, and the raids—and so defense against them—became organized. Then came philosophers to work out why and when defensive war, or even raiding itself, was justified by religion and morality.

WHAT IS WAR?

It has been said that only two species out of all the billions on earth fight wars: humans and ants. (Recent observations have put our closest evolutionary kin, chimpanzees, on this short and infamous list as well.)

It's a matter of meaning, of course. Many animals fight for food, mates, self-protection, to protect their young, to guard their territory, and if carnivores, to eat. But these are one-on-one struggles, or at the most disorganized brawls. Following several leading authorities, we define war to mean organized combat between groups large enough to allow for a division of duties within the ranks of each, movement into battle in organized formation, and deployment of such strategies as encirclement or ambush.

Arthur Ferrill, for example, opines that "'organized warfare' can best be defined with one word. . . *formation*." "When warriors are put into the field in formation, when they work as a team under a commander or leader rather than as a band of leaderless heroes, they have crossed the line (it has been called 'the military horizon') from 'primitive' to 'true' or 'organized' warfare."[4]

Similarly, Roy Prosterman characterizes war as "A group activity, carried on by members of one community against members of another community," in which the primary goal is to inflict serious or lethal injury on the other community, or at least to make that result sufficiently likely as to accomplish the first group's overall objective.[5] As Douglas P. Fry observes in adopting this definition, the emphasis on battle between communities indicates war as such is not primarily focused against particular individuals or kin groups. The definition therefore excludes individual homicides and feuding, and "clarifies that *war entails relatively impersonal lethal aggression between communities.*"[6]

Keith Otterbein, in *The Evolution of War*, spoke of war simply as "armed combat between political communities"[7]—"political" of course implying a fairly well-regimented organization. Later, in his monumental *How War Began*, the same author declared that "Warfare consists of the activities of military organizations, groups of men—under the direction of leaders—who engage in armed combat."[8] In the present work, we will mean by war, in contrast to other kinds of fighting, combat between political communities (though not necessarily nations, so as to not to exclude civil wars and insurgencies) using reasonably well-defined formations, leadership, and strategies requiring such organization.

THE FEEL OF WAR

What is war like? Here let us focus just on what it is like to be an ordinary soldier at the field of battle.

Many writers have forcefully evoked the peculiarly intense emotion, the profound awareness of vulnerability, and sense of confusion of war up close. The participant feels this war-world is wrong, the breakdown of human order, the place of powerful emergence of something almost alive that should not be, yet is. Nonetheless, the soldier can only do what he is trained to do, and keep loyalty to his comrades. Stephan Crane, in his great novel of the American Civil War, *The Red Badge of Courage*, called up with especial vividness the comradeship strangely coexisting with sheer anarchy amid the horror of combat itself; this closeness and chaos is, in its own time, the great fact of the soldier's life; and over that chaos, in the line of Poe, "Death looks gigantically down."[9] Crane's central character, Henry Fleming, an ordinary Union blue, felt:

> There was a consciousness always of the presence of his comrades about him. He felt the subtle battle brotherhood more potent even than the cause for which they were fighting. It was a mysterious fraternity born of the smoke and danger of death. . .
>
> Presently he began to feel the effects of the war atmosphere—a blistering sweat, a sensation that his eyeballs were about to crack like hot stones. A burning rage filled his ears. . .
>
> Buried in the smoke of many rifles his anger was directed not so much against the men who he knew were rushing toward him as against the swirling battle phantoms which were choking him, snuffing their smoke robes down his parched throat. He fought frantically for respite for his senses, for air, as a babe being smothered attacks the deadly blankets.[10]

Nonetheless, war happens, and many are the ways in which it is justified. Why do we do what we say we hate?

JUST WAR THEORY

In Western thought, the concept of a just war, one that can be waged without moral or ethical offense, goes back at least to Cicero in ancient Rome. It was since developed by such Christian thinkers as Augustine and Thomas Aquinas, becoming a part of authoritative Roman Catholic teaching.

The current Catholic Catechism speaks of the obligation of all citizens and governments to work for the avoidance of war, and praises "those who renounce violence and bloodshed" and "make use of those means of defense available to the weakest," so bearing witness of gospel charity, and bearing "legitimate witness to the gravity of the physical and moral risks of recourse to violence, with all its destruction and death." Here the stance of many saints and other conscientious objectors to participation in war is evidently acknowledged and honored.

Nonetheless, the Catechism goes on to outline the traditional criteria of a just war. It must be ordered by legitimate authority, and it can only be defensive, in order to repel unjust aggression against one's own country or another otherwise helpless people; the damage that would be inflicted by the aggressor must be "lasting, grave, and certain"; all other means of putting an end to the aggression must have been shown to be ineffective; the defenders must have serious prospects of success; and the use of arms must not inflict evils greater than those to be eliminated. The last point is particularly stressed in light of the modern ability to destroy "whole cities or vast areas with their inhabitants."[11]

Just war theory in Judaism today is comparable. Jewish thinkers surveying its development from the beginning to the present note that, in the Hebrew Scriptures, the ancient Israelites felt entitled to fight total war against the Canaanites inhabiting the land they believed God had promised them, but wars against other nations outside this territory were only defensive and pursued only to the extent necessary to preserve that inheritance. The views of modern Jews on war have, like those of modern non-Jews, ranged from absolute pacifism to militarism, but the middle position concedes that war may sometimes be necessary, but that only defensive war is morally acceptable.[12]

Jewish ethicists, understandably, have a special concern regarding war and the state of Israel. Questions remain open as to in what way modern Israel has special religious as well as political meaning, where its boundaries should be from the religious point of view, and if the contemporary curse of "terrorism" ever justifies "preventive" war as defensive in a morally acceptable sense.

In Judaism, examples of attitudes toward warfare range from the already mentioned wars fought by ancient Israel to conquer and defend the Holy Land, to a nonviolent act of resistance to the Roman occupation of Palestine in 26 CE. According to the historian Flavius Josephus, to protest the procurator Pontius Pilate's plan to set up Roman standards to Jupiter in the temple, extreme blasphemy and idolatry to the Jewish mind, masses of Jewish peasants refused to plant crops and sat down in a protest around the ruler's palace until he was forced to relent.[13]

Mention should also be made of the Islamic concept of Jihad, or Holy War that, as defined by respected commentators, is not dissimilar to Just War in Jewish and Christian thought. Jihad may be used to spread or defend Islam, but only after a call to belief has been extended, and there is a reasonable possibility of success for the jihad. The medieval jurist Ibn Taymiyyah declared that "lawful warfare is essentially jihad," and urged soldiers to avoid hatred but to "Fight in God's cause those who fight you; but do not provoke hostility, for God does not love aggression."[14]

Many just war precepts like the foregoing, building also on the work of the Dutch Protestant Hugo Grotius (1583–1645), have been adapted into international law endorsed by the United Nations. Grotius wisely adds to considerations like those above, "It is necessary to observe that a war may be just in its origin, and yet the intentions of its authors may become unjust in the course of its prosecution. For some other motive, not unlawful IN ITSELF, may actuate them more powerfully than the original right, for the attainment of which the war was begun. It is laudable, for instance, to maintain national honour; it is laudable to pursue a public or a private interest, and yet those objects may not form the justifiable grounds of the war in question."[15]

Let us take as an example the German invasion of Poland on September 1, 1939, the beginning of World War II. By just war theory, the Polish attempt at military defense against this aggression was justified. Their nation had been attacked, essentially because of Hitler's desire to expand the Reich eastward; diplomacy had failed; the Poles believed, wrongly, that they could mount an effective resistance; and they also believed, very rightly, that Nazi victory would utterly devastate the Polish nation and people.

(I recall, as a small child safe in central Illinois that fateful late summer day, hearing a strange voice speaking on the radio in a foreign language: harsh, vibrant with excitement, and oddly hypnotic. My mother said, "That's Hitler. He's starting a war." I could not understand a word of the German, but I have never forgotten the outlandish passion in those tones. Here is another side to war from the rather dry reasoning of just war theory: the role of the charismatic leader, intense feeling, and partisan loyalty. Later in this chapter we look at what Aldous Huxley called "crowd intoxication," a spell Adolf Hitler was well able to cast over many of his countrymen.)

There were complications. German radio claimed their attack was in retaliation for a repulsed Polish assault on a German radio station near the border. After the war it was learned that the incident had been faked, and that the "Polish" assailants, left dead on the ground for the benefit of news photographers, were actually unfortunate German concentration camp inmates dressed in Polish uniforms. But this "justification" shows at least how just war concepts can be manipulated in propaganda, as well as by the passions of the hour.

France and Great Britain declared war on Germany September 3 in support of Poland, because they believed by then that Hitler could not be stopped except by force. Reflect on whether, and how, these secondary declarations by powers not directly attacked could be justified by just war rules. Were there other options?

TO THE RIGHT AND LEFT OF JUST WAR

Other principles have also been invoked in relation to war. Those called *realists* contend that moral concepts appropriate to individuals cannot be applied to nations, which operate simply out of their need for security and in their self-interest. For these purposes war may sometimes be required.

Then there is militarism as a principle. Militarism is one name for the notion that war is not necessarily bad, but can be healthy for society, teaching bravery, self-sacrifice, and loyalty to the greater good. This view is close to that of the warrior code, to be discussed later. A Christian example of the idea that righteous war is holy and need not be fought with the constraints of just war theory is found in the rhetoric of the English Puritan preacher William Gouge (1575–1653) who, drawing heavily from the example of Israel's wars in the Hebrew Scriptures, allowed that offensive wars are permitted for the "Maintenance of Truth, and purity of Religion," pointing out that "God himselfe is stiled A man of warre, and the Lord of hosts."[16]

The German general Friedrich von Bernhardi, writing on the eve of World War I, and whose influential thinking characterized much of the attitude behind that military effort, declared, "War is a biological necessity of the first importance, a regulative element in the life of mankind which cannot be dispensed with, since without it an unhealthy development will follow, which excludes every advancement of the race, and therefore all real civilization."[17]

At the opposite pole is pacifism, the belief that war is never righteous or holy. An early modern example would be George Fox (1624–1691), a younger contemporary of William Gouge, and like him tested by the bitter English civil wars of religion in the seventeenth century. Fox was the major founder of the long-lasting Religious Society of Friends (the Quakers), traditionally pacifist. Though his views on the wrongness of war evolved gradually, by 1651 Fox could say, when asked to serve in Cromwell's Puritan army fighting against the royalists, that he "lived in the virtue of that life and power that took away the occasion of all wars. . . I told them I was come into the covenant of peace which was before wars and strife were."[18]

Nonviolent struggle may be advocated in place of war, as it was by Mohandas K. Gandhi (1869–1948). Gandhi's term was *satyagraha*, "holding to truth." This principle, he said, "excludes the use of violence because man is not capable of knowing the absolute truth and, therefore, not competent to punish."[19] The practice can include disobedience of laws regarded as egregiously unjust, passive resistance (such as lying down before British troop trains), and noncooperation with authorities considered illegitimate, as when supporters of Gandhi refused to accept appointments or honors from the British government of India.

Mohandas K. Gandhi, 1931   (India Images/Dinodia Photos/Alamy)

But the basic principle behind "holding to truth" is simply speaking to the heart of the opponent, less by words than through the active demonstration, as in strikes, marches, and Gandhi's fasting, of one's own willingness to suffer in preference to acceptance of what the *satyagrahi* regards as profoundly wrong. The Gandhian way proved its worth in the struggle for Indian independence, and in the 1960s Civil Rights movement under Dr. Martin Luther King, Jr., in the United States.

Those two activities, in India and the United States, were essentially internal conflicts within a nation. Just war principles, laid out with war between two sovereign states primarily in mind, are challenged anew in the cases of civil war and revolution or insurgency. They need to be rethought, whether on Gandhian or other lines, in the twenty-first century, for it now looks as though traditional warfare, between one more or less equal nation and another, is becoming more and more obsolete. Wars since World War II ended in 1945 have typically been undeclared border skirmishes, or internal resistance, insurgency, or revolution leading to civil war, though outside powers have often been heavily involved. These facts raise such theoretical questions as what is just cause for rising up against one's own government, or an occupying power; who has legitimate authority to declare a revolution (the people as a whole?); how does one gauge probability of success; and what means to rectify the situation peacefully must be tried first, and for how long? (For one answer, read the U.S. Declaration of Independence.)

Another issue that ought to be mentioned, though we cannot discuss it here in detail, is the role of passages in major religious scriptures that appear to endorse or glorify war and even genocide. One thinks of those in the Bible concerning the Israelites' conquest of Canaan and the extermination of peoples who stood in the way, those verses in the Qur'an counseling war against unbelievers and those who persecute Islam, or a passage like that from the Hindu Bhagavad Gita cited below on righteous war and the righteous warrior.

Within these respective religious traditions, and others, some have interpreted such lines in a symbolic way, saying they really mean in inner battle against evil and unbelief all of us must fight. Others say they refer to times long past, but are no longer really applicable today. Philip Jenkins, in *Laying Down the Sword: Why We Can't Ignore the Bible's Violent Verses*, about such texts, says that, "As religions grow in scale and sophistication, they evolve to the point that they realize the failings of those original scriptures. . . the uglier we come to find [such] texts. . . the more evidence we have of the *success* of the biblically based religions, rather than of their primitivism or blood lust."[20] The same can be said of the attitude of many Muslims and Hindus toward their violent verses.

But whether such an explanation would satisfy every adherent or critic of these scriptures may be open to question, and indeed Jenkins also gives plentiful examples of their invocation on behalf of war and genocide in recent as well as ancient times. It may be a matter of circumstances. As Jenkins states, most of the time "most believers can and do live with outrageous scriptures without pursing their implications." But when war looms and draws you into it, the verses are there. "If the circumstances in which you live make you seek such justifications, then you will find them. . . If you don't need them, you won't find them."[21]

When you do need them, another world awaits. For a quite different way to look at the human proclivity for war slips in beside the just war debate and alongside the scripture debate, and demands its chance to be heard. Here is what it has to say.

Why is it that, despite all the high-sounding philosophy of just war theory and the paeans regularly addressed to peace, people nonetheless seem so attracted to war and violence? Look at the bestseller books and blockbuster movies, of this year or the last or 10 years ago—a great proportion will have to do with war, and though the good guys may win, these works many of us love to read and see hardly disguise the fact that it is the battle scenes and things blowing up that get our blood coursing. Is it that somehow, deep down, we really like war? Would the liking have anything to do with religion, or at least with mythological themes?

If so, we had better come to terms with that before we finish with discussing religion and war.

A REMARKABLE DISCOVERY

In 2009, the largest hoard of Anglo-Saxon gold ever unearthed was found in a farmer's field in Staffordshire, north-central England. The fortunate finder was a hobbyist using a metal detector he had bought at a jumble sale. Worth millions in sterling or dollars, this collection contained over 11 pounds of gold and more than 5 of silver.[22]

Moreover, this particular cache consisted almost entirely of military objects. Their trim was studded with gems and all worked with such exquisite beauty it brought tears to the eyes of one expert. Although some Anglo-Saxon collections have contained such finely wrought items as jewelry, brooches, chalices, and of course there is the famous Sutton Hoo funeral ship, apart from two or three crosses the Staffordshire assemblage represented war gear: sword fittings, harness ornaments, parts of armor, elaborately decorated with animal figures and swirls, all of consummate craftsmanship. The only significant inscription, on a strip of gold and in occasionally misspelled Latin, was martial as well as biblical. Translated and completed, it offered this prayer: "Rise up, O Lord, and let thine enemies be scattered; and let them that hate thee flee before thy face" (Numbers 10:35).

The remarkable treasure is probably from the seventh- or eighth-century Anglo-Saxon kingdom of Mercia, though it may represent booty taken by the Mercians, people nominally Christian by this time but primarily known as an energetic and aggressive folk. The history and culture of "Dark Age" Mercia has heretofore been obscure, but no doubt remains now that this ancient realm was a center of wealth and war.

However, our main concern, as we turn attention to the mythology of war, is simply this: Why were these objects, the fittings of warriors and dedicated to war, so beautifully crafted? What means all this artistry?

Consider the jewels, mostly garnets, embedded in the armor cladding. Jewels are often thought traditionally to concentrate spiritual power, like a battery. Their use today in rings signifying commitment—engagement rings, fraternity and sorority rings—may reflect a trace of this idea. Certainly

Gold sheath and folded cross, from the hoard of Anglo-Saxon gold found in England, 2009 (UPPA/ZUMAPRESS/Newscom)

the bejeweled crowns of kings suggest as much even more directly and powerfully. So do the "stones of fire" enclosed in settings of gold filigree (Ezek. 28:14, 16), in the breastplate worn by Aaron and his successor High Priests in ancient Israel (Ex.39:8–18).

The beauty, symbolism, and splendid craftsmanship of these instruments of self-protection and death to others—shield and sword—clearly mediated values of virtually ultimate importance to the warrior people. Although the animal-form symbols also found on Anglo-Saxon and Nordic implements (apart from those of Christian provenance) are not too well understood, undoubtedly on one level, like the cross and biblical charm, they are to be counted as supernatural guardians.

PROTECTION AND MORE THAN PROTECTON

Being a fighting man is an anxious business. On the field of battle wariness—being alert to every unexpected motion or sound beside or behind, as the hand sweats on sword hilt or trigger—can make the difference between victory or defeat, life or death. Fear gnaws at one's insides; the eternal struggle between caution and need to strike first blurs one's brain. Even in camp or on parade ground, under martinet superiors themselves anxious about being obeyed, the common soldier has little real peace till victory is assured, or he enjoys a few well-earned hours or days of leave.

Moreover, the warrior knows that no matter how wary or skilled one may be, the field of battle is finally a gruesome lottery. A few inches, a few seconds, can be the difference between fatal or superficial blow, and who can totally control all such variables? Even if one endures beyond fatigue and never really sleeps, the moment will come when some sign is missed and the enemy is upon one. The decision, in other words, is finally in the hands of the gods or fate. Therefore, it is vitally important that, while the man of arms takes care to be prepared in terms of weapons and the skill to use them, he be no less forearmed in the face of the invisible powers that also govern the field. He must be sure that he is guarded by the right amulets and charms, has articulated all possible protective spells and rituals, and has the best divine names and chants on his lips.

So it was that the Anglo-Saxon's gems with their magic guarded the bearer, as did the fighting beasts with their ferocity. So it was that Homer's proud Greeks and Trojans in the *Iliad* knew that the favor or displeasure of one god or another could save or curse a mere mortal, so the knights of King Arthur were careful to attend mass before setting out on an adventure and to ask the prayers of hermits.

Even the help of another's spirituality can be of benefit. David Finkel, in his splendid chronicle of a single unit of U.S. troops in Iraq 2007–2008, *The Good Soldiers* (a volume one enthusiastic commentator declared "may be the best book on war since the *Iliad*"[23]), mentions a soldier who, though wounded, said that, "thanks to God, and Jesus, and a wife who tithes and sings hymns and reads the Bible for two hours a day, sometimes three, he was fine."[24]

LIVING THE DREAM

Two parallel strands of ethical and moral philosophy have accompanied the fighting man from the first wars down to the present. One strand is the thinking behind the "just war" discussions, that peace is good and war is evil, even if at times a necessary evil.

The other strand is the ancient warrior ethic, which extols the virtuous warrior and presents him as supremely good if he simply follows his own code. While the cause ought to be righteous, that decision is really in the hands of others, and his task is merely to do what a warrior is supposed to do. As he does it, his values are courage, honor, and victory. They shape the ideal warrior, and to be that person is the true soldier's dream.

The commander of the battalion followed in *The Good Soldiers*, cited above, Lt. Col. Ralph Kauzlarich, liked to say, virtually as a mantram, "It's all good." In a meeting of his company commanders, at a time when the situation in the part of Baghdad under his guard was far from encouraging, Kauzlarich spoke "in the slow, precise diction he used when he was all about persuasion." "You guys are living the dream right now," he pronounced. "You truly are living the dream. Talk to your people about that. Make sure they understand why we do what we do."[25]

Living the dream. That would be the dream evoked by armaments like those of the Mercians, arms lovingly manufactured as objects of beauty. Beauty, the portal of timeless reality, the outpost of the archetypes that underlie that changing world, suggests that what one does under its aegis is greater than oneself. Armed beauty is part of "the dream" and helps war become a kind of mysticism. It makes the battles one fights, all one does, part of a myth that explains in narrative form the way the world works, perhaps even how it came into being through struggle and how the gods fought demons at the beginning. We today can be part of that eternal struggle.

"Living the dream" elevates one into participation in the eternal myth of the hero, discussed in Chapter 3, one who undergoes the initiation of blood and (even if oneself imperfect), by cunning, skill, bravery, and strength overcomes minions of darkness: the heroes Hercules, Rama, Beowulf, Lancelot, the Maid of Orleans. Insofar as the Anglo-Saxon armor was embellished with the metal of light, set with the fiery jewels of cosmic power, and enlivened with beasts caught in undying moments of action, it bespoke its wearer as engaged in the world's unending drama of heroic war. The warrior's code was never put better than when Krishna addressed Prince Arjuna in the Bhagavad Gita, as the latter mooted whether he should go into battle against his kinsmen.

> [T]o a warrior, there is nothing nobler than a righteous war. Happy are the warriors to whom a battle such as this comes: it opens a door to heaven.
>
> But if you refuse to fight this righteous war, you will be turning aside from your duty. You will be a sinner, and disgraced. People will speak ill of you throughout the ages. To a man who values his honor, that is surely worse than death. The warrior-chiefs will believe it was fear that drove you from the battle; you will be despised by those who have admired you so long. Your enemies, also, will slander your courage. They will use the words which should never be spoken. What could be harder to bear than that?
>
> Die, and you win heaven. Conquer, and you enjoy the earth.[26]

(It might be mentioned that Gandhi read the Bhagavad Gita as his favorite scripture, but took its war to be allegorical of the eternal battle against evil, and admonitions like the above as addressed to his nonviolent warriors, who could be the strong or weak, young or old, men, women, or children, but who all the more needed a special sense of courage and honor.)

Or, as the early eighteenth-century Japanese *Hakakure*, a manual for samurai warriors, put it more succinctly:

Japanese samurai warrior   (Photo Japan/Alamy)

The most important thing for a warrior is to keep death ever foremost in his mind. . . Therefore, you should live every day as though it were your last. Live every hour as though you had only a few more minutes to live. . . [T]he warrior has nothing else to worry about, because he realizes that he has only to live in the present moment with the utmost intensity. . . The way of the warrior is fulfilled in death.[27]

How do myths of the warrior help in living up to such an exacting standard? In that great modern epic, J.R.R. Tolkien's *The Lord of the Rings*, when Frodo and his companion Sam find themselves on the way into a horrible cavern called Cirith Ungol, they firm up their morale by recalling old heroic stories. Sam, thinking of the no less perilous adventure they were themselves on, acutely observed, "Why, to think of it, we're in the same tale still! Don't the great tales never end?" To this Frodo replied that, while the tales continue without cease, the people in them come and go, generation after generation, as each fights the particular shape taken in its own time by the Dark Lord.[28]

In this endless warfare, we can only do what we can in our own time. As Gandalf, Frodo's wizard-mentor, noted, "[E]ven the very wise cannot see all ends."[29] And again, while we may not have wished for the battle given us in our time: "But that is not for [us] to decide. All we have to decide is what to do with the time that is given us."[30] For a warrior of sword or spirit, that "what to do" is taking part in the ongoing mythic battle of which he or she is a part, whose beginnings and endings may be lost in the mists of time, but whose present field is clear enough.

So it was that a modern warrior could see himself and his men, battling the almost daily bombers and snipers met in the treacherous half-war that followed "Operation Iraqi Freedom," as still "living the dream."

THE JOY OF BATTLE

For Ralph Kauzlarich, the dream he was living was clearly dream in the sense of an inner terrain that lifts the soul into the larger world of archetype and myth, making the dreamer spiritually a moving part within a great dream, and "It's all good."

That is because another facet of the mythology of war is realization that, as in all truly mythical living—in contrast to our flat ordinary ambivalent lives—a deep joy is called up, deeper even than the fear and grief—at least for some, some of the time. One may recall George C. Scott, playing General George S. Patton in the film *Patton*, saying half to himself as he surveyed a smoking scene of deadly battle, "I love it. God help me I do love it so. I love it more than my life."[31]

General John J. Pershing, commander of U.S. forces in France in World War I, quashing a proposed Army study on the causes of war, reportedly said the answer was obvious: "Men go to war because they enjoy it."[32] Perhaps not all, there is also the observation of the brilliant but sardonic Union general in the American Civil War, William T. Sherman, that "War is hell"; an adversary of his, the Confederate general Robert E. Lee, put it more judiciously, "It is well that war is so terrible, otherwise we would become too fond of it."

Not a few civilian commentators have assumed that the cause of war lies in the negative side of human nature. We fight, they say, out of lust for power, to prove our strength, out of insatiable greed for the goods of another, or simply out of the evil that stems from original sin or flawed karma. In this view, improve the human condition, or elevate moral character, and our perverse lust for war will wither away.

But there is that other "militarist" side. Is the occasional war good for us? Does it awaken among those in whom they had been too long dormant such virtues as patriotism, heroism, self-sacrifice, bonding man to man, and idealism about a noble cause?

Like General von Berhardi, previously cited, the philosopher G.W.F. Hegel averred that through war "the ethical health of peoples is preserved. . . just as the blowing of the winds preserves the sea from the foulness which would be the result of a prolonged calm, so also corruption in nations would be the product of a prolonged, let alone 'perpetual', peace."[33] John Adams, later second president of the United States, said as the American Revolution began, that war was the only way "to prevent luxury from producing effeminacy. . ."[34] Though no longer intellectually fashionable, one can hear similar views expressed now almost as much as ever, even if half-apologetically, on various internet blogs, on talk shows, in after-dinner conversations.

TERRORISM

A word should be said also about "terrorism," much in the news now and in a real sense the most provocative form of warfare active in the twenty-first century. Terrorism means indiscriminate destruction of enemy life and property by underground groups, with a view to expressing rage and demoralizing the foe, they hope leading them to make concessions or just give up. Terrorism is frequently practiced in the name of religion, often by groups identified as "fundamentalist" though usually disavowed by the religious mainstream. What motivates them?

Terry Eagleton has pointed out that such groups, like "fundamentalists" generally (though most are not violent), believe truth is absolute.[35] For such believers, truth and error are at opposing ends of the spectrum, and there is no gray in between. "You're either with us or against us, and evil." The terrorists' truth means theirs is a perfect society, and the other's error is total and no better than nihilism, believing in nothing. Error's political expression inevitably leads to anarchy, the lawless chaos of a society without absolute rules based on absolute truth.

But the terrorist also recognizes that in such a polarized world, chaos may well bring in its opposite in the end, so work for good. Creating conditions of nihilism and anarchy through terror could induce the world to "flip" to pure belief and the perfect society. This is similar to the closely related apocalyptic mentality. It says that conditions are only going to get more and more terrible, with wars and rumors of wars, until—when it seems like they couldn't get any worse—in a sudden, wonderful reversal the kingdom of God breaks through.

Probably not all so-called terrorists have thought their actions through in this way. But like revolution—which is often a secular version of apocalyptic—the prospect of forcing radical, even total, social change through sudden violence has a crypto-religious side. We are here dealing with actions and forces that are far greater than those of ordinary, everyday life, but like war are living a myth.

MYTHIC TIME AND OURSELVES AGAIN

Going back to joy, several recent books on war, such as Lawrence LeShan's *The Psychology of War* and Chris Hedges' *War Is a Force That Gives Us Meaning*, have confirmed Pershing's remark by emphasizing the fascinating pull of war. LeShan stressed that battle enables us to move into what he terms "mythic" as opposed to "sensory" reality. In the "mythic" world, and that is the world of the terrorist also, one is "living the dream," and feels tremendously alive, whether in the face of hell or glory, in a way we never do in our humdrum everyday lives.[36]

Perhaps no one said it better than a woman who survived the London blitz: "It was a marvelous time. You forgot about yourself and you did what you could and we were all in it together. It was frightening, of course, and you worried about getting killed, but in some ways it was better than now. Now, we're just ourselves again."[37]

That "ourselves again" of the London woman after the blitz is what LeShan called "sensory reality," that is, the world as it is seen by the ordinary senses, in ordinary time, with all its usual dimness and drabness, without the glamor of the heightened mood with adrenaline flowing brought by the danger, the thrill of occasional victory, and the overarching common purpose of wartime. Come wartime, and the gray ambiguities of most human issues, including when and when not to kill, are wiped away, to be replaced by a world of bright colors and stark contrast between good and evil: "mythic reality." Our side and the enemy are clearly defined over against each either, like gods and demons, and all moral imperatives are subordinated to one: Victory! War in effect suspends the Ten Commandments, and substitutes its own supreme precept: Whatever it takes, Win!

Much that in ordinary time would be wrong—murder, grievous injury, capture, deception, destruction of property—is now justified if those terrible means bring victory closer. Innumerable ugly impulses usually kept caged, the tigers and pythons of the mind, can be unlocked to have their day in war, whether with grim acceptance or fierce joy.

Other drives break the bars as well. War permits, even encourages, excessive use of alcohol, tobacco, and other drugs when available, whether as escape from its dread or to fortify oneself for action. Moreover, it is well known that the alternative consciousness of war frequently allows for greater sexual license than ordinarily; by the same token, psychoanalytic commentators have frequently pointed to the phallic significance of the sword, and no less of the gun with its explosive discharge.

LeShan concluded:

> [T]he promise of war offers a clean conscience, full membership in a group, meaningfulness to one's actions and intensity in one's life, and a chance to change to an easier, less stressful, more magical way of organizing reality. Where else can you get all that at once?[38]

The other writer cited, Chris Hedges in *War Is a Force That Gives Us Meaning*, imparts much the same message. As a reporter who had covered war zones for the *New York Times*, he came to feel conflict's addictive power. Even after being sickened by war's horrors, he has found himself going back time and again, trying to reach and comprehend the core of this human affliction. He came up with the following summary.

> The enduring attraction of war is this: Even with its destruction and carnage it can give us what we long for in life. It can give us purpose, meaning, a reason for living. Only when we are in the midst of conflict does the shallowness and vapidness of much of our lives become apparent. Trivia dominates our conversations and increasingly our airwaves. And war is an enticing elixir. It gives us resolve, a cause. It allows us to be noble.[39]

No wonder a dedicated warrior could call it "living the dream." In this connection, we ought to set alongside the comment of LeShan and Hedges one by the popular writer on mythology Joseph Campbell:

> People say that what we're all seeking is a meaning for life. I don't think that's what we're really seeking, I think that what we're seeking is an experience of being alive, so that our life experiences on the purely physical plane will have resonances within our own innermost being and reality, so that we actually feel the rapture of being alive. That's what it's finally about. . .[40]

To be alive, to be sure, but is all rapture the same? Here are some lines from a remarkable autobiographical novel, *Storm of Steel* by Ernst Jünger, based on the author's life as a German soldier in World War I. His vivid narrative depicts not only the endless anxious tedium, the fear, the sickening horror of what is seen and done on the battlefield, but also moments of another kind. In the midst of one engagement:

> I was to observe that there is a quality of dread that feels as unfamiliar as a foreign country. In moments when I felt it, I experienced no fear as such but a kind of exalted, almost demoniacal lightness; often attended by fits of laughter I was unable to repress.[41]

Commencing the great offensive of March 1918:

> The immense desire to destroy that overhung the battlefield precipitated a red mist in our brains. We called out sobbing and stammering fragments of sentences to one another, and an impartial observer might have concluded that we were all ecstatically happy.[42]

Certainly not all would agree. Finkel records not only his Iraq commander's "living the dream," but also his troops' incessant cursing—like that of all soldiers everywhere—at everything from the food to the regular danger and the filth, heat, and stink of their part of Iraq's dismal capital. Finkel's book goes on to record the hideous lifelong deformities from wounds, and the posttraumatic stress disorder, suffered by some of these men. Their dream soon enough became a nightmare.

THE HORROR OF WAR

The meaning of war is clearly intense, but is it horror or fear or joy? It is as though emotion is raised to such a pitch that ordinary distinctions fall away, like elements heated to the plasma state and no longer solid, liquid, or gas.

C.S. Lewis, later famous as a writer on religion, was on the other side from Jünger as a British lieutenant at the time of that 1918 confrontation. Here is what he faced on the field of battle:

> . . . the frights, the cold, the smell of H. E. [high explosives], the horribly smashed men still moving like half-crushed beetles, the sitting or standing corpses, the landscape of sheer earth without a blade of grass. . .[43]

Many others have commented on what it is like to see, and smell, a field littered with bodies, many twisted into grotesque shapes, many horribly mutilated or in various stages of decomposition, among them some still moving, perhaps trying to crawl without arms or legs, moaning piteously; over all the pungent odors of gunpowder, feces released in death, swelling and decaying human flesh.

So it is that the dream can quickly, like the turn of a page, switch from glory to a lifetime of blindness, or in a wheelchair or, almost worse, to a haunting hallucination repeated mechanically in virtually every sleep, as the gunshots or dive bombers or helicopters roar down out of an ashen sky, over and over, night after night. Innumerable veterans have returned with post-traumatic stress disorder, a serious condition that involves frequent highly emotional flashbacks to the traumatic situation, anxiety, inability to sleep or concentrate, to establish solid relationships, and a drifting, purposeless life that often leads to dependence on drugs or alcohol. To put it another way, nothing back home is like the war in its intensity; one hates it yet is lost without it.

Warriors who go forth to war full of chivalry, a sense of dedication to a righteous cause, and with the cheers of their compatriots in their ears, can within 6 months of their "baptism of fire" find themselves continually tense, anxious, full of a cold, ceaseless fear that gets into the marrow of the bones, to be only expunged in the occasional explosion of anger, till the field of battle is left behind. They learn to see before and behind, start and shoot at anything unknown that moves, feel no real loyalty except to their comrades at arms, realize no one else will ever understand the extreme they were at, none except those who have themselves been there.

The myth of war, like all myth a narrative reflecting timeless truth, turns around after the heroic moment has passed to reveal a deeply ominous side as it becomes not only myth but also personal story. As one veteran put it, "Every day I was in Vietnam, I thought about home. And, every day I've been home, I've thought about Vietnam." Max Cleland, Vietnam amputee and former U.S. senator, commented, "Wars are not over when the shooting stops. They live on in the lives of those who fight them. That is the curse of the soldier. He never forgets."[44]

THE NONVIOLENT HIGH

It remains to indicate that nonviolent action in deadly conflict can induce the same ultra-intensity of unforgotten feeling as that besetting the soldier armed with sword or gun. Here is an example.

In March of 1965, the eyes of the world were on Selma, Alabama. As part of the Civil Rights movement under the leadership of the Rev. Martin Luther King, Jr., a large group of African Americans from Selma were planning a peaceful march from that town to the state capital, Montgomery, to present petitions for the redress of their many grievances under brutal racial segregation and discrimination. On March 7, called "Bloody Sunday," they set out, only to be stopped on the Edmund Pettus Bridge, just outside town, by white law officers who claimed the march was illegal and who, mounted on horseback, wielded whips, truncheons, and tear gas till the demonstrators were forced back to a church in the black section of Selma. Among the marchers were two young girls, Sheyann Webb, 8, and Rachel West Nelson, 9, both eager volunteers, who later recalled the event for an oral history project. Here is Sheyann's account of what happened in that church.

> So the church was the place to be, I thought. So we just stayed there and we stared straight ahead. And we cried. It just seemed in that moment that everything was so hopeless. . . I didn't think that crying and sobbing was ever going to stop. . .

But then later in the night, maybe nine-thirty or ten, I don't know for sure, all of a sudden somebody there started humming. I think they were moaning and it just went into the humming of a freedom song. It was real low, but some of us children began humming along, slow and soft. . . But it just started to catch on, and the people began to pick it up. . .

We was singing and telling the world that we hadn't been whipped, that we had won.

Just all of a sudden something happened that night and we knew in that church that—Lord Almighty—we had really won, after all. We had won!

I think we all realized it at the same time, that we had won something that day, because people were standing up and singing like I'd never heard them before.[45]

Indeed that night was a turning point. The next day Dr. King returned to Selma, while people of both races and from all over the country flocked to the beleaguered city to join the undefeated marchers. Finally a Federal Court order permitted the Selma to Montgomery march. It set out triumphantly, with King at its head, on Sunday the 21st.

Sheyann recalls the tremendous throng, perhaps 25,000 or even more, massed in front of the capitol building at its climax, King speaking, and at the end all shouting with him, "Glory, glory hallelujah," with a deafening roar. It was Martin Luther King, the nonviolent warrior, who as if in complement to the soldiers' "living the dream" through war, had famously proclaimed, "I have a dream." But Sheyann added later:

As I look back on it, I think the real victory wasn't the fact that we went to Montgomery and had that rally. . . The real triumph had been on March the seventh at the bridge and at the church afterwards, when we turned a brutal beating into a nonviolent victory.[46]

The editor of these reminiscences, Frank Sikora, wrote that

Rachel West Nelson, in recalling those turbulent days in 1965, said it seemed to her that something "divine" was taking place, and that even today she can stand on the street by Brown Chapel AME church and "hear" the sounds of the freedom songs that were so loved and so hated in those times in Alabama.[47]

WAR AND MORAL MEANING

By now it should be clear that the human meaning of war embraces far more than rational ethical discussion based on the principles of just war, conventional patriotism, the idealism of the pacifist, or the cool calculations of the "realist." War seems to engage feelings and motivations about as primal as any one can get at, from loyalty to kin and friend to emotion so intense it is hard to distinguish fear from joy, all so extreme as to become a lure. We may want to sample that loyalty and that dreadful rapture because it is so different from anything else. Yet we know that war and its ghastly results are so terrible many who have seen will not speak—of those mangled and mutilated bodies, those starving children, those leveled cities, those nights of sickening fear.

How do we think about war? The principles of course are important, for without them reasonable discussion could hardly begin. Think about them, and analyze wars past and present of which you have essential knowledge in terms of the various criteria for a just war, or for resistance to all war.

But would not the next step have to be dealing with the drives that make people want to live the hero myth as exemplified by the warrior, and to know the extremes intimately? That makes us want war even as we hate it? We would need not only an alternative means of conflict resolution, but also a force powerful enough to displace the ancient lure of war as a way of "living the dream" of intensity, meaning, and mythic power. By now we should realize that, until these drives are answered in some other way, humankind will probably find a way to continue fighting no matter how many noble resolutions are passed and peace conferences held.

Philosophers have talked about the need for a "moral equivalent to war," in William James' term. James thought it could be the "war" against nature—an unfortunate term, in these ecological times, but what he meant was simply the campaign to make our planet a better place for humans to live on through international cooperation rather than conflict.[48] The great science fiction writer Arthur C. Clarke proposed that the exploration of space could be that alternative to war.[49]

Some have also found a comparable intensity of life in nonviolent action for justice such as that of Gandhi and King, mentioned above, and we have seen how that alternative resounded in Selma.

Back to war, the novelist/philosopher Aldous Huxley wrote of the kind of "crowd intoxication" that excites and dehumanizes people in the mass till they "will believe any nonsense and obey any command, however senseless or criminal." Though he does not explicitly mention war, Huxley, writing in 1952, was undoubtedly thinking of the demagogic dictators who led the world into World War II. Huxley set those intoxicating political passions—which in my view should certainly include the rapture of war as depicted above—alongside alcohol, debauched sexuality, and drugs as means of getting outside the prison house of the self through "downward self-transcendence." But such poisons, he thought, are only surrogates for what we really want, something higher, loss of the ego-self in true liberation and transcendental spiritual experience, as known by the great saints and mystics. Would then the intensity of war be false and idolatrous mysticism substituting for the real thing?[50] The alternative a truly authentic spiritual life? Or nonviolent campaigning fueled by the spiritual resources of a Gandhi or King?

On the other hand, certain of the "new atheists" like Richard Dawkins, Christopher Hitchins, and Sam Harris, discussed earlier, have blamed religion, above all monotheism, for a great part of the world's wars. They claim that religions sometime use wars to attain their goals of converting and dominating nations. Religious leaders, they say, contribute to the fervor behind war and terrorism by proclaiming violence to be justified when used toward righteous ends or to fulfill the will of God, and their faiths promote irrational, emotional ways of thinking and acting that encourage fighting and killing for God.

In particular, say the antireligious, religion encourages the kind of tribalism, or nationalism, that exalts fierce bonding to one's own land, faith, and way of life, and then seeing those of other creeds and cultures as infidels and potential or actual enemies. Sam Harris wrote, ". . . faith inspired violence in at least two ways. First, people often kill other human beings because they believe that the creator of the universe wants them to do it. . . Second, far greater numbers of people fall into conflict with one another because they define their moral community on the basis of their religious affiliation."[51]

Against that, careful historical scholarship like that of William T. Cavanaugh has demonstrated that most conflicts that came to be identified as "wars of religion"—because the combatants on the two sides were predominantly of different faiths, and religion often featured in their respective propaganda—actually had far more complex and secular causes.[52]

Then there was George Fox's ability to say, out of his deep religious faith, that he "lived in the virtue of that life and power that took away the occasion of all wars."

What do you think?

SUMMARY

War is often defined as fighting based on organization, strategy, and division of roles. Its human origin is debated, but the prevailing opinion is that it is really a result of the discovery of agriculture and establishment of settled communities that attracted pillagers.

By many accounts being in war is an incomparable experience, extreme in all ways. It can be incredibly horrible and yet also fascinating.

War has been justified by just war theory, which says it is legitimate as defense against unjust aggression under certain conditions. Other theoretical response has ranged from militarism, saying war is good in its own right, to pacifism, which says it is never right.

The moral-religious issue of war is also closely related to the myth of the hero and the warrior code, which exalt the nobility of heroic struggle.

Some thinkers have endeavored to find a "moral equivalent to war," ranging from the improvement of living conditions on earth to space exploration.

JOURNEY'S END

We have just completed a long wandering exploration through the mysterious realm of religion past and present. We have looked at the manifestations of faith from its outer expression in the structure of temples and the organization of society to its ramification in the innermost places of the heart. In all this we may have found there to be no one concept or definition of religion that equally suits all its forms, but a core of meaning lies in its insistence, through countless clues and rules, that we humans live in a larger context of meaning than that of time, space, and matter alone. As William James declared, for religion an unseen order also envelopes our lives, and we must conform to it as well as to our everyday needs.

In this writing, it is hoped we have offered some sense of how that unseen order has been perceived by the inner eye, and how its arrangements have been mapped, throughout the world and the ages. However one feels personally about religion, it is an imposing picture.

APPENDIX

Studying Religion

Here are suggested projects to help you study, understand, and experience some of the material in this book. They are presented in connection with selected chapters. For further help, see Donald E. Miller and Barry J. Seltser, *Writing and Research in Religious Subjects* (Englewood Cliffs, NJ: Prentice Hall, 1992).

Paper or Report on Myth (Chapter 3)

Select a particular myth. Then do the following with it:

1. Introduce it briefly in terms of type (creation, hero, etc.), setting, and cultural background.
2. Tell the story of the myth. Include significant variants, remembering that Claude Lévi-Strauss said a myth must be known in all its variants to be fully understood.
3. Tell how we know about it—when, where, and how it emerged, when it was first recorded and published, and any modern influence it has had, including in movies, or in names such as Hercules that have become virtual bywords.
4. Describe the original historical and cultural setting of the myth, showing how it fits into that setting and expresses its values.
5. Give a modern interpretation of the myth, if you wish one that appeals to you personally, whether psychological (Freud, Jung, Hillman, etc.), structuralist (Lévi-Strauss, Eliade), political, economic, moral, scientific, whatever.

Meditation Experiment (Chapters 5 and 6)

Although various states of consciousness can be given religious value, one of the easiest and most beneficial to try out as an exercise in sampling religiously important states is the meditative. As an exercise to use in connection with academic study, however, it should be regarded as a psychological experiment, not a religious or spiritual practice. Don't do this experiment unless you feel very comfortable with it on all levels, and stop it if anything about it bothers you or feels wrong. But comprehending something about meditation is important for understanding many of the world's religious traditions, since it is a key practice in them, one that is a royal road to realizing the kind of consciousness they would consider liberated or enlightened. Even more generally, intentionally entering a meditative state can help one grasp how practices such as chanting or focusing can significantly alter feelings, perceptions, and the experience of space and time.

To try meditation, first find a quiet, uncluttered place where you are not likely to be disturbed and there is little to distract you. For your first efforts, 12 to 15 minutes should probably be about the right duration of time to allow.

Sit cross-legged on a cushion on the floor or the bed or, if you prefer, in a fairly hard chair. Fold or rest the hands gently, and close the eyes or focus them softly on a single point. Keep the spine and neck straight but not rigid. As far as posture is concerned, the important thing is to find the right balance between too much strain from rigidity and too much relaxation that will lead to corresponding mental sloppiness. Be free of pain and strain, but poised and alert.

On the mental level, the key is to stop the activity of the "monkey mind," as some Zen people call it, the stream of consciousness always running from one thing to another, in order to allow your mind a little quiet time just to be itself as pure consciousness. The way to do this, many teachers say, is to stop the onrushing activity of the mind by focusing on just one thing, sometimes called "one-pointed consciousness."

One focus of one-pointed concentration can be the breath. Either count the breaths from one to ten, as some Zen practitioners do, or just maintain "mindfulness" of breathing, following it in and out. You can also concentrate visually on a candle flame or some other object that will permit a calming yet focused gaze. Or you can have an audio focus, repeating a word or phrase very quietly over and over, or listening to a natural sound such as falling rain.

Keep up the practice until the mind is very still, then hold the stillness without—so far as possible—thinking about anything for a time. Then gently bring yourself out of the meditation state.

During meditation, you will undoubtedly experience wandering thoughts. Everyone does. Don't worry about them. Just let them go, following them away like released balloons disappearing into the sky, till they are gone.

You may want to write up this experiment as a paper or report, or a journal item for your own future reference. If so, here is a brief outline that may be of help in organizing and touching on important points.

1. Give the time and place, and describe the setting. Tell how you felt that day, especially when you went into the experiment. How was your health? Were there any major problems you were contending with?
2. Tell what technique (counting breaths, visual focus, etc.) you used.
3. Describe concisely what happened from beginning to end, particularly shifts in mood, emotion, and self-awareness. Include reference to internal or external distractions, and any especially vivid images that arose in your mind.
4. Analyze your experience of time and space. Did the 12 minutes, or whatever, seem especially short or long? What kind of awareness, if any, did you have of your spatial and physical environment, including your own body? (For some people this awareness falls away; for others it becomes especially acute.)

Give your overall reaction to the experiment. How did you feel about it afterward? Did it help you understand anything about religion?[1]

Visiting and Analyzing a Religious Service (Chapters 4 and 11)

A very helpful exercise you might do is visit a religious service in a tradition that is unfamiliar to you and write it up as a report. Here is an outline you could follow.

A preliminary note. For this exercise it would usually be best to select a group about which you do not have strong positive or negative feelings, but which would be fairly neutral for you and about which you can be objective. When you visit, be sure to dress appropriately and be respectful. If you take notes, do so very inconspicuously, and do not make a recording or video without first asking permission. It is best just to try to remember what transpired. On the other hand, it is usually all right to ask leaders or members questions afterward if anything is unclear. But depend on what you actually get from this experience for the paper, not what a book or Internet source says about the group—this is a field research project, to be based on what you actually see and hear; individual members or bodies may deviate quite a bit from the official teaching and practice of a denomination or tradition.

Background Information   Give the full name, exact address, and religious affiliation, including exact denomination, of the group; give the date and time of your visit; and give the name and type of service attended.

General Information   Describe the outside and inside appearance of the building, giving special attention to particularly important symbols and distinctive architectural features. Then describe the way visitors are greeted, and the sort of people in this group—their apparent social class, lifestyle type, ethnic background, average age, gender, and approximate number present. Describe in the same way the leadership conducting the service.

Account of Service   Describe what happened in the service from beginning to end. Try to give some sense of the emotional tone and subjective spiritual meaning of the activity. For example, was the opening dramatic or casual? Was the congregational participation emotional or reserved? Was much of the service spontaneous? Did it seem to be ancient ritual or contemporary?

Analysis   Analyze the worship experience in terms of the three forms of religious expression: theoretical (teaching), practical (worship), and sociological. At least one-third of the paper should be this part.

Theoretical.   What, essentially, does this religion teach? As far as you could tell from this one experience, from the sermon, practices, symbols, and so on, what seems to be the main message of this religion? You may need to distinguish between what was "officially" said in creeds or the like, and what really seemed to be most important to the people in the congregation as they took part.

Practical.   What was the basic nature of the worship? Formal or informal, old or new, structured or spontaneous, intellectual or emotional, or something of all of these. What message about how this group conceives of the role of religion, and the best way for humans to build bridges to Ultimate Reality, did this worship communicate?

Sociological.   What kind of group was it? As well as you could tell from this one experience, was it close-knit or diffuse? Was this group composed of mostly people drawn to the religion by family or ethnic ties, or mostly committed converts of different backgrounds? What role did the priest or leader play? What message about religious experience was communicated by the nature of the group?

Conclusion   How would you summarize your interpretation of this group in terms of the three forms of religious expression? (This does not mean your personal opinion of it, but how the forms fit together and how it served the persons for whom it is important.)

Reading a Novel (Chapter 8)

One possible project in conjunction with this chapter would be a paper analyzing a novel from a religious and literary point of view. Here is an outline you could probably use with almost any novel suitable for analysis in this way. I hope you find it helpful.

Give full bibliographical information about the novel: author, title, place of publication, publisher, date, and number of pages.

Give a little information about the author, particularly data about his or her background, personality, life experiences, beliefs, and commitments that would help understand why the author wrote this novel and the points of view—religious, political, psychological, and the like—that seem to be expressed in it. You may need to go to other sources for some of this information.

Summarize the story of the novel.

Analyze the plot. Describe the main events and how they came about. Which characters contributed what elements to the way the plot developed? How aware were they of what they were doing? Note important plot symbols (if any) and comment on their probable meaning.

Then look at the plot in religious terms. Do the symbols have any relation to important religious symbols: cross, tree, tomb, or the like? Does the plot seem to follow any important religious scenario: Joseph Campbell's hero myth, fate or destiny in classical mythology, Christian redemption by suffering and death, the Buddhist quest for enlightenment, or similar religious themes?

Look next at the characters. Describe them, with specific references, showing how they relate or fail to relate to one another and what they experience. Notice especially how they change. Is there religious symbolism or significance in any of this? Do they, like Dostoyevsky's characters, represent character types, good or bad or mixed, that can be understood in common religious terms?—as sinners of the flesh, of the passions, of the intellect, or of the spirit? as penitents or converts? Christ figures or Buddha figures? saints?

Summarize whatever fundamental messages or perspectives—on religion, human nature, society—appear to come through from the author.

Perhaps an optional but possibly very fruitful task would be to look at moral and ethical decisions that are made by one or more of the characters in terms of the categories in Chapter 14 of this book. How are they made? On deontological or consequentialist grounds, or other grounds? What are the results of these decisions? And what about religious decisions, in terms of Chapter 12? Are they made on the basis of reason, experience, empiricism, authority, sociological factors, or existential choice? How do they stack up against the idea that religious choices are really irrefutable?

Finally, look at the novel in terms of a definition of religion that seems appropriate: as scenario for the real self, experience of the holy, salvation, finding a meaningful community, or whatever. Discuss.

Analyzing Religion in Popular Culture (Chapter 9)

For a paper or report, select a topic from out of the vast array of popular culture: a popular song, performer, movie or TV show, comic strip, "superhero," style of dress, urban legend, advertising motif, etc.

First describe it fully for the purpose.

Then present any overt religious content, including religious or mythological allusions.

Then talk about any subliminal religious motifs you see. For example, light can allude to the religious significance of light, beautiful scenes to paradise, and the like.

Then discuss the possible meaning of this image in its context, for its presumed audience. What does it say about values in contemporary culture? Does its religious meaning suggest ways in which religion might be changing, especially on a personal level? How do you feel about it?

Religion on the Internet (Chapter 10)

For a paper or report, select a particular site from one of the several levels described in this chapter: practical religious information; intellectual information; religious conversion, discussion, and dating; Internet religious services and religions; games; virtual reality; and beyond.

Describe that site, with examples of how it works. If the art, symbolism, design, and sound are especially effective, bring that up, suggesting subliminal ways people might be influenced by it.

Talk about its presumed audience, why people would turn to it, and what effect it might have on users.

As appropriate to the particular topic, offer views on religious, archetypal, and mythological allusions. Remember much can really be religion, or affect religious attitudes, without saying so.

Discuss the site's place in a world in which more and more of life, including perhaps religion, is lived on line. Then go on to debate what it may say about a spiritual future in which, some say, more and more of our lives will be lived on the Internet and in virtual reality.

Looking at a Religious Group (Chapter 11)

This project will be a study of a particular religious group looked at in terms of several kinds of sociological questions. It should be undertaken only after discussion with your instructor, and probably also only after a conference with the clergyman or other leadership of the group. It is not recommended that you undertake a study of a religious group in this way without the full knowledge and consent of the group as expressed through its leadership, and also that of your instructor. This is a big project, requiring several weeks of fairly intensive research. It could be undertaken as a team project by several people working together.

First, here are some things to do during the period of research.

Attend most meetings of the group, business as well as worship.

Keep notes of what happened at each, and also on attendance—number, age, gender, ethnic background, dress, attitude. Note whether key individuals come alone or with others, and the nature of participation.

Pick out those who you find to be leaders in the group, whether officially or unofficially. In meetings and discussions especially, look at how power is distributed and exercised. Observe the symbols of relative prestige of different people, as well as the behavioral clues as to how people are regarded in the group and how they regard it.

In worship settings, also look for the things called for in the project above for Chapter 4.

Read the important books and literature on the group, both those by the group or sympathetic to it (including its magazines, which can give very helpful insights) and those by outside researchers.

Set up several interviews with leaders, key people, and people representative of different classes—for example, age, gender, background, length of experience, basic attitude—in the group. In these interviews, ask them for:

Their own personal life stories, and the stories of their relationships to the group.

History of the group as they know it.

Its teaching as they understand it, especially in terms of what in it is especially significant for them.

What aspects of the worship or other spiritual practices (meditation methods, prayer methods, etc.) are particularly important?

What interpersonal relationships, or relations to leaders and pastors or spiritual teachers, are especially important (sociologically), and why?

Something of how interviewees see the sociology of the group—how they perceive the kind of people in it, how leadership is exercised and decisions made, what tensions exist, and the group's relationship to the larger community.

Then, correlating all this information, do a paper on the group. It could be outlined as follows:

Identification of Group   Give its full name and location, and fundamental data: denominational affiliation, size, ethnic makeup, type of building and services, nature of surrounding community, and unusual features.

Nature of Study   At the outset, tell why you wanted to study this particular group, and what questions you had in mind, or ideas about it you wanted to test. Discuss fully your methodology and the progress of the study, including any problems you ran into. Give exact dates and places of your attendance, interviews, and so on. Tell everything necessary for the reader to fully know how the research was carried out.

History   As background, give the history of the group and, more briefly, of the denomination or tradition out of which it came. Be sure the history tells *why* group has the doctrinal and social features it presents today. Include perceptions of its history by members.

Theoretical Expression   Give the group's doctrinal and narrative expression (e.g., formal teachings, significant myths, stories, memories, conversion and healing accounts, and religious "folk wisdom" you heard). This may be based partly on reading, but it will be important to contrast and compare the group's formal statements of belief with what seems to emerge from services and interviews as really significant beliefs to members today. How are these related to the tradition? Analyze sources of authority in teaching, the role of charismatic teachers, and the role of sacred texts.

Practical Expression   Describe services, using queries similar to those outlined in the project for Chapter 4 above.

Sociological Expression   Again, use queries for analysis similar to those outlined in the project for Chapter 4. Deal with the initiation of new members, leadership, relationship with the larger community, and tensions within the group. Be sure to use interview data—but cautiously, remembering that each person's statements are only one point of view.

Individual Case Studies   This may be optional, but if you have time and sufficient data, you could select a few individuals within the group and discuss them as case studies in terms of conversion, varying relationships over the years within the group, moving into positions of leadership, and finally, serving as models to others. Ask what problems and tensions they had to overcome, and why the group was so important to them.

Analyzing a Religious Argument (Chapter 12)

Write a paper on a religious question, or even present the issue as a live debate in class. Examples could be as follows:

Does a God exist?

Do human beings (or animals) have an immortal soul? Is it possible to be fully enlightened?

Is there an absolute standard of morality?

Is it possible to live a joyous secular life?

You will first need to define exactly what you mean by the key terms: for example, what do you mean by God, by a soul, by enlightenment?

Then, taking the existence of God as an example, first present arguments from reason for the existence of God. Then respond with, or if it is a live debate, let the other person respond with, arguments from reason against the existence of God.

Next, in a real debate, each person would have a chance to rebut the other for a few minutes.

After that, go on to present arguments for and against the existence of God from the standpoints of the other means of determining truth in religion presented in this chapter: experience, empiricism, authority, sociological factors, and existential choice. (On the last, you will have to ask why anyone would choose to make an existential choice for or against belief in God.) Be sure to define each of these terms, tell what kind of evidence they bring to bear, and what its value and limitations are.

At the end, you may determine which side has scored the most debating points if you wish—and if you can!

Analyzing the Afterlife (Chapter 13)

Two possibilities: You could write a paper or report on a particular concept of the afterlife in the outline for the paper or report on myth given for Chapter 3 above.

Or you could set up a mock or live debate in the manner described above for Chapter 11 for the pros and cons of one of these topics: the afterlife generally, reincarnation, a theocentric or anthropocentric heaven, the reality of hell, whether we can have any knowledge of life beyond the grave.

Analyzing an Ethical Problem (Chapters 14 and 15)

Write a paper that analyzes a specific case in which an ethical decision must be made. It can be a hypothetical case, one you have read or heard about in the media, or, if you are free to discuss it without violating anyone's confidentiality, a case you know personally. This argument could also be set up as a debate, as presented in Chapter 11 above. Here are some possible examples. Fill in the specifics.

> Should an employee report misconduct by another employee of which he or she has knowledge, such as misusing company funds or sexual harassment?

> Should a lawyer suppress or misrepresent important information she or he has uncovered while researching a case in order to help his or her client, even though the suppression of this information will damage an innocent person?

> Should an abortion be performed, or euthanasia permitted, in a particular case?

Moving on to Chapter 15, the argument could be about just war theory, whether it is valid as presented, whether changes need to be made in it for contemporary conditions; the application of just war theory to a particular case, hypothetical or actual; the validity of pacifism; why people fight wars; the question of whether war can be ended in human life.

After describing the case in sufficient detail, being sure to include every fact that could conceivably be relevant to an ethical judgment, give the arguments on both the pro and con sides. Be sure to include the relevant meta-ethical principles behind each:

concepts of God and divine command, ideas of personhood, of what life really means, and what you mean by quality of life.

Then tell how a decision would be reached, and what the decision might be, using both deontological and consequentialist principles.

Then give your own judgment and defend it in terms of what principles and methods of deciding seem most important to you. Be sure you make clear why you consider them the most important, and how they work in terms of the specific facts of the case as you have presented it.

GLOSSARY

Here are some words used in this book that may be new to you or whose use in religious studies may not be clear. If there are any others, be sure to look them up in a dictionary.

Abrahamic Religions Religions tracing a common spiritual lineage back to the biblical and Qur'anic figure of Abraham: Judaism, Christianity, and Islam.

Actualizing Acts and attitudes that make a reality visible and felt.

Animism Belief in finite spirits influencing life, as of ancestors or nature.

Anthropomorphic Having human form.

Apocalyptic Belief about and texts concerning sudden, dramatic acts of God, particularly in the End Times.

Archetype A form that especially emphasizes the original, eternal, supreme significance of something. In religious studies that are influenced by Jungian thought, it may refer especially to the psychological *type* represented by a deity or other sacred figure: for example, the Great Mother, the Wise Old Man, the Hero, the Maiden, the "Shadow" or Satan.

Audio Symbols Symbols in the form of sounds or words rather than something seen.

Authority In religion, acceptance of a particular source of knowledge as reliable beyond doubt because of divine guarantees.

Bhakti The devotional tradition in Hinduism, especially noted for its emotional love and fervor.

Cargo Cults Religious movements, usually under the leadership of a native prophet, common in colonial areas. They believed that if the natives followed certain prescriptions, such as a dance or destroying their present possessions, they would be sent abundant new riches like those on the white man's ships.

Chanoyu The Japanese "tea ceremony" associated with the Zen Buddhist tradition; its way of doing simple, natural acts gracefully and mindfully is expressive of Zen spiritual values.

Civil Religion Beliefs and practices presenting a country as a whole, such as the United States, as having a sacred meaning apart from the sacredness of individual religious institutions.

Conceptual Verbal Audio Symbols Words having symbolic power in which the emphasis is on the meaning of the words and their associations, such as in story, myth, doctrine, and religious rhetoric.

Consequentialist Ethics Another name for **teleological ethics**.

Conservative Style Religion holding to an unchanging view of religious truth and its expression, regardless of tension with the outside world.

Content Message What a statement says explicitly, in contrast to the **structural message**.

Conversion In religion, a major change in one's faith often effected by a powerful experience, long or short, in which the new symbols of transcendence come through strongly as true and vital.

Cosmogonic Myth A myth of the origin of the universe.

Deconstructionism A philosophical school that rejects looking for common underlying structures in a field such as religion, in favor of seeing the unique difference in each example or person involved.

Denomination A structurally independent institutional and sociological organization within a larger religious tradition, usually holding an interpretation of the religion distinctive in certain particulars and frequently having its main strength in a particular country or culture.

Deontological Ethics The ethics of "ought," based on a prior sense of duty or obligation, usually seen as deriving from divine command, from right reason, and/or from what is made incumbent on humans by their nature or natural law.

Disciple A special type of religious personality in his or her own right; essential to the founder of a particular religion by providing an intimate audience for the message in a group that will prepare the lasting institutionalization of the newly founded religion.

Doctrine Expression of the beliefs of a religion in propositional verbal form, as statements of truth.

Emergent Religion A new religious movement arising out of established religion, typically characterized by a charismatic leader, a simple definite belief and practice, and future orientation.

Empiricism Direct observation and experimentation in the external world as a means for determining truth.

Eschatology Doctrine of the "Last Things" or "End Times," such as a final resurrection and judgment, in religion.

Essentialism The much-criticized idea that all entities in a supposed class, such as religion, have a common essence or nature.

Established Religion The dominant institutional religion of a society.

Existential Choice Religious faith recognized as freely given commitment, on the grounds that religious truth is not discoverable by outside means but only in the context of commitment through faith. The existential choice is made on the basis of no external "proof" that acts as a compulsion, but as a free decision.

Existentialism Philosophy popular just after World War II but having its roots in the work of earlier thinkers such as Kierkegaard. Existentialism emphasizes the need for each person to determine his or her own real being not just through ideas but through decision and corresponding action. In religious existentialism, it means a free decision for faith and acting in accordance with it.

Expansive Emergent Religion Religious movements that borrow from several sources, often combining new and familiar features.

Experience In religion, what has happened to one or what one has lived through, particularly "religious experience"—moments of great realization, awakening, and emotional power attributed to direct encounter with transcendent reality—used as a basis for determining truth.

Folk Religion The religion of ordinary people, usually peasants and illiterate, in traditional societies.

Founder The originator of a major new religion.

Fundamentalist Style Way of understanding authoritative religious statements, which indicates they must be taken literally and consistently with each other within the religious system, regardless of tension with outside worldviews. Similar to conservative styles.

God or god A conscious center of being, knowledge, and power superior to humanity, upon which ordinary humans must depend and have relations of prayer and offerings for their well-being.

Great Tradition The religious life of a religion's elite, oriented toward the values of literacy, historical awareness, and the culture's artistic and political traditions.

Guilt In religion, a sense of having done wrong by violating the laws or expectations of God or Ultimate Reality; a sense of guilt may be followed by repentance or serious renouncing of that wrongdoing and by conversion or rebirth.

Hero/Savior Myth A myth of a person who, through great ordeal, works to restore the right relations between humanity and Ultimate Reality by defeating forces of evil, effecting redemption, or clearing and showing the way back to right relations with the Ultimate.

Icon In the Eastern Orthodox tradition of Christianity, a stylized portrait of a religious figure used as a focus of worship.

Impersonal Absolute The divine conceived of as a pure being and consciousness without particularized thoughts or personality.

Initiation A rite of passage that marks a transition from one stage of life to another. In religion, rites of initiation from childhood to adulthood are very common, as are rites of initiation (or experiences of initiation) into a vocation as a specialist in the sacred, such as that of a shaman or priest. Initiatory scenarios vary, but often they are quite intense experiences, involving isolation of the candidate, an ordeal such as fasting or even scourging, a physical transformation such as circumcision or knocking out a tooth, and an opportunity for experiencing the divine in dream or vision. After initiation, one is incorporated into society again in the new role.

Intensive Emergent Religion Religious movements that stress a strict, devout following of the prevailing religion.

Intentionalism The doctrine that ethics should be judged by the doer's intentions as well as, or instead of, the consequences.

International Religion A religious movement or institution, such as Buddhism, Christianity or Islam, spread through many countries.

Layperson An ordinary member of a religion with no special office.

Liberal Style Way of understanding religious statements, which indicates their meaning must be consistent with the best current scientific and philosophical thought; often emphasizes a nonliteral interpretation of them.

Liminality, Liminal State Being outside the ordinary structures of society, as is a novice during initiation or a wanderer during most of life; also called *marginality.*

Little Tradition Folk or popular religion; the nonliterate religion of ordinary people oriented toward the present, the seasonal round, the local place.

Liturgy The text of a structured, frequently conventional and traditional religious rite, such as the Roman Catholic Mass or Anglican worship. Many parts of this kind of worship are often sung.

Magic In religious studies, this word is generally used to mean producing desired results or controlling events by manipulating supernatural forces or beings through symbols such as charms, spells, and rituals thought to have an irresistible power over them. Magic differs from religion by working for particular limited ends rather than expressing the full nature of transcendent reality; it stresses power over the supernatural rather than oneness with it or devotional service toward it; and it desires that power for particular goals rather than full salvation, liberation, or real selfhood. But in practice, the line between magic and religion is often blurry.

Mahayana The "northern" tradition of Buddhism, predominant in China, Korea, Japan, Vietnam, and neighboring areas; it has many Buddhas and bodhisattvas and emphasizes many paths to enlightenment, Nirvana here and now, and the "buddha nature" in all things.

Mantra In Hinduism and Buddhism, a short chanted formula held to have particular sacred power, as for evoking a particular deity.

Meditation Calming the mind through withdrawal of sensuous stimuli and focusing awareness on one thing or voidness; often used to induce religious states of consciousness or valued in itself as religious and a means of getting in touch with religious reality.

Meta-ethics The philosophical or religious worldview, the view of God, nature, or Ultimate Reality, that underlies an ethical system.

Monism Philosophical view that emphasizes the oneness of all, including the oneness of God and the universe; one basic universal substance or God manifested in all things.

Monk and Nun Men and women, respectively, who live lives wholly devoted to spirituality; to this end they may be celibate, embrace poverty, and live in communities of persons devoted to the same end. They dedicate much time to prayer and meditation, though they may also study, do manual labor, and administer monastic holdings. Some, like the sadhus of India, may be wanderers or hermits as well as members of communities.

Monotheism Belief in one God.

Mufti A Muslim authority on religious law.

Mystic One whose spiritual life emphasizes states of consciousness considered direct, unmediated experience of religious reality.

Mystical, Mysticism In religion and religious studies, mysticism is usually taken to mean an experience interpreted by the experiencer as direct, immediate contact with Ultimate Reality, usually in terms of a profound awareness of oneness with that reality. In their classic form, mystical experiences are not so much emotional—as conversion and various other religious experiences may sometimes be—as deep, quiet experiences of awareness and of unity with that of which one is aware; commonly the experience is said to be beyond words.

Myth In religious studies, a story that expresses in narrative form important aspects of the religion's and the culture's view of the universe and the human place in it, in relation to God or the gods.

National Religion A religion basically limited to one country, often supported by political authority and embodying important aspects of the country's history and culture.

Natural Law Principles with ethical implications derived from nature by reason alone, based on what appears to be the given predisposition or purpose of a thing, such as that humans are meant to live in families and that sexuality is intended for procreation.

Natural Rights Rights, such as the right to life, liberty, or self-defense, held to pertain to all persons by virtue of their humanity, in contrast to legal rights granted by custom or law.

Nirvana The Buddhist term for absolute unconditioned reality.

Nonconceptual Verbal Audio Symbols Words, such as chants, having symbolic power in which the emphasis is on the sound rather than the meaning.

Nonverbal Audio Symbols Sounds such as music, bells, or drums that have symbolic power but are not verbal.

Numinous A quality of mystery, terror, and fascination often ascribed to the sacred.

Ontological Argument A argument for the existence of God based on the idea that if a God is possible, he must exist.

Peak Experience Abraham Maslow's term for a "self-validating" state of intensity and joy in which one is completely fulfilled in the present; often compared to mystical states in religion.

Personal Monotheism Belief in one God who is personal, that is, able to think particular thoughts, with particular ends, and favor particular things deliberately, as well as give and respond to love and service.

Pluralistic Having more than one example, as a society in which it is evident there is more than one religion.

Polytheism Belief in many gods; a different way of experiencing the transcendent than monotheism, polytheism stresses the different nature of the divine in different times, places, and situations.

Popularizer One who labors to bring the central message of a religion, as he or she understands it, to ordinary people.

Priest A person who performs religious rites and services as a specialist; their effect does not depend on his or her fervor or psychic state but only on the office. Priesthood may be hereditary, and facility is acquired by training, not necessarily by shamanistic call and initiatory ordeal.

Private Symbol A symbol that has special meaning for a particular individual because of its association with his or her personal life.

Prophet A religious speaker or writer who is believed to speak with the voice of God to denounce evils, predict future events, call for justice, and comfort the afflicted.

Public Symbol A symbol that has a generally accepted meaning for a community, usually through association with a major institution.

Reason The unbiased use of logical analysis based on objectives, unquestioned premises to establish truth.

Rebirth A spiritual experience that is interpreted as spiritually parallel to physical birth, in that the individual is seen as a "new person" before God or the gods, now in the right relationship with Ultimate Reality, whereas before he or she was not.

Reformer One who strives to make major changes of faith, practice, and organizational structure within an ongoing religious tradition.

Religion Human networks or collections of ideas, attitudes, acts, social patterns, and other symbols expressing the nature of transcendent reality and what humans are in relation to it, and intended to draw power from that reality and that relation.

Religious Expression, Three Forms of:
    Practical Expression in practices, such as worship, rite, prayer, meditation, pilgrimage, and costume.
    Sociological Expression in groups, institutions, social relations (as between spiritual leader and follower), and relation of the religion to the larger social order.
    Theoretical Expression in words and ideas, as in doctrines, philosophies, myths, and lore.

Religious Group A set of people whose interpersonal relations are a part of one another's religious experience and who enact some religious activity together.

Religious Rhetoric Religious language, as in preaching or inspirational writing, intended to trigger responses of belief and experience in recipients.

Rite A religious performance, such as a sacrifice or worship service, usually done by and for a group and usually "orchestrating" symbols in several media—for example, words, music, symbols together—which enacts the transcendent reality of the religion, making it seem present or easily accessible.

Ritual The pattern of words and actions through which a rite is carried out.

Sacrament A specific, visible action and object believed to convey divine grace and power, such as baptism or Holy Communion in Christianity.

Sacred Dedicated to religious purposes, as a shrine; in religious studies, the sacred often refers to the whole network of elements which stands against the ordinary or "profane" to symbolize the transcendent, as in the concepts of sacred space and sacred time.

Shaman A religious specialist in primitive religion who typically attains his or her vocation by divine call and arduous initiation, then with the aid of helping spirits heals, tells the future and contacts gods and departed souls in rites involving trance.

Sign An indicator that merely points to what it indicates but does not share in its nature.

Sociology The study of human societies or social units large and small in terms of their structure, processes, and interaction with other social units, with a view to looking for general principles that govern them.

Soul An immaterial substance often conceived by religions to be within the self, as its ultimate identity, its place of rapport with transcendent reality, and often as that which bears one's moral record and leaves the body to incarnate in another body after death or to experience heaven or hell.

State of Consciousness A particular separate, discrete activity or "feel" of mind, such as concentration, daydreaming, or sleep.

Structuralism The study of deep patterns of symbolism and behavior that cut across many traditions.

Structural Message What a statement says implicitly by the way it is put and its context.

Subjective Having to do with one's inner feelings, attitudes, ideas, and state of consciousness or with the life of the mind and emotions; subjectivity can be expressed outwardly only through some symbol: behavior, gesture, rite, speech.

Subuniverses Areas of life in which particular "rules" and attitudes prevail which do not occur outside that realm, such as play, work, worship, etc.

Sufi Common name for a mystic in the Islamic tradition.

Supernatural Belief in that which is "above nature"; although the term can refer to ghosts and anything else that does not conform to natural law; in religious philosophy supernature is much the same as the transcendent.

Symbol That which properly both reminds one of something, such as the transcendent or a loved one, and evokes feelings and behavior appropriate to it. A symbol therefore is more than a sign. It does not just give information; it calls forth a response and, like the image of a deity, may even virtually become that which it symbolizes. Religious symbols are often polyvalent, that is, having more than one meaning at the same time.

Teleological Ethics Ethics based on the principle that the result of an action is that by which it should be judged.

Theology The study of God.

Theriomorphic Having animal form.

Traditionalism Way of putting religious statements that emphasizes their being part of a long-standing religious tradition with strong links to the society's culture and history, and in which many people participate out of deep-rooted family or ethnic ties.

Transcendence Being above ordinary human knowledge and ordinary perception and reality; in religion the transcendent is usually identified with Ultimate Reality, that which one cannot go beyond: God, the absolute, existence itself. All else is partial and "conditioned," or limited by being in only one place, one time, and one mode of being, and by boundaries of knowledge and ability.

Utilitarianism The doctrine that ethics should be based on "the greatest good for the greatest number."

Yantras In Hinduism, abstract diagrams that can represent certain deities.

Zen An East Asian tradition of Buddhism emphasizing mindfulness and closeness to nature.

NOTES

Chapter 1

1. See Gregory Curtis, *The Cave Painters*. New York: Knopf, 2006; David Lewis-Williams, *The Mind in the Cave*. London: Thames and Hudson, 2002; Werner Herzog, *Cave of Forgotten Dreams*. New York: Sundance Selects, 2011.
2. Friedrich Schleiermacher, *The Christian Faith*. New York: Harper & Row, 1963, p. 17.
3. Émile Durkheim, *The Elementary Forms of the Religious Life*. New York: Macmillan, 1915, p. 47.
4. Ibid., p. 383.
5. William James, *The Varieties of Religious Experience*. New York: Modern Library, n.d., pp. 31–32. Orig. pub. 1902. Italics in original.
6. Ibid., p. 53.
7. Karl Marx, "Toward the Critique of Hegel's Philosophy of Right," in Lewis S. Feuer, ed., *Basic Writings on Politics and Philosophy: Karl Marx and Friedrich Engels*. Garden City, NY: Doubleday Anchor Books, 1959, p. 262.
8. Sigmund Freud, *The Future of an Illusion*. Garden City, NY: Doubleday Anchor Books, 1964, p. 47. First pub. in German 1927.
9. Rudolf Otto, *The Idea of the Holy*. New York: Oxford University Press, 1958, p. 76. First pub. in German 1917.
10. Mircea Eliade, *The Sacred and the Profane*. New York: Harcourt Brace Jovanovich, Inc., 1959, p. 13.
11. Jonathan Z. Smith, "'Religion' and 'Religious Studies': No Difference at All," *Soundings* 71, 1988, p. 234. See also Smith, *Imagining Religion*. Chicago: University of Chicago Press, 1982.
12. Russell McCutcheon, *Manufacturing Religion*. New York: Oxford University Press, 1997, p. 208. See also John F. Wilson, "The Study of Religion: A Family of Academic Disciplines," in Paul Ramsey and John F. Wilson, eds., *The Study of Religion on the Campus of Today*. Princeton, NJ: Princeton University Press, 1967, p. 36.
13. Talal Asad, *Genealogies of Religion*. Baltimore: Johns Hopkins University Press, 1993.
14. Wilfred Cantwell Smith, *The Meaning and End of Religion*. Minneapolis, MN: Augsburg Fortress, 1991. First pub. 1963.
15. Joachim Wach, *Sociology of Religion*. Chicago: University of Chicago Press, 1944, pp. 17–34.

Chapter 2

1. The Jane Goodall Institute. http://www.janegoodall.org/chimp-central-waterfall-displays.
2. Mircea Eliade, *Shamanism: Archaic Techniques of Ecstasy*. New York: Pantheon Books, Inc., 1964.
3. Karl Jaspers, *The Origin and Goal of History*. London: Routledge & Kegan Paul, 1953, pp. 1–27, 51–60.
4. See Robert S. Ellwood and Barbara A. McGraw, *Many Peoples, Many Faiths: Women and Men in the World Religions*, 10th ed. Upper Saddle River, NJ: Pearson Prentice Hall, 2012.
5. See Robert Ellwood, *Cycles of Faith: The Development of the World's Religions*. Walnut Creek, CA: Altamira Press, 2003.

Chapter 3

1. Summarized in Walter J. Ong, *Orality and Literacy: The Technologizing of the Word*. New York: Routledge, 1982, pp. 49–56. See Aleksandr Romanovich Luria, *Cognitive Development: Its Cultural and Social Foundations*. Trans. Martin Lopez-Morillas and Lynn Solotaroff. Cambridge, MA: Harvard University Press, 1976.

2. Walter J. Ong, *Orality and Literacy*, pp. 43–45.
3. Claude Levi-Strauss, "The Structural Study of Myth," *Journal of American Folklore*, LXXVIII, 270, Oct.–Dec. 1955, pp. 428–444. Reprinted in Richard and Femande DeGeorge, eds., *The Structuralists: From Marx to Levi-Strauss*. Garden City, NY: Doubleday Anchor Books, 1972, pp. 169–194.
4. William Shipley, *The Maidu Indian Myths and Stories of Hánc'ibyjim*. Berkeley, CA: Heyday Books, 1991, pp. 51–52. This account is based on my treatment of the story in Robert Ellwood, *Myth: Key Concepts in Religion*. London and New York: Continuum, 2008, pp. 108–111.
5. Baldwin Spencer, and F.J. Gillen, *The Native Tribes of Central Australia*. London: Macmillan, 1939, pp. 38–91.
6. Hesiod, *Theogony and Works and Days*. Trans. Stanley Lombardo and Robert Lamberton. Indianapolis, IN: Hackett, 1993, pp. 64–66.
7. Alexander Heidel, *The Babylonian Genesis: The Story of Creation*. Chicago: University of Chicago Press, 1963.
8. Antony Alpers, *Legends of the South Seas*. New York: Crowell, 1970, pp. 51–54.
9. Joseph Campbell, *The Hero With a Thousand Faces*. New York: Bollengen Foundation, 1949.
10. Susanne Langer, *Form and Freedom*. New York: Scribner's, 1953, p. 307.

Chapter 4

1. Paul Tillich, *Systematic Theology*. Chicago: University of Chicago Press, 1951, vol. I, p. 239.
2. See, for example, the description of Nichiren chanting in Robert Ellwood, *The Eagle and the Rising Sun: Americans and the New Religions of Japan*. Philadelphia: The Westminster Press, 1974, pp. 69–75.
3. Richard Schechner, *Environmental Theater*. New York: Hawthorn Books, Inc., 1973.
4. Victor Turner, *The Ritual Process: Structure and Anti-Structure*. Ithaca, NY: Cornell University Press, 1977; Arnold van Gennep, *Rites of Passage*. Chicago: University of Chicago Press, 1960.
5. Andreas Lommel, *Shamanism: The Beginnings of Art*. New York: McGraw-Hill, 1967, p. 29.
6. James G. Frazer, *The Belief in Immortality*. London: Macmillan, 1913, vol. I, pp. 250–254.

Chapter 5

1. Stanley Krippner, "Altered States of Consciousness," in John White, ed. *The Highest State of Consciousness*. Garden City, NY: Doubleday & Company, Inc., 1972, pp. 1–5.
2. William James, *The Principles of Psychology*. New York: H. Holt & Co., 1890, vol. II, chap. 21.
3. Alfred Schutz, *Collected Papers*, in Maurice Natanson, ed. The Hague, the Netherlands: Martinus Nijhoff, 1973, vol. I, pp. 207–259.
4. Ibid., p. 232.
5. Frederick J. Streng, *Understanding Religious Life*, 2nd ed. Encino, CA: Dickenson Publishing Co., Inc., 1976, pp. 7–9.
6. For examples see Mircea Eliade, *Rites and Symbols of Initiation*. New York: Harper Torchbooks, 1965.
7. Evelyn Eaton, "Towards Initiation," *Parabola* 1, 3 (Spring 1976), pp. 42–46.
8. Eliade, *Rites and Symbols of Initiation*, pp. 106–108.
9. Luk, *Ch'an and Zen Teaching*. London: Rider & Co., 1962, vol. 3, pp. 19–20.
10. C. B. Purdom, *The God-Man*. London: George Allen & Unwin, 1964, pp. 18–19.
11. See Abraham Maslow, *Toward the Psychology of Being*. New York: Van Nostrand Reinhold Company, 1968; and *Religion, Values, and Peak Experiences*. Columbus, OH: Ohio State University Press, 1964.

12. Victor Turner, *The Ritual Process*. Chicago: Aldine Publishing Co., 1969, chaps. 3–5. See also Arnold van Gennep, *Rites of Passage*. Chicago: University of Chicago Press, 1960.
13. William James, *The Varieties of Religious Experience*. New York and London: Longman, Green, 1902. See also G. William Barnard, *Exploring Unseen Worlds: William James and the Philosophy of Mysticism*. Albany, NY: SUNY Press, 1997.
14. See Sigmund Freud, *Totem and Taboo*. Trans. James Strachey. London: Routledge and Kegan Paul, 1950; and *The Future of an Illusion*. Trans. W.D. Robson-Scott. Garden City, NY: Doubleday & Company, Inc., 1957.
15. For summaries of the position see Carl G. Jung, et al., *Man and His Symbols*. Garden City, NY: Doubleday & Company, Inc., 1969; and Frieda Fordham, *An Introduction to Jung's Psychology*. Harmondsworth, England: Penguin Books, 1956.
16. See James Hillman, *Re-Visioning Psychology*. New York: Harper Perennial, 1976, 1992; and *The Dream and the Underworld*. New York: Harper & Row, 1979.
17. Dean Hamer, *The God Gene: How Faith Is Hardwired Into Our Genes*. New York: Doubelday, 2004.
18. See, for example, Andrew Newberg and Mark Robert Waldman, *Why We Believe What We Believe*. New York: Free Press, 2006; and Newberg and Waldman, *How God Changes Your Brain: Breakthrough Findings From a Leading Neuroscientist*. New York: Ballantine, 2010.
19. James, *The Varieties of Religious Experience*. New York: Modern Library, n.d., p. 14.

Chapter 6

1. See Paul Ricoeur, *The Symbolism of Evil*. Boston: Beacon, 1969, especially "Conclusion: The Symbol Gives Rise to Thought," pp. 347–357, and also as Ricoeur "The Symbol Gives Rise to Thought," in Giles B. Gunn ed., *Literature and Religion*. New York: Harper & Row, 1971, p. 214.
2. Ricoeur, *Symbolism of Evil*, pp. 351–352.
3. Gordon Allport, *The Individual and His Religion*. New York: Macmillan, 1950.
4. Abraham H. Maslow, *Toward a Psychology of Being*. New York: Van Nostrand Reinhold, 1968, pp. 103–104. See also his *Religion, Values, and Peak Experiences*. Columbus, OH: Ohio State University Press, 1964.
5. *The Life of Saint Teresa* [her autobiography]. Trans. J.M. Cohen. Harmondsworth, England: Penguin Books, 1957, p. 122.
6. Tom S. Cleary and Sam I. Shapiro, "The Plateau Experience and the Post-Mortem Life: Abraham H. Maslow's Unfinished Theory," *The Journal of Transpersonal Psychology* 27 (1), Nov. 1995, p. 2.
7. Ibid., p. 19.
8. Evelyn Underhill, *Mysticism*. London: Methuen, 1911. Many later editions.
9. St. John of the Cross, *Dark Night of the Soul*. Trans. E. Allison Peers. New York: Doubleday, 1959. First trans. by Peers pub. 1933.
10. Bhadantacariya Buddhaghosa, *The Path of Purification (Visuddhimagga)*. Trans. Bhikku Nyanamoli, 2nd ed. Colombo, Ceylon: A. Semage, 1964. Reprint Berkeley, CA: Shambhala, 1976. For a summary see also Daniel Goleman, *The Varieties of the Meditative Experience*. New York: Dutton, 1977, pp. 24 39.
11. Achaan Chah, *A Still Forest Pond: The Insight Meditation of Achaan Chah*. Wheaton, IL: Quest Books, 2004; *Food for the Heart: The Collected Teachings of Ajahn Chah*. Somerville, MA: Wisdom Publications, 2002.
12. Buddhaghosa, *Path*, p. 704.
13. Goleman, *Varieties*, pp. 34–35.
14. *Bhagavad Gita: The Song of God*, 4th ed. Trans. Swami Prabhavananda and Christopher Isherwood. Hollywood, CA: Vedanta Press, 1987, p. 82.

15. Ibid., p. 83.
16. Roland H. Bainton, *Here I Stand: A Life of Martin Luther*. New York and Nashville: Abingdon, 1950, p. 45.
17. Ibid., p. 59.
18. Ibid., p. 65.

Chapter 7

1. Ruth Finnegan, *Limba Stories and Story-Telling*. Oxford, UK: Clarendon Press, 1967, pp. 234–235.
2. Harold Courlander, *Tales of Yoruba Gods and Heroes*. New York: Crown, 1973, pp. 15–20.
3. David Adams Leeming, *The World of Myth: An Anthology*. New York: Oxford University Press, 1990, pp. 147–153.
4. Mircea Eliade, *Rites and Symbols of Initiation*. New York: Harper & Row, 1965, p. 84.
5. H. R. Ellis Davidson, *Scandinavian Mythology*. New York: Peter Bedrick, 1988, pp. 36–38.
6. Peggy Sandy, *Fraternity Gang Rape: Sex, Brotherhood, and Privilege on Campus*. New York: University Press, 1990, pp. 152–153.
7. Mary Baker Eddy, *Science and Health, With Key to the Scriptures*. Boston: The First Church of Christ, Scientist, 1875, 1994, p. 330.
8. Gershom G. Scholem, *Major Trends in Jewish Mysticism*. New York: Schocken Books, 1941, 1954, pp. 244–286.

Chapter 8

1. Note, however, that philosophical Hindus and Buddhists do not conceive of Brahman or Nirvana as having personal consciousness in the way that Jewish, Christian, or Muslim monotheists think of God as possessing.
2. This painting is presented and discussed in Beverly Moon, ed., *An Encyclopedia of Archetypal Symbolism*. Boston: Shambhala, 1991, pp. 454–457.
3. A useful introduction to this topic is Kathleen J. Regier, compiler, *The Spiritual Image in Modern Art*. Wheaton, IL: Theosophical Publishing House, 1987.
4. *The Analects of Confucius*. Trans. Arthur Waley. London: George Allen & Unwin, 1938. Vintage book ed., p. 69.
5. "The Voice of the Devil," in Alfred Kazin, ed., *The Portable Blake*. New York: Viking, 1953, pp. 250–251.
6. Lynn Ross-Bryant, *Imagination and the Life of the Spirit: An Introduction to the Study of Religion and Literature*. Ann Arbor, MI: Scholars Press, 1981, p. 85.
7. Ross-Bryant, *Imagination and the Life of the Spirit*, 87; citing Giles B. Gunn, "Introduction: Literature and Its Relation to Religion," in Giles B. Gunn, ed., *Literature and Religion*. New York: Harper & Row, 1971, p. 23. A later version of this essay appears as Chapter 2 of Giles Gunn, *The Interpretation of Otherness: Literature, Religion and the American Imagination*. New York: Oxford University Press, 1979.
8. Yukio Mishima, *The Temple of the Golden Pavilion*. Trans. Ivan Morris. New York: A.A. Knopf, 1958.
9. Fyodor Dostoyevsky, *The Brothers Karamazov*. Translated with an Introduction by David Magarshack. London: Penguin Books, 1958, 1982.

Chapter 9

1. See Colleen McDannell, *Material Christianity: Religion and Popular Culture in America*. New Haven, CT: Yale University Press, 1995, pp. 27–32, 189–192.

2. Ibid., p. 30.
3. Nancy T. Ammerman, "Golden Rule Christianity: Lived Religion in the American Mainstream," in David Hall, ed., *Lived Religion in America*. Princeton, NJ: Princeton University Press, 1997, pp. 196–217.
4. Wladyslaw Piwowarski, "The Guarantor of National Identity: Polish Catholicism," in Norbert Greinacher and Norbert Mette, ed., *Popular Religion*, Concilium, vol. 186. Edinburgh, UK: T & T Clark, 1986, pp. 20–27.
5. David K. Jordan, *Gods, Ghosts, and Ancestors*. Berkeley, CA: University of California Press, 1972, pp. 31–33.
6. I would not want to suggest that strong belief in life after death is necessarily inconsistent with working for righteousness in this world. Innumerable persons deeply involved in good works, from early slavery abolitionists to Salvation Army officers today, have been motivated by firm religious commitment of which afterlife belief was an important component.
7. Todd Burpo with Lynn Vincent, *Heaven Is for Real*. Nashville, TN: Thomas Nelson, 2010; Don Piper, *90 Minutes in Heaven*. Grand Rapids, MI: Revell, 2004. On Lynn Vincent, see Ariel Levy, "Annals of Authorship; Lives of the Saints; The Religious Right's Leading Ghostwriter," *The New Yorker*, Oct. 15, 2012, pp. 30–36.
8. Dr. Eben Alexander, "Heaven Is Real: A Doctor's Experience With the Afterlife," *Newsweek*, Oct. 8, 2012; thedailybeast.com/newsweek/.../proof-of-heaven-a-doctor's. . . . Eben Alexander, *Proof of Heaven: A Neurosurgeon's Journey into the Afterlife*. New York: Simon & Schuster, 2012.
9. Belief in the importance of childhood faith is a salient aspect of popular religion. The Lotus Sutra, a Buddhist scripture, affirms that a small child who simply presents a few flowers crushed in his tiny hand to an image of the Buddha, or makes a crude clay stupa (shrine) our of devotion, is closer to enlightenment than a learned monk attempting to do all the right meditations. Why? Because the monk is clinging to ego by wanting enlightenment even as he tries to get rid of it, while the child simply forgets himself in enthusiasm for the act of devotion, and what is enlightenment but the forgetting of self—the egolessness of which the scriptures speak. A momentary enlightenment, perhaps, but a start. Jesus spoke of a little child as greatest in the kingdom of heaven and said that to enter it we must become as little children. (Matt. ch. 18)
10. See Gracia Fay Ellwood, *The Uttermost Deep*. New York: Lantern Books, 2001.
11. Carmie Lynn Toulouse, "Modern Navajo Witchcraft Stories," in David M. Brugge and Charlotte J. Frisbie, *Navajo Religion and Culture: Selected Views*. Santa Fe, NM: Museum of New Mexico Press, 1982, p. 86.
12. See David Bromley, *The Satanism Scare*. Piscataway, NJ: Aldine Transactions, 1991; Robert S, Hicks, *In Pursuit of Satan*. Buffalo, NY: Prometheus Books, 1991; Gareth J. Medway, *Lure of the Sinister*. New York: New York University Press, 2001; Jeffrey S. Victor, *Satanic Panic*. London: Open Court, 1993; W. Scott Poole, *Satan in America*. Lanham, MD: Rowman and Littlefield, 2009.
13. Martin E. Marty, "The Revival of Evangelicalism in Southern Religion," in David E. Harrell, Jr., ed., *Varieties of Southern Evangelicalism*. Macon, GA: Mercer University Press, 1981, pp. 9–21.
14. John Storey, *Cultural Theory and Popular Culture: An Introduction*, 4th ed. Athens: University of Georgia Press, 2006, pp. 4–6. See also Dominic Strinati, *An Introduction to Theories of Popular Culture*. London and New York: Routledge, 1995.
15. Leonid Heretz, *Russia on the Eve of Modernity*. Cambridge: Cambridge University Press, 2008, p. 114.
16. Robert Redfield, *Peasant Society and Culture*. Chicago: University of Chicago Press, 1973. orig. pub. 1956. The distinction is not entirely new; see Max Weber, *The Sociology of Religion*. Trans. Ephraim Fishoff. Boston: Beacon Press, 1963, chap. 7, "Castes, Estates, Classes, and Religion." First German pub. 1922.

17. Ibid., 46.

18. These are based on Robert Ellwood, *Cycles of Faith*. Walnut Creek, CA: AltaMira, 2003, pp. 150–153.

19. See Ann Braude, *Radical Spirits: Spiritualism and Women's Rights in Nineteenth-Century America*. Boston: Beacon Press, 1989. See also Ann Douglas, *The Feminization of American Culture*. New York: Farrar, Straus, and Giroux, 1998.

20. Peter W. Williams, *Popular Religion in America*. Englewood Cliffs, NJ: Prentice Hall, 1980.

21. Tom Beaudoin, *Virtual Faith: The Irreverent Spiritual Quest of Generation X*. San Francisco: Jossey-Bass, 2000, pp. 60, 81. Cited in Pete Ward, *Gods Behaving Badly: Media, Religion and Celebrity Culture*. Waco, TX: Baylor University Press, 2011, pp. 78–79.

22. Quentin J. Schultze, "Touched by Angels and Demons: Religion's Love-Hate Relationship With Popular Culture," in Daniel A. Stout and Judith M. Buddenbaum, eds., *Religion and Popular Culture*. Ames: Iowa State University Press, 2001, pp. 39–48.

23. Alyson Shontell, "Apple Is a Religion." *Business Insider*/SFGate.com, May 21, 2011. www.sfgate.com/cgi-bin/article.

24. Mircea Eliade, *The Sacred and the Profane*. Trans. Willard R. Trask. New York: Harcourt Brace Jovanovich, 1959, pp. 204–205.

25. Ibid., p. 204.

26. Eric Michael Mazur and Tara K. Koda, "The Happiest Place on Earth," in Eric Michael Mazur and Kater McCarthy, eds., *God in the Details: American Religion in Popular Culture*. New York and London: Routledge, 2001, pp. 304–305.

27. Gregory L. Reece, *Elvis Religion*. London and New York: L. B. Tauris, 2006, pp. 12–13.

28. Ted Harrison, *Elvis People: The Cult of the King*. London: Fount, 1992; John Strausbaugh, *E: Reflections of the Birth of the Elvis Faith*. New York: Blast Books, 1995. See also Erika Doss, *Elvis Culture: Fans, Faith, and Image*. Lawrence: University Press of Kansas, 1999.

29. Strausbaugh, *E*, pp. 11–12.

30. Raymond A. Moody, Jr., *Elvis After Life*. New York: Bantam Books, 1989, p. 20, 23.

31. Mircea Eliade, *Shamanism: Archaic Techniques of Ecstasy*. New York: Pantheon Books, 1964, p. 45, 81.

32. Adam Possamai, "Superheroes and the Development of Latent Abilities: A Hyper-real Re-enchantment?" in Lynne Hume and Kathleen McPhillips, eds., *Popular Spiritualities*. Aldershot UK and Burlington VT: Ashgate, 2006, pp. 53–62; R. Reynolds, *Super Heroes: A Modern Mythology*. London: B. T. Batsford, 1992; Jeffrey J. Kripal, *Mutants and Mystics: Science Fiction, Superhero Comics and the Paranormal*. Chicago: University of Chicago Press, 2011. See also Trina Robbins, *The Great Women Superheroes*. Northampton, MA: Kitchen Sink Press, 1996.

33. Pete Ward, *Gods Behaving Badly: Media, Religion, and Popular Culture*. Waco, TX: Baylor University Press, 2011, p. 69. I owe several of the references in this section to this work.

34. Paul Heelas, ed., *Religion, Modernity, and Postmodernity*. Oxford, UK: Blackwell, 1998, pp. 4–5.

35. Cathy Lynn Grossman, "More Americans Designing a Make-Your-Own Religion," *The Washington Post*, Sept. 15, 2011. http://www.washingtonpost.com/on-faith/more ame.

36. George Barna, *Futurecast: What Today's Trends Mean for Tomorrow's World*. Carol Stream, IL: Tyndale BarnaBooks, 2011.

37. Wade Clark Roof, *Spiritual Marketplace: Baby Boomers and the Remaking of American Religion*. Princeton, NJ: Princeton University Press, 1999, p. 69.

38. Meredith McGuire, *Lived Religion: Faith and Practice in Everyday Life*. Oxford, UK: Oxford University Press, 2008, p. 5.

39. John D. Caputo, *On Religion*. London: Routledge, 2001, p. 90.

Chapter 10

1. See Helen A. Berger and Douglas Ezzy, "The Internet as Virtual Spiritual Community: Teen Witches in the United States and Australia," in Lorne L. Dawson and Douglas E. Cowan, eds., *Religion Online*. New York and London: Routledge, 2004, pp. 175–188.
2. June 1, 2010, Business. http://dealbook.nytimes.com/2010/06/14/merely-human-thats-so-yesterday.
3. www.pewinternet.org/Media-Mentions/2004.
4. James Glieck, *The Information*. New York: Pantheon, 2011
5. Lisa Miller, "My Take: How Technology Could Bring Down the Church." CNN Belief Net. http://religion.blogs.cnn.com/2011/05/15.
6. Amy Frykholm, "Loose Connections," *The Christian Century*, May 31, 2011, pp. 20–23.
7. Heidi A. Campbell, *When Religion Meets New Media*. London and New York: Routledge, 2010, pp. 142–143.
8. Berger and Ezzy, "The Internet as Virtual Spiritual Community," pp. 181–82.
9. Mohammed el-Nawawy and Sahar Khamis, *Islam Dot Com: Contemporary Islamic Discourses in Cyberspace*. New York: Palgrave Macmillan, 2009.
10. Brenda E. Brasher, *Give Me That Online Religion*. San Francisco: Jossey-Boss, 2001, p. 54
11. Ronald L. Grimes, et al., eds., *Ritual, Media, and Conflict*. Oxford, UK: Oxford University Press, 2011, pp. 141–147. http://www.lourdes-france.org.
12. Morten T. Højsgaard, "Cyber-Religion: On the Cutting Edge Between the Virtual and the Real," in Morten T. Højsgaard and Margit Warburg, eds., *Religion and Cyberspace*. London and New York: Routledge, 2005, p. 60.
13. Arianna Huffington, "The Internet Grows Up: Goodbye Messy Adolescence," Huffington Post 06/16/2011. http://www.huffingtonpost.com/arianna-huffington/the-internet-grows-up-goo_b_878157.html.
14. Seth Schiessel, "Exploring Moral Consequences, the Obvious and the Unintended," *New York Times,* June 22, 2011. http://www.nytimes.com/2011/06/22arts/video-game.
15. On the popularity of medieval fantasy, see David W. Marshall, ed., *Mass Market Medieval: Essays on the Middle Ages in Popular Culture*. Jefferson, NC: McFarland, 2007. See also Laurie N. Taylor, "Gothic Bloodlines in Survival Horror Gaming," in Bernard Perrin, ed., *Horror Video Games*. Jefferson, NC: McFarland, 2009, pp. 46–61.
16. See Simon Egenfeldt Nielsen, "Video Game Culture," in Simon Egenfeldt Nielsen, Jonas Heide Smith, and Susana Pajares Toscam, eds., *Understanding Video Games*. London and New York: Routledge, 2008, pp. 140–141.
17. Jane McGonigal, *Reality Is Broken: Why Games Make Us Better and How They Can Change the World*. New York: Penguin Press, 2011.
18. Stephanie Rosenbloom, "It's Love at First Kill," *The New York Times*, Apr. 24, 2011. http://www.nytimes.com/2011/04/24/fashion.
19. Elias Aboujaoude, *Virtually You: The Dangerous Powers of the E-Personality*. New York: W. W. Norton, 2011, pp. 144–145.
20. Stephen King, *Danse Macabre*. New York: Berkeley Books, 1981, pp. 395–396.
21. Jennifer J. Cobb, *CyberGrace: The Search for God in the Digital World*. New York: Crown, 1998.
22. Ibid., p. 33.
23. Ibid., p. 31. See also Michael Heim, *The Metaphysics of Virtual Reality*. New York: Oxford University Press, 1993.
24. Patrick French, *India: A Portrait*. New York: Knopf, 2011, p. 355.
25. Second Life, Spirituality and Belief. http://secondlife.com/destinations/belief.
26. Erik Davis, *TechGnosis: Myth, Magic and Mysticism in the Age of Information*. New York: Harmony Books, 1998; David Noble, *The Religion of Technology: The Divinity of Man and the Spirit of Invention*. New York: Penguin, 1999.

27. Ray Kurzweil, *The Age of Spiritual Machines: When Computers Exceed Human Intelligence*. New York: Viking, 1999; and *The Singularity Is Near: When Humans Transcend Biology*. New York: Penguin, 2006.
28. Stephan D. O'Leary, "Utopian and Dystopian Possibilities of Networked Religion in the New Millennium," in Højsgaard and Warburg, eds., *Religion and Cyberspace*, p. 47.
29. Ibid., p. 48.
30. Freeman Dyson, *Imagined Worlds*. Cambridge, MA: Harvard University Press, 1997, p. 121.
31. Ibid., p. 135.
32. Ibid., pp. 135–136.

Chapter 11

1. See Ernst Troeltsch, *The Social Teaching of the Christian Churches*. Trans. Olive Wyon. New York: The Macmillan Company, 1931, vol. 2; and J. Milton Yinger, *Religion, Society, and the Individual*. New York: The Macmillan Company, 1957.
2. See Andrew M. Greeley, *The Denominational Society: A Sociological Approach to Religion in America*. Glenview, IL: Scott, Foresman, 1972.
3. Mark Chaves, *American Religion: Contemporary Trends*. Princeton, NJ: Princeton University Press, 2011, pp. 57–58.
4. See Russell E. Richey and Donald G. Jones, eds., *American Civil Religion*. New York: Harper & Row, Publishers, Inc., 1974.
5. Conrad Cherry, *God's New Israel: Religious Interpretations of American Destiny,* rev. ed. Chapel Hill, NC: University of North Carolina Press, 1998.
6. These types are suggested by those in Joachim Wach, *Sociology of Religion*. Chicago: University of Chicago Press, 1944, and *The Comparative Study of Religion*. New York: Columbia University Press, 1958; and G. van der Leeuw, *Religion in Essence and Manifestation*. New York: Harper & Row, Publishers, Inc., 1963, 2 vols.
7. Robert Wuthnow, *After the Baby Boomers: How Twenty- and Thirty-Somethings Are Shaping the Future of American Religion*. Princeton, NJ: Princeton University Press, 2007.
8. See also Mark Chaves, *American Religion*, p. 40.
9. Laurie Goodstein, "Percentage of Protestant Americans Is in Steep Decline, Study Finds," *The New York Times*, Oct. 9, 2012. www.nytimes.com/2012/10/10/us/study-finds-that-percentage.
10. Pew Research Religion in Public Life Project, "'Nones' on the Rise," Oct. 9, 2012. www.pewforum.org/2012/10/09/nones-on-the-rise/
11. Mark Chaves, *American Religion,* p. 40.

Chapter 12

1. "American Piety in the 21st Century: New Insights to the Depth and Complexity of Religion in the U.S. Selected Findings from the Baylor Religion Survey," Sept. 2006. http://www.baylor.edui/content/services/document.php/33304.pdf.
2. H. Richard Niebuhr, *Radical Monotheism and Western Culture*. New York: Harper & Row, Publishers, Inc., 1970.
3. Charles Hartshorne, *Anselm's Discovery*. La Salle, IL: Open Court, 1965.
4. Alvin Plantinga, *The Nature of Necessity*. Oxford, UK: Clarendon Press, 1974; *God and Other Minds*. Ithaca, NY: Cornell University Press, 1967. See also Alvin Plantinga, ed., *The Ontological Argument, from St. Anselm to Contemporary Philosophers*. Garden City, NY: Anchor, 1965.
5. See Frank B. Dilley, "The Irrefutability of Belief Systems," *Journal of the American Academy of Religion,* June 2, 1975, pp. 214–223.
6. Charles Hartshorne, *A Natural Theology of Our Time*. LaSalle, IL: Open Court Publishing Co., 1967, p. 30.

7. Richard Rorty, "Anticlericalism and Atheism," in Richard Rorty and Gianni Vattimo, eds., *The Future of Religion*. New York: Columbia University Press, 2005, pp. 30–32.

8. John D. Caputo, "Jacques Derrida (1930–2004)," *Journal for Cultural and Religious Theory*, 6 (1), Dec. 2004, p. 7.

9. John D. Caputo, *Deconstruction in a Nutshell: A Conversation with Jacques Derrida*. New York: Fordham University Press, 1997, pp. 165–167.

10. Richard Dawkins, *The God Delusion*. Boston: Houghton Mifflin, 2006; Victor J. Stenger, *God: The Failed Hypothesis*. Amherst, NY: Prometheus, 2007; Christopher Hitchens, *God Is Not Great*. New York: Twelve Books, 2007; and Sam Harris, *The End of Faith*. New York: Norton, 2004.

11. See Jim Holt, *Why Does the World Exist?* New York: Liveright, 2012.

12. Richard Dawkins, *The Selfish Gene*. New York: Oxford University Press, 1989.

13. G. Levine, ed., *The Joy of Secularism*. Princeton, NJ: Princeton University Press, 2011.

Chapter 13

1. Francis Mading Deng, *Africans of Two Worlds: The Dinka in Afro-Arab Sudan*. New Haven, CT: Yale University Press, 1978, p. 47.

2. David Ferry, *Gilgamesh: A New Rendering in English Verse*. New York: Farrar, Strauss and Giraudoux, 1993.

3. A J Spencer, *Death in Ancient Egypt*. Harmondsworth, England: Penguin, 1982.

4. Alwyn Rees and Brinley Rees, *Celtic Heritage: Ancient Traditions of Ireland and Wales*. New York: Grove Press, 1961.

5. The twelve novels of the "Left Behind" series, all published Wheaton, IL: Tyndale House, are (short titles): *Left Behind* (1995), *Tribulation Force* (1996), *Nicolae* (1997), *Soul Harvest* (1998), *Apollyon* (1999), *Assassins* (1999), *The Indwelling* (2000), *The Mark* (2000), *Desecration* (2001), *The Remnant* (2002), *Armageddon* (2003), and *Glorious Appearing* (2004), plus a sequel, *Kingdom* (2007), and three prequels, *The Rising* (2005), *The Regime* (2006), and *The Rapture* (2007), together with various other spin-offs in the form of children's versions, interpretations, and the like. See also Glenn W. Shuck, *Marks of the Beast: The Left Behind Novels and the Struggle for Evangelical Identity*. New York: New York University Press, 2005.

6. For more on apocalyptic, including contemporary versions, see Robert Ellwood, *Tales of Lights and Shadows: Mythology of the Afterlife*. London and New York: Continuum, 2010, pp. 55, 111–120.

7. Hal Lindsay, with C. C. Carlson, *The Late Great Planet Earth*. Grand Rapids, MI: Zondervan, 1970. New York: Bantam Books, 1973, pp. 124–125.

8. Pew Forum on Religion and Public Life, "Many Americans Not Dogmatic About Religion," Dec. 10, 2009. http://pewresearch.org/pubs/1434/multiple-religious-practices-reincarnation-astrology-psychic.

9. Morey Bernstein, *The Search for Bridey Murphy*. New York: Doubleday, 1956.

10. Friedrich Nietzsche, *The Gay Science*. Trans. Walter Kaufmann. New York: Random House, 1974, pp. 273–274. See also, Lawrence J. Hatab, *Nietzsche's Life Sentence: Coming to Terms With Eternal Recurrence*. London and New York: Routledge, 2005.

11. On this see Ned Lukacher, *Time-Fetishes: The Secret History of Eternal Recurrence*. Durham, NC: Duke Univeristy Press, 1998, p. 119.

12. Colleen McDannell and Bernhard Lang, *Heaven: A History*, 2nd ed., New Haven, CT: Yale University Press, 2001, p. 148.

13. Ibid., p. 93.

14. Letter to Hans, reproduced in Roland H. Bainton, *Here I Stand: A Life of Martin Luther*. New York and Nashville: Abingdon Press, 1950, p. 303. Conversation with Magdalene cited in McDannell & Lang, *Heaven*, p. 153.

15. *Vita Nuova.* Trans. Mark Musa. New York: Oxford University Press, 1992, p. 36.
16. See Emanuel Swedenborg, *Heaven and Hell.* Trans. George F. Dole. West Chester, PA: Swedenborg Foundation, 2000.
17. Nina Baym, ed., *Three Spiritualist Novels by Elizabeth Stuart Phelps.* Urbana and Chicago: University of Illinois Press, 2000.
18. Raymond A. Moody, Jr., *Life After Life.* Atlanta, GA: Mockingbird Books, 1975, pp. 56–57.

Chapter 14

1. Peter Singer, *Animal Liberation.* London: Jonathon Cape, 1976.
2. Marjorie Spiegel, *The Dreaded Comparison.* New York: Mirror Books, 1988.
3. Joseph Fletcher, *Situation Ethics.* Philadelphia: Westminster Press, 1965.
4. See Harvey Cox, ed., *The Situation Ethics Debate.* Philadelphia: Westminster Press, 1968.
5. For the statements of many churches and other significant religious groups, including Jewish and Muslim bodies and dissidents such as Catholics for a Free Choice, see J. Gordon Melton, *The Churches Speak on Abortion.* Detroit, MI: Gale Research, 1989.
6. Edward Batchelor, Jr., ed., *Abortion: The Moral Issues.* New York: Pilgrim Press, 1982. This book is a useful anthology of many perspectives, both Catholic and Protestant, on the question. For feminist perspectives, see Rosalind Pollack Petchesky, *Abortion and Woman's Choice.* New York and London: Longman, 1984; and Beverly Harrison, Our *Right to Choose: Toward a New Ethic on Abortion.* Boston: Beacon Press, 1983.
7. Reported in Gregory F. Pence, *Classic Cases in Medical Ethics.* New York: McGraw-Hill, 1990, pp. 3–24. On the Quinlan case, see also Paul Ramsey, *Ethics at the Edge of Life.* New Haven, CT: Yale University Press, 1978, pp. 268–299.
8. On such difficult cases as deformed newborns, see Paul Ramsey, *Ethics at the Edge of Life,* pp. 189–267; and on the ethical allocation of limited medical resources, see John F. Kilner, *Who Lives? Who Dies?* New Haven, CT: Yale University Press, 1990.
9. Pence, *Classic Cases in Medical Ethics,* pp. 25–44.
10. Joseph Fletcher, *Morals and Medicine.* Boston: Beacon Press, 1961, pp. 85–86.
11. Pence, *Classic Cases in Medical Ethics,* pp. 45–63.
12. Rosemary Radford Reuther, *Sexism and God-Talk: Toward a Feminist Theology.* Boston: Beacon Press, 1993.
13. Judith Plaskow, *Standing Again at Sinai.* San Francisco: Harper, 1991.
14. Seyyed Hossein Nasr, "Islam, the Contemporary Islamic World, and the Environmental Crisis," in Richard C. Foltz, Frederick M. Denny, and Azizian Baharuddin, eds., *Islam and Ecology: A Bestowed Trust.* Cambridge, MA: Center for the Study of World Religions, Harvard Divinity School, distr. Harvard University Press, 2003, p. 104.
15. Stephanie Kaza, "The Gridlock of Domination: A Buddhist Response to Environmental Suffering," in John E. Carrol, Paul Brockelman, and Mary Westfall, eds., *The Greening of Faith: God, the Environment, and the Good Life.* Hanover, NH: University of New Hampshire Press, 1997, pp. 147–148.
16. Jonathan Helfand, "The Earth Is the Lord's: Judaism and Environmental Ethics," in Eugene C. Hargrove, ed., *Religion and the Environmental Crisis.* Athens, GA: University of Georgia Press, 1986, pp. 38–52.
17. Wesley Granberg-Michaelson, *Redeeming the Creation. The Rio Earth Summit: Challenges for the Churches.* Geneva, Switz.: World Council of Churches Publications, 1992, p. 28.
18. John Cobb, Jr., "Christian Existence in a World of Limits," *Environmental Ethics* 1 (2), 1979, p. 152.
19. See, for example, Loren Wilkinson, *Earthkeeping: Christian Stewardship of Natural Rsources.* Grand Rapids, MI: Eerdmans, 1980.
20. See Robert Booth Fowler, *The Greening of Protestant Thought.* Chapel Hill, NC: University of North Caroline Press, 1995, p. 157.

21. John Chryssavgis, *Cosmic Grace—Humble Prayer: The Ecological Vision of the Green Patriarch Bartholomew I.* Grand Rapids, MI: Eerdmans, 2008. http://www.patriarchate .org/news/media/links/quotes.
22. Fazlun M. Khalid with Joanne O'Brien, ed., *Islam and Ecology*. New York: Cassell, 1992; and Foltz, Denny, and Baharuddin, *Islam and Ecology: A Bestowed Trust,* 2003.
23. Nasr, "Islam, the Contemporary Islamic World, and the Environmental Crisis," p. 96.
24. Bron Taylor, *Dark Green Religion: Nature Spirituality and the Planetary Future.* Berkeley, CA: University of California Press, 2010.

Chapter 15

1. Douglas Fry, *The Human Potential for Peace: An Anthropological Challenge to Assumptions About War and Violence.* New York: Oxford University Press, 2006. Summarized in Fry, *Beyond War*, pp. 237–238. See also Raymond Kelly, *Warless Societies and the Origin of War.* Ann Arbor, MI: University of Michigan Press, 2000.
2. Fry, *Beyond War*, p. 68.
3. Kirk Endicott, "Property, Power, and Conflict Among the Batek of Malaysia," in Tim Ingold, David Riches, and James Woodburn, eds., *Hunters and Gatherers.* Oxford, UK and New York: Berg, 1991, vol. 2, p. 122.
4. Arthur Ferrill, *The Origins of War, From the Stone Age to Alexander the Great,* rev. ed. Boulder, CO: Westview Press, 1997. See also H. H. Turney-High, *Primitive War: Its Practice and Concepts,* 2nd ed. Columbia, SC: University of South Carolina Press, 1971, p. 23.
5. Roy Prosterman, *Surviving to 3000: An Introduction to the Study of Lethal Conflict.* Belmont, CA: Duxbury-Wadsworth, 1972, p. 140.
6. Douglas P. Fry, *Beyond War: The Human Potential for Peace.* New York: Oxford University Press, 2007, p. 17.
7. Keith Otterbein, *The Evolution of War: A Cross-Cultural Study.* New Haven, CT: Human Relations Area Files Press, 1970, p. 3.
8. Keith Otterbein, *How War Began.* College Station, TX: Texas A&M University Press, 2004, p. 4.
9. From "The City in the Sea," by Edgar Allan Poe.
10. Stephen Crane, *The Red Badge of Courage.* Pleasantville, NY: The Reader's Digest Association, 1982, pp. 44–45. Original pub. 1895.
11. *Catechism of the Catholic Church,* 2nd ed. Vatican City: English translation for the U.S. by United States Catholic Conference, 1994, 1997, pp. 555–557. See also Richard J. Regan, *Just War: Principles and Cases.* Washington, DC: Catholic University of America Press, 1996; and Roland H. Bainton, *Christian Attitudes toward War and Peace.* New York and Nashville: Abingdon, 1960.
12. A useful summary is Norman Solomon, "The Ethics of War: Judaism," in Richard Sorabji and David Rodin, eds., *The Ethics of War.* Aldershot, UK and Burlington, VT: Ashgate, 2005, pp. 108–137.
13. Flavius Josephus, *The Jewish War*, 2.9.2-4. in Abraham Wasserstein, ed., *Flavius Josephus: Selections From His Works.* New York: Viking, 1974, pp. 180–181.
14. Alia Brahimi, *Jihad and Just War in the War on Terror.* New York: Oxford University Press, 2010, p. 101. See also Majid Khadduri, *War and Peace in the Law of Islam.* Baltimore: Johns Hopkins Press, 1955; and John Kelsey and James Turner Johnson, eds., *Just War and Jihad.* New York and Westport, CT: Greenwood Press, 1991.
15. Hugo Grotius, *The Rights of War and Peace.* Trans. A.C. Campbell. New York and London: Dunne, 1901, p. 273. Original Latin ed. 1625.
16. Lisa Sowell Cahill, *Love Your Enemies: Discipleship, Pacifism, and Just War Theory.* Minneapolis, MN: Fortress Press, 1994, pp. 144–145.
17. Friedrich von Bernhardi, *Germany and the Next War.* Trans. Allen H. Powles. New York: Longmans, Green, 1914.

18. George Fox, *Journal of George Fox*, rev. ed., in John L. Nickalls, ed. Philadelphia: Religious Society of Friends, 1997, p. 65. 1st ed. by Nickalls 1952. Original by Fox, ed. Thomas Ellwood, 1694.

19. M.K. Gandhi, *Non-Violent Resistance*. New York: Schocken Books, 1951, p. 3.

20. Philip Jenkins, *Laying Down the Sword: Why We Can't Ignore the Bible's Violent Verses.* New York: HarperOne, 2011, p. 17.

21. Ibid., p. 244.

22. "Largest Ever Hoard of Anglo-Saxon Gold Found in Staffordshire," *The Guardian*, Sept. 24, 2009; http://www.guardian.co.uk/uk/2009/sep/24/anglo-sax. . .; other media sources.

23. Back cover comment by Geraldine Brooks; David Finkel, *The Good Soldiers*. New York: Farrar, Straus and Giroux, 2009.

24. Finkel, *The Good Soldiers*, p. 56.

25. Ibid., p. 112.

26. *The Bhagavad-Gita: The Song of God*. Trans. Swami Prabhavananda and Christopher Isherwood. Hollywood, CA: Vedanta Press, 1944, 1987, pp. 41–42.

27. Yamamoto Tsunetomo, *The Hagakure*, in D. E. Tarver, ed. New York and Lincoln, NE: Writers Club Press, 2002, pp. 3, 18, 43–44.

28. J. R. R. Tolkien, *The Two Towers*, Part II of *The Lord of the Rings*. Boston: Houghton Mifflin, 1954, pp. 696–697.

29. Ibid., *The Fellowship of the Ring*, Part I of *The Lord of the Rings*, p. 69.

30. Ibid., p. 60.

31. Though attributed to Patton, and allegedly characteristic, to the best of my knowledge the quote has not been reliably documented.

32. Cited in Lawrence LeShan, *The Psychology of War*. New York: Helios Press, 2002, pp. 71–72.

33. G. W. F. Hegel, *Hegel's Philosophy of Right*. Transl. T.M. Knox. Oxford, UK: Clarendon Press, 1942, p. 210.

34. Michael C. C. Adams, *The Great Adventure*. Bloomington, IN: Indiana University Press, 1990, p. 51.

35. Terry Eagleton, *Holy Terror*. Oxford, UK: Oxford University Press, 2005, p. 26.

36. LeShan, *op. cit.*

37. Cited in LeShan, *Psychology of War*, p. 29.

38. LeShan, *Psychology of War*, p. 160.

39. Chris Hedges, *War Is a Force That Gives Us Meaning*. New York: Public Affairs Press, 2002, p. 3.

40. Joseph Campbell, with Bill Moyers, *The Power of Myth*. New York: Doubleday, 1985, p. 5.

41. Ernst Jünger, *Storm of Steel*. Trans. Michael Hofmann. London: Penguin Classics, 2004, p. 93. Orig. German pub. 1920; later slightly revised.

42. Ibid., p. 232.

43. C. S. Lewis, *Surprised by Joy*. Orlando, FL: Harvest Books, 1955, p. 196.

44. Max Cleland, "The Forever War of the Mind," *The New York Times*, Nov. 7, 2009.

45. Sheyann Webb and Rachel West Nelson, *Selma, Lord, Selma: Childhood Memories of the Civil-Rights Days*, as told to Frank Sikora. University, AL: University of Alabama Press, 1980, pp. 104–106.

46. Ibid., p. 126.

47. Ibid., p. xiv.

48. William James, "The Moral Equivalent of War" (1906). www.constitution.org/wj/meow.htm.

49. Arthur C. Clarke, "Space Flight and the Spirit of Man" (1961), collected in Clarke, *Voices From the Sky*. London: Mayflower Books, 1969, pp. 11–18.

50. Aldous Huxley, "Substitutes for Liberation" (1952), collected in Jacqueline Hazard Bridgeman, ed., *Huxley and God: Essays*. San Francisco: Harper San Francisco, 1992, pp. 124–125.

51. Sam Harris, *Letter to a Christian Nation.* New York: Knopf, 2006, pp. 80–81. See also Hector Avalos, *Fighting Words. The Origins of Religious Violence.* Amherst, NY: Prometheus, 2005. Regina M. Schwartz, *The Curse of Cain. The Violent Legacy of Monotheism.* Chicago: University of Chicago Press, 1997. David Livingston Smith, *The Most Dangerous Animal: Human Nature and the Origins of War.* New York: St. Martin's Press, 2007.
52. William T. Cavanaugh, *The Myth of Religious Violence: Secular Ideology and the Roots of Modern Conflict.* New York: Oxford University Press, 2009.

Appendix

1. For more on meditation by the author, including some accounts of student experiments with it, see Robert Ellwood, *Finding the Quiet Mind.* Wheaton, IL: Quest Books, 1983.

CREDITS

pp. 34–35: Based on Lévi-Strauss Claude. "The Structural Study of Myth," Journal of American Folklore, October-December 1955: 428–44.

pp. 35–36: Shipley, William. The Maidu Indian Myths and Stories of Hancibyjim. Berkeley, CA: Heyday Books, 1991. Reprinted courtesy of Heyday, www.heydaybooks.com.

p. 70: Maslow, Abraham. From Toward the Psychology of Being. New York: VanNostrand Reinhold Company, 1968.

p. 70: Based on Maslow, Abraham. Religions, Values, and Peak Experiences. Columbus: Ohio State University Press, 1964.

p. 79: Maslow, Abraham. From Toward the Psychology of Being. New York: VanNostrand Reinhold Company, 1968.

p. 80: Based on Cleary, T.S. and S.I. Shapiro. "The Plateau Experience and The Post-Mortem Life: Abraham H. Maslow's Unfinished Theory", The Journal of Transpersonal Psychology 27, 1 November 1995.

p. 80: Underhill, Evelyn. Mysticism. London: Methuen, 1911.

pp. 85–86: © Daniel Goleman, Excerpted from The Meditative Mind, (Tarcher, Putnam, 1988).

p. 87: Here I Stand ©1950 Abingdon Press. Used by permission. All rights reserved.

p. 100: Sanday, Peggy. Fraternity Gang Rape: Sex, Brotherhood, and Privilege on Campus. New York University Press, 1990: pp. 152–153.

p. 109: Shelly, Percy. Adonis. Charles Ollier. 1821.

p. 120: Bainton, Roland H. Here I Stand: A Life of Martin Luther. New York and Nashville: Abingdon, 1950.

p. 121: Blake, William. "The Tiger" Songs of Innocence. Basil Montagu Pickering. 1789.

pp. 121–122: Hopkins, Gerald. God's Grandeur. London: Humphrey Milford. 1918.

p. 123: Excerpt from "Tsunemasa" by Zeami from The No Plays of Japan, copyright © 1922 by Arthur Waley. Used by permission of Grove/Atlantic, Inc. Any third party use of this material, outside of this publication, is prohibited.

p. 161: (c) 1981 by Stephen King. Published originally by Playboy.

p. 164: O'Leary, Stephan D. "Utopian and Dystopian Possibilities of Networked Religion in the New Millennium" Religion and Cyberspace. Eds. Morten T. Hojsgaard and Margit Warburg, Routledge, Taylor and Francis Group, 2005: 47, 48.

pp. 215–217: Excerpt from pp. 68–9 [293 words] from Life After Life: The Investigation Of A Phenomenon–Survival Of Bodily Death By Raymond A. Moody, Jr.. Copyright ©2000 by Raymond Moody. Reprinted by permission of HarperCollins Publishers.

p. 245: Crane, Stephen. The Red Badge of Courage. Pleasantville, New York: The Reader's Digest Association, 1982: 44–45.

p. 252: The Bhagavad-Gita: The Song of God. Trans. Swami Prabhavananda and Christopher Isherwood. California: Vedanta Press. 1944, 1987: 41–42.

pp. 258–259: Webb, Sheyann and Rachel West Nelson. Selma, Lord, Selma: Childhood Memories of the Civil Rights Days. Ed. Frank Sikora. University of Alabama Press. 1980: 104–106, 126.

BIBLIOGRAPHY

The following lists of books present a few suggestions for further reading in several of the areas touched on in this introduction to religious studies. This bibliography should not be thought of as more than a sampling. It is therefore limited to ten books for each chapter.

I am well aware that many pages could be filled with worthwhile titles in any one of these areas. In assembling this bibliography, the needs of undergraduates and other interested but beginning students have been kept uppermost in mind. Thus, I have tried to include not only such books as would be considered best or most significant by specialists, but also books that do an especially good job of whetting a budding interest in an area, or providing an introductory aperture to it, or a useful general overview of its history and current state. Many of the books given in footnotes have not been repeated here, except for the most important; they are, however, also recommended. Many of these books themselves contain extensive bibliographies in their own fields, to which the reader is referred.

Chapter One: How to Study Religion

BERGER, PETER L., *The Sacred Canopy.* Garden City, NY: Doubleday Company, Inc., 1969.
DEAL, WILLIAM E. and TIMOTHY K. BEAL, *Theory for Religious Studies.* London and New York: Routledge, 2004.
ELIADE, MIRCEA, *The Sacred and the Profane.* New York: Harcourt Brace Jovanovich, Inc., 1959.
HINNELLS, JOHN, ed., *The Routledge Companion to the Study of Religion*, 2nd ed. London and New York: Routledge, 2010.
MOMEN, MOOJAN, *The Phenomenon of Religion: A Thematic Approach.* Oxford, UK: Oneworld, 1999.
OLSON, CARL, *Religious Studies: The Key Concepts.* London and New York: Routledge, 2011.
SHARPE, ERIC J., *Comparative Religion: A History.* LaSalle, IL: Open Court, 1986.
SWIDLER, LEONARD and PAUL MOJZES, *The Study of Religion in an Age of Global Dialogue.* Philadelphia: Temple University Press, 2000.
PALS, DANIEL Z., *Eight Theories of Religion.* New York: Oxford University Press, 2006.
WACH, JOACHIM, *Sociology of Religion.* Chicago: University of Chicago Press, 1944.

Chapter Two: History of Religion on Planet Earth

ARMSTRONG, KAREN, *The Great Transformation: The Beginning of Our Religious Traditions.* New York: Anchor, 2007.
BELLAH, ROBERT N., *Religion in Human Evolution: From the Paleolithic to the Axial Age.* Cambridge, MA: Harvard University Press, 2011.
BOWIE, FIONA, *The Anthropology of Religion: An Introduction.* Malden, MA and Oxford, UK: Blackwell, 2006.
ELIADE, MIRCEA, *History of Religious Ideas*, 3 vols. Chicago: University of Chicago Press, 1978–1985.
ELLWOOD, ROBERT, *Cycles of Faith: The Development of the World's Religions.* Walnut Creek, CA: Altamira, 2003.
GLAZIER, STEPHEN, *Anthropology of Religion: A Handbook.* Westport, CT: Praeger, 1999.
LESSA, WILLIAM A. and EVON Z. VOGT, *Reader in Comparative Religion: An Anthropological Approach.* New York: Harper & Row, Publishers, Inc., 1979.

LEWIS-WILLIAMS, DAVID, *Conceiving God: The Cognitive Origin of Evolution and Religion.* London: Thames and Hudson, 2010.

SMITH, HUSTON, *The World Religions: Our Great Wisdom Traditions.* San Francisco: Harper San Francisco, 1999.

WADE, NICHOLAS, *The Faith Instinct: How Religion Evolved and Why It Endures.* New York: Penguin, 2009.

Chapter Three: Myth: Our Lives, and the World's, Are Stories

CAMPBELL, JOSEPH, *The Mythic Image.* Princeton, NJ: Princeton University Press, 1974.

DONIGER, WENDY, *The Implied Spider.* New York: Columbia University Press, 2011.

DOTY, WILLIAM, *Myth: A Handbook.* Westport, CT: Greenwood, 2004.

_____, *Mythography.* Tuscaloosa, AL: University of Alabama Press, 2010.

ELIADE, MIRCEA, *Myth and Reality.* New York: Harper & Row, 1965.

ELLWOOD, ROBERT, *Myth: Key Concepts in Religion.* London and New York: Continuum, 2008.

_____, *Tales of Darkness: The Mythology of Evil.* London and New York: Continuum, 2009.

_____, *Tales of Lights and Shadows: The Mythology of the Afterlife.* London and New York: Continuum, 2010.

LEEMING, DAVID ADAMS, *The World of Myth: An Anthology.* New York: Oxford University Press, 1990.

SEGAL, ROBERT S., *Theorizing About Myth.* Amherst, MA: University of Massachusetts Press, 1999.

Chapter Four: Magic Doorways: Symbol, Rite, and Religion

BERNBAUM, EDWIN, *Sacred Mountains of the World.* San Francisco: Sierra Club Books, 1990.

EDSON, GARY, *Masks and Masking: Faces of Tradition and Belief Worldwide.* Jefferson, NC: McFarland, 2005.

ELIADE, MIRCEA, *Images and Symbols.* London: Harvil, 1961.

_____, *Rites and Symbols of Initiation: The Mysteries of Birth and Rebirth.* New York: Harper & Row, 1975.

GRIMES, RONALD, et al., *Ritual, Media, and Conflict.* New York: Oxford University Press, 2011.

JUNG, CARL, et al., *Man and His Symbols.* Garden City, NY: Doubleday, 1964.

TRESIDDER, JACK, ed., *The Complete Dictionary of Symbols.* San Francisco: Chronicle Books, 2005.

TURNER, VICTOR, *The Ritual Process.* Chicago: Aldine, 1969.

_____, *Dramas, Fields, and Metaphors: Symbolic Action in Human Society.* Ithaca, NY: Cornell University Press, 1974.

WOMACK, MARI, *Symbols and Meaning: A Concise Introduction.* Walnut Creek, CA: AltaMira, 2005.

Chapter Five: Oases of the Mind: The Psychology of Religion

FREUD, SIGMUND, *The Future of an Illusion.* Garden City, NY: Doubleday, 1957.

HILLMAN, JAMES, *Re-visioning Psychology.* New York: Harper, 1992.

HOOD, RALPH W., PETER C. HILL, and BERNARD SPILKA, *The Psychology of Religion: An Empirical Approach.* New York: Guilford, 2009.
JAMES, WILLIAM, *Varieties of Religious Experience.* New York and London: Longmans, Green, 1902. (Many reprints.)
JUNG, C.G., *Modern Man in Search of a Soul.* New York: Harcourt, Brace, 1933.
MASLOW, ABRAHAM H., *Religions, Values, and Peak Experiences.* Columbus, OH: Ohio State University Press, 1964.
NEWBERG, ANDREW and MARK ROBERT WALDMAN, *How God Changes Your Brain: Breakthrough Findings From a Leading Neurosurgeon.* New York: Ballantine, 2010.
PALOUTZIAN, RAYMOND F. and CRYSTAL L. PARK, eds., *Handbook of the Psychology of Religion and Spirituality.* New York: Guilford, 2005.
PARGAMENT, KENNETH J., *Psychology of Religion and Coping: Theory, Research, Practice.* New York: Guilford, 2001.
WULFF, DAVID M., *Psychology of Religion: Classic and Contemporary.* New York: Wiley, 1997.

Chapter Six: Inner Adventure: The Way of Realization, the Way of Faith

BAINTON, ROLAND II., *Here I Stand: A Life of Martin Luther.* New York and Nashville, TN: Abingdon, 1950.
BUCKE, RICHARD MAURICE, *Cosmic Consciousness.* New Hyde Park, NY: University Books, 1961.
DICKENS, ANDREA JANELLE, *The Female Mystic.* New York: Tauris, 2009.
ELLWOOD, ROBERT, *Mysticism and Religion.* New York: Seven Bridges, 1999; Berkeley, CA: Apocryphile Press, 2012.
FORMAN, ROBERT K.C., *Mysticism, Mind, Consciousness.* Albany, NY: State University of New York Press, 1999.
GOLEMAN, DANIEL, *The Varieties of the Meditative Experience.* New York: Dutton, 1977.
HARDY, ALISTER, *The Spiritual Nature of Man.* Oxford, UK: Clarendon Press, 1979.
JOHN OF THE CROSS, *Dark Night of the Soul.* Trans. E. Allison Peers. New York: Doubleday, 1990.
JONES, RICHARD H., *Mysticism Examined: Philosophical Inquiries Into Mysticism.* Albany, NY: State University of New York Press, 1993.
RANKIN, MARIANNE, *An Introduction to Religious and Spiritual Experience.* London and New York: Continuum, 2008.

Chapter Seven: Why Evil?

ADAMS, MARILYN McCORD and ROBERT M. ADAMS, eds., *The Problem of Evil.* Oxford, UK: Oxford University Press, 1990.
FRANKFURTER, DAVID, *Evil Incarnate: Rumors of Demonic Conspiracy and Satanic Abuse in History.* Princeton, NJ: Princeton University Press, 2006.
INWAGEN, PETER van. *The Problem of Evil.* Oxford, UK: Oxford University Press, 2006.
DONIGER [O'FLAHERTY] WENDY, *The Origins of Evil in Hindu Mythology.* Berkeley, CA: University of California Press, 1976.
LING, TREVOR, *Buddhism and the Mythology of Evil.* London: Allen & Unwin, 1962.
MEDWAY, GARETH, *Lure of the Sinister.* New York: New York University Press, 2001.

PARKIN, DAVID, *The Anthropology of Evil*. Cambridge, MA and Oxford, UK: Basil Blackwell, 1985.
RICOEUR, PAUL, *The Symbolism of Evil*. Boston: Beacon, 1967.
RUSSELL, JEFFREY, *The Prince of Darkness: Radical Evil and the Power of Good in History*. Ithaca, NY: Cornell University Press, 1988. (See also other works by this author.)
STIVERS, RICHARD, *Evil in Modern Myth and Ritual*. Athens, GA: University of Georgia Press, 1982.

Chapter Eight: Faith Through Form: Religion and Art

BRANDON, S.G.F., *Man and God in Art and Ritual*. New York: Scribner's, 1975.
BRITTON, KARLA, *Constructing the Ineffable: Contemporary Sacred Architecture*. New Haven, CT: Yale University Press, 2010.
DILLENBERGER, JANE, *Image and Spirit in Sacred and Secular Art*. New York: Crossroad, 1990.
GROOVER, KRISTINA K., ed., *Things of the Spirit: Women Writers Constructing Spirituality*. Notre Dame, IN: University of Notre Dame Press, 2004.
GUNN, GILES, *The Interpretation of Otherness: Literature, Religion and the American Imagination*. New York: Oxford University Press, 1979.
HUGHES, GLENN, *A More Beautiful Question: The Spiritual in Poetry and Art*. Columbia, MO: University of Missouri Press, 2011.
HUNGERFORD, AMY, *Postmodern Belief: American Literature and Religion since 1960*. Princeton, NJ: Princeton University Press, 2010.
NORMAN, EDWARD, *The House of God*. New York: Thames and Hudson, 1990.
ROSS, LESLIE, *Art and Architecture of the World's Religions*. Santa Barbara, CA: Greenwood Press/ABC-CLIO, 2009.
ROSS-BRYANT, LYNN, *Imagination and the Life of the Spirit: An Introduction to the Study of Religion and Literature,* Chico, CA: Scholars Press, 1981.
SCOTT, NATHAN, *The Broken Center*. New Haven, CT: Yale University Press, 1966.

Chapter Nine: Ghost Marriages and Country Music: Popular Religion

BERGESEN, ALBERT J. and ANDREW M. GREELEY, *God in the Movies*. New Brunswick, NJ: Transaction, 2000.
CUSACK, CAROLE M., *Invented Religions: Imagination, Fiction, and Faith*. Aldershot, UK and Burlington, VT: Ashgate, 2010. (Church of the SubGenius, Church of the Flying Spaghetti Monster, Jediism, and others.)
HUME, LYNNE and KATHLEEN McPHILLIPS, *Popular Spiritualities*. Aldershot, UK and Burlington, VT: Ashgate, 2006.
LADERMAN, GARY, *Sacred Matters: Celebrity Worship, Sexual Ecstasies, the Living Dead, and Other Signs of Religious Life in the United States*. New York: New Press, 2009.
MAZUR, ERIC MICHAEL and KATER McCARTHY, eds., *God in the Details: American Religion in Popular Culture*. New York and London: Routledge, 2001.
McDANNELL, COLLEEN, *Material Christianity: Religion and Popular Culture in America*. New Haven, CT: Yale University Press, 1995.
McGUIRE, MEREDITH, *Lived Religion: Faith and Practice in Everyday Life*. Oxford, UK: Oxford University Press, 2008.

STORY, JOHN, *Cultural Theory and Popular Culture: An Introduction.* Athens, GA: University of Georgia Press, 2006.

STOUT, DANIEL A. and JUDITH M. BUDDENBAUM, eds., *Religion and Popular Culture in America.* Ames, IA: Iowa State University Press, 2001.

WILLIAMS, PETER, *Popular Religion in America.* Englewood Cliffs, NJ: Prentice Hall, 1980.

Chapter Ten: Infinite Information, Worlds Without End: The Internet, Religion, and Virtual Realities

ABOUJAOUDE, ELIAS, *Virtually You: The Dangerous Powers of the E-Personality.* New York: W. W. Norton, 2011.

BRASHER, BRENDA E., *Give Me That Online Religion.* San Francisco: Josey-Boss, 2001.

CAMPBELL, HEIDI A., *When Religion Meets New Media.* London and New York: Routledge, 2010.

CARR, NICHOLAS, *The Shallows: What the Internet Is Doing to Our Brains.* New York: Norton, 2010.

COBB, JENNIFER J., *CyberGrace: The Search for God in the Digital World.* New York: Crown, 1998.

DAWSON, LORNE L. and DOUGLAS E. COWAN, eds., *Religion Online.* New York and London: Routledge, 2004.

EGENFELDT-NIELSEN, SIMON, JONAS HEIDE SMITH, and SUSANA PAJARES TOSCAM, *Understanding Video Games.* London and New York: Routledge, 2008.

HØJSGAARD, MORTEN T. and MARGIT WARBURG, *Religion and Cyberspace.* London and New York: Routledge, 2005.

KURZWEIL, RAY, *The Age of Spiritual Machines.* New York: Viking, 1999.

THISTLETHWAITE, SUSAN BROOKS, *Dreaming of Eden: American Religion and Politics in a Wired World.* New York: Palgrave Macmillan, 2010.

Chapter Eleven: Traveling Together: The Sociology of Religion

BECKFORD, JAMES A. and JOHN WALLISS, *Theorising Religion.* Aldershot, UK and Burlington, VT: Ashgate, 2006.

CHAVES, MARK, *American Religion: Contemporary Trends.* Princeton, NJ: Princeton University Press, 2011.

CLARKE, PETER B., ed., *The Oxford Handbook of the Sociology of Religion.* Oxford, UK: Oxford University Press, 2009.

ELLWOOD, ROBERT S., and HARRY B. PARTIN, *Religious and Spiritual Groups in Modern America,* 2nd ed. Englewood Cliffs, NJ: Prentice Hall, Inc., 1988.

GREELEY, ANDREW, *The Denominational Society.* Glenview, IL: Scott, Foresman and Company, 1973.

HAAR, GERRIE TER and YOSHIO TSURUOKA, *Religion and Society: An Agenda for the 21st Century.* Leiden, Netherlands: E. J. Brill, 2007.

SWENSON, DONALD S., *Society, Spirituality, and the Sacred: A Social Scientific Introduction.* Peterborough, ON: Broadview, 1999.

WACH, JOACHIM, *Sociology of Religion.* Chicago: University of Chicago Press, 1944.

WEBER, MAX, *Sociology of Religion.* Boston: Beacon Press, 1963.

WUTHNOW, ROBERT, *After the Baby Boomers: How Twenty- and Thirty-Somethings Are Shaping the Future of American Religion.* Princeton, NJ: Princeton University Press, 2007.

Chapter Twelve: Truth Messages: The Conceptual Expression of Religion

DEUTSCH, ELIOT, *Advaita Vedanta: A Philosophical Reconstruction*. Honolulu, HI: East-West Center Press, 1969.

DREYFUS, HUBERT and SEAN DORRANCE KELLY, *All Things Shining: Reading the Western Classics to Find Meaning in a Secular Age*. New York: Free Press, 2011.

EDELGLASS, WILLIAM and JAY L. GARFIELD, *Buddhist Philosophy: Essential Readings*. Oxford, UK and New York: Oxford University Press, 2009.

FORD, DAVID F., *The Modern Theologians*. Cambridge, MA: Blackwell, 1997.

JONES, DAVID and E.R. KLEIN, *Asian Texts, Asian Contexts: Encounters With Asian Philosophies and Religions*. Albany, NY: State University of New York Press, 2010.

JORDAN, JEFFREY J., *Philosophy of Religion: The Key Thinkers*. London and New York: Continuum, 2011.

MACKINTOSH, HUGH ROSS, *Types of Modern Theology: Schleiermacher to Barth*. London: Nisbet and Co., 1947.

MBITI, JOHN S., *Concepts of God in Africa*. New York: Praeger, 1970.

ROWE, WILLIAM L., ed., *God and the Problem of Evil*. Malden, MA: Blackwell, 2001.

RUNZO, JOSEPH and NANCY M. MARTIN, *The Meaning of Life in the World Religions*. Oxford, UK: Oneworld, 2000.

Chapter Thirteen: Worlds to Come: Religious Eschatology and the Afterlife

BAYM, NINA, ed., *Three Spiritualist Novels by Elizabeth Stuart Phelps*. Urbana, IL and Chicago: University of Illinois Press, 2000.

BECKER, CARL B., *Breaking the Circle: Death and the Afterlife in Buddhist Thought*. Carbondale, IL: Southern Illinois University Press, 1994.

BRANDON, S.G.F., *The Judgment of the Dead: The Idea of Life After Death in the Major Religions*. New York: Charles Scribner's Sons, 1967.

BRAUDE, ANN, *Radical Spirits: Spiritualism and Women's Rights in Nineteenth Century America*. Boston: Beacon, 1989.

HICK, JOHN, *Death and Eternal Life*. New York: Harper & Row Publishers, Inc., 1977.

JORDAN, DAVID K., *Gods, Ghosts, and Ancestors: The Folk Religion of a Taiwanese Village*. Berkeley, CA: University of California Press, 1972.

KINSLEY, DAVID R., *The Divine Player: A Study in Krsna Lila*. Delhi, India: Motilal Banarsidass, 1979.

McDANNELL, COLLEEN and BERNHARD LANG, *Heaven: A History*, 2nd ed. New Haven, CT: Yale University Press, 2001.

SPENCER, A.J., *Death in Ancient Egypt*. Harmondsworth, UK: Penguin, 1982.

ZALESKI, CAROL, *Otherworld Journeys*. New York: Oxford University Press, 1987.

Chapter Fourteen: How Shall We Live? Religion and Ethics

ANCESCHI, LUCA, et al., eds., *Religion and Ethics in a Globalizing World: Conflict, Dialogue, and Transformation*. New York: Palgrave Macmillan, 2010.

ARNOLD, DENIS G., ed., *The Ethics of Global Climate Change*. New York: Cambridge University Press, 2011.

BRAUN, KATHRYN L., JAMES H. PIETSCH, and PATRICIA L. BLANCHETTE, eds., *Cultural Issues in End-of-Life Decision Making*. Thousand Oaks, CA: Sage Publications, 2000.

DALTON, ANNE MARIE and HENRY C. SIMMONS, *Ecotheology and the Practice of Hope*. Albany, NY: State University of New York Press, 2010.

GRAHAM, FORDON, *Eight Theories of Ethics*. London & New York: Routledge, 2004.

LEE, WENDY LYNNE, *Contemporary Feminist Theory and Activism: Six Global Issues*. Peterborough, ON, and New York: Broadview, 2010.

MATHEWES, CHARLES, *Understanding Religious Ethics*. Chichester, UK and Malden, MA: Wilcy-Blackwell, 2010.

MORGAN, PEGGY and CLIVE A. LAWTON, *Ethical Issues in Six Religious Traditions*, 2nd ed. Edinburgh, UK: Edinburgh University Press, 2007.

PENCE, GREGORY F., *Classic Cases in Medical Ethics*. New York: McGraw-Hill, 1990.

TAYLOR, BRON, *Dark Green Religion: Nature Spirituality and the Planetary Future*. Berkeley, CA: University of California Press, 2010.

Chapter Fifteen: Horror and Glory: Religion Confronting War

CAHILL, LISA SOWELL, *Love Your Enemies: Discipleship, Pacifism, and Just War Theory*. Minneapolis, MN: Fortress Press, 1994.

FRY, DOUGLAS, *Beyond War: The Human Potential for Peace*. New York: Oxford University Press, 2007.

GANDHI, MOHANDAS K., *Non-violent Resistance*. New York: Schocken Books, 1951.

HEDGES, CHRIS, *War Is a Force That Gives Us Meaning*. New York: Public Affairs Press, 2002.

KELLY, RAYMOND C., *Warless Societies and the Origin of War*. Ann Arbor, MI: University of Michigan Press, 2000.

KHADDURI, MAJID, *War and Peace in the Law of Islam*. Baltimore: Johns Hopkins Press, 1955.

LeSHAN, LAWRENCE, *The Psychology of War*. New York: Helios, 2002.

MARLANTES, KARL, *What It Is Like to Go to War*. New York: Atlantic Monthly Press, 2011.

REGAN, RICHARD J., *Just War: Principles and Cases*. Washington, DC: Catholic University of America Press, 1996.

SORABJI, RICHARD and DAVID RODIN, eds., *The Ethics of War*. Aldershot, UK and Burlington, VT: Ashgate, 2005.

INDEX

A

Abortion: The Moral Issues (Batchelor), 230
Abortion controversy, 228–31
Aboujaoude, Elias, 161
Abrahamic religions, 207–8
Abstraction, 33
Adulthood, religious development in, 66–67
Afterlife, 203–4
Algonquin initiation rite, 67, 70
Allport, Gordon, 78
al-Masih ad-Dajjal, 208
Amida Buddha, 89
Ammerman, Nancy T., 133
Analects of Confucius, 118, 226
Ancient empires, 21–22
Anglo-Saxon, 250
Animal Liberation (Singer), 224
Animal-rights issue, 224
Animism, 17, 24, 240
Anselm of Canterbury, 191
Anthropological evidence for war, 243
Anthropomorphic deities, 114
Apocalyptic, 209
Apostolic period, 27–28
Aquinas, Thomas, 190, 199, 213
Archaic agriculture, 20–21
Archetype, 113
Architecture, religious, 116–18
Arhant, 85–86
Art, religion and, 107–28
Artificial intelligence, 163–64
Ash'arism, 102
Atheists, 199–200, 260
Audio symbols, 51
Augustine, St., 69, 105, 213
Australian aboriginals, 37
Authority, determination of truth by, 193
Awakening, 81–82
Awareness of self, 70
Axial age, 22–25
Axis mundi, 141

B

Baba, Meher, 69
Babajan, Hazrat, 69
Baptism, Christian, 58
Baroque church, 117
Bartholomew, Ecumenical Patriarch, 239–40
Basho (poet), 120
Basilica, 117
Batchelor, Edward, Jr., 230
Beaudoin, Tom, 140
Bentham, Jeremy, 224
Berger, Peter L., 63
Bernhardi, Friedrich von, 247
Bernstein, Morey, 212
Bhagavad Gita, 86–87
Bhakti, 119, 134
Blake, William, 120–22
Bouvia, Elizabeth, 232–33
Brasher, Brenda E., 155
Brothers Kilramazov, The (Dostoyevsky), 126–28
Buddha, 115
Buddhism, 25, 51, 53, 69, 74, 97, 102, 112, 169–71, 176–77, 188
    arts of, 112, 114
    compassion, 225
    insight, 84–86

nature worship, 237–38
poetry of, 120
reincarnation, 210–11

C

Camouflages of the sacred, 140–44
Campbell, Joseph, 41, 124, 143, 257
Caputo, John, 145
Cargo cults, 174
Carr, Nicholas, 152
Centesimus Annus, 238–39
Chagall, Marc, 112
Change, capacity for development and permanent, 64–69
Chanoyu, 112
Chants, 119
Charismatic personality, 175
Childhood, religion and, 66–67
China, religions in, 69, 118, 182
Chinvat Bridge, 206
Christianity, 26, 136–37, 176–77
    in America, 169, 171, 176
    art of, 110–11
    baptism in, 58
    environmental ethics, 238–39
    Gnostic school of, 121
    judgment, 208–9
    Roman Catholic church, 169
    sexual images and roles in, 236
    war according to, 247
Christian Old Testament, 204
Church architecture, 117–18
Civil religion, 171
Conceptual expression of religion, 186–200
Conceptual verbal audio symbols, 51–53
Conceptual verbal expression, 52–53
Conditioned reality, 108–9
Confucianism, 26, 118, 182
Consciousness, states of, 61–62, 69–71
Consequentalist ethics, 223
Conservatism, 172
Content message, 193
Conversions, 68–69, 71
Cosmic egg, 38
Cosmogonic myth, 37
Cosmological argument, 190
Coyote, 35–37
Creed, Nicene, 208
Critical distance, 78
Cults, 124, 174
Cyber apocalyptic, 163–65
Cyberheaven, 155
Cybernetic revolution, 149
Cybernetic science, 162
Cyborgs, 151, 164

D

Dance, music and, 119
Dark Green Religion (Taylor), 240–41
Davis, Erik, 163
Deconstructionism, 198
Denominational founder, 180
Denominations, 170–71, 181
Deontological ethics, 222–23
Deprivation state, 79
Derrida, Jacques, 198
Development, psychological stages, 80–83
Devil's share, 135–36
Devotionalism, 28

Dinka, 204–5
Disciple, 25
Disneyland, as sacred place, 141–42
Doctrine, 52–53
Dostoyevsky, Fyodor, 126
Drama, religious, 122–23
Dreaded Comparision, The (Spiegel), 224
Dreamtime, 37
Dukha, 97
Durkheim, Émile, 6
Dyson, Freeman, 164

E

Eagleton, Terry, 255
Earthmaker, 35–36
Eastern orthodox churches, icons in, 110–11
Ecology, religion and, 236–41
e-correspondents, 150
Effervescence, social, 6
Egyptian religions, 21, 114
   life after death, 205
Eliade, Mircea, 8, 18, 140–41
Emergent religions, 169, 172–77
Empiricism, 193
Enuma Elish, 38
Eschatology, 23–24, 37, 103, 175, 202–17
Essentialism, 197–98
Essentialist, 10
Established religion, 169–72, 176
Eternal recurrence, 212–13
Ethics, religion and, 218–41
   abortion controversy and, 228–31
   contemporary issues, 227–34
   defined, 220
   environmental ethics, 236–41
   guidance on practical issues, 219–20
   kinds of ethical thought, 222–26
   law and love, tension between, 226–27
   medical revolution and, 227–28
   morality and, 220–21
   right to die and, 231–34
   role of women in religion and, 234–36
   similarities and differences in ethical traditions,
      226–27
   social enactment of, 221
   social ethics, 220
Euthanasia, 231, 233–34
Evangelicalism, 140
Everystudent.com, 154
Evil, 93
   initiation of, 98
   origin of, 94–98
   religion to create, 98–100
   religious thought and, 100–105
Existentialism, 89, 194–96
Expansive emergent religion, 176
Experience, finding truth through, 192–93

F

Faith, 2, 4, 172
Ferrill, Arthur, 244
Fiction, 124–28
Finkel, David, 251
First Naïveté, 77
Fletcher, Joseph, 226, 233
Folk religion, 138–39
Founders, religious, 22–25, 176, 179
Fox, George, 247 48
Friends, religious society of, 247
Freud, Sigmund, 7, 72
Fundamentalism, 137, 138, 145, 172, 255

G

Gaia, 38
Gamesmanship, 157–61
Gandhi, Mohandas, 181, 248
Genesis, 37
Georgian church, 117
Ghost marriages, 133–34
Giotto, 110
Gnostic school of Christianity, 121
God is creator, 196
God or gods
   belief in, 72, 188–89
   in relation to creation, 37
   and Satan, 37
Goleman, Daniel, 85–86
Gouge, William, 247
Great religions, 25–27
Great traditions, 133, 138, 169
Greek sculpture, 114–15
Greene, Graham, 125
Grotius, Hugo, 246
Groups, religious, 168–69
Grünbaum, Adolf, 199
Guilt, 71

H

Hafez, 77
Haiku, 120
Hakakure, 252
Hamlet (Shakespeare), 122 23
Handel, 131
Hartshorne, Charles, 191, 197
Harvest festival, 3
Heaven, 213–15
Hebrew scriptures, 182, 204
Hedges, Chris, 256
Heelas, Paul, 144
Hercules, 41–44
Hermes, 35
Hero/Savior myth, 46
Hero with a Thousand Faces, The (Campbell), 41, 124
Hillman, James, 74
Hinduism, 25, 71, 97, 102, 112, 181, 188, 221
Historical impact of religion, 181
History, interpretation of, 182
Højsgaard, Morten T., 156
Hominization, 230
Hopkins, Gerard Manley, 121–22
Huffington, Arianna, 156
Hui-Neng, 69
Humanistic psychology, 73
Humanity, 20
Hume, David, 191, 196
Hunter and gatherer societies, 17–19
Huxley, Aldous, 260
Hymns, 119

I

Iconoclasm, 51
Icons, 110–11
Illiterates vs. literates, 34
Illuminative stage, psychological development, 83
Impersonal absolute, God as, 188
Implicit faith, 172
India, religions in, 21, 25, 69
Individuation, religion as quest for, 72
Initiation, 18, 67, 70, 98
Inner adventure, 76–91
   ways to go, 77–80
Intensive emergent religion, 176
Intentionalism, 225
Intercultural religion, 169

International religions, 3–4, 169–70
Internet
  for everyday information, 149
  religion and, 148–49
  as a source of information, 149, 151–53
Irish celts, 205–6
Ise shrine (Japan), 3
Islam, 26
  end time, 207–8

J

Jainism, 227
James, William, 6, 62, 72, 260
Japan, religions in, 3, 3–4, 26, 119–20, 126, 169–70,
    173–74
Japanese No drama, 122
Jaspers, Karl, 22
Jenkins, Philip, 249
Jesus, 26, 44–45
Jewish, environmental ethics, 238
Jihad, 246
Jodo, 89
Joy of battle, 254–55
Judaism, 26, 176, 236, 246
  environmental ethics, 238
Jung, Carl Gustav, 7, 72, 113
Justice, religious demands for, 181

K

Kali-yuga, 39
Kanu, 95
Karma, 102
Kaza, Stephanie, 238
Kierkegaard, Søren, 89, 195
King, Martin Luther, 181
Kinkakuji (The Temple of the Golden Pavilion)
    (Mishima), 126, 128
Krippner, Stanley, 61–62
Krishna, 134
Krishna consciousness movement, 28
Kurzweil, Ray, 163–64
Kyoto, Japan, 57

L

Langer, Susanne, 46
Language games, 197
Laozi, 26
Law, natural, 222–23
Law and love, tension between, 226–27
Layperson, 178–79
Left Hand of Darkness, The (LeGuin), 234
Leguin, Ursula, 234
Lévi-Strauss, Claude, 34, 198
Liberal style, 172
Lienardt, Godfrey, 204–5
Life after death, 102–3, 135
Life after Life (Moody), 215–17
Liminality, 70–71
Linde, Anrei, 199
Lindsay, Hal, 209
Literature, religious, 124–28
Little traditions, 138, 169
Liturgical music, 119
Liturgy, 119
Living the dream, 251–54
Living will, 232
Loki, 35
Love and law, tension between, 226–27
Luria, Issac, 104
Luther, Martin, 87–89, 214

M

Magic, 16
Magog, 208
Mahayana Buddhism, 112, 188, 225
Mahdi, 208
Maidu people, 35–36
Mantras, 119
Marx, Karl, 6–7
Maslow, Abraham, 70, 78–80
Mayan religion, 138
McCutcheon, Russell, 8, 198
McGonigal, Jane, 160
McGuire, Meredith, 145
Mecca, Muslim pilgrimage to, 56–57
Medical revolution, 227–28
Meditation, 71
Memory, articulation of, 16
Mercy killing (euthanasia), 231, 233–34
Meta-ethics, 221
Militarism, 247
Mill, John Stuart, 224
Miller, Lisa, 152
Mishima, Yukio, 126
Mondrian, Piet, 113
Monism, 188
Monk, 178
Monotheism, personal, 189
Monotheistic god, 24
Moody, Raymond, 143, 215
Morality, ethics and, 220–21
Mortal Kombat, 157
Moses, 24
Mt. Fuji, 133
Mufti, 223
Muhammad, 24
Music, religious, 51–52, 118–20
Mystic, 19, 179
Mystical experience, 11
Mysticism, 7, 80
Myth, 16–17, 31–46, 52, 94–98, 124, 254, 258
  of comic book, 143
  creation, 37
  of the end of days, 37
  of the hero, 37, 40–41
  kinds of, 37
  meaning, 45–46
  origin of evil, 37

N

Nagarjuna, 191
Nakayama, Miki, 174
Nasr, Seyyed Hossein, 236–37
National religions, 170
Natural law, 222–23
Natural rights, 222
Nature worship, 237
Nazi euthanasia practices, 232–34
Near-death experiences, 134–135, 215–17
Nembutsu, 89
Netherlands, euthanasia law in, 233–34
Newberg, Andrew, 74
Nichiren Buddhism, 52
Niebuhr, H. Richard, 188
Nietzsche, Friedrich, 212
Nirvana, 84, 108, 112, 211
Noble, David, 163
No drama of Japan, 122
Nonconceptual verbal expression, 52
Nonliterate oral culture, 34
Nonverbal symbols, 51–52
Normative nature of society, 180–81
Novels, religious, 124–28

Numinous, the, 7
Nun, 178

O

Odyssey, 203–4
O'Leary, Stephan D., 164
Ong, Walter J., 34
Ontological argument, 191
Otterbein, Keith, 244
Otto, Rudolf, 7
Ouranos, 38

P

Pacifism, 247
Painting, religious, 110–13
Paley, William, 193
Palladian church, 117
Pargament, Kenneth I., 74
Path of bhakti, 87
Paul (apostle), 65, 67
Peak experience, 70–72
Pentecostalism, 136–37, 140
Performance music, religious, 119–20
Personalities, religious, 177–80
Personal monotheism, 189
Pharaoh, 21, 97, 205
Phelps, Elizabeth Stuart, 214
Philosopher, 179
Pilgrimage, 56–57
Piwowarski, Wladyslaw, 133
Plantinga, Alvin, 191
Plateau experience, 79–80
Pluralistic, 170
Poetry, religious, 120–22
Polish Catholicism, 133
Polytheism, 22, 101, 189
Popular culture (little traditions), 137–40
Popularizer, 180
Power and the Glory, The (Greene), 125
Practical religious expression, 9
Preference, religious, 194
Preparation, psychological development, 83
Presley, Elvis, 142–43
Priest, 3, 177
Private symbols, 49–50
Process Theology, 239
Profane, the sacred vs. the, 8
Prophet, 26, 179
Prophetic teaching, 181
Prosterman, Roy, 244
Protestantism, 51
Pseudonirvana, 85
Psychological interpretations, 72–75
Psychology of religion, 60–75
Public symbols, 49–50
Public worship, 54–55
Pure Land Buddhism, 28, 89–90
Purgatory, 209

Q

Quaker meeting, 54
Quinlan, Karen, 231–32

R

Reason, finding truth through, 190–92
Rebirth, 67, 70
Redfield, Robert, 138–39
Reformation, 28–29
Reformer, 179–80
Reincarnation, 102, 209–12
Religion confronting war, 242–61

Religion(s)
  as another reality, 5
  artistic representations, 131–32
  defining, 3
  emergent, 169, 172–77
  established, 169–72, 176
  history of, 14–30
  Internet and, 148–49
  online talks, 154–56
  present status, 182–84
  sociology of, 6, 167–84
  study of, 8
  theories of, 137–40
Religious belief, 196–97
Religious expression, forms of, 3–5, 8–11
Religious groups, 155, 168–69
Religious liberalism, 172
Resurrection of the dead, 205, 207
Rheotoric, religious, 53
Ricoeur, Paul, 77
Right to die, 231–34
Rites, 3, 53–58
Ritual, 3
Roe vs. Wade, 229–30
Roles, sexual, 234–36
Roman Catholic church, 169
Romanesque church, 117
Roof, Wade Clark, 145
Rorty, Richard, 197
Rosenbloom, Stephanie, 161
Ross-Bryant, Lynn, 125

S

Sacraments, 171
Sacred, the, 6, 8
Sacred and the Profane, The (Eliade), 8
Sallman, Warner, 131–32
Samatha, 85
Satan, 37, 95
Satanic panic, 136
Saussure, Ferdinand de, 198
Savior hero, 44–45
Schechner, Richard, 54
Schleiermacher, Friedrich, 6
Schultze, Quentin J., 140
Schutz, Alfred, 62
Sculpture, religious, 113–15
Second Naïveté, 78
Self-awareness, 70
Self-centered, 79
Sesshu (artist), 112
Sexual images and roles, 234–36
Shakespeare, William, 122–23, 131
Shaman, 18–19, 177
Shinran, 89–90
Shintoism, 3, 26
Shodo, 89
Shradh, 134
Siberia, Altaic shaman in, 18
Signs vs. symbols, 48–50
Sila, 85
Singer, Peter, 224
Situation Ethics (Fletcher), 226
Skin walkers, 135
Smith, Jonathon Z., 8, 198
Social class, 221
Social effervescence, 6
Social ethics, 220
Society, transformation by religion, 180–81
Sociological factors in religious preference, 194
Sociological religious expression, 9–10
Soul, 16–17

Spiegel, Marjorie, 224
Spiritism, 17, 18
Stained-Glass windows, 108–10, 117
States of consciousness
    mental shifts in, 61–62
    religious, 70–72
    subuniverses and their corresponding, 62–64
Storey, John, 137
Stories, religious, 124–28
    as myth, 32–33
Streng, Frederick, 67
Structuralism, 8
Study of religion, 8
Subjective experiences, 3–5
Subuniverses, 62–64
Suffering, 97
Sufi, 118
Suicide, 232–33
Sun Buddha, 133
Superheroes, 143–44
Supernatural allies, 18
Swedenborg, Emanuel, 214
Symbol(s), 48–59
    audio, 50–53
    categories of religious, 49–50
    change of, in great religions, 25
    distinction between signs and, 48–50
    doctrine as, 52–53
    myth as, 52
    orchestration of, in rite, 53–59
    public and private, 49–50
    transcendent experience expressed as, 8

T

Talmud, 238
Tangaroa, 38
TechGnosis (Davis), 163
Teleological argument, 190
Teleological ethics, 222–26
Tenrikyo, 173–74
Terrorism, 255
The Dark Night of the Soul, 83
The Epic of Gilgamesh, 205
Theologian, 179
Theoretical religious expression, 9
Theravada, 84
The Religion of Technology (Noble), 163
Theriomorphic form in sculpture, 114
The Search for Bridey Murphy (Berstein), 212
The Shallows (Carr), 152
The Witcher 2: Assassins of Kings, 157
Thinking about god, 187–88
Tillich, Paul, 49, 120, 124, 189
Tir nan Og, 206
Toyouke, 3
Traditionalism, 172
Transcendence, 8–9
Transformation
    of society by religion, 180–81
    transformative process of rite, 54
Transitions of life, religious parallels to, 64–69

Tribe's crucial information, 33–34
Trickster, 35–37
Truth in religion, determining, 189–93
Tsunemasa (No play), 122–23
Turner, Victor, 58, 70
Twelve Labors of Hercules, 42–43

U

Unconditioned reality, 108–9
Underhill, Evelyn, 80–83
Unitive state, psychological development, 83
Universal law, concept of, 21
Utilitarianism, 224–25

V

Van Gennep, Arnold, 58, 70
Verbal expression, 52–53
Video game, 157–61
Vipassana, 84
Virtually You, 161
Virtual religions, 156
Visuddhimagga, 84–85
Voluntary death, 232–33

W

Wach, Joachim, 9
Waley, Arthur, 118
War
    defining, 244
    the feel of, 244–45
    horror of, 257–58
    joy of battle, 254–55
    and moral meaning, 259–61
    protection during, 251
    theory of, 245–47
Warcraft, 157
Warrior hero, 41–44
Way of Faith, 86–90
Way of Realization, 80–83
Weber, Max, 176, 182
Wicca, 154
Williams, Peter, 140
Wisdom, 28
Witch doctor, 18
Witches, 135
Wittgenstein, Ludwig, 197
Women, role in religion, 234–36
Worship, 181
    public, 54–55
Wut, 99

Y

Yantras, 112
Yawm ad-Din, 207–8
Yoga, 67–68

Z

Zarathustra, 24
Zen tradition, 112
Zoroastrianism, 205–6